W9-AUR-504

Parable

One dark night, two horseback rider's road across a drought-filled land. As they came to a dry riverbed, a voice cried out to them to halt. Being strangers in that part of the world, they stopped. Then the voice commanded them to dismount their horses, pick up a handful of pebbles, put them in their pockets and remount. So they did as they were commanded, dismounted their horses, picked up a handful of pebbles, put them in their pockets and remounted. The voice said, "Tomorrow at sunrise, you will be both glad and sorry." So off into the night they rode.

At sunrise, they put their hands in their pockets, and lo and behold, the pebbles had turned into diamonds, rubies and other precious stones. Then they remembered the warning: "Tomorrow at sunrise you will be both glad and sorry." And that they were—glad they had taken some, but sorry they had not taken more.

Fourth Edition

On Becoming a Teacher

Part I

Some Important Things You'll
Need to Know and Use

Dr. Frank Paoni
Brookdale Community College

Name ____

Section Number ______________ Day ______________ Time ______________

KENDALL/HUNT PUBLISHING COMPANY
4050 Westmark Drive Dubuque, Iowa 52002

Copyright © 1995, 1999, 2002, 2007 by Kendall/Hunt Publishing Company

ISBN 978-0-7575-4778-2

All rights reserved. No part of this publication may be reproduced, stored in a retrieval system, or transmitted, in any form by any means, electronic, mechanical, photocopying, recording, or otherwise, without prior, written permission of the copyright owner.

Printed in the United States of America
10 9 8 7 6 5 4 3 2 1

DEDICATION

To my parents,

Buster & Bernice

My sisters,

Carol & Pat

My wife, son and daughter-in-law,

Maureen, Sebastian & Irene

TABLE OF CONTENTS

Making the Difference

From a Small Seed a Garden Grows

Through the generosity of small, local grants, the hard work of a Principal and his students, and the expertise of local craftsmen, a garden idea became a reality for the children of an elementary school. It began with a few fifth grade students planning a creative, outdoor space that included planting a variety of horticulture specimens, and creating a cascade of water over rocks in a reflection pond. The special garden offered seating among oaks and cedars, in a serene setting meant for reflection and reading. It soon became a popular place for teachers and students to share literature, read poetry and enjoy the beauty of nature.

As the garden idea grew in popularity, so did its design. Plans are now in the making to expand the small garden into a center courtyard, overlooking a new library extension. An amphitheater is taking shape in the garden, turning an outdoor space into a classroom with wireless Internet access points for study. Local volunteer groups and organizations are assisting small children with plans to add memorial waterscapes, bird feeders and wind chimes. A small pond is being expanded into an in ground pool filled with Koi and water plants. Speaker plants will pipe soft music into this unique learning space.

Exercise:

What purpose does this garden serve?

____

____

How does the garden change school and enrich the curriculum?

____

____

What would you add to the garden?

____

____

What gardening ideas do you have?

____

____

List other types of gardens.

____

____

Chapter 1:

Introduction To Philosophies of Education

Chapter Topics:

Definition
Asking Why
Sample Question
Philosophical Thoughts
Philosophy Unit Terminology
Comparison of Philosophies
Two Views of Education
Parochial School Philosophy
Public School Philosophy
Philosophy/Teaching Inventory
Statements of Philosophical Belief
Philosophy of the Arts
Example of Class Project—My Teaching Philosophy

Definition: ***An educational philosophy is a series of value statements that guide the teacher in classroom decisions.*** As with a philosophy of life, an educational philosophy establishes guidelines, point of reference parameters when decisions are to be made.

In life, a value or morals governs a person's will to take the correct action.

The classroom also provides an opportunity for values to guide the teacher in following a consistent pattern. If a teacher believes (values) that students should be active learners, then he or she would select teaching methods that would allow students to participate in games, field trips, role-playing and discussions.

Having an educational philosophy provides for a consistent pattern of actions in the classroom that will help the teacher become more confident in decision making.

Exercise:

What is your most important teaching value?

____

____

____

____

____

Asking "Why?"

As a student, you have probably questioned why a teacher was doing things in a certain way or even questioned why you were learning a given subject or required to take this course.

Why do I have to take this test?
How come we have to take Gym?
Why can't I wear these. . .?
Why do I always have to sit in this same seat?

Every "***why***" deserves an answer. And every answer should lead back to a philosophy of schooling—a set of values that supports or guides the reasons for making those choices. ***School should be designed by choice, not by chance.*** Choices should be by reason, not by chance!

Sample Question

Why do schools begin at 7:30 A.M.? What are other choices?

Considering a Later School Bell

- A number of school districts are considering a later start time of 8:30 A.M. for high school students.
- Students have to wake up as early as 5:00 A.M. to get ready for a 7:20 A.M. start time.
- Research seems to support teacher observations that students sleep through their early morning classes.
- Students who start at later times are more alert and responsive during morning classes. They are reported to gain an hour or more sleep time per night, and as a result have fewer mood swings. There has also been a drop in absenteeism.
- A later start does have scheduling concerns for sporting event start times.
- There is an additional concern of busing at times that overlap with start times of middle and elementary schools. Often, districts would have to increase budget requirements to include double or triple the number of buses needed to accommodate the scheduling change.

Exercise:

Write your own questions and possible alternative solutions.

Philosophical Thoughts

Exercise:

Highlight and explain the key words representing each philosophy.

A truly educated environment is one in which there is ***a balance*** between ***factors*** under the learner's control and those that he could not influence. A learner's situation in which the learner can exercise no control in terms of his purposes, teaches him to conform or to rebel, but not to master. A learning situation in which all the factors are under the learner's control leads to whimsical or undisciplined behavior. Desirable learning results from the learner recognizing factors in the situation to which he must adopt and the others that he can manipulate in terms of his purposes.

John A. Dewey

Pragmatism

____

____

____

Education should leave the student to consider the ***universal*** questions and ***aspirations*** of mankind throughout the study of the great works of literature, philosophy, history and science in which they have been expressed.

George F. Kneller

Realism

____

____

____

I took a piece of ***plastic clay***,
And ***idly*** fashioned it one day,
And, as my fingers pressed it still,
It moved and yielded to my will.

It came again when days were passed
The bit of clay was hard at last
The form I gave it, still it bore
But I could change that form no more.

I took a piece of ***living clay***
And ***deftly*** formed it day by day
And molded with my power and art
A young child's soft and yielding heart.

It came again when years were gone
It was a man I looked upon
He still that early impress bore
By I could change it never more.

Author Unknown

Idealism

____

____

____

It seems to me that anything that can be taught to another is relatively ***inconsequential***, and has little or no significant influences on ***behavior***.

Carl Rogers

Existentialism

____

____

____

Philosophy Unit Terminology

- **Educational Philosophy:** A statement that reflects the values/principles that guide a teacher in making choices[1] in the classroom.

Exercise:

Explain choices in a relationship to dress code.

- **Metaphysics:** The nature of reality or what is real is the concern of metaphysics. Such questions as: Is there a meaning to life? Why do I exist? Why do we educate? What is the purpose of education? These are all possible questions that are raised in the discussion of ***"reality."***

- **Epistemology:** The study of knowledge and how to acquire knowledge or how to know that things are true. There are several types or ways of acquiring knowledge:

  Revealed: Knowledge that has been ***disclosed*** to man by God. Books such as the Koran, the Bible, and Bhagavad-Gita house these eternal truths.

  Rational: Knowledge that is derived from using ***reasoning*** powers. A logical thinking process using formal logic and mathematics is intuitive.

  Empirical: Knowledge that is ***confirmed*** through our senses—seeing, hearing, smelling, feeling, and tasting; knowledge that can be duplicated or that reflects our powers of observation.

  Authoritative: Knowledge that we accept as true comes from ***noted*** experts in their respective fields—things that have been proven true and we accept without question; (U.S. Capitals, the speed of sound, and George Washington's presidency).

  Intuitive: Knowledge that comes from within. I know things are true, inner feelings and insight.

[1] Choices and decisions are used interchangeably.

- **Axiology:** The study of values. What we teach and how we teach are reflective of our value system. The study of values includes the following aspects:

  Objectivity of Values: Are values objective or subjective? If values are objective, then they exist in their own right, regardless of personal choices. If values are subjective, then they reflect personal preference, not external views.

  Absoluteness of Values: Are the values permanent and unchanging, or are they consistently changing? Values can be viewed as absolute or changing. Absolute values were true three thousand years ago and will be true throughout our eternity.

  Hierarchy of Values: Does one value hold more importance than another? If there were a value conflict (choice between values), which value would be selected? If there is a hierarchy, then the choice is already made. What decisions should students be given in learning?

Exercise:

1. List the types of decisions you will make as a teacher in the classroom (grading).

2. Explain the most important decision that you will make.

3. What decisions should students be given in learning?

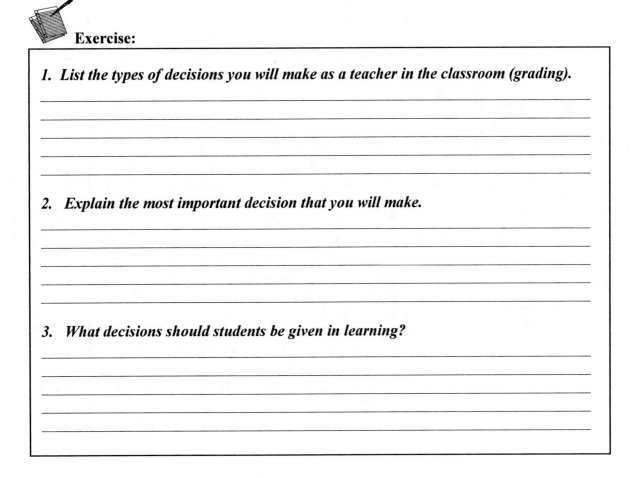

Comparison of Various Philosophies

Directions: Highlight your individual choices for each category.

	Reality	Curriculum Emphasis	Teaching Methods	Values Making	Classroom	Decision
	Classical - Traditional - Authoritarian - Convergent					
Realist	Physical World Natural	3 Rs Math & Science	Lecture, Drill Books Laboratory	Permanent Well-Rounded Man	Structured Rows of Chairs	Teacher 90%
Idealist	World of Ideals Form Spiritual	3 Rs Humanities "The Ideal Man Great Books	Informal Lecture and Discussion	Permanent Ideal Man	Semiformal "Schoolish"	Teacher 75%
	Forward - Liberal - Nonauthoritative - Divergent					
Pragmatist (Constructivism)	Experiencing World	3 R's Social Sciences Social Exp. A need to improve the social order	Problem-Solving and Groups Any Method that works Projects	Changing "Whatever Works"	Laboratory for Learning Informal "Well Used" Open Space	Teacher 55% Student 45%
Existentialist	Lived Reality Freedom	3 Rs Humanities "The Ideal Man" Great Books	Socratic Discussion & Role-Playing	Changing Personal Freedom & Choices	Open Space Community	Teacher 20% Student 80%

Two Views of Education

Exercise:

Highlight the views that you favor most.

Traditional View of Education

- ***Student:***
  - Reasoning is learned through mental exercises.
  - The student can learn through conditioning.
  - The mind is capable of integrating pieces of learning.
  - Mental calisthenics are important to develop the mind.
- ***Teacher:***
  - A model of excellence, scholarliness, expert.
  - Demonstrator of content and knowledge.
  - Mental disciplinarian and spiritual leader.
  - Curator of knowledge and tradition.
- ***Curriculum:***
  - Literature and history are subjects of symbol.
  - Mathematics and science are physical world subjects.
  - Language and logic are subjects of the intellect.
  - Great books and doctrine are subject matter.
- ***Method:***
  - Master facts and information.
  - Rote learning and memorization are stressed.
  - Assigned reading and homework.
  - Study is a means of intellectual discipline.

Progressive View of Education

- ***Student:***
  - Learner is an experiencing person.
  - Learner has freedom of choice.
  - Student awareness and acceptance highly esteemed.
  - Human experiences important as related to change.
  - Learn through experience.
- ***Teacher:***
  - Research project director.
  - Teacher serves as a guide for learned activities.
  - Teacher is ***never*** obtrusive.
  - Teachers ***always*** respectful of the rights of others.
  - A motivator.
- ***Curriculum:***
  - Content should not be compartmentalized.
  - Interest of pupils may demand what is to be studied.
  - Group learning and field trips are valuable.
  - Subject matter of social experience.
- ***Method:***
  - Maximum of self-expression and choice.
  - Formal instruction is minimal in favor of learning areas that appeal to the student.
  - Problem solving.
  - Teach how to manage change.

Philosophy and Goals of a Parochial School

We're seeking to build a Christian community rooted in the Gospel of Jesus Christ. It is our acceptance of this spiritual mandate that gives meaning to the academic, athletic, cultural and social programs. A hallmark of Catholic education is a belief that "the glory of God is the human person fully alive, is lived throughout in our daily experience of love, learning and service to others."

As Christians in the community, we commit ourselves to providing a comprehensive education for students entering the twenty-first century. As educators, we live this commitment by providing instruction in a caring and nurturing environment.

To implement the above, the administration and staff must promote the following goals:

1. ***Sustain*** an environment where Christian tradition and Catholic identity form the basis of all endeavors.
2. ***Provide*** a comprehensive curriculum that recognizes the individual's needs, talents and differences.
3. ***Stimulate*** students by providing opportunities for self-expression, critical thinking, problem-solving, and aesthetic appreciation.
4. ***Provide*** through student, teacher, community and diocesan interaction, a variety of curricular and co-curricular activities that promote respect for individual differences.
5. ***Encourage*** students to assume responsibility for their learning and actions so that they will become lifelong learners and contributing members of a democratic society.
6. ***Improve*** student communication skills in reading, writing, speaking and listening.
7. ***Help*** students access their academic and vocational goals and the means for realizing them.
8. ***Prepare*** students to accept the challenges of a rapidly changing, pluralistic society by providing a knowledge base and opportunities for the practical application of social awareness.
9. ***Nurture*** personal growth by providing opportunities for physical, intellectual, social and spiritual development preparatory to accepting adult responsibilities related to self-sufficiency, home life and leisure pursuits.

Exercise:

Explain how goal number three could be implemented.

Public School Philosophy

We believe that each child is endowed with his or her own individual capacities and characteristics, and that our schools, to the best of our ability, should provide each child with the kind of education best fitted to him or her as an individual. We know that the needs of children are similar, but not identical, and we try to adapt our program to this knowledge.

As children become older and more mature, we try to provide them with the opportunities to make choices for themselves, as we believe that the making of wise choices is a necessary part of living in a democracy. We try to avoid asking children to make choices too difficult for their level of development and maturity.

We believe a spirit of free inquiry is essential to education in a democracy. To establish the climate essential for freedom, teachers and administrators need to follow book selection practices calculated to provide a wide variety of reading experiences.

Your High School Philosophy

Exercise:

From a high school handbook, list three philosophical goals. Use direct quotes.

1. ____

____

2. ____

____

3. ____

____

Philosophy/Teaching Inventory

The following inventory concerns your feelings about some teaching practices. Its purpose is to provide you with meaningful information about your own possible philosophy of education.

There are no right or wrong answers. The best answer is the one most descriptive of your feelings and opinions. Therefore, answer each item honestly, because only realistic answers will provide you with useful information about your philosophy of education.

Statements of Philosophical Belief

Exercise:

Each of the following statements represents different philosophical thoughts. Read each statement and rate the statements on how they represent your philosophical viewpoint.

Strongly Value (SV)	Moderately Value (MV)	Little Value (LV)

_____ 1. Students should be helped to understand that the world exists as an expression of a supernatural power.

_____ 2. The basic need for man is to understand the physical and psychological forces that control the universe.

_____ 3. Man must learn through trial and error to adapt himself to his environment in whatever manner he chooses.

_____ 4. Man must learn to develop ideas and assumptions that enable him to control his own destiny.

_____ 5. Man must predict problems that occur and ***adjust*** his society to meet them.

_____ 6. Change is quite inevitable; man must learn to alter his ideas and institutions to fit present problems.

_____ 7. Change represents an uneven but consistent system process for ***improving*** life for mankind.

_____ 8. The teacher serves primarily to transmit the best of man's accumulated knowledge and beliefs.

_____ 9. The school must develop in students the academic and intellectual skills demanded by present culture.

_____ 10. The school must make cultural problems real to the students and assist them in arriving at tentative solutions.

_____ 11. The basic job of the school is to acquaint learners with the greatest minds and most valid ideas known to mankind.

_____ 12. Students must learn to develop novel ideas and approaches to the unique problems that will occur in their lifetimes.

_____ 13. Students must be helped to develop a sense of right or wrong that is acceptable to them in their daily lives.

_____ 14. Students must learn to apply fundamental, moral ideas to present problems.

_____ 15. Students must learn to alter traditional ideas of right and wrong whenever they become irrelevant to existing problems.

_____ 16. Students must learn to live with a basic and unchanging moral code.

_____ 17. The school must identify the skills and ideas needed in the coming society and help students to develop them.
_____ 18. The school exists solely to help students apply reason and knowledge in their daily lives.
_____ 19. The school should perform the role expected of it by the culture.
_____ 20. The school must equip all students to know and understand the great, classical ideas as well as their ability permits.
_____ 21. Institutions and social customs change, but man is and always has been fundamentally the same.
_____ 22. The teacher serves primarily to organize curricular experience and to direct students toward efficient learning processes.
_____ 23. The teacher serves primarily to guide and direct students in the process of organizing learning experiences.
_____ 24. The teacher is variously a source of information, a planning director and a disciplinarian, depending on the needs of the class. The teacher's prime role is to keep the class interested, excited and open to ideas.
_____ 25. Students must learn to make decisions, relate them to others and accept responsibility for their own ideas.
_____ 26. Students must become aware of the traditional beliefs that underlie and give meaning to daily life.
_____ 27. Students must learn to test their ideas and determine whether they are valid.
_____ 28. Students must learn to make decisions, relate them to others and accept responsibility for their own ideas.
_____ 29. Our schools neglect the bright students and cater to average and below average learners.
_____ 30. Our schools fail to develop fundamental academic skills.
_____ 31. Our schools fail to deal with the problems of importance to students.
_____ 32. Our schools are tuned to the past and teach much that is outdated and useless.
_____ 33. We plan to meet the unique cultural and personal problems that will hurt in the near future.
_____ 34. We should involve students more actively in planning and executing curricular ideas.
_____ 35. We should return to a more concentrated emphasis on fundamental subjects.

Notes:

____

____

____

____

Exercise:

For the top two statements that you strongly value, complete the following exercise using the format indicated.

Statement: "The basic need for man is to understand the physical and psychological forces that control the universe."

Explanation: We need to know the laws of science and math that make the world as it is. How do things grow? What is rain? How does it function? Why and how do planes fly? What causes disease? Man has a thought process, and it's important to understand how he thinks for living, social impact and basic human relations.

Practice: Require science, math and psychology courses for all students. Have laboratories for the students that will allow students to discover some of the answers and raise questions.

The statement you strongly value most.
Statement:

Explanation:

Practice:

Your second choice.
Statement:

Explanation:

Practice:

Philosophy and the Arts

All the philosophies teach art, but each will approach the subject in a different manner both from a subject and style perspective. Your task is to classify the works of art from a philosophical point of view. (Classroom exercise)

	Realism	**Idealism**	**Pragmatism**	**Existentialism**
Subject	Nature Man posed Forced Fixed	Ideal person Religion myths Truths	Life, Natural movement In/Outdoors with action	Emotion, Feeling, Concepts, Places, Dreams, Unknown
Style	Clear, "Photo," Bright colors Smooth brushstrokes	Clear, "Photo," Bright colors Smooth brushstrokes	Blurry, Fuzzy, Dots, Pastels, Unique color combinations	Abstract, Concrete, Blurry, Clear, Pastels, Sharp color
Artist				
Process	Repetition	Repetition	Use your senses to see and feel	Allow your emotions to free your talent

Exercise:

Classify each of the following painting titles as to the philosophy they represent. (Notes will be given by the instructor.)

Title of Painting	**Artist**	**Philosophy**

What is your favorite painting and why?

Example of Class Project

Philosophy Project
My Teaching Philosophy
by Kathy N.

I have decided, after many years of working in a different field that the course in my life I most want to pursue is to become a teacher. It's in this profession that I feel I'll find the most fulfillment as a human being. I believe that teaching is one of the most important roles anyone can have in society, as education is the foundation in everyone's life. From the moment a child takes their first steps into a classroom, what takes place there is what helps mold him or her into the adult that they will eventually become.

I believe that every individual, no matter what their culture, race, religion or other circumstances may be, has a right to an equal education. Everyone is worthy of a teacher's time and effort and should never be made to feel otherwise. There is so broad a spectrum of possibilities that lie within each individual, that the outcome of their education can inspire any kind of greatness. It is well within each of us that is the focus of my desire to become a teacher. I think it is a great challenge to invoke not only the best from each student, but to give their uniqueness the inspiration it deserves.

The importance of the teaching profession is like no other, and that the care, the guidance and the physical and mental well-being of society's children are put into the teacher's hands. The number of hours spent with a teacher each day, during the school year, naturally influences the course of the students' lives outside of the classroom. The teacher becomes not only the interpreter of knowledge, but a counselor and role model in moral behavior and acceptable social skills. In this aspect, the significance of the lessons taught becomes even greater as you see them applied in the students' everyday lives.

In today's society, the importance of the teacher has become even greater. With the necessity in many cases for both parents to maintain a career, the need of the students for guidance, acceptance, motivation and reassurance is much more extreme. A teacher must now take on more of a parental role that was not necessarily required as much in the past. The teacher may become more of a confidant to a student than the actual parent is. In this case, the role that the teacher plays, and the limitations he or she sets on their involvement, is of greater consequence to the student than it ever used to be. With this added responsibility, the teacher's job assumes a more importance than it has ever had before.

The accomplishment of a teacher is measured today not only on the basis of traditional knowledge that a student accumulates from him or her, but from the values gained or lost in the experience. Therefore, it is critical that the teacher have definite ideas and values to impart on his or her students that are well thought out, and most important, defensible. It will be with these ideas and values that a teacher will make good decisions that will lead to his or her success.

I think it is imperative for a teacher to stay up-to-date and on top of his or her field. With the world always changing, new technologies becoming available, and new methods of teaching being discovered, it's important to stay abreast. New ideas and techniques to motivate children can only bring more excitement to the classroom and improve their success as well as the teachers.

The value I feel most critical to the success of teaching is the recognition of each individual as a human being, with the equal right to education. It is with this strong belief, assisting a teacher in decisions that would give every student an equal chance in the classroom, no matter what their level or special needs. Along with this comes acknowledgement of each student's right to respect and fair treatment by others. I believe that social standards are absolute in this regard and my classrooms policies would have to be based with this, and as it's most important principle, in mind. In these beliefs I come closest to the Realists' philosophy in that "what is right is right for man in general, not simply for the members of a particular race or society."[2]

Another value that I believe to be important in decision-making is the evaluation of the students' progress. I think fair practices, those that encompass the whole class (perhaps at different levels), are those that are the best. Effort above all should be rewarded, as with none there would be no achievement. The recognition of this effort, or the failure of, should be considered along with the student's individual ability in the evaluation process. There are a lot of complications in the evaluation of some students, as I have seen firsthand in my field experience. I think it is crucial for a teacher to develop a full background on the nature of the student and his or her particular problems to be able to best recognize the effort they're capable of.

The uniqueness of each student, as I mentioned in my opening, is something I would personally value as a teacher and am sure would guide me in the decision-making process. I would stress in my classroom the need to develop the individualized strengths that each of the students possess and search for motivational techniques to inspire their own ideas and pride in their individuality. I think it is critical for the students to be able to recognize and accept differences as a positive rather than a negative force in their lives. This will equip them with social skills that will enhance society's tolerance for uniqueness in the future.

The intent of my ideas and value system would be, in summary, to prepare my students for their adult life in society, according to age-appropriate lessons. There are many things that I have learned from my teachers that I will carry with me today, and still assist me in making wise choices. I hope to be able to arm my students with lessons they will carry into adulthood that will aid them in making the right decisions in their lives.

Every teacher, I am sure, has his or her own ideas about what changes they would make to enhance education for children. Mine may be similar to many, but they are ideas that I feel strongly about. The first thing I would look to change in classroom teaching is the increasing size of students per classroom. With the growth of curriculum, it gets more

---

[2] Dr. Frank Paoni, *On Becoming a Teacher*, Dubuque, IA Kendall/Hunt, 1975, p. 28.

difficult for one teacher to cover all that is necessary in the school year with a larger amount of students. If this were impossible I think co-teaching is a valid solution to the problem. As we saw in the film *Teacher/Teacher*, a larger class is better accompanied by a pair of instructors. This also gives the teachers the opportunity and time to work individually with any students that require extra help. On the other end of the spectrum those students that are ready to move ahead will have the opportunity to do so with more ease and guidance. Co-teaching or smaller class sizes also give the teacher the occasion to get to know the students better. This can only assist in the understanding of each of their abilities, strengths and weaknesses.

With the escalation of two-career families, and time constraints on parental involvement, I think a system has to be better developed to inform parents about their child's grade point average with increased frequency. In elementary schools the problem may not be as pronounced as it is at the middle school and high school levels. At this stage children are less likely to share their scholastic difficulties with parents; I'm sure for several different reasons. Many times the parent is informed about problems at a stage in the marking period that is too late to assist in any way. I like the idea of a biweekly or monthly status report filled out by the teacher on each student's progress, to be signed and then commented on by the parent. If this were done, teachers defenses of their rating systems would decrease considerably, early warning signs would be well established and both students and parents would be made aware in a timely fashion to institute changes essential to earning a higher average. With this type of frequent communication required, a teacher may come to a better understanding of situations in the students' home life and possibly provide assistance to a student that otherwise may not have been deemed necessary.

The last thing I believe is important enough to change is the way that the Basic Skills children are taken in and out of the regular classroom. I recognize the need for children to be segregated for their special needs and am a strong supporter of the Basic Skills Program, but believe a more organized and efficient way of doing this has to be established. In many cases in the classroom I am doing my field work in, the two boys who go to basic skills for reading return only to sit while the class is doing something else. During a lesson I was presenting they returned, and when I included them in what we were doing they informed me that they didn't have to do any work when they came back. I find this distressing as they are more than capable of completing a lot of work that they are missing. I think it is essential that a schedule be worked out between the teachers for a well-established time frame. Lesson plans can be prepared and implemented to include these children in whatever is being done while they are present in their regular classrooms. I feel by not doing this, the foundation for the Basic Skills program is being torn down.

In every profession, a person begins with high expectations of what he or she will accomplish in their field. Our ambitions are what drive us to become a success. In addition, every new teacher has certain expectations and ambitions for his or her students as well as themselves. I think it is important though, for these expectations to be realistic, in this field especially, as frustration on both the student's part and the teacher's can easily set in.

In order for students in my class to obtain what I consider academic success, they will have to show me above all, their strongest effort for staying on task and completing the assigned work. It will be my job to recognize what each individual is capable of and to consider this in their evaluations. I will empress upon my students the significance of their active participation in all of the classes' activities, as this will influence their grades. The art of communicating is a great one, and I hope to build confidence in each child by encouraging the free expression of their thoughts through controlled discussions, artwork, writing, and other projects. It will be imperative, with consideration to different levels, that everyone be involved.

I will require that a mutual respect be established among all of us in the classroom, where no one is ever made to feel ashamed or embarrassed of any of their contributions. This respect will encompass personal property, the use of proper language, and manners that I believe are appropriate for the atmosphere. With definite standards set up that are religiously adhered to, I think the classroom can be a wonderful social experience for all of those included. In summary, my expectations of my students will be to be the best that they can be. I can expect no more from them and will expect no less. Again each individual's level, special needs, and ability will have to be considered. I feel that this is a realistic requirement and one through which frustration can easily be thwarted by the motivation of the students enthusiasm for learning.

School and Classroom Design

While considering the possibilities of incorporating my own ideas into a design of a classroom, I kept having one persistent thought, and that was light. I have been in several schools that are dark and dreary, and I believe this can be a deterrent to learning. This is the reason there is both a design for a school and a classroom included. I felt that I had to show how to bring outside light into a building, then a single room. Air conditioning will be imperative, as the natural light will also produce heat that has to be stabilized.

In the school design there is a wide hallway (in black) that surrounds the core facilities of the building. The ceiling structure above this hallway will include a dome-shaped skylight to cover the entire hall. Each classroom lining the hallway will have a glass (safety) wall from the ceiling to the floor in order to allow this light to come in. The classrooms that border the exterior line of the building will also have this glass wall facing out. Each room will include its own skylight to further enhance the natural lighting.

Classroom

The library/conservatory sections of the building, on each side of the entrance, will be two stories and again have glass walls on the exterior. I have allowed maximum space for this section of the school, as I think a library with this atmosphere would be very conducive to learning. The enlarged area would also increase the amount of time each student would be able to spend there.

Two computer labs have been included to make it possible for each student within the school to have maximum exposure and time for applications. With changing technology a constant, it is a necessity that cannot be overlooked in the design of new school buildings.

Finally are the core facilities. An auditorium is in the front of the building that you step down into. This is to allow the rows of seats to accumulate in height for the viewer's sake. Behind this are the two gym areas. I think both gyms are necessary to avoid too many combinations of more than one class. The wall dividing the two can be opened to accommodate spectators for sporting events.

The last of the core facilities is the cafeteria. This modernized style with glass walls will give the students more of a break from the mood of the traditional classroom.

The classroom design is one that I would find ideal. It allows maximum space for separate areas within groupings of students, this kind of room would be conducive to them being able to work at their own pace with less pressure. It is also large enough to accommodate a large class and could easily work well if team-teaching were to be necessary.

As you enter the classroom, there are students' lockers lining the first two walls and sofas for gathering before and after the start and finish of class time, I like the idea of having lockers within the homeroom, as there is always an adult presence close by. The teacher's desk is placed in the middle to oversee student activities no matter where they are in the room.

The separate areas include individualized seating in the traditional style, a group area with counter space and storage, and relaxed seating with bookshelves lining the walls. This area would also be used for the viewing of any media. Computers are also included in each classroom as again, technology is demanding. The exterior wall, be it lining the outside of the school or the hallway, will be glass from ceiling to floor. Over the center of the room is the skylight mentioned in the school design, depicted by the dotted line.

Both the school and the classroom layouts were designed with the middle school or high school level in mind. Depending on the amount or students proposed for attendance, it could easily be build as a two-story building with classrooms on the upper level as well.

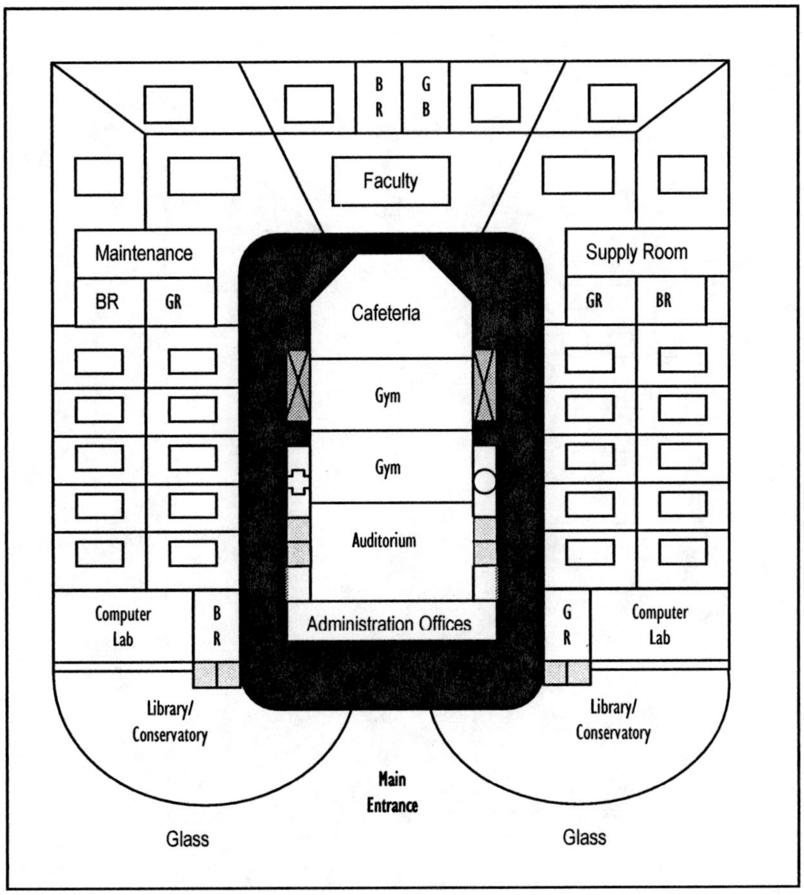

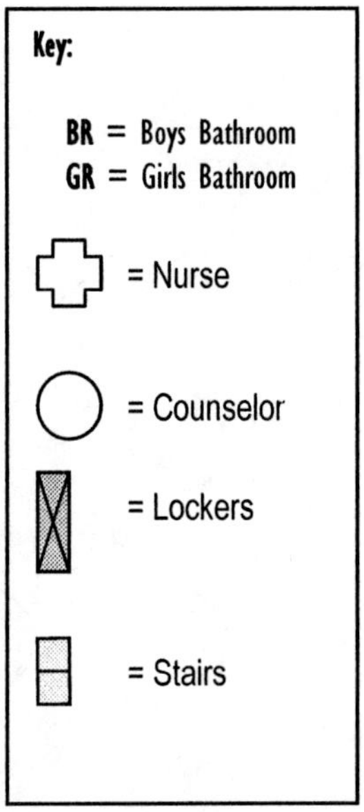

School Layout

Exercise:

What are the advantages and the disadvantages to the above layout?

Advantages:

____

____

____

Disadvantages:

____

____

____

Classroom Layout

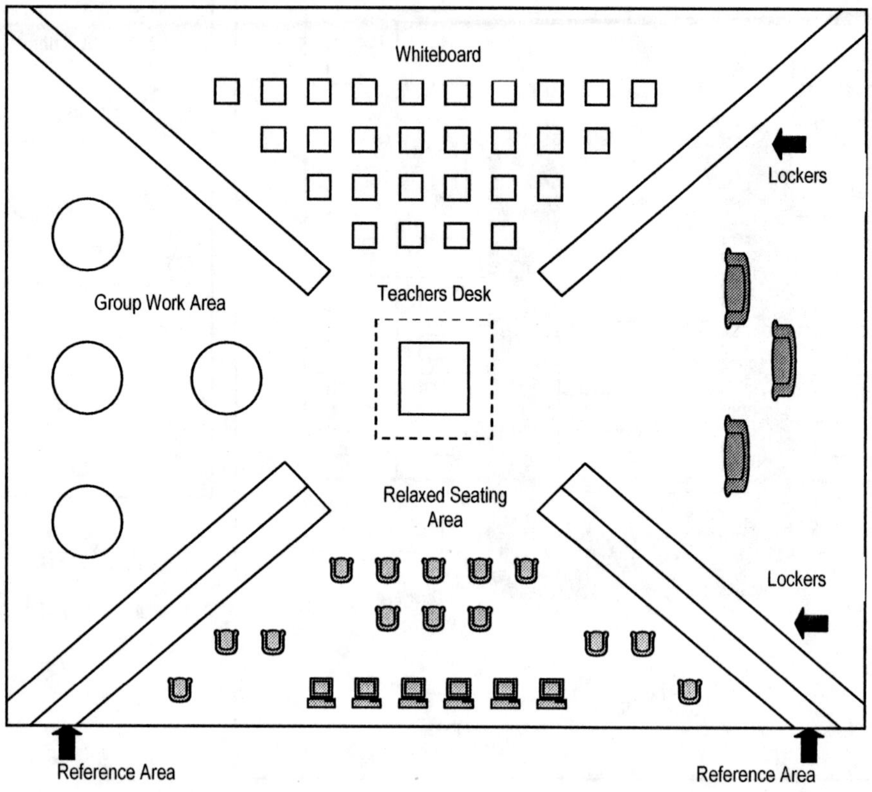

Chapter Notes & Additional Information:

Chapter 2:

Philosophies of Education

Chapter Topics:

This chapter will focus on four philosophies and one theory of education that have influenced the American educational system. Pragmatism and Realism have had the greatest impact on both public and private institutions. Existentialism and Idealism have had more impact on the private sector of American education. Constructivism, based upon Jean Piaget's theories, offers a unique view of schooling.

Pragmatism

"Man is the measure of all things"

Pragmatism (Dewey, James)

Basic Beliefs

1. Utility or usefulness is the key to an effective philosophy.
2. Learning is essentially the interaction between man and his environment.
3. "***Right***" and "***wrong***" are relative, rather than absolute terms.
4. Education is experiencing, whereas mastery of content is incidental.

General Aims

1. Based on the activity and goals of members of society and the interest of the learner.
2. Help the individual become a socially efficient member of society.
3. Help man bring meaning to the world through himself.
4. Become a flexible human being.
5. Prepare a student for life because education is life.

Subject Matter

1. Socially desirable activities.
2. Knowledge and skills of interest are useful to the learner.
3. Rather than teaching the traditional subjects directly, the teacher tends to draw on them only as they contribute to the solution of the problems at hand.

4. The pragmatist does not reject the study of logically, organized subject matter, but maintains that this should come later, rather than earlier, in the student's education.
5. Intelligence is best trained by being applied to what interests it.

Methodology

1. The use of problem-solving approach and letting the students select the problem.
2. The use of ***project method*** so that a student draws on the aspects of knowledge that are particularly useful to the task.
3. Reading, writing and arithmetic become more meaningful and more easily mastered when they help the people fulfill their purposes.
4. The ***solution*** to the problem is not as important as the steps by which the student arrived at the problem.

Pragmatist education is ***not opposed to discipline,*** but rather discipline grows out of interest.

1. ***Provide*** experience that will motivate excitement. Field trips, movies, CDs and guest experts are examples of activities designed to awaken student interest in an important problem.
2. ***Guide*** the student into formulating a specific definition of the problem. Since each student approaches the problem from his or her own experimental background, the teacher should encourage all students to formulate their own aims and goals.
3. ***Plan*** individual and group objectives with the class to be used in solving the problem.
4. ***Assist*** the students in collecting information pertaining to the problem. Essentially, the teacher serves as a guide by introducing skills, understanding, knowledge and appreciation through the use of books, compositions, letters, research speakers, movies, field trips, television or anything else that may be appropriate.
5. ***Evaluate*** what the class learned and how they learned it, what new information occurred, and what each student discovered for himself or herself.

Exercise:

Highlight the thoughts or statements that you favor. Describe your view of the Pragmatist classroom.

Student's Role

The learner is an individual who grows or develops from within the activity in a social setting and through the use of intelligence. Learners would well adjust to their environment and know a great deal about solving problems with little factual information. An individual would follow his own interests and probably resist directions. The students' interests and ***curiosity*** principally motivate their learning.

Teacher's Role

The role of the teacher is that of a guide or counselor. There is no room for indoctrinations or leadership. The teacher is to assist the student when he or she is in difficulty and to guide general development in the light of a superior wisdom, which the student ***does not yet possess.*** The teacher teaches the student to adapt himself or herself to a community of individuals and their needs and ideas.

In Experimentalism, learning is always considered to be an individual matter. Teachers ought not to try to pour the knowledge they have into the student because such efforts are fruitless anyway. What each student learns depends on their own personal needs, interests and problems. In other words, the content of knowledge is not an end in itself but a means to an end. Thus, students who are faced by a problem may be able to reconstruct their environment in order to solve this felt need.

Values

Values are ***relative***. There are no absolute principles on which we can lean, irrespective of their consequences for other. The values to be taught in school are those that advance human welfare. The student should learn how to make difficult, moral decisions, not by falling back on rigidly prescribed principles, but rather by determining which course of intelligent action is likely to produce the best results in human, finite terms.

Self-realization is the supreme end of all men.

Education is never-ending and is the means to self-realization. The student is evaluated by progress of the learner in terms of a native ability to master the facts, skills and attitudes demanded by the social group of which they are a part. The degree to which students grasp crucial concepts, problems or values, which have been and should be operating in today's society, is important.

Additional Notes for Pragmatism:

Pragmatism Thoughts and Ideas

Principal Themes: The reality of change, man is a social and biological being, the relativity of values, and the use of critical intelligences.

Reality is the interaction of man with his environment. Is what we experience. Man and his environment are "coordinates." They are equally responsible for what is real.

(George Kneller)

Man gives new meaning to the universe.

The student must study a world as it affects him or her.

Human nature is plastic and changeable.

Children only grow by associating with others. They must learn ***to live in a community of individuals,*** cooperate with them and adapt to social needs and goals.

Knowledge is produced by a transaction between man and his environment.

We grasp things best by locating and solving problems.

Education is all one with growing. He has no end by itself.

The value of schooling is the extent to which it encourages a desire for continued growth.

A child is a natural learner, because he or she is curious. The teacher's role is to stimulate that curiosity.

Values are relative and the child should learn how to make different moral decisions, not by relying on rigidly stated principles, but by deciding which action is likely to produce the most favorable consequences for the greatest number of human beings.

Education should be life itself, not preparing for living.

Learning should be directly related to the interests of the child.

Learning through problem-solving should take precedence over the inculcating of subject matter.

The teacher's role is not to direct, but to advise.

The school should encourage cooperation rather than competition.

Only democracy permits, indeed encourages, the free interplay of ideas and personalities that are a necessary condition of true growth.

Exercise:

Explain the boldfaced statements:

____

____

____

Pragmatism

Teachers' Roles	Teaching Methods	Curriculum Subject Matter	Students' Roles
A resource person in the classroom who directs the students to reliable sources of information A comrade and a counselor to students. A guide on leading students to discover correct methods for solving problems. Directs and assists students in acquiring sensitivities and competencies that are necessary for social change and leadership. Acts as a stimulus of natural curiosity in students. Assists students in creating and focusing on social problems in their environment so that they can control and/or change it.	Free and open classroom discussion. **Use of projects constructed around social problems.** **Team and interdisciplinary teaching.** Use of independent student programs. Field trips. **Construction and use of many problem-solving activities.** **Heavy reliance on the scientific method to solve problems.**	Social Sciences Curriculum is divided into units of study that are based on the interests and needs of the student. A variety of elective subjects in the learning program. Experience-oriented subject matter. Interdisciplinary arrangement of subject matter Topics, themes and/or subject matter is socially oriented.	An active participant in the learning process. An experiencing organism capable of using native intelligence to solve the problems of the environment. A social member of a group potentially capable of actively participating in the realization of future social objectives. Must learn to make difficult moral decisions by decoding which courses of action are likely to produce the best results for society.

Exercise:

Explain one concept from each category.

Teacher's Role: ______________________________

Teaching Methods: ______________________________

Curriculum Subject Matter: ______________________________

Students' Roles: ______________________________

Realism

"Schools should produce students who are well rounded."

Realism (Aristotle, St. Thomas Aquinas, Adler, Hutchins)

Basic Beliefs

1. The universe has physical reality. It is not an accumulation of ideas.
2. Man learns about his universe through his senses.
3. We learn ***through systematic observation*** and ***experimentation.***
4. Learning should have some practical application.

General Aims and Objectives:

1. To develop the rational power of man; to reason, judge and discriminate.
2. Reasoning differentiates man from lower animals.
3. To perfect man through the development of his intellect and through humanistic endeavors.
4. To relate teaching to the present, instead of the past.

The purpose of education is not to convert each student into something where an individual, but to enable him or her to become a tolerant and well-adjusted person, in harmony, both mentally and physically, with the physical and cultural environment.

Subject Matter

Besides the three Rs, physical science would have the most important place in school. The great amount of thought (the classics) are included as well as subjects of a practical nature (typing, industrial arts and driver training), but not those of the behavioral sciences (psychology, sociology and anthropology) because they are not yet reliable enough to warrant major attention in the school.

Methodology

The initiative in education rests with the teacher. Intelligence demands discipline and the learning of the scientific method and problem solving.

1. Recognizing a problem.
2. Designing a method for reaching a solution
3. Carrying out the essential steps toward a solution.

Memorization is a learning strategy that is often employed.

The teaching method recommended by the Realist is ***authoritative.*** The teacher must require that the student be able to ***recall, explain and compare facts; to interpret relationships; and to infer new meanings.*** Evaluation is an essential aspect of teaching according to the realism.

The teacher must use objective methods by evaluating and giving the type of test that lends itself to accurate measurement of the student's understanding of essential material. Frequent tests are highly desirable. For motivational purposes, Realists stress that it is important for the teacher to always reward the success of each student. A teacher who rewards the accomplishments of students, reinforces what has been learned.

Exercise:

> ***Highlight the thoughts or statements that you favor. Describe your view of the Realist classroom.***
>
> ____
>
> ____
>
> ____

Student's Role

A mind to be trained. It is the student's responsibility to master those elements of knowledge that have stood the test of time. Before deciding what can be done with the world, the students should learn what experts say the world is really like. The students should ***not be allowed to find out*** whatever they want to know because often what they want to know is less important than what they should know.

Teacher's Role

The umpire between true and false logic. It is the teacher's responsibility to decide what knowledge the students should learn, to teach the students to face reality and to be able to adapt to their own circumstances, to be able to figure their way out when confronted with problem situations, and to impart to the student the substantive knowledge of the actual world.

The Realist classroom is ***teacher centered.*** Students are taught by a teacher who is impersonal and objective and who knows the subject fully. The teacher must utilize student interest by relating material to students' experience and by making the subject matter as concrete as possible. The teacher maintains discipline by rewarding efforts and achievements.

Values are ***permanent and objective.*** All educational systems should be geared to certain well-defined values. Similarly, the moral standards that we teach the child should be influenced as little as possible by the teacher's views. Instead, they should conform to what has proven to be the enduring values of man throughout history. The child should be taught to live by ***absolute moral standards*** in knowledge of what is right for man in general, not simply for the members of a particular race for society. It is also important for the child to acquire good habits, for virtue does not come automatically: it has to be learned.

Realism Thoughts and Ideas

Matter is the alternate reality; hills, trees, cities and stars are not simply ideas in the mind of observing individuals. They exist in and of themselves, independently of the mind.

The principle of ***independence*** is that there exists a world of things, events and relations among these things and events, and this world is not dependent for its existence and character on its being known.

The universe is ***permanent*** and enduring. Change is real, but it takes place in accordance with permanent laws of nature that give the universe continued structure.

All Realists believe that values are ***permanent and objective***; they differ in their reasons for thinking so.

Realists agree that all educational systems should be geared towards certain well-defined values. Since values themselves do not vary, neither do the true ends of education.

The purpose of education is not primarily to convert each child into something rare and individual; it is to enable him or her to become a ***tolerant and well-adjusted*** person, in harmony mentally and physically with the physical and cultural environment.

It is the student's responsibility to master those elements of knowledge that have ***stood the test of time***. Before deciding what can be done with the world, he or she should learn what experts say the world is really like.

Since man is a rational being, the school should be given priority to the cultivation of ***reason.***

Learning necessarily involves ***hard work and application.***

The initiative in education should lie with the teacher rather than the student.

The heart of the educational process is the ***absorption*** of prescribed subject matter.

The school should retain ***traditional methods*** of mental discipline.

The school should be a training ground to do ***necessary but unattractive tasks***.

Authority begins by being external. It is significant if it ends, through habit formation and self-control, thus becoming internal.

"The will must be developed in the individual before he can exercise free will. He does not know what he desires."

Exercise:

Explain the above italicized quote.____

____

Realism

Aristotle (382–322)

Teachers' Roles	Teaching Methods	Curriculum Subject Matter	Students' Roles
To introduce the student to the "natural world" by acting as a guide. Provide the student with the regularities of nature (the rhythm) and understand the "natural laws." Teacher is a spectator (observer) of the universe. A servant of the learner, nature and society. Provides the student with a set of self-defined values. Assists students in becoming intellectually well-balanced individuals.	Extensive employment of drills and exercises. Lecture–demonstrations and other sensory related techniques. Controversial dialogue. Use of the scientific method to develop logical thinking skills. Field trips. Audiovisual materials and equipment.	Subject matter oriented toward self-development and fulfillment. Emphasis on knowledge that deals with human condition. Curriculum is comprised of those kinds of subjects that can be measured and/or quantified. Social Sciences in the curriculum are studied from the point of view of the natural force that bears on human behavior. The curriculum is composed of the essential facts of knowledge that have with stood the test of time.	A biologically functioning organism who experiences the natural world through sensory experiences. Must be subject to the discipline of natural law (the coercive order of nature). A machine to be conditioned and programmed A mind to be trained and filled with enduring facts and principle.

Exercise:

Explain one concept from each category.

Teachers' Role: ______________________________

Teaching Methods: ______________________________

Curriculum Subject Matter: ______________________________

Students' Role: ______________________________

Existentialism
"I should seek not the way, but my way."

Existentialism

Basic Beliefs

It is a philosophy of ***personal freedom*** and responsibility. Man is the sum of his own actions, for each of which he is fully responsible, because he could have chosen otherwise.

General Aims and Objectives

1. To help the student learn to live life in the knowledge that someday, on a day like this one, ***life is going to end.***
2. Let the students ask themselves what they are living for. Are they living to the full as free men, or are they content simply to exist? When they die, will it have mattered whether they lived at all, or should they, as Blaise Pascal said, "Live today as if you were to die tomorrow?"

Methodology

1. Any method that is desired by the students.
2. Group work is discouraged in favor of individual work.
3. The ***end*** of group education is the education of the individual. The individual uses the group for his or her own personal fulfillment.

The Existentialist also deplores the tendency of parents to surrender more and more of their educative responsibilities to the school. At home, the child can be an individual. At school he or she must share the attention of the teacher with many other students.

The ***problem-centered approach*** of experimentalism is rejected on the grounds that the problems chosen concern students chiefly in their role as a social being.

The Existentialist teacher must be democratic and thus utilize a nondirective technique.

- **Democratic:** The teacher never imposes personal goals on the student. The teacher's function is to guide the student. The teacher is a research person and must therefore make plans along with the students (democratically) on the basis of their individual needs and goals.

- **Nondirective:** Exact and detailed lesson plans are not necessary; this would be imposing adult interests and values on the student. With the teacher as a guide, each individual must be free to develop his or her own purposes and work out his or her own learning. ***Problems the individual student directs to***

the teacher should be reflected back in such a way as to arouse the student's insight into the nature of the problem.

Subject Matter and Curriculum

The whole emphasis of the curriculum must shift from the ***world of objects*** to the ***world of the person***.

Knowledge, properly conceived, brings freedom because it delivers man from ignorance and prejudice and enables one to see oneself as he or she really is. The school must, therefore, completely revise its conception of knowledge. It must cease to regard subject matter as an end in itself, or as an instrument to prepare the student for a future career, and should consider it instead as ***a means for the cultivation of the self.*** Great importance is attached to the humanities, since history, literature, philosophy and art are revealed in greater depth than any other subjects revealing the nature of humanity and its conflict with the world. A considerable body of traditional subject matter must be mastered, but overspecialization is a mistake because it stunts the growth of the student's total inner life.

Student's Role

Learning is no longer regarded primarily as mental discipline. The students should be urged to involve themselves intellectually and ***emotionally*** in whatever they study. The students must appropriate to themselves and exercise a problem or study they tackle.

Ideally the student should use any career occupation as primarily a means for the exercise of freedom and only secondarily for immediate and tangible rewards.

Teacher's Role

The role of the teacher is to assist each student personally in a journey toward self-realization. A good teacher acts as a free agent. The teacher's influence is not temporary, but persists into adult life. A good teacher urges students to challenge and criticize their own ideas. The teacher advises them not to be discouraged by fear or error. He or she pleads with them never to take the opinions of others for granted. The teacher must also encourage the students to commit themselves to their work, to reflect on each item of knowledge until it is of importance to them personally.

When dealing with the rebellious adolescent, the teacher should not seek to humiliate them or hold them up to the ridicule of the rest of the class. By all means the teacher must punish the student, pointing out that certain behavior will not be tolerated. Do not talk down to the student or seek to rid the student of self-respect.

The teacher should impress each student with the need to be himself or herself rather than a stereotype of the group. He should point out that in order to be a man, it is not necessary merely to fill a T-shirt, but to also have courage, values and independence.

Values

The only values acceptable to the individual are those that he or she freely has adopted.

Existentialism provides no cover for self-egoism, for to seek selfishly one's own freedom, regardless of its effect on that of other people, is to violate the very meaning of freedom.

The teacher should not impose his or her own values, but should present the principles in which he or she believes and the reasons for them, and then ask the student to choose whether he or she will accept them or not.

The teacher should bring home vividly to the students that, whatever they do, they cannot escape the ***consequences of their actions***. The students must accept their actions as the issue of their own free choice, however thoughtless that choice may be.

Classroom

When introducing a subject, the teacher seeks to introduce as many points of view as possible. He or she seeks to present the subject as a product of the thoughts of many people and as a focus of continuing thought.

It is not the teacher's intention to let the students use whatever view of the subject he or she desires. The teacher does not impose an interpretation either. Instead, after a full discussion the teacher offers the student what he or she believes to be the best view of the subject and asks whether the students will accept it.

Process

The teacher presents the class with a variety of views. The teacher is well read and knowledgeable about the subject and submits the subject for discussion. After discussions, the teacher offers a personal view and asks each student to test their view against their own experience. If the students reject the view, it is put forth as their right to do so.

Existentialism insists not that the teacher be successful, only that he or she be honest.

Subject matter

No subject is more important (in itself) than any other. The subject that matters is the one in which the individual finds self-fulfillment and an awareness of the world.

The ***humanities*** loom large in Existentialism because they deal with the essential aspects of human existence.

Concern is not for what is taught but for its purpose.

The teacher encourages the students to think for themselves. He or she questions the students about their ideas, proposes other ideas and so leads them to choose between alternatives.

Learning/knowledge is not ***"soaking up"*** but is acquired by **active effort**, by never closing the mind or heart, and by seeking more profound truth than those one possesses.

Methods

The Socratic method is the ideal mode of education, since by it, the student learns what he or she personally asserts to be true.

Teacher

The teacher should impress each student with the need to be himself or herself rather than a stereotype of a group. By word and deed the teacher should express the student's independence.

The teacher is not in the classroom primarily to impart knowledge (realism) or as a consultant in problem solving (pragmatism) or a personality to emulate idealism. The teacher's function is to assist each student personally in a journey toward self-realization.

Exercise:

Highlight the thoughts or statements that you favor. Describe your view of the Existentialist classroom.

____

____

____

____

Existentialism Thoughts and Ideas

Metaphysics

Reality is ***lived***. To describe the real, we must describe not what is beyond, but what the human condition is.

Philosophy should be reason informed by passion. It is in passion, in states of heightened feeling, that ultimate realities are disclosed.

The physical universe, the world apart from man, has neither meaning nor purpose—just something that ***happens to be there.***

In the universe, man happens by chance. There is no natural scheme of things. Man owes nothing to nature but existence. Existence then precedes essence, in the sense that he or she must exist to become.

"Man is nothing other than what he makes himself."

As free men and free teachers, we must seek to expose in combat all those forces in culture and society that tend to dehumanize men by denying them their freedom.

Choosing

"Freedom" is neither a good nor an ideal. It is a potential for action. Serious choices are between values, both good and bad.

Freedom is never exhausted in a single act. It leads to further choices. True freedom implies communion and not egoism. The egoist is driven by narrow self-interest.

"Man is condemned to be free—Man is free, therefore he is totally responsible and has no excuse, no exit."

Exercise:

Explain the boldfaced, italicized quote.

____

____

____

____

Knowing

My knowledge depends on my understanding of reality, on my own interpretation of the nature of being. Subject matter (codified knowledge) should be treated neither as an end in itself nor as a means of preparing the student for an occupation and career. It should be used, rather, as a means toward self-development and self-fulfillment.

Let the growing person think out troubles for him or herself. One must find truths true to oneself. Specialization diminishes the man. He is a creature of knowledge, not the masters of it.

Teaching and Learning

"A dialogue is a conversation between persons in which each person remains a subject for the other, a conversation."

Teaching cannot be a true dialogue if the teacher were construed as instructor, one who simply meditates between a student and the subject matter. When teaching is understood as instructing, the teacher is devalued into a means for the transfer of knowledge, and the student is devalued into the product of this transfer.

Existentialism

Friedrich Nietzsche (1845-1900)

Teachers' Roles	Teaching Methods	Curriculum Subject Matter	Students' Roles
Acts as an interrogator in the classroom. Offers knowledge from previous subject matter from areas that students may make choices. Is also an active learner. Urges students to take responsibility for and to deal with the results of their actions. Seeks to make students active and critical thinkers about their existence in the world they live in. Director in the learning process. Encourages free play and physical activity in a noncompetitive manner and atmosphere.	Role-playing Psychodrama Much reading and "Socratic discussion." Controversial dialogue. Use of the scientific method to develop logical thinking skills. Field trips. Audiovisual materials and equipment.	Subject matter oriented toward self-development and fulfillment. Emphasis on knowledge that deals with the human condition. A broad curriculum that would include some rough and difficult academic subjects. Students are exposed to diverse cultural patterns and lifestyles in the subject matter. The curriculum material would be composed of information that stresses the individual and his or her capacity for making decisions. Subjects might be organized around themes that deal with the individual and his or her world.	An active and spontaneous learner. The ultimate chooser for learning. Responsible for choices and actions. An interrogator of the Teacher. Actively seeks knowledge and truth by never closing the mind or the heart. Is an actor in the entire drama of learning. Chooses values and ethics that are consistent with being an authentic, unique, individual person with both private and public Needs.

Exercise:

Explain one concept from each category.

Teachers' Role: ______________________________

Teaching Methods: ______________________________

Curriculum Subject Matter: ______________________________

Students' Role: ______________________________

Idealism
"To see things as they should be rather than as they are."

Idealism (Socrates, Plato, Hart, Butler and Hegel)

Basic beliefs

1. Ideas are of the ultimate importance.
2. Man is basically good.
3. Faith is dominant over proof.
4. Certain truths are eternal.

General Ames and Objectives

1. To form an intellectual elite.
2. To develop a unit between the spirit of man, nature, tradition (what has withstood the test of time), cultural heritage and the state.

Subject Matter and Curriculum

1. To develop the student's ability to read, write and discuss.
2. Ideas included are the arts, music, ethics and literature.

The curriculum should reflect the wholeness of knowledge and a more concentrated effort toward subjects such as philosophy, history and religion. Science should be taught less as factual information than as a way of thinking.

Methodology

Develop a student's mind through basic method of lecture and drill. It is based on the following reasoning:

1. I have mastered certain of society's great ideas.
2. My students have not learned these ideas.
3. I will pass along this part of their heritage by the written and spoken word.
4. Theory does not lead to mastery, therefore ***repetition*** is necessary.

The classroom structure and atmosphere and should provide the student with opportunities to think and to apply the criteria of moral evaluation to concrete situations within the context of the subjects. The teaching methods must encourage the acquisition of facts as well as skill in reflecting on these facts. It is not sufficient to teach students how to think. ***It is very important that students think about why they are acquiring information;*** otherwise, they will simply compound their ignorance.

Teaching methods should encourage students to enlarge their horizons, stimulate reflective thinking, encourage personal choices, provide skills in logical thinking, provide opportunities to apply knowledge to moral and social problems, stimulate interest in the subject content and encourage students to accept the values of human civilization.

Student's Role

The student is a plastic mind to mold. Much attention is given to the child and to the individual differences. The purpose of teaching is not so much to familiarize the students with the mass of information, as to stimulate them to ***discover the meaning of information*** for themselves, relating the known to what is around oneself.

Teacher's Role

The teacher is the selector of information and a person the student may emulate. He or she seeks to bring out knowledge from students rather than pouring into them, although the content of education is not something that the students decide for themselves.

In idealism, the teacher is ***deemed more important*** than in other educational philosophies.

Idealists have high expectations of the teacher. The teacher must be ***excellent***, in order to serve as an example for the student, both intellectually and morally. No other single element in the school system is more important than the teacher. The teacher must excel in knowledge and in human insight into the needs and capacities of the students and must demonstrate moral excellence in personal conduct and convictions. The teacher must also exercise great ***creative skill*** in providing opportunities for the students mind to discover, analyze, unify, synthesize and create applications of knowledge to life and behavior.

Values

Values are absolute and unchanging. School policy must therefore be founded on enduring principles. "There are no really bad children, but only those who have strayed away from or do not yet fully comprehend the fundamental moral order of the universe," or as Hart stated in his categorical imperative:

> ***We shall all act always as though our actions were to become a universal law of nature, binding on all men in similar circumstances.***

The evolution of a student is in terms of how nearly the student has attained the ideal standards established by the best work, achievement and tradition of the past and the specific standards set by the instructor.

Idealism Thoughts and Ideas

Ultimate reality is spiritual rather than physical, mental rather than material.

Coherence Theory of Truth: The more comprehensive the system of our knowledge and the more consistent the ideas it embraces, the more truth it may be said to possess. (***Henkel***)

The purpose of a teacher is not so much to present the student with a mass of information as to help him impose order and meaning on it.

(Kant)

Values and ethics are absolute. They are not man-made, but are part of the very nature of the universe.

Evil is incomplete good, ugliness is beauty, incomplete or disorganized.

(Butler)

There are really no bad children, but only those who have strayed or don't comprehend the fundamental moral order of the universe.

"The world is my idea."

(Schopenhauer)

Exercise:

Explain the above boldfaced, italicized quote.

____

____

____

____

Man is both free and determined; free as in spirit, determined to the extent that he is also a physical being subject to natural laws.

The idealist teacher presides like Socrates over the birth of ideas—developing possibilities within the student.

Education is the eternal process of superior adjustment of the physically and mentally developed, free, conscious human being to God, as manifested in the intellectual, emotional environment of man.

(Horne)

Interest, Effort and Discipline: Effort is the will to do things when one does not want to.

Strengths of idealism

- High level of cognitive education
- Concern for morality and character.
- Stress on the human and personal side of life.
- Approach to education is holistic.

Additional Idealism Notes:

____

____

____

____

____

____

____

____

Idealism

Socrates (469–399BC)

Teachers' Roles	**Teaching Methods**	**Curriculum Subject Matter**	**Students' Roles**
The most important person in the classroom. An example for students to follow and imitate. Wrings out knowledge from students. Assists students in imposing order and meaning on all information and knowledge. Presents enduring values to live by. Responds to students as individuals to develop each student's individual destiny. Maker of decisions.	Socratic discussions. Textbook readings. Drills. Memorization. Recitation Any technique that instills physical, mental and moral discipline. Informal lecture. Controlled discussion.	Idea-centered. The Humanities (history, modern and classical language, philosophy, literature and the arts). The subject matter of ideas, as found in books. Curriculum is primarily literary and is concerned with the "Ideal Man" and the "Ideal Society" (the accumulated heritage of the human species).	A spiritual being in the process of becoming a representation of the "Absolute Self." Attempts to get closer to the absolute by imitating his teacher. A plastic mind to be molded in accordance with his spiritual destiny. Relates information (knowledge) "wrung out" by the teacher to previous personal experiences.

Exercise:

Explain one concept from each category.

Teachers' Role: ______________________________

Teaching Methods:______________________________

Curriculum Subject Matter: ______________________________

Students' Role: ______________________________

Constructivism

Definition: ***A philosophical belief and practice that asserts that each individual understands and interprets the world differently and create personal knowledge based on experiences.***

According to Jean Piaget, a noted psychologist and anthropologist, children move through several stages of development. As each day progresses the child constructs knowledge and enhances understanding to the processes of assimilation and accommodation. Guided instruction, scaffolding and problem-solving practices enable the teacher to present a learner-focused environment, rich in experiences and created on exploration and discovery.

A noted psychologist, Howard Gardner, suggest that there are four approaches to understanding.

- ***Observational Approach:*** An apprenticeship where children learn by doing often using multiple-input diverse settings.

- ***Confrontational Approach:*** Direct involvement where the learners consider their beliefs. The teacher encourages understanding by pointing out misconceptions and asking students to reflect on consequences. The student gradually learns to monitor intuitive thought and cultivate habits of understanding.

- ***Asystematic Approach:*** The teacher possesses specific understanding goals that are correlated through performance. Stressing generative topics central to specific disciplines in interest, the teacher promotes personal learning environments. Students gain understanding through questioning and practical applications. Their understanding is assessed through regular interim practice performances.

- ***Focused Approach:*** Through the use of multiple intelligences, the teacher is able to use different pedagogical approaches to reach more students in more effective ways. This implies more time being spent on topics of discovery, a portrayal of the topic in a variety of ways to illustrate its intricacies and to reach various students, the use of multiple approaches to learning and teaching that explicitly call on the range of intelligences, skills and interests.

An essential component of the constructivist environment is the notion that we do not learn in a vacuum. For us to understand the world, we must interact with other humans. Central to the constructivist philosophy is the need to involve children in socially appropriate activities relying on peers and adults to help share a clear understanding of the world around us.

Central to this theory our practices such as cooperative group activities, peer tutoring, reciprocal teaching, workshop environments and free exploration periods where conversation and active involvement are encouraged.

Creating a Field Trip for Each Philosophy

Exercise:

For each philosophy create a field trip that represents the philosophy (in any subject area) and explain how it represents that philosophy's values.

Example:

Realism: A field trip to San Diego to study the environment via scientific investigation. Take water samples, collect specimens and try seining. Write a description for each specimen found. Conduct experiments concerning tides, etc.

Rationale: The Realist believes in scientific investigation through laboratory research and the scientific method. He or she also believes that this is a physical, natural world governed by physical, natural laws. Therefore, we should study the physical universe/environment and the laws that govern it.

Pragmatist:

Trip: ____

____

____

____

Rationale:

____

____

____

Existentialist:

Trip: ____

____

____

____

Rationale:

____

____

____

Idealist:

Trip: ______________________________

____

____

____

Rationale:

____

____

____

Chapter Notes & Additional Information:

____

____

____

____

____

____

____

____

____

____

____

____

____

____

____

Personal Thoughts & Ideas

Chapter 3:

Schools That Are Different

Chapter Topics:

School Makes a Difference

This chapter will explore the elements that make schools different. Why is one school better than another? Even when all are equal, especially when it comes to money, there seems to be an inequality among schools.

There are key characteristics among the better schools that can be applied to all schools for improvement. Each of the quality schools may seem to have a different focus, but what drives them is a steady belief in what they are doing and a clear ***philosophy*** of schooling.

As you build your classroom and your school, reflect on the possibilities and the dreams. Do not be constrained by money considerations or what was, think only of what can be.

Chapters 1 and 2 gave a theoretical framework for your ideas. This chapter will focus on how they can be implemented and give examples of possible dreams.

As a starting point for creating a dream school or classroom, reflect on your previous school experiences. Go back from the earliest to your most recent school days and focus on those aspects that gave you the strongest positive images.

Exercise:

What were your favorite years in school and why?

My Favorite years in school was when I was in grammar school. I found it more Fun and interesting than High School. I participated alot in activites and sports and was less shy to particapate.

School Images

Things I like Best About Schooling

Exercise:

Reflect on personnel, curriculum, teaching methods, experiences, clubs, sports and students.

I enjoyed playing soccer, art, reading etc...
I remember my 4th grade teacher very well. Her name was Mrs. Harris. She was a very dedicated teacher and really try to help each individual student. She made everything Fun and interesting.

Things I Dislike About Schooling

Exercise:

Reflect on personnel, curriculum, teaching methods, experiences, clubs, sports and students.

The five changes I would make in education or schooling would be: (Ex: Require all teachers to know their students' names. Utilize more interesting ways of teaching.)

____
____
____
____
____

Describe your academic abilities and how your teachers viewed you as a student.

____
____
____
____
____

Multiple Intelligence: A New Way of Looking at Students

"What all children need begins early in their lives, someone who believes in them and supports the way in which they learn best."

Thomas Armstrong

Howard Gardner identified eight different intelligences that each person possesses to some degree. Circle the ones you feel most likely represent your intellectual strengths.

1. ***Linguistic Intelligence***
2. ***Logical Mathematical Intelligence***
3. ***Spatial Intelligence***
4. ***Musical Intelligence***
5. ***Bodily-Kinesthetic Intelligence***
6. ***Interpersonal Intelligence***
7. ***Intrapersonal Intelligence***
8. ***Naturalist Intelligence***

Howard Gardner's definition of intelligence supersedes that of learning styles. It is through our intelligences that we possess, associate and create understanding and knowledge. Our learning styles are favored avenues of taking in new ideas. In effect, learning styles operate within our separate intelligences.

Descriptions of Intelligences

1. ***Linguistic Intelligence:*** People with this intelligence exhibit the ability to recall, understand and use language, native, or perhaps other languages in both verbal and written form. They are sensitive to the sounds, rhythms, inflections and

meters of words. They have sensitivity to the different functions of language—its potential to excite, convince, stimulate, and convey information or simply to please.

2. ***Logical Mathematical Intelligence:*** The ability to think logically and to view the world in mathematical relationships. Those with mathematical intelligence can set up a string of symbols and carry out a set of operations using these symbols for solving a problem. They are guided by reason and have a feeling or sense for the order of operations. They may have the ability to create new combinations using mathematical entities with the desire to change the way others think about mathematical order. They love to deal in abstract thought and find enjoyment proving theories relevant to physical reality that have long been considered unsolvable.

3. ***Spatial Intelligence:*** The ability to think in visual with spatial imagery. This ability transcends verbal, written or graphic forms with the capacity to perceive the visual world accurately and to transform and modify one's perceptions to recreate visual experiences even in the absence of a physical stimulus. They have a sensitivity to the various lines of force that act on the visual or spatial display; a feeling for tension, balance and composition.

4. ***Musical intelligence:*** This intelligence finds strength in the ability to think musically, to have understanding and application with the use of pitch, volume and timbre (tone quality). They have a strong auditory sense, can remember music easily and cannot get music out of their minds. Through the use of music, they can capture emotion and forms of feeling. In composition musical intelligences is evident in the ability to have schema or "frame" for hearing music and creating pieces that convey well-structured phrases in a musical sense.

5. ***Bodily-Kinesthetic Intelligence:*** The ability to move through space, to use one's body in different skilled ways for expression and goal-directed purposes, to work skillfully with objects both involving fine motor and gross motor movements. They develop a keen mastery in the motions of their bodies to possess a fluidity of motion. They have a strong sense of timing and direction. When used in elegant ways, this intelligence produces a desired effect where there is an end to one action for a second action to occur.

6. ***Interpersonal Intelligence:*** The ability to notice and make distinctions among other individuals, particularly among their moods, temperaments, motivations and intentions. The individual who is sensitive to others and the outside community can act on this knowledge to influence a group of others.

7. ***Intrapersonal Intelligence:*** Those who have a strong sense of self and are secure in their strengths and weaknesses. They attract others because of their ability to know themselves and they exhibit a strong central focus with the capacity to set goals for self-growth. They are able to cope with their surroundings and feel a

sense of self-assurance in performing the tasks they set. People who exhibit intrapersonal intelligence have the ability to access their feelings over a range of emotions. They can instantaneously discriminate, understand and guide their behavior. They gain deep sense of their own feelings and can symbolize complex sets of emotions.

8. ***Naturalist Intelligence:*** The ability to recognize and classify animals, minerals and all variety of flora and fauna. The ability to recognize cultural artifacts and to classify them accordingly to distinct characteristics. Having sensitivity to other features of the natural world and to value the interrelationship among natural systems.

Types of Activities to Enhance Multiple Intelligences

Verbal	Visual	Logical	Musical	Inter-personal	Intra-personal	Bodily-Kinesthetic	Naturalist
Bibliographies	Cartoons	Analogies	Acappella	Arguments	Affirmations	Body language	Bird watch
Biographies	Collages	Calculations	Choirs	Challenges	Creative	Dancing	Catch
Books	Constructions	Codes	Choral reads	Collages	Goals	Dramatization	Categorize
CDs	Doodles	Computations	Chords	Communication	Insight	Experiments	rocks
Crosswords	Drawings	Equations	Compositions	Consensus	Interpretations	Facial	Collect shells
Debates	DVDs	Formulas	Harmonies	Conversations	Intuiting	expressions	Ecology
Essays	Illustrations	Fractions	Instruments	Debates	"I" statements	Field trips	studies
Fiction	Maps	Games	Jingles	Dialogs	Journals	Games	Explore caves
Internet	Mobiles	Logical	Melodies	Games	Logs	Gestures	Field studies
Jokes	Models	Matrices	Musicals	Group projects	Meditations	Interviews	Field trips
Listening	Mosaics	Mazes	Neat	Group tasks	Poetry	Lab work	Fish
Magazines	Murals	Outlines	Performance	Mosaics	Quotations	Pantomime	Forecast
Newspapers	Paintings	Patterns	Quartets	Murals	Records	Role-play	Identify plants
Nonfiction	Photographs	Probabilities	Raps	Observation	Reflections	Skits	Nature walks
Poetry	Posters	Puzzles	Rhythms	charts	Self-	Sports	Observe nests
Printouts	Sculptures	Sequences	Scores	Round robins	assessments		Photography
Readings	Sketches	Syllogisms	Songs	Social			Plant
Reports	Statues	Theorems	Trios/Duos	interactions			Star gaze
Research	Storyboards	Timelines		Sports			
Speeches	Symbols						
Storytelling	Visual aids						
Symbols							

From Robin Fogarty, *Problem Based Learning & Other Curriculum Models*

Notes:

Parent's Role for Good Schooling

Exercise:

What are the two most critical things parents must do to support education?

1. ____
____

2. ____
____

Some Ideas for Parents

1. **Be a role model.** Your children should see you reading, working through problems and learning from the mistakes you make.

2. **Do not jump ahead.** Preschool is not high school; the emphasis should be on play. Elementary school is not college; too much time on homework can be counterproductive.

3. **Keep on reading.** Read to children when they are babies and do not stop even when they are excellent readers themselves.

4. **Be involved.** Know what is going on in the school and in the classroom. Be supportive and enrich it. Do not do your kids' work for them!

5. **Applaud the effort.** Parents need to praise hard work and persistence, not just the outcome. Make praise specific, and do not just offer generic esteem boosting.

6. **Allow for mistakes.** Errors are learning opportunities and they can be good practice for dealing with life's setbacks.

7. **Respect your children's style.** Although educators advise a quiet, homework spot without distractions, some kids work better to background noise. Let them do their homework their way, unless their work is suffering.

8. **Do not forget morals.** A strong ethical framework, religious or otherwise, will help your children resist the ever-present siren call of negative peer pressure.

A Collection of Ideas to Improve School

As you read the following suggestions for improving "schools", consider:

- What does it mean?
- How it would be implemented?
- What is the cost of implementation?
- What would it replace?
- What problem does it address?
- What factions would support or oppose it?

Exercise:

Rate the following ideas.

Strongly Value	***Moderately Value***	***Little Value***
SV	***MV***	***LV***

_____ 1. Establish a national examination or curriculum for our students.

_____ 2. Raise the standards for testing; have quality standards.

_____ 3. Give additional time to students who need it.

_____ 4. Make a stronger commitment to professional development of school employees.

_____ 5. Grant school staff and parents more authority over decisions affecting the teaching of our children.

_____ 6. Provide a quality, early-childhood program for all disadvantaged students.

_____ 7. Expand services to eliminate health and social barriers to learning.

_____ 8. Access and make available technologies that support teaching.

_____ 9. Call for more accountability in schooling.

_____ 10. Abolish the student-teaching system.

_____ 11. Establish a Common Core of Learning.

_____ 12. Place less emphasis on the basal reading series and the related tests and more on true reading.

_____ 13. Make assessment of students more practical. (Assessment of students' knowledge to solve problems, think critically and demonstrate their abilities by writing essays or performing experiments versus memorization of material.)

_____ 14. Graduate students on performance not on seat time.

_____ 15. Make sure students are responsible for learning. Four years of C's in English will not gain you a diploma if you cannot write an essay, read for Comprehension, or speak accurately and effectively.

_____ 16. Communicate to parents and students exactly what is expected of them in each course.

_____ 17. Promote interdisciplinary teaching and learning.

_____ 18. Decrease the emphasis on standardized testing and place more emphasis on a meaningful curriculum.

_____ 19. Bring back and reintroduce geography to the schools.

_____ 20. Decrease the size of large schools by having "schools within schools."
_____ 21. Decentralize: Allow more ownership of the school to the teachers, principals and students.
_____ 22. Create magnet schools—specially designed schools that attract students interested in a particular emphasis.
_____ 23. Eliminate tracking and ability grouping, with more emphasis on heterogeneous grouping.
_____ 24. Improve interrelationships of schools, teacher-to-student and student-to-teacher.
_____ 25. Rethink the school calendar.
_____ 26. Finance schools through state income tax first versus property tax.

Rank your top five ideas:

1. ____
2. ____
3. ____
4. ____
5. ____

Three-fourths of high school students in the U.S. enter the workforce without the skills necessary to succeed in the changing workplace.
Twenty percent of college students are in remedial education courses.
A reported 52 percent received a B.A. after six years.
A reported a 30 percent of community college students have a B.A.

New Jersey School Choice

New Jersey joins merely 20 other states where students can cross district lines for their schooling, tuition free.

Under the new proposal, districts with room in their classrooms could sign up within the state to accept outside students. The program would be phased in, with up to 10 districts participating in the first year, 15 in the second and 21 in the third through fifth years.

Parents who wish their children to attend a participating district would apply a year ahead of time. If there are more candidates than openings, they would be chosen through a lottery system. There were also be limits on the number of students leaving anyone district, with a cap of no more than 7 percent of the district's enrollment. Officials estimate that as many as 2,000 students overall could end up participating in the program.

In a new provision, students could not be older than ninth graders before entering the program, to ensure that they will not be in the program for just a year or two.

Charter Schools in New Jersey

The Charter School Program Act of 1995 enacted January 11, 1996, encourages innovation in educating public school children. Private not-for-profit schools are established though state-contracted, district-supportive programs by innovative educators, committed parents and entrepreneurs. The purpose of the charter school is to stimulate reform in the public school system. To date, New Jersey has contracted more than 50 charter schools. Currently, three schools are functioning in Monmouth County.

The charter school operates within its own philosophy and specializes in a certain curriculum or addresses a certain student population. Often centered near at-risk districts, charter schools challenge current public school practices.

"The introduction of charter schools is not just part of an isolated reform effort, but it is one innovative strategy in a broad effort to bring out significant improvements in student achievement.

The charter school program enables teachers, parents, community leaders, private entities and institutions of higher education, to take the lead in designing public schools that will provide unique and innovative approaches toward the achievement of higher academic standards." (The New Jersey Charter School Application, August 1999.)

Characteristics of New Jersey Charter Schools

- Charter schools may not charge tuition.
- A private or parochial school may not convert to a charter school.
- A charter school is open to all students on a space-available basis with preference being given to students from the district of residence or region of residence of the charter school.
- All classroom teachers and professional support staff must hold appropriate New Jersey certification.
- 10,538 students in preschool through grade 12 were attending charter schools in New Jersey as of October, 2000.
- 8,184 of those students attended charter schools in the Abbott districts.
- The highest number of operating charter schools are in Newark, Trenton and Jersey City.
- Charter schools are extending choice to ***predominantly minority students*** (88 percent).
- The average enrollment in a charter school is 193 students.
- The average school year for a charter school is 186 days.

- The average length of the school day in a charter school is slightly over seven hours; students are engaged in instruction for an average of slightly over six hours.
- Ten of the charter schools that opened in 1997 were granted renewals in February, 2001.These renewed charters are for a five-year period.
- Monmouth County hosts three charter schools:

1. **Academy Charter High School**
   Opened 1998 in South Belmar
   Director: Ms. Mary Jo L. Kapulko
   Grades 9–12; first graduating class 2001

2. **Hope Academy Charter School**
   Opened 2001 in Asbury Park
   Director: Ms. Alexis C. Harris
   Grades K–5; emphasis with projected K–8 students

3. **Red Bank Charter School**
   Opened 1998 in Red Bank
   Director: Ms. Meredith Pennotti
   Grades K–8 projected

Sample of a Charter School

Academy Charter High School

Academy Charter High School is a public high school open to all students who reside in towns of Allenhurst, Asbury Park, Avon, Belmar, Bradley Beach, Deal, Interlaken and South Belmar. An extensive outreach program will see a representative cross section of the communities. It opened in September, 1998 with 100 ninth- and tenth-grade students, adding one grade each year to have enrollments of 150 ninth, tenth, and eleventh graders in the 1999–2000 school year, and reaching a maximum amount of 200, ninth, tenth, eleventh and twelfth graders in the 2000–2001 school year.

As a child-centered school, Academy Charter High School is dedicated to providing a challenging, nurturing environment, founded on the virtues of courage, respect, truth and honor, in which each child's social and academic potential is maximized. The nontraditional design of the Academy Charter High School allows the school to function as a community, with the child always at its main focus. Students will be provided with the support and guidance necessary to reach their maximum potential, both socially and academically. The students who graduate from Academy Charter High School will have the self-esteem, self-discipline and intellectual curiosity needed to maintain their status as lifelong learners.

The educational program of Academy Charter High School is designed to meet and exceed core curriculum content standards. The curriculum for each grade level is closely integrated and is based on the interdependency of academic skills. The majority of the school day is block scheduling, resulting in 90-minute class periods. This facilitates the infusion of technology as well as allowing for greater emphasis on the use of creative teaching methods and assessments. Technology is incorporated into all subject areas. Our goal is one computer for every two students. The ability to use and adapt technology is an indispensable skill for survival in the real world.

Various methods of assessment of student work, based on real-life standards are used. Students will demonstrate mastery of material through the use of presentations (both oral and written) and portfolios as well as traditional testing. They will also have the opportunity to design their own projects to demonstrate proficiency. Students and parents are provided with monthly reports reflecting the students' progress toward mastery of the clearly defined goals of each course. Students are able to improve their score on each goal throughout the duration of the course. Allowing students to achieve mastery in this way, along with increased class time in student–teacher interactions, enables teachers to maximize learned potential of the students of various abilities.

Every student will be mentored by a faculty member from their first day of school through graduation. Students will meet with their mentors weekly, both individually and as part of small-group discussions.

Much of the philosophy and governance structure of Academy Charter High School is based on Dr. James Comer's School Development Program (SDP) of the Yale Child Study Center. The STD is under contract to provide staff development (especially in the areas of child development and behavior) and guidance in the areas of school governance, parental involvement, assessment, technology utilization and curriculum development. The SDP model has proven successful in over 300 schools across the country.

It's Not the Money, It's the Principal

Canton Middle School occupies an austere, brick building in a blue-collar neighborhood overlooking an industrial stretch of Baltimore's Inner Harbor. The school's windows are grated; the front entrance is an unwelcoming barricade of steel doors. Canton has 750 students, 55 percent white, typically of Polish, Italian or Greek ancestry; 35 percent black; 5 percent Hispanic; and 5 percent Native American. The only thing they have in common is poverty. Eighty-six meet federal requirements to receive a free lunch. Anyone who visits the school expecting a scene from ***The Blackboard Jungle*** is in for a surprise. With classes in session, the halls are quiet. Bright floors gleam. Most importantly, the school has become an academic showcase with test scores advancing year to year—all of this within a broader school system described by its own interim chief executive officer as "academically bankrupt."

One man gets the credit for Canton's current condition—school Principal Craig Spilman, a 33-year veteran of the system. Spilman was assigned to Canton in 1989, a time when on any given day, one out of every five children was likely to be absent. Today's attendance is at 88 percent. Suspensions are down; test scores are up and in some cases dramatically. The last month, for example, Canton reported that its students had tripled the rate at which they passed a battery of state school-performance tests.

To achieve this improvement, insiders and outsiders agree, Spilman had to break every rule of the system, spoken and unspoken. When he arrived at Canton, he said, "I had to clear the deck." He fired four teachers. "They did not want to work and did not want to change. It did not matter. I wanted them out."

Instead of hiring from within, long the practice in Baltimore, he went outside. He hired teachers from Teach for America, a nonprofit organization that recruits, selects and trains college graduates to work in urban schools. He recruited men and women exiting the Peace Corps or the downsized military, including a former military intelligence specialist and an Arabic translator.

Spilman long ago abandoned traditional classroom models, but this year took an especially daring leap. He adopted the New American Schools' "Expeditionary learning" protocol in which children working as a team, conduct actual field research aimed at producing a final product, such as an exhibition or presentation.

Exercise:

What other changes do you think Craig Spilman made other than firing teachers?

The Copernican Plan

A plan that has the potential of reducing average class size by 20 percent, increasing the number of courses per semester by 20 percent, reducing the number of students a teacher works with every day by 60 to 80 percent, providing students with seminars on complex issues and a more favorable teaching and learning environment.[3]

"Wow! Let's do it"

- **Macro scheduling:** Students take one or two classes over a 30- or a 60-day period. In blocks of 2 to 4 hours—allowing for ***more creative teaching and fewer students.***

- **Individual instruction:** Teachers teach six instead of five classes, and class size drops.

- **Complex issues:** Regular, academic personal interest seminars are built into afternoon "I seminars," which stands for integration as well as interest issues. Students are grouped by interests and not ability.

- **Differentiated diplomas:** Academic Honors, Academic, Occupational, Standard and Completion Diplomas. Each diploma has its own special characteristics.

Exercise:

Rationale for differentiated diplomas:

Mastery Based Credits Verses Letter Grades:

- Each student enrolled 6 macro, 24 courses in 4 years
- 10 mastery credits for successful completion of each course
- I-credit awarded for participation and attitude rather than mastery
- Physical Education, chorus, band, and health education alternate with seminar on prep/help/study.
- 200 days of schooling per year
- Use of IEP (Individualized Education Plan)

[3] Notes from *The Copernican Plan: Restructuring the American High School*, by Joseph M. Carroll, *Phi Delta Kappan*, January 1990, pp. 358-365.

Sample Class Schedule

<table>
<tr><th>Time:</th><th>Schedule A</th><th>Schedule B</th></tr>
<tr><td>7:46</td><td rowspan="3">Macroclass
(226 min.)
for 30 days</td><td>Macroclass I (110 min.)
for 60 days</td></tr>
<tr><td>9:36</td><td>Passing (6 min.)</td></tr>
<tr><td>9:42</td><td>Macroclass II (110 min.)</td></tr>
<tr><td>11:32</td><td>Passing</td><td>(6 min.)</td></tr>
<tr><td>11:38
12:13</td><td>First Lunch (35 min.)</td><td>Seminar I
Music/Phys. Ed.
(70 min.)</td></tr>
<tr><td>12:48</td><td>Seminar II
Music/Phys. Ed.
(70 min.)</td><td>Second Lunch (35 min.)</td></tr>
<tr><td>1:23</td><td>Passing</td><td>(6 min.)</td></tr>
<tr><td>1:29</td><td>Preparation/Help/Study
(70 min.)</td><td>Physical Education/Music</td></tr>
<tr><td>2:39</td><td>Departure</td><td>(6 min.)</td></tr>
<tr><td>2:45
5:00</td><td colspan="2">Activities and Sports
(135 min.)</td></tr>
</table>

Exercise:

What are the advantages and disadvantages to the previous schedule?

Looping: What is it? Does it work?

Looping, in its many forms has been used in education for a number of years. First described in 1913 under the name of ***"teacher rotation,"*** looping allows the teacher to advance with the same students over a period of time, generally within a two-year interval. In theory, looping provides consistency for the students and the teacher as there is no need to ***"get to know one another"*** at the beginning of the second school year. Oftentimes this practice is used at lower grade levels, providing consistency for learning and teaching, particularly when children have wide developmental differences within an emotionally stable learning environment that supports success. For example, a first-grade teacher will remain with his or her class for two years as the children begin reading skill development. Looping also encourages alternative practices such as teaching within a whole language approach or within a cooperative learning structure.

What Are the Benefits of Looping?

- Students remain on task longer at the end of the first year.
- Students gain learning time at the beginning of the second year.
- Teachers accumulate more in-depth understanding of individual students learning styles, strengths and weaknesses.
- More teacher/student contact time.
- Less time spent on pre-assessment activities.
- Parents and teachers can often build strong working relationships.
- It provides stability for students and builds a sense of community.
- Reduces student anxiety about new situations.
- Allows students to focus on skill and social development.
- It has a positive effect on student confidence levels and attitudes.
- Teachers report fewer discipline problems, improved attendance and test results, and reduced retention.
- Teachers, students and parents are more apt to resolve problems rather than allowing them to continue until the end of the first year.
- Looping can easily be established among individual teachers as part of the school structure, or in a schoolwide system approach.
- Looping is easier to implement and fund than any other school reform efforts.

What Are Some Problems Associated with Looping?

- Parents worry the teacher and their child may have an ineffective teacher/learner relationship that might be perpetuated over a longer period of time than the traditional one-year assignment.
- Time might exacerbate problems with teacher/student personality clashes.
- Newcomers may find it difficult to fit into a looping class.

- Teachers and students may find separation after two years emotionally difficult to handle.
- Not all teachers are willing to participate in this approach.
- There needs to be strong, consistent, professional development support for success.
- Avoid a tendency to overload the looping classrooms with special needs students.

Carnegie Foundation for the Advancement of Teaching

The Carnegie notes that ***"good"*** should:

- Agree on and teach children a core of math, science and language and then test to measure results.

  "You cannot expect a nation to continue putting in billions of dollars unless you have some way to measure results," Boyer, the Director of the Carnegie Foundation, said.

- Create a sense of community, stressing discipline and caring to children while reaching out to parents and local businesses.

  "An effective school absolutely has to have parents as full partners," Boyer said

- Provide health, counseling and other services to children and find a way to provide resources such as books, maps, plans, computers and telephone lines.

- Teach children ethics along with academics.

"Schools are often hesitant to do this because of idealistic controversies in the nation's constitutional separation of church and state," Boyer noted.

"But the result is we are leaving students confused about what behavior and conduct is expected," Boyer said. "And sadly, the vacuum is being filled with negative signals."

Exercise:

Explain this concept.

The Ideal Secondary Curriculum

The former Education Secretary William J. Bennett outlined his ideas for the American high school.

Graduation Requirements for a Model High School

English

One year of each of the following (arranged sequentially):

- Introduction to Literature
- American Literature
- British Literature
- Introduction to World Literature

Fine Arts

- Art History (one semester)
- Music History (one semester)

Foreign Language

Two years required in a single language

Mathematics

Three years required from among the following choices:

- Algebra I
- Plane and Solid Geometry
- Algebra II and Trigonometry
- Statistics and Probability (one semester)
- Precalculus (one semester)
- Calculus AB or BC

Physical and Health Education

Two years required

Science

Three years required from among the following choices:

- Astronomy and Geology
- Biology
- Chemistry
- Physics or Principles of Technology

Social Studies

One year of each of the following (arranged sequentially):

- Western Civilization
- American History

One semester of each:

- Principles of American Democracy
- American Democracy and the World

Exercise:

1. ***Explain the strengths of this curriculum.***

____

____

____

2. ***Explain the weaknesses of this curriculum.***

____

____

____

3. ***What subjects are left out (psychology)?***

Creating Lifelong Learners

Probably the most significant goal for schooling is to develop in students the capacity and desire to learn. Yet most of the time spent in the classroom is on the content, not the process. All students have the capacity to learn, but few achieve their full potential.

The reasons are numerous, and often the school has no control over many of them (poor home environment, poor nutrition and ill health), though we can and should teach the process of learning. Casey and Tucker, in their article *"Problem Centered Classroom," Phi Delta Kappan,* October 1994, stated that school is a place where children need to learn the skills of being effective learners, and that being an effective learner is being a ***"creative problem solver."***

Effective learners have the following characteristics:

- Constantly curious and questioning
- Enjoys figuring things out
- Seeks out problems or challenges
- Persistent in working and spending time on tasks
- Flexible in creating how they approach tasks and are independent and seek help when blocked
- Confident about themselves and are risk-takers

Teachers can ensure that students become better problem solvers by:

- Posing open-ended questions
- Teaching the steps of thinking
- Incorporating problem solving in the curriculum
- Connecting lessons to student interests
- Challenging and questioning the students to defend their views
- Focusing on concept development over rote memorization
- Bringing theory into practice and making connections to real-life situations

Exercise:

What teaching strategies are geared toward problem solving?

School Days

Sentiment is growing for U.S. schools to lengthen their academic year. Proponents say a lengthened school year will provide a better education and let the United States keep pace in an increasingly high-tech, global economy.

School Year Length in Days

Japan	243
Israel	261
Germany	210
England (UK)	192
France	185
United States	180

Higher Education*

Number of postsecondary students per 100,000 people

Japan	2,006
Israel	2,769
Germany	2,546
England (UK)	1,795
France	2,362
United States	5,145

Literacy*

Percentage of total population that is literate

Japan	100.0 %
Israel	91.8 %
Germany	100.0 %
France	98.8 %
United States	95.5 %

School Spending*

Percentage of national GNP spent on education

Japan	5.6 %
Israel	8.5 %
Germany	4.6 %
England (UK)	5.2 %
France	5.8 %
United States	6.8 %

Sources: Education Commission of the States; **Britannica World Data Annual*.

School Nutrition

Research shows that up to one-third of American children skip breakfast. Poorly nourished and hungry students create classroom behavior problems that affect the entire classroom's learning time. Research indicates that breakfast program benefits include improved educational achievements and improved health outcomes (less stress, obesity, fatigue and illness). In addition, children who eat breakfast at school have sufficiently reduced absence or tardiness rates, fewer trips to the school nurse and better disciplinary records than those who do not.

Exercise:

How would you implement a school nutrition program?

____

____

Classroom of the Future

Exercise:

Layout of a model classroom designed for New York City that provides separate special project and independent study areas that can be supervised from the teacher's desk, without occupying any more space than the traditional rectangular classroom.

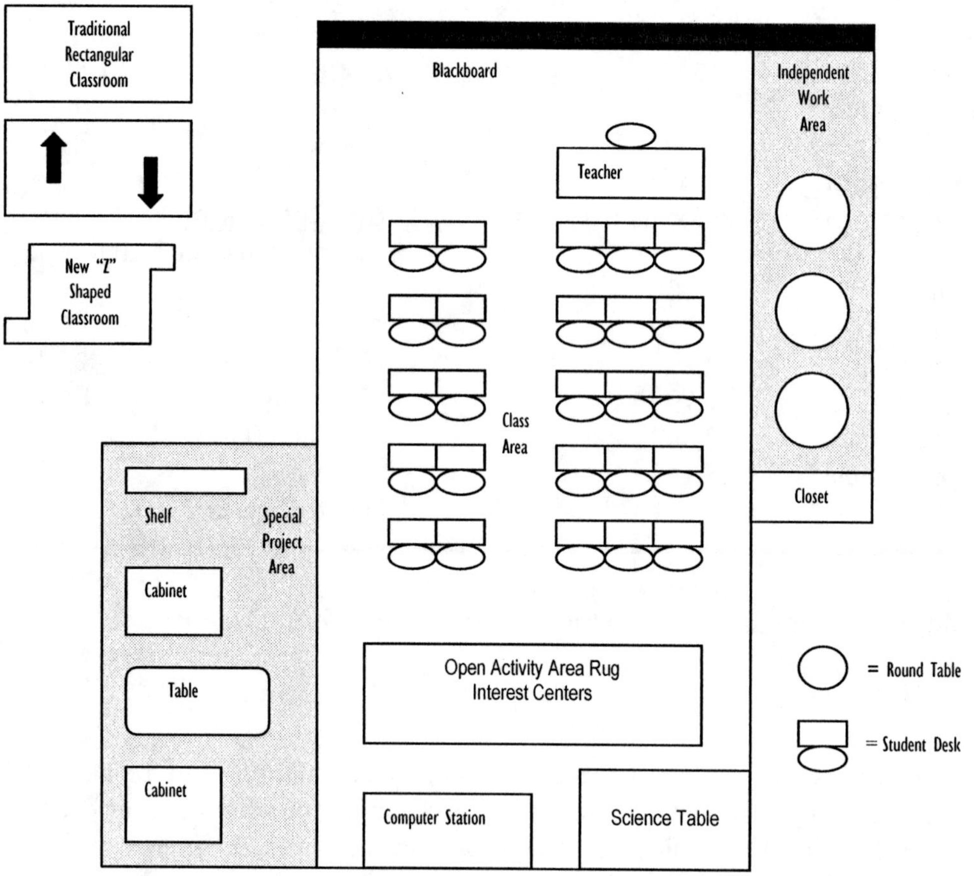

What are the advantages over the old classroom?

____

____

____

____

____

Redesigning Schools

An alternative school for middle and high school students is designed with learning communities meant to keep students calm and limit distractions. Bathrooms are in every classroom. Classrooms surround a common area for eating lunch. Short hallways and one-way traffic patterns keep students from moving room to room and stop them from lingering. Classes are segregated by grade.

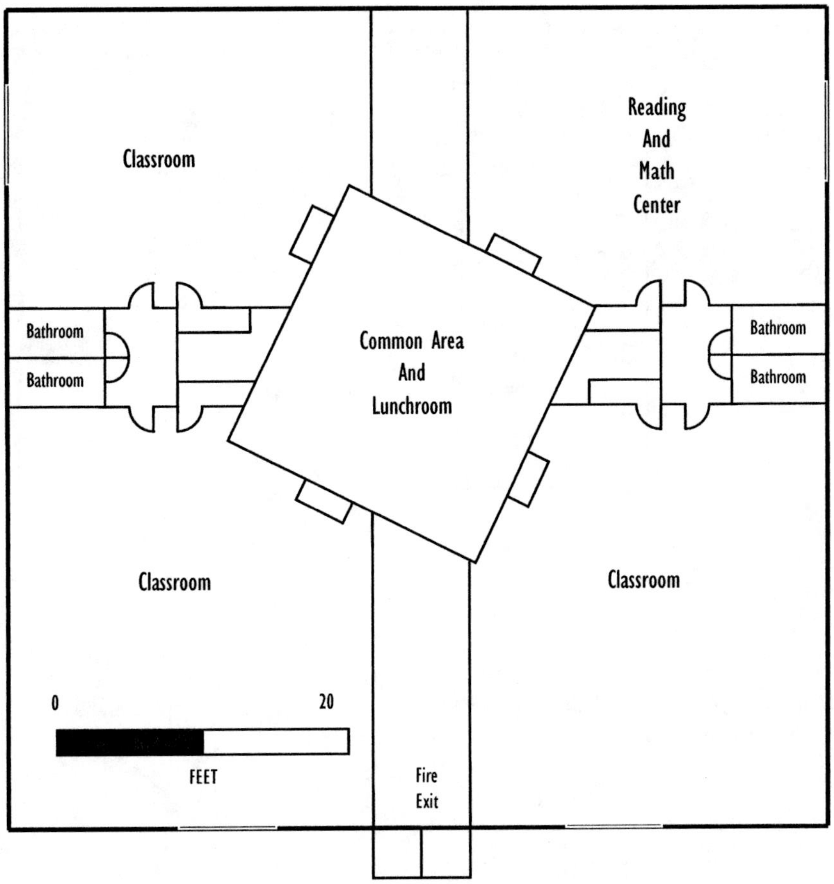

Exercise:

Design and explain the interior of the Common Area and Lunchroom.

____

____

____

____

____

____

____

Sam Hwang's Ideal Future School Floor Plan

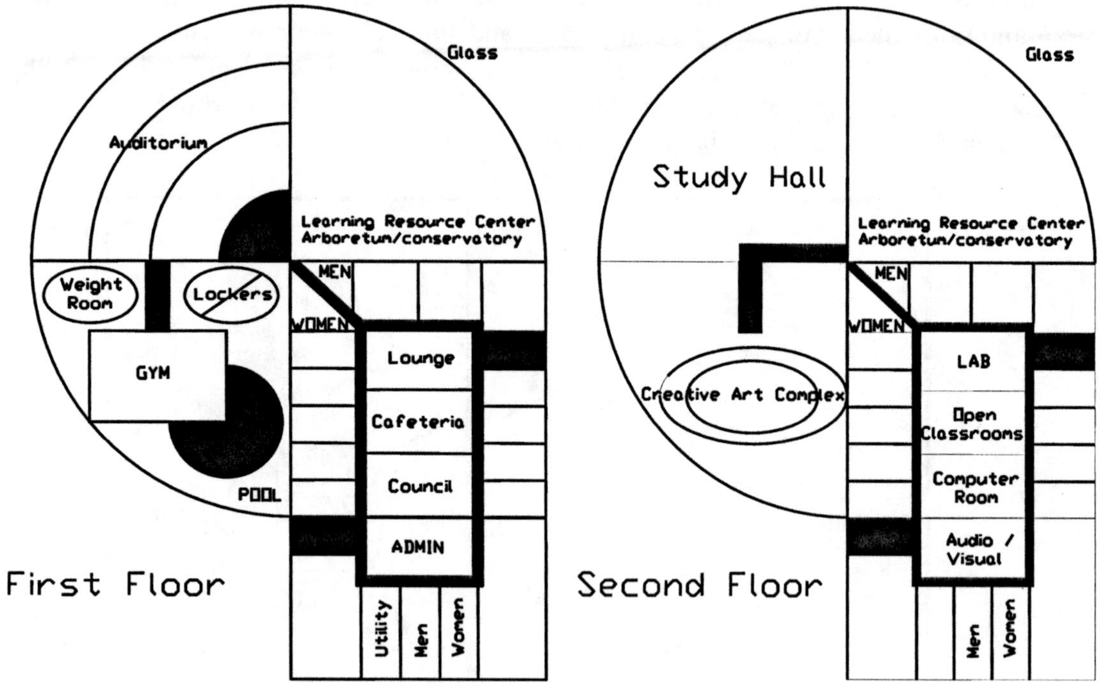

Exercise:

Design and explain what you would include in the ideal study hall.

____

____

____

____

____

____

____

____

____

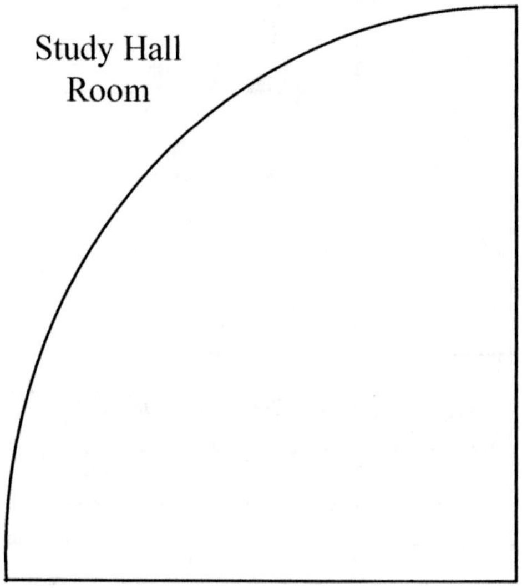

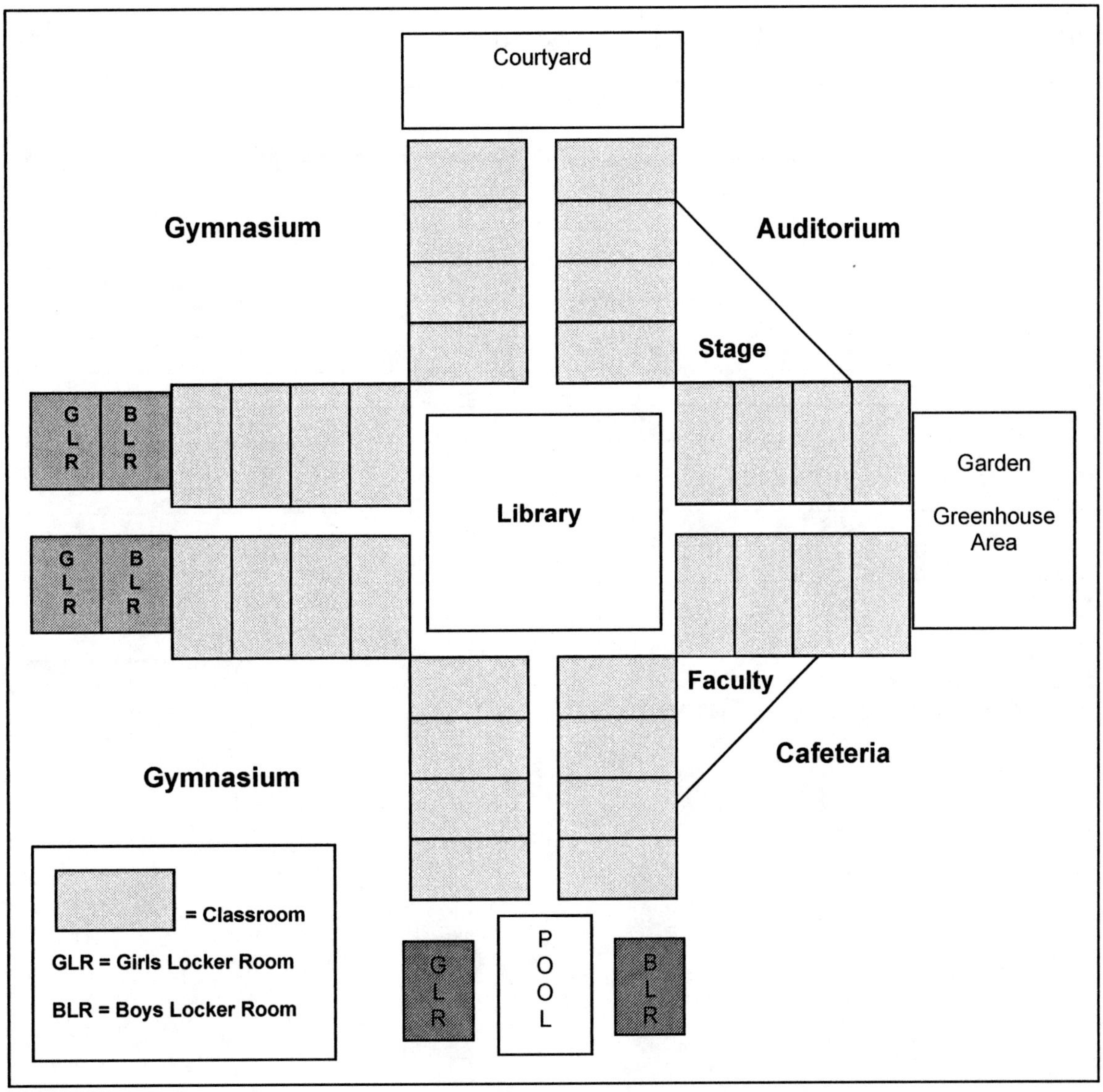

Exercise:

Explain the advantages and disadvantages of the above space.

Advantages:

____

____

____

Disadvantages:

____

____

____

Chapter Notes & Additional Information:

Personal Thoughts & Drawings

Chapter 4:

Certification

Chapter Topics:

Definition	**Provisional Requirements**
Types of Teaching Certificates	**Authorization**
County Substitute Certificate	**Routes to Certification**
Local School District Requirements	**Traditional Route**
Paraprofessional	**Alternate Routes**
Paraprofessional Approval	**Requirements Covering Certification**
Standard Certificate Requirements	**Continuing Education Rules**

Certification of teaching varies from state to state, and the requirements may be diverse or very similar, depending upon the states in comparison. This chapter will focus only on the requirements for certification in the state of New Jersey.

Definition: ***Reciprocity—"mutual exchange of privileges"***

New Jersey is party to the Interstate Certification Compact for reciprocity purposes with member states. Certificates from other states and transcripts are reviewed to determine if the applicants are eligible (content and professional education requirements and Praxis) for reciprocity.

Alabama	**Kentucky**	**Oklahoma**
California	**Maine**	**Pennsylvania**
Connecticut	**Maryland**	**Rhode Island**
Delaware	**Massachusetts**	**South Dakota**
District of Columbia	**Michigan**	**Utah**
Florida	**Nebraska**	**Vermont**
Hawaii	**New Hampshire**	**Virginia**
Idaho	**New York**	**Washington**
Indiana	**Ohio**	**West Virginia**

Exercise:

How might reciprocity affect you?

____

____

____

____

____

____

Types of Teaching Certificates

N.J.A.C. 6:11-4.5 County Substitute Certificate

A. Persons who do not hold a standard instructional certificate issued by the State Board of Examiners, but who can present a minimum of 60 semester hour credits completed in an accredited college, may be granted a county substitute certificate for day-to-day substitute teaching in the county that grants the certificate.

B. Each district board of education will submit to the county superintendents for review and approval, each applicant's official transcripts, oaths of alliance and credentials.

C. The certificate will be issued for a three-year period, but the holder may serve for no more than 20 consecutive days in the same position in one school district during the school year. Such certificates are issued by the county superintendent of schools, and are granted only when the supply of properly, certified teachers is inadequate to staff the school. They carry none of the accrued benefits, such as pension and tenure, to which a regularly employed teacher is entitled and are intended only for persons temporarily performing the duties of a fully certified and regularly employed teacher.

D. For specific vocational-technical skills, a vocational county substitute certificate may be issued to an applicant on the basis of appropriate work experience in lieu of 60 semester hour college credits. Such work experience will be substantiated by a notarized statement of previous employment.

E. Persons who hold a standard New Jersey instructional certificate issued by the State Board of Examiners may serve as a substitute in areas outside the scope of the certificate, for no more than 20 consecutive days in the same position in one school district during the school year. A substitute certificate will not be needed for this service.

F. The holder of a valid New Jersey registered nurse license may be issued a county substitute certificate to serve as a substitute for a school nurse.

G. The holder of a county substitute certificate is authorized to serve as an athletic coach in the district in which he or she is employed. The 20-day limitation noted in (C) above does not apply to such coaching situations. Issuance of a certificate under these conditions will be subject to the approval of the county superintendent of school as specified in N.J.A.C. 6:29-3.3.

Local School District Requirements

Substitute Requirements:

Oath of Allegiance
Proof of T.B. test (Mantoux) within the last three years
Additional requirements for your school district

Paraprofessional

The state of New Jersey Abbott districts require paraprofessional applicants to hold either 45 credits, have an associate's degree or attain a passing grade on the Parapro exam. This requirement applies to those paraprofessionals who are working in classrooms serving Title I funding from the federal government. Individual districts set passing scores for the Parapro examination as well as college credit level requirements.

6:11-4.6 Paraprofessional Approval

A. School aides and/or classroom aides, assisting in the supervision of student activities under the direction of a principal, teacher or other designated, certified, professional personnel, will be approved by the county superintendent of schools.

B. Certain rules require school district employee aides to develop job descriptions and standards for appointment. These descriptions and standards should be based on the study of ***local needs.***

6:11-5.2 Requirements for the standard certificate

Standard or Regular: A permanent certificate (lifetime) issued to those who have met all requirements for certification.

To be eligible for the standard certificate in any instructional area, the candidate shall:

1. Possess a provisional certificate pursuant to **N.J.A.C. 6A:9-8.2**; and

2. Successfully complete a State-approved district training program pursuant to **N.J.A.C. 6A:9-8.3** and **8.4** while employed provisionally in a position requiring the appropriate instructional certificate.

A. A candidate who has completed the requirements pursuant to **N.J.A.C. 6Aa:9-8.1(b)** and at least one year of appropriate teaching experience under a valid out-of-state license or certification will be eligible for a standard certificate on completion of the test requirement.

B. For the candidate who has completed the requirements pursuant to **N.J.A.C. 6A:9-8.1(b),** but hasn't meant the GPA (Grade Point Average) requirements pursuant to **N.J.A.C.6A:9-8.1(a)2**, three years of successful teaching experience under a valid out-of-state certificate are necessary.

C. Successful teaching experience will be demonstrated by the offer of contract renewal from the employing district; or submission of satisfactory performance evaluations; or submission of letters of experience on official school letterhead.

D. A candidate who holds National Board for Professional Teacher Standards (NBPTS) certification and the corresponding out-of-State license or out-of-State certificate will be eligible for the standard certificate in the NBPTS certificate field without additional requirements.

E. A brief listing of certifications is available through the New Jersey Department of Education (State code reference number provided) (www.state.nj.us/education)

Standard Certificates

Elementary K–5 must carry two majors; one being education such as elementary education or special education, with a recommended second major from among the Core Curriculum Content Standard areas. (See the New Jersey Department of Education Licensing and Standards code for detailed information on this process. www.state.nj.us/education.)

Standard Certificates with Special Requirements

- **6A:9-11.1** Preschool through grade 3 (Praxis exam under construction; due out in 2008)
- **6A:9-11.2** Vocational-technical education
- **6A:9-11.3** Special Education
- **6A:9-11.4** Bilingual/Bicultural Education
- **6A:9-11.5** English as a Second Language (ESL)
- **6A:9-11.6** Driver Education
- **6A:9-11.7** Military Science
- **6A:9-11.8** Health and Physical Education
- **6A:9-11.9** Physical Science
- **6A:9-11.10** World Language
- **6A:9-11.11** Elementary schools with subject matter specialization (often referred to as ***Middle School Certification***). Applicants for this endorsement must hold:

    1. ***At least a CE in elementary K-5 to be eligible for this endorsement!***

    2. In addition, candidates for the elementary school with subject matter specialization endorsements must complete a study in adolescent development to obtain this standard certificate. Alternate route

teachers study adolescent psychology in their Alternate Route training classes and therefore, meet this requirement.

- 6A:9-11.12 Swimming and Water Safety
- 6A:9-11.13 Technology Education

6:11-5.1 Requirements for the Provisional Certificate

A. To be eligible for the provisional certificate instructional fields, except as indicated in **N.J.A.C. 6:11-8,** The candidate shall:

1. Hold a CE or CEAS.

2. Obtain and accept an offer of employment in a position that requires certification.

B. ***Certificate of Eligibility (CE):*** Candidates who complete the requirements above will be issued a CE that will permit them to seek provisional employment in the positions requiring instructional certification. Eligibility for a CE in instructional areas requires that the candidate shall:

1. **Hold a bachelor's or an advanced degree** from a regionally, accredited college or university.

2. Achieve a cumulative **GPA of at least 2.75** when a GPA of 4.0 equals an A in a baccalaureate degree program.

3. **For subject area endorsements**, complete at least 30 credits in a coherent sequence of courses appropriate to the instructional area. At least 12 semester-hour credits must be at the advanced level of study, including junior, senior or graduate level study.

4. **For the elementary school endorsement**, complete a liberal arts, science, dual-content or interdisciplinary academic major for a minimum of 60 semester-hour credits in liberal arts and/or science. ***(All course work must appear on the transcript of a regionally accredited four-year college or university.)***

5. **Pass the appropriate state test** of subject matter knowledge (Praxis II exam; various formats exist).

6. **Pass an examination** in physiology, hygiene and substance abuse. In lieu of this examination, the applicant may present basic military training or college-level study in the areas such as biology, health or nutrition.

C. ***Certificate of Eligibility in Instructional Fields (CEAS—Certificate of Eligibility with Advance Standings):*** The candidate will meet the requirements in of all of the preceding and complete one of the following programs of teacher preparation:

1. A New Jersey college program, graduate or undergraduate, that is approved by the Department for the Preparation of Teachers pursuant to **N.J.A.C. 6A:9-10;**

2. A college preparation program included in the Interstate Certification reciprocity system of **NASDTEC**:

3. An out-of-state teacher education program approved by **NCATE**, **TEAC**, or any other national professional education accreditation body recognized by the Council on Higher Education Accreditation approved by the Commissioner;

4. A teacher education program approved for certification by the Department in one of the states party to the **NASDTEC** Interstate Contract, provided the program was completed on or after January 1, 1964 and the state that the program is located in will issue the candidate comparable endorsement; or

5. An out-of-state college teacher education program approved by the State Department of Education in which the program is located.

Exercise:

1. Describe your short-term (AS, AAS, BA or certificates) education goals to include your perceived level of interest.

Major:________________________
Minor: ________________________
Elective courses I wish to take:
____
____
____
____
Possible schools to transfer to:
____
____

Certificates I want to achieve:
____
____
____
Program of study: ______________
Recommended major courses at BCC:
____
____
____
____

2. Describe your long-term (master's or higher) goals in education to include degrees as well as new areas of study, subject and level of teaching.

Masters Program:	Subject Areas:
______________________________	______________________________
______________________________	______________________________
Doctorate Program:	______________________________
______________________________	______________________________
______________________________	Level of teaching:
Other:	______________________________
______________________________	______________________________
______________________________	______________________________

Routes to Certification

There are two basic routes to become a certified teacher in the New Jersey—***Traditional and Alternative.*** Each has its pluses and minuses for the recipient and both take approximately the same period time to qualify.

Traditional Route

6:11-7.2 Admission, Retention and Graduation of Students

A. Teacher preparation programs are those curricula that lead to a recommendation for a New Jersey Certificate of Eligibility with Advanced Standings in instructional fields pursuant to **N.J.A.C.6:11-5.1**, irrespective of the organizational unit of the college in which the curriculum is offered. Formal admission to teacher preparation programs will be reviewed at the beginning of the junior year and will be granted to those students who have:

1. Maintain a cumulative grade point average **(GPA)** of at least **2.75** where a **4.0** equals an A, for the first two years of college. It is the intent of this and other standards that refer to minimum grade point average to ensure that institutions determine intellectual competence of those recommended for certification. The required average of **2.75** should be viewed as only a minimal means of achieving this goal; the variability of the GPA among institutions should also be recognized. Therefore, institutions are encouraged to exceed the standard, when appropriate, and to develop additional criteria for ensuring that perspective teachers are intellectually capable.

2. Achieved ***acceptance levels of proficiency*** in the use of English language (oral and written) and mathematics. Students with deficiencies in these areas on admission to college will be

required to demonstrate the elimination of such deficiencies through an oral or written assessment by the beginning of the junior year.

3. Demonstrated ***aptitude for the profession of teaching*** through successful completion of an appropriate, practical experience in an elementary or secondary school. This requirement would normally have to be met before the student is granted status as a junior in the program.

B. Each student will be evaluated at the end of the semester, prior to student teaching, by college faculty (both education and subject matter) and confirmed as a candidate for certification on the basis of a comprehensive assessment of relevant indicators which shall include:

   1. Maintains cumulative grade point average of at least 2.75 (4.0 equals an A); and

   2. Demonstrates acceptable levels of teaching proficiency in junior field experience as indicated by the evaluation reports of college and school faculty. Such evaluations will be communicated to the student and will be included in the student's permanent file.

C. Only students who have been confirmed as candidates for certification will be assigned to student teaching.

D. College shall recommend for certification to the Department of Education only those students who have completed the certification program and have:

   1. Maintains a cumulative grade point average of 2.75 (4.0 equals an A); and

   2. Demonstrates continued confidence, aptitude, motivation and potential for outstanding success in teaching as indicated by assessments of student teaching performance by college and school supervisors. Such assessments will be communicated to the student and will be part of the student's file.

E. All standards will be applied equitably to all students, ***including transfer students,*** and without discrimination based on legally prohibited criteria.

F. Students completing an approved program must be recommended for a Certificate of Eligibility with Advanced Standing by their college or university and must pass a state test pursuant to **N.J.A.C. 6A:11-5.1(a)3** before one will be issued by the State Board of Examiners.

6:11-7.3 Curriculum

A. Each ***approved undergraduate teacher*** preparation program will provide approximately 60 semester credit hours of general education, including electives. General education courses are distributed among the arts, humanities, mathematics, science, technology and social sciences. The inclusion of technology as an aspect of general education is intended to allow for the inclusion of courses and topics (such as computer literacy, the history of technology and the sociological impact of technological advancement) which would contribute to the general technical literacy of students. The purpose of general education is to develop the prospective teacher as an educated person, rather than to provide professional preparation. This component of the program will exclude courses that are clearly professional or vocational in nature.

B. Each approved teacher preparation program will require its students to complete a major in the arts, humanities, social sciences, mathematics, science or technology disciplines.

C. At least 96 credits of the total program must be distributed among the general education, academic major and behavioral/social science aspects of the program.

D. For purposes of certification, a central focus of the undergraduate teacher education program is the professional component. This component must meet appropriate standards and study requirements of the National Association of State Directors of Teacher Education and Certification. In addition, each approved undergraduate teacher preparation program will provide study in the essential behavioral/social science and professional education areas listed in **N.J.A.C. 6:11-5.3(g)** through 3. Approximately 30 credit hours of instruction shall be devoted to professional preparation; a minimum of nine credits must be devoted to the study in the behavioral/social sciences and may be included in the professional or liberal arts component of the program.

E. The student teaching experience of each approved undergraduate program will be the equivalent of a full-time experience of one semester's duration and will be included within the professional component.

F. In accordance with the provisions of **N.J.S.A.198A:26-8,** ***students must take an examination in physiology and hygiene,*** including the effects of narcotics and alcohol. In lieu of this examination, the applicant may present basic military training or study in the areas such as biology, health or nutrition.

Teachers Seeking New Jersey Teaching Licenses

- Bachelor's degree from an accredited college or university.
- Passing score in the Praxis II appropriate tests.
- Completion of at least 30 credits in a coherent major in the instructional subject teaching field. The elementary education endorsement requires a major in the liberal arts or pure science.
- Successful completion of one of the following:
    - The alternate route ***Provisional Teacher Program***; or
    - A state-approved college teacher preparation program and one year of full-time mentored teaching under a New Jersey provisional license; or
    - A state-approved college teacher preparation program and one year of full-time teaching under a valid out-of-state license.

Brookdale Community College

Brookdale Community College has created articulation with Georgian Court University and New Jersey City University (NJCU) that offers a variety of teacher certification degree programs through the Communiversity. Successful associate degrees candidates who meet articulation requirements may transfer into the following third- and fourth-year teacher certification programs either in a P–3 or a K–5 urban education certificate; or in a K–5 Special Education dual certificate. Please contact the Communiversity, academic advisement personnel or your education instructor for further information. Further information for these certification opportunities is available at the Brookdale Web site www.brookdalecc.edu.

Alternate Route

6:11-5.3 Requirements for State-Approved District Training Programs

A. Each district, school, or consortium seeking to hire a provisional teacher must submit a plan to the Department of Education and receive approval in accordance with the same procedures used for initial approval of collegiate preparation programs.

B. Each state-approved, district training program will provide essential knowledge and skills to provisional teachers to the following phases of training:

1. A full-time seminar/practicum of no less that 20 days' duration that takes place prior to the time the professional teacher takes full responsibility for a classroom. This seminar/practicum will provide formal instruction in the

essential areas for professional study listed in (4) below. It should introduce basic teaching skills through supervised teaching experiences with students. The seminar/practicum components of the experience will be integrated and will include an orientation to the policies, organization and curriculum of the employee district. This requirement does not apply to provisional teachers who are holders of certificates of eligibility within and standing pursuant to **N.J.A.C. 6:11-5.1 (c).**

2. A period of intensive on-the-job supervision beginning the first day that the provisional teacher assumes full responsibility for a classroom and continuing for a period of at least ten weeks. During this time the provisional teacher will be visited and critiqued no less than one time every two weeks by members of a Professional Support Team and will be observed and formally evaluated at the end of ten weeks by the appropriately certified members of the team. At the end of the ten-week period, the official teacher will receive a formal written progress report from the chairperson of the support team. This requirement is waived for candidates in the Community College Alternate Route New Pathways to Teaching program.

3. An additional period of continued supervision and evaluation of no less than 20 weeks' duration. During this period, the provisional teacher will be visited and critiqued at least four times and will be observed formally and evaluated at least twice. No more than two months will pass without a formal observation. Opportunities will be provided for the provisional teacher to observe the teaching of experienced colleagues.

4. Approximately 200 hours of formal instruction in the following topics will be provided in all three phases of the program combined. This requirement does not apply to provisional teachers who are holders of Certificates of Eligibility with Advanced Standings pursuant to **N.J.A.C.6:11-5.1(c).**

    a. ***Curriculum:*** Studies designed to foster an understanding of the curriculum taught and the assessment of teaching, including topics such as the following:

        1. the organization and representation of subject matter,
        2. the development in use of tests and other forms of assessment,
        3. the evaluation and selection of instructional materials in the appropriate use of textbooks and teachers' guides,
        4. the use and interpretation of standardized tests and teacher-developed instruments,
        5. the readiness process and other language arts skill development appropriate to the field of specialization and grade level, and

6. a knowledge of techniques and materials for fostering the development of reading and language arts skills.

b. ***Student Development and Learning at all Levels:*** Studies designed to foster an understanding of students, their characteristics as individuals, and the ways in which they learn, including topics such as:

1. student interests,
2. motivation,
3. preventing classroom disruption,
4. creating a healthy learning climate,
5. individual and group learning,
6. language development,
7. individual differences, and
8. the role of technology in early learning.

c. ***The Classroom and the School:*** studies designed to foster an understanding of the school as a social unit and classroom management, including such topics as:

1. the bureaucratic/social structure of student education,
2. the making of teaching decisions,
3. allocation of instructional time,
4. setting priorities,
5. pacing of instruction,
6. setting of goals,
7. questioning techniques,
8. student practice, and
9. independent work.

Exercise:

What are the advantages and disadvantages of the alternate route?

Advantages: ____

____

____

Disadvantages: ____

____

____

Other Requirements Covering Certification

6:11-3.5 District Reporting Responsibility

In cases where teaching staff members are accused of misdemeanors, crimes or conduct unbecoming that might warrant revocation or suspension, and then resign or retire from their positions, either before tenure proceedings have been brought or prior to the conclusion of such proceedings, it is the responsibility of the school chief administrator of the district to notify the State Board of Examiners of alleged, conduct pursuant to **N.J.A.C.6:11-3.6 (a)2.** Should the State Board of Examiners issue an order to show cause, it is the responsibility of the district that reported the conduct to cooperate with the State Board of Examiners in ascertaining and representing the facts underlying such allegations.

6:11-3.6 Procedures for Revocation or Suspension of Certificates

The procedure for issuance of an Order to Show Cause will in all cases afford the individual notification of the charges and an opportunity to be heard with respect thereto. The following procedures are applicable to cases brought to the State Board of Examiners by reason of specific statutes and regulations.

Upon the decision of the Commissioner of Education, cases contested before the Commissioner of Education, resulting in loss of tenure or dismissal of a teacher or teaching staff member for inefficiency, incapacity, conduct unbecoming a teacher or other just cause, will be forwarded to the State Board of Examiners for determination of possible revocation or suspension.

Accredited Two-Year College Credits

Courses taken at an accredited two-year college are accepted toward meeting requirements for certification only if such courses of should appear on official transcripts of accredited four-year colleges approved for teacher education (no more than six credits in Professional Education.)

6:11-3.8 Suspension of Certificates

A. A teacher employed by a district board of education who shall, without the consent of the district board of education, leave the school before the expiration of the term of his or her employment will be deemed guilty of unprofessional conduct.

B. The Commissioner of Education may, upon receiving notice of the fact, suspend the certificate for a period not exceeding one year.

6:11-3.9 Oath of Allegiance Required

A. Every person whose application is pending or who hereafter applies for a license, or any renewal thereof, to teach or supervise in any of the public schools of this State, will subscribe to the oath of allegiance and office prescribed in **N.J.S.A.41: 1.3.**

B. Any person who is a citizen or subject of any country other than the United States, such as an exchange teacher, is required to file an oath to support the Constitution of the United States while so employed.

6:11-3.11 Minimum Degree and Age Requirement

Applicants for teacher certificates must be at least 19 years old, have graduated from an approved high school, or have an equivalent education as determined by the State Board of Examiners, and have received the baccalaureate degree from an accredited institution of higher education. The requirement of a baccalaureate degree does not apply to applicants for the vocational endorsements in **N.J.A.C. 6:11-8.1.**

6:11-3.10 Citizenship Requirement

To be eligible for a certificate, the applicant must be a citizen of the United States (except a teacher of foreign languages, unless such teacher has been a resident of the United States for more than 10 years; or an applicant for temporary employment under a special program approved by the Commissioner of Education) or have preliminary citizenship status.

6:11-3.12 Teachers in Evening Schools

Teachers of academic subjects in accredited public evening schools and teachers in evening schools for foreign-born residents require a valid New Jersey elementary or subject teacher's endorsement authorizing the teaching of the specified subject(s) in public day schools.

Continuing Education Rules

Required Professional Development for Teachers

Each active teacher will be required to complete 100 clock hours of state-approved continuing professional development and/or in-service every five years. The initial five-year period will extend from September 2000 to September 2005. General categories of professional development are:

- ***Formal courses*** offered online or offline and conferences (including, but not limited to, workshops, seminars, institutes or other such programs) sponsored by colleges and universities, district boards of education, professional associations, training organizations, or other entities approved through the local district plan process or are part of the provider registration system. (Time eligible: hour for hour. Only one hour per week can be counted for time spent in serving as a mentor or cooperating teacher).

- ***Courses, seminars or other activities*** that are required for maintaining licenses or certificates issued by professional organizations or government entities. (Time eligible: hour for hour). If the same course must be taken twice within a five-year period, the hours only count once toward fulfilling the continuing requirement.

- ***Action research, study, development*** and other activities related to curriculum writings that focus on the Core Curriculum Content Standards. (Time eligible: hour for hour.)

- Activities that serve the profession, including but not limited to grant writing, mentoring a preservice or novice teacher, professional service on boards or committees, and teaching a course or workshop. (Time eligible: limited to 75 hours out of the 100 hours, with the following limits also in force):

    - ***Hours for service*** on board/committees (Time eligible: limited to 10 hours per year of professional development credit, provided that such services identified in the PIP with the specific goals of the experience outlined.)

    - Hours served as a member to a provisional teacher or as a ***cooperating teacher*** for a preservice teacher. (Time eligible: limited to one hour of professional development credit for each week of supervision.)

    - ***Clock hours*** spent as a presenter or teacher of courses or workshops delivered for the first time. (Time eligible: hour for hour.) Teaching or presenting the same or a similar course or workshop will only come once in a five-year cycle.

    - Eligible preparation time for delivering ***first presentation***. (Time eligible: two hours of preparation for every hour of delivery time.) Will only count once in a five-year cycle.

    - ***Independent, professional studies***, including, but not limited to, action-research, study groups, sabbaticals, fellowships, internships, teacher exchanges, textbook review, portfolio development and online workshops or programs.

Chapter Notes & Additional Information:

Personal Thoughts & Drawings

Chapter 5:

Boards of Education

Chapter Topics:

- Powers to the State
- Laws and Policies
- NJ Constitution
- Local issues
- Administration of School Laws
- The Role of the Local Board
- Authorities and Powers of the Board
- Qualifications of the Board Members
- Election and Number of Board Members: Terms
- Board Meetings
- Typical Meeting Agenda
- Types of Board Meetings
- The Sunshine Law
- Good News about Public Schools
- NJ Takeovers
- NJ Takeovers Update
- Proficiency—Minimum Standards
- Monmouth County High School HSPA
- Graduation Requirements
- Eighth Grade Proficiency Exam
- Monmouth County/NYC Test Results
- Mandated School Curriculum—NJ Public Schools
- NJ Core Curriculum Content Standards
- School Improvement AYP
- Adequate Yearly Progress
- Sanctions Process
- School Category
- List of Schools Not Meeting AYP
- AYP Sanctions Timeline
- Commissioner Comment on AYP
- The Changing Faces of American Schools
- Academic Performance HSPA
- Other Board Policies

Powers to the States

"The powers not delegated to the United States by the Commissioner, nor prohibited by it to the States, are reserved to the States respectively, or to the people."

—Tenth Amendment to the U.S. Constitution

The structure in the United States will flow very similarly to the following schema:

Laws and Policies

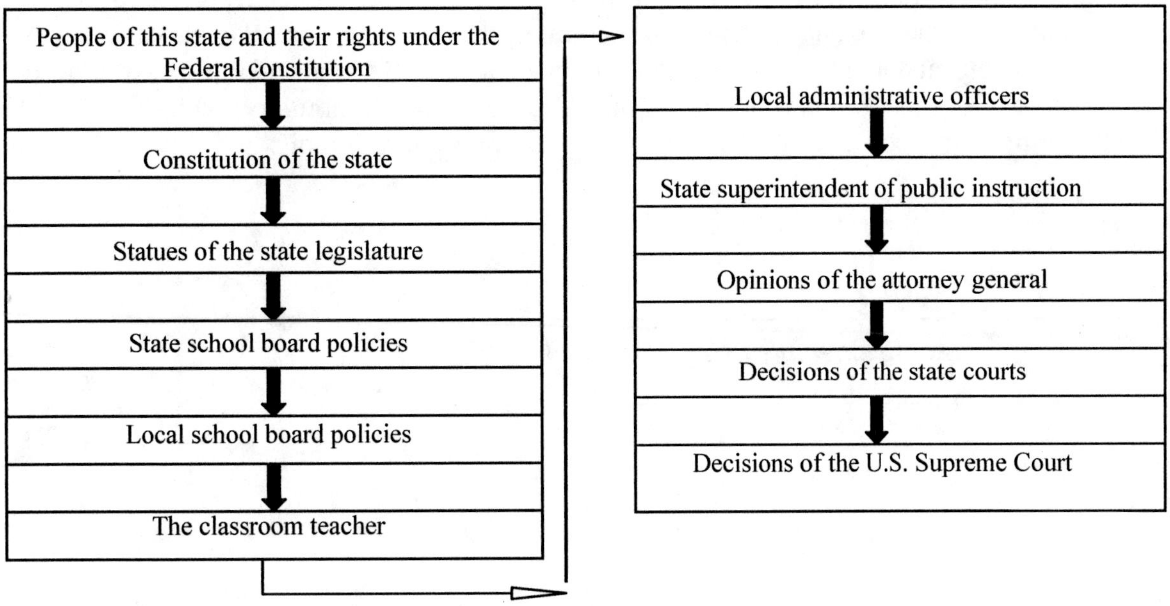

New Jersey Constitution

As in the rest of the 50 states, the power and legal responsibility for education lies within each respective state. The New Jersey Constitution lays the foundation for education in the state with the following phrase:

"The Legislature shall provide for the maintenance and support of a thorough and efficient system of free public schools for the instruction of all children in this state between the ages of five and eighteen years."

Exercise:

What is your interpretation of thorough and efficient?

____

____

____

____

Local Issues

Local school boards of education face difficult decisions when balancing their district needs to education mandates set by federal and state legislature. As state budget requirements increase, funding has decreased. In fact, New Jersey state government has paid only 40 percent of education costs on average. Increased mandates, along with stagnant state aid to education since 2001, has worsened the problem, by forcing communities to increase property taxes to cover more of the costs that the state should be paying. The current over reliance on property tax causes great concern for school boards, as well as for the citizens they serve. Oftentimes, these tensions are played out in day-to-day decisions about program operations, extracurricular offerings and other school needs. As a result, school board members have to face the community with unfavorable decisions. The tensions caused by their position can become complex.

Exercise:

1. ***What issues are currently being addressed at the local level?***

____

____

____

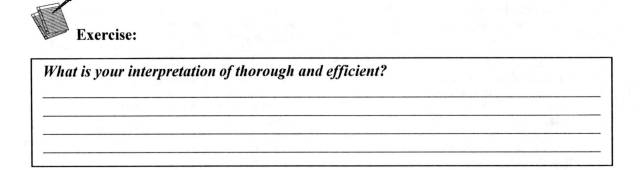

2. ***How has the local school board addressed these issues?***

____

____

____

3. ***What tensions have been raised through school board decisions or action taken?***

____

____

____

The Administration of the School Laws

The Role of the Local Board

The local board of education is the prime enforcer of the school laws. Local boards have quasi-judicial powers. Any member of a local board may administer oaths to witnesses in any hearing that the local board has jurisdiction. The president of any local board of education may issue a subpoena at the request of any party to such a hearing and to compel the presence of witnesses for the production of documents. The president of the board, as a whole, may apply to the courts for relief against recalcitrant witnesses. Parties are guaranteed the right to be represented by counsel, to testify and produce witnesses on their behalf, and to cross-examine witnesses against them.

Authority and Powers of the Board

Every local board of education is obligated as part of its mandatory powers and duties to:

1. Adopt an official seal.
2. Enforce the rules of the State Board of Education.
3. Make, amend and repeal rules for its own government, the transaction of business, the government and management of public schools and public school property in the district, for the employment and regulation of conduct and discharge of employees.
4. Perform all acts and do all things, consistent with law and state board roles, necessary for the proper conduct, equipment and maintenance of the public schools. (**N.J.S.A. 18:11.1**)

Power is usually granted or implied to local school boards including the power to act as follows:

1. Obtain revenue
2. Maintain schools
3. Purchase sites and construct buildings
4. Purchase materials and supplies
5. Organize and provide programs of studies

6. Employ necessary workers and regulate their services
7. Admit and assign students to schools and control their conduct

Certain acts of a board of education require a majority vote of all members of the board. The following actions require a majority vote of the full membership of the board (selective packs):

1. Appointing a teaching staff member
2. Transferring a teaching staff member
3. Adopting or altering the course of study
4. Selecting textbooks
5. Withholding a prescribed employment or adjustment increment
6. Determining the sufficiency of charges to dismiss or reduce the salary of a tenured employee
7. Disposing of land owned by the board, or the rights or interests therein
8. Fixing and determining the amount of money in the budget to be submitted to the voters in a Type II district
9. Authorizing the issuance of school bonds in a Type II district (**N.J.S.A. 18A:15.2)**

Definition: ***Quorum of membership.***
For a quorum to be established you must have a majority of members of the full board.

Exercise:

What constitutes a quorum?

____

____

What is the quorum for the following?

Nine member boards: ______________________________
Seven member words: ______________________________
Five member board: ______________________________

Qualifications of Board Members

Each member of any board of education will be a citizen and resident of the district, or of such constituent district of a consolidated or regional district as may be required by law, and will have been such for at least one year and immediately preceding his appointment or election, he will be able to read and write, will be registered to vote in the district, and, not withstanding the provisions of **N.J.S.A. 2C:51-1** or any other law to the contrary, he is not disqualified as a voter pursuant to **U.S. 19:4-L.**

Exercise:

1. ***Explain the phrase "read and write."***

____

____

2. ***What requirements do you think would be necessary to be a board member?***

____

____

3. ***Why should you run for the local school board? State your reasons.***

____

____

Civic attitude spurs most candidates

School boards are neighborhood politics at their most, or at least, neighborly. At any given meeting, parents will stand up to praise a school board or panic. Some will read carefully prepared speeches and others will be moved by the moment to speak. Meetings often last past midnight, debate then spilling out into the parking lot. Topics can be routine, like policy changes, paying the bills, or more controversial, school construction plans or boundary changes.

Board members don't make any money; it is a volunteer job in New Jersey. They get little glory. Their names may be put on a plaque when a new school goes up and sometimes they appear on cable TV or get scorched by criticism in the letters to the editor of the local weekly.

J got a real education in public service as during his three years on a school board.

From the hate-mail:

Twenty-five or thirty pieces of it arrived after he backed a plan to build a $22.4 million worth of new schools through lease purchase financing.

From the vandalism: Three mailboxes bashed in and a deep "doughnut" dug on his front lawn by a driver who punctuated the act with an obscene gesture as he drove off.

From the children who came up to his then second-grade daughter and said, "Your daddy's going to raise taxes and drive us all out of here." There was even a letter in the local newspapers suggesting that J and his family leave town.

"It was kind of scary, to tell you the truth," he said. "When you live in a town like this, you don't think there are people like them."

It might have been enough to scare him away from school boards for good, but two years after his term ended, J is back, one of five school board candidates in the same town, and thousands in the running for the 1,566 seats available in the April elections.

When asked what makes them run, moves board hopefuls talk about their interest in the schools. They only want to improve their kids' education and wish to serve the community.

"It may sound corny," said J, father of two and former board president, "but it's the honest-to-God truth. I am a strong believer in public education and I'm just willing to roll up my sleeves and play a role in that."

New Jersey has over 570 districts with elected boards of education. According to the New Jersey School Boards Association, three people usually run for every two seats.

Exercise:

What is your reaction?

Election and Number of Board Members; Terms

The board of education will consist of nine members, or it will consist of three, five, or seven members as, and if, it has been so determined pursuant to law or shall be so determined by referendums as provided in this chapter, who shall be elected at the annual school elections in the district for terms of three years, except as otherwise herein provided.

18A:14-9. Nomination by petition and number of signers

Each candidate to be voted on at a school election will be nominated directly by petition, signed by a least ten persons, none of whom shall be the candidate himself, and filed with the secretary of the board of education of the district on or before 4:00 PM on the 54th day preceding the day of the election. The signatures need not all appear on a single petition, and any number of petitions may be filed on behalf of any candidate but no petition shall contain the endorsement of more than one candidate.

Board Meetings

All board meetings shall be public, and each board will hold a meeting at least once every two months during the period that the schools in the district are in session.

All meetings will be called to commence not later than 8:00 PM of the designated day, but if a quorum be not present at the time that the meeting is called, the member or members present may recess the meeting to a time not later than 9:00 PM of the said day and, if no quorum be present at that time, the member or members present may adjourn the meeting to commence not later than 8:00 PM of another day, not more than seven days following the date that the original meeting was called, but no further recess or adjournment of the meeting will be made.

Public announcements of time and day that any meeting is so recessed or adjourned will be made at the time of the recess or adjournment.

Typical Meeting Agenda (Public Meeting)

The order of business will be as follows unless altered by the president or a majority of those present and voting:

- Call to order
- Flag salute
- Roll call
- Statement of notice given (**C10:4-10**)
- Approval of minutes of the previous meeting(s)
- Acceptance of secretary's financial report and report of custodian
- Payment of bills and requisitions of taxes for school purposes
- Secretary's report
- Superintendent's report
- Communications
- Report of committees and new business
- Hearing of public: Any persons wishing to be heard during the public session of the board meeting will first be recognized by the chairman. He shall then identify himself by name and proceed with his comments. The chairman is responsible for the orderly conduct of the meeting and will rule on such matters as the speaker's right to address the board, the time to be allowed for public discussion, the appropriateness of the subject being presented and the suitability of the time for such a presentation. Any person may make a formal, written request to the chairman to be heard on an agenda item, prior to an official vote. The board, as a whole, will have the final decision on the appropriateness of all such rules.
- Adjournment

18A:11-2. Power to sue and be sued; consensus of schoolchildren

The board may sue or be sued by its corporate name and likewise submit to arbitration and determination disputes and controversies in the manner provided by law.

Types of Board Meetings

Regular or Special Meeting: The board conducts official business and the public has the opportunity to speak.

Agenda for Workshop Meeting: The board cannot conduct official business but may discuss items for regular meetings. The public can attend but not speak unless invited to.

Closed for Executive Sessions: The board can exclude the public to discuss "personnel or contracts for litigation" at closed or executive sessions.

Minutes of the board meetings must be kept and made part of the public records and must be open to inspection at reasonable times and places by the public.

Exercise:

> ***What is your interpretation of the three types of board meetings?***
>
> Regular or Special Meeting:
>
> ____
>
> ____
>
> Agenda or Workshop Meeting:
>
> ____
>
> ____
>
> Closed or Executive Meeting:
>
> ____
>
> ____

The Sunshine Law: The Open Public Meetings Act.

N.J.S.A. 10:4-6

The law requires all public bodies organized by law and collectively empowered as a voting body to spend public funds or affect people's rights to be given adequate notice of and be permitted to attend all meetings except those exempted by the law itself. All discussions and official actions of the public body must take place in public.

- A committee is exempt from action if it is without effective authority to act (cannot be a majority of the board).
- Annual and 48-hour notice is required of meetings, giving time, date, location, and to the extent known, the agenda of any regular, special or rescheduled meetings and stating whether formal actions may be taken.
- Agenda refers solely to the list of subject matter to be discussed and acted on at the meeting.
- A board can, however, act on items not included in the published agenda if the need for action on such matters was not known to the board until the date of the meeting.
- Emergency meetings may be held without adequate advanced written notice if three-quarters of its members present vote in favor of holding the meeting—must post as soon as possible.
- Public participation is not required, but the opportunity to be present is. (The public can speak at regular/special meetings, but has no right to speak at the agenda, workshop-only meetings.)

- Minutes must be kept of meetings, including: presiding person, time and place, members present, subjects considered, actions taken and vote of each member.
- Closed (executive) sessions can take place only after a "resolution" is adopted at the public meeting stating the general nature of the subject to be discussed. Reasons or exceptions for excluding the public are:

    - Any matter that is an express provision of federal law or state statue or a rule of court will be rendered confidential.
    - In discussion of any materials, the disclosure would constitute an unwarranted invasion of privacy (individual can request an open session).
    - Discussion of collective bargaining agreements.
    - Purchase, lease or banking rate, for disclosure would adversely affect the public interest.
    - Discussion and tactics in protecting safety and property.
    - Litigation, pending or anticipated.
    - Employment recommendations and terms.

Good News about Public Schools

- New Jersey's public school students are required to pass a rigorous state test in order to earn a high school diploma, and 94 percent passed it last year.

  New Jersey Department of Education
- Eight out of ten New Jersey high school graduates plan to continue their education after high school.

  New Jersey Department of Education
- The number of New Jersey students taking AP exams increased 6 percent last year. The state's average AP scores rank fifth in the nation and is well above the passing standard for college credit.

  Educational Testing Service
- In the last five years, the average, combined SAT score for New Jersey public school students has increased thirteen points.

  College Board
- In 1995, 1996 and 1997, average SAT math scores for New Jersey public school students exceeded those of parochial school students.

  College Board
- New Jersey's high school completion rate for young adults (ages 18 to 24) has risen to over 91 percent, the highest rate ever.

  U.S. Census
- On a typical school day, the attendance rate of New Jersey's public school exceeds 94 percent.

  New Jersey Department of Education

Exercise:

How can these statistics be deceiving?

New Jersey School Takeovers

Several years ago, New Jersey officials decided that they were tired of watching from the sideline as Jersey City school and city officials seemed more concerned with providing jobs for friends than with following student test scores. State officials took charge of the system, taking out the superintendent and the board of education members.

A decade into state control, attendance is up slightly in Jersey City schools, and test scores have improved, but there has been no dramatic turnaround in student performance. The state is seen by many residents as little more than an occupying force.

The Department of Education is now running the state's three largest school districts, yet state officials are still without a plan to return the schools to local control, a detail that was not addressed in the legislation that gave the state authority to take over schools. Even those New Jersey officials involved with the regional takeover in 1989 now acknowledge that the state was armed with more good intentions than practical strategy.

"There was a vague assumption on our part that if we fixed the central office and replace the people who were there with good people, those good people would solve the problems of urban education," said Leo F. Klagholz, New Jersey's Commissioner of Education, who was the head of teacher certification for the state in 1989. "It turns out to be not that simple."

New Jersey was the first state to take over a school system after it decided that it was inept and corrupt. Twenty-one other states have followed suit, but because they haven't seen New Jersey's model at work, they are shying away from taking control of all day-to-day operations. Instead, those states favor takeovers that give local mayors control of the school systems.

New Jersey State Takeover: 1999 Update

- New Jersey was the first state to take over failing urban school districts. In 1989, New Jersey gained control over the Jersey City, Newark (1995) and Paterson (1991) school systems.

- In June of 1999, then-commissioner Hespe announced a plan to return Jersey City school district over to local control. He made no announcement for Newark or Paterson districts.
- Commissioner Hespe claimed mixed results, with successes cited in management and business practices. Crumbling schools have seen major repairs. There have been successful expansions of magnet schools, preschool and kindergarten programs and after-school activities.
- Academic improvements have had weak results with marginal improvements in test scores and a dismal dropout rate of over 50 percent.
- Based on the New Jersey model, other states have attempted to gain control of failing school districts, including the most recent takeover of Detroit schools.
- Unlike New Jersey, most states takeover plans allow local school board members and superintendents to remain in an attempt to control local racial tensions.
- Recent state takeovers have attempted to add additional financial support along with in-school team support requiring improvement plans.
- Other states have turned over school district responsibility to city mayors. Chicago's Mayor Daley's appointees have improved maintenance, reorganized central office staff, privatized some services and put 109 schools on probation.

Proficiency—What are Minimum Standards?

New Jersey mandatory state tests assess skills in reading, writing, math and science. In the next few years, social studies and other core curriculum content areas will be formally assessed. The tests required by the state are given in grades three through seven (**NJASK**), grade eight (**GEPA**), and grade eleven (**HSPA**). Additional assessment tools are used in preschools (**ELAS**) as well as the Alternate Assessment Process (**ASP**) and Special Review Assessment (**SRA**). The function of the state test is to evaluate the students' progress and to determine if the school is succeeding in teaching the necessary skills. As an early indicator of success, the tests determine whether the students need additional support in basic skills areas, reading, math, written language and science.

Unless students pass the **HSPA** with proficiency, they will not be allowed to graduate with a New Jersey high school diploma. State test scores are reported to the public through the media, in the New Jersey report card process and to the parent. School scores are compared against state averages with parents receiving their child's scores and corresponding explanations about their strengths and areas of concern.

Students who need alternate testing environments due to severe disabilities, have the opportunity to take the Alternate Proficiency Area Assessment. The Alternate Proficiency Assessment (**APA**) is a portfolio assessment designed to measure progress toward achieving New Jersey's state educational standards for those students with severe disabilities, who are unable to participate in the New Jersey Assessment of Skills and Knowledge (**NJASK**), the Grade Eight Proficiency Assessment (**GEPA**), or the High School Proficiency Assessment (**HSPA**). It is administered in each contact area where the nature of the student's disability is so severe that the student is not receiving instruction in any of the knowledge and skills measured by the general, statewide assessment and the student cannot complete any of the types of questions on the assessment, in the content areas, even with accommodations and modifications.

The Special Review Assessment (**SRA**) is an alternate assessment that provides students with the opportunity to exhibit their understanding and mastery of the **HSPA** skills and contexts that are familiar and related to their experiences. The **SRA** content is linked to the **HSPA** test specifications to ensure that students who are certified through the **SRA** process have attained the same skills and competencies, at comparable levels, as students who pass the written HSPA test. This test is available in English as well as Spanish, Portuguese and Gujaratu.

For information about New Jersey Core Content Standards, assessment and alternate testing options can be found at www.state.nj.us/education under assessments and standards.

- **ELAS —Early Learning Assessment System**
- **NJASK—New Jersey Assessment of Skills and Knowledge**
- **GPA—Grade Eight Proficiency Area Assessment**
- **HSPA—High School Proficiency Assessment**
- **APA—Alternate Proficiency Assessment**
- **SRA—Special Review Assessment**

Monmouth County High School HSPA 2005 Reports

State standard 79% Proficient School district HSPA 2004–2005 reports	Verbal (meeting proficiency or advanced proficiency)	Math (meeting proficiency or advanced proficiency)
Allentown High	88.4 %	80.0 %
Asbury Park	34.7 %	24.6 %
Freehold Township District	92.7 %	89.2 %
Henry Hudson Regional	72.3 %	61.9 %
Long Branch	65.7 %	61.7 %
Matawan Regional	86.4 %	77.7 %
Monmouth Regional	87.2 %	79.7 %
Neptune Township	74.4 %	68.9 %
Red Bank Regional	88.4 %	77.8 %
Rumson Fairhaven Regional	97.8 %	93.6 %
Shore Regional	97.8 %	88.4 %

Graduation Requirements

- Completion of at least 110 credits (equivalent of 22 courses)
- At least 20 credits in language arts literacy
- At least 15 credits in mathematics
- At least 15 credits in science
- At least 15 credits in social studies
- At least 3.75 credits per year in health, safety and physical education (distributed over 150 minutes per week)
- At least 5 credits in visual and performing arts
- At least 5 credits in technological literacy, career education and life skills
- At least 5 credits in world languages

Other Requirements

- Length of school year: 180 days
- Length of school day: minimum of 4 hours of instructional time (2.5 hours for kindergarten)
- Credits in world languages.

Sample Eighth Grade Proficiency Exam

Grammar (time, 1 hour)

1. Give nine rules for the use of capital letters.
2. Name the parts of speech and define those that have no modifications.
3. Define verse, stanza and paragraph.
4. What are the principal parts of a verb? Give principle parts of lie, play, and run.
5. Define case. Illustrate each case.
6. What is punctuation? Give rules for principle marks of punctuation.

7–10. Write a composition of about 150 words and show therein that you understand the practical use of the rules of grammar.

Arithmetic (time, 1.25 hours)

1. Name and define the Fundamental Rules of Arithmetic.
2. A wagon box is 2 ft. deep, 10 ft. long and 3 ft. wide. How many bushels of wheat will it hold?
3. If a load of wheat weighs 3,942 lb., what is it worth at 50¢ per bushel, deducting 1,050 lb. for tare?
4. District No. 33 has a valuation of $35,000. What is the necessary levy to carry on a school seven months at $50 per month and have $104 for incidentals?
5. Find the cost of 6,720 lb. of coal at $6 per ton.
6. Find the interest of $512.60 for 8 months and 18 days at 7 percent.

7. What is the cost of 40 boards that are 1 ft. wide and 16 ft. long and cost $20 per meter?
8. Find the bank discount on $300 for 90 days (no grace period) at 10 percent.
9. What is the cost of a square farm at $15 per acre, the distance of which is 640 rods?
10. Write a bank check, a promissory note and a receipt.

U.S. History (time, 45 minutes)

1. Give the epochs in which U.S. history is divided.
2. Give an account of the discovery of America.
3. Relay the causes and effects of the Revolutionary War.
4. Show the territorial growth of the United States.
5. Tell what you can of the history of New Jersey.
6. Describe three of the most prominent battles of the Rebellion.
7. Who were the following: Morse, Whitney, Fulton, Bell, Lincoln, Penn and Howe?
8. Name events connected with the following dates: 1607. 1620, 1800, 1849, 1865.

Orthography (time, 1 hour)

1. What is meant by the following: alphabet, phonetic, orthography, etymology and symbolization?
2. What are elementary sounds? How are they classified?
3. What are the following, and give examples of each: *trigraph, subvocals, diphthong cognate letters* and *linguals*?
4. Give four substitutes for the caret *u*.
5. Give two rules for spelling words with a final *e*. Name two exceptions under each rule.
6. Give two uses of silent letters in spelling. Illustrate each one.
7. Define the following prefixes and use them in connection with a word: *bi-, dis-, mis-, pre-, semi-, post-, non-, inter-, mono-* and *sup-*.
8. Mark diacritically and divide into syllables the following words, and name the sign that indicates the sound: *card, ball, mercy, sir, odd, cell, rise, blood, fare* and *last.*
9. Use the following correctly in sentences: *cite, site, sight, fane, feign, fain, vane, vein, vain, raze, raise* and *rays*.
10. Write ten words frequently mispronounced and indicate pronunciation by the use of diacritical marks and syllabication.

Geography (time, 1 hour)

1. What is climate? On what does climate depend?
2. How do you account for the extreme climates in Kansas?
3. Of what use are rivers? Of what use is an ocean?
4. Describe the mountains of North America.
5. Name and describe the following: Monrovia, Odessa, Denver, Manitoba, Hecla, Yukon, Saint Helena, Juan Fernandez, Aspinwall and Orinoco.

6. Name and locate the principal trade centers of the United States.
7. Name all the republics of Europe and the capital of each.
8. Why is the Atlantic coast colder than the Pacific in the same latitude?
9. Describe the process by which the water of the ocean returns to the sources of rivers.
10. Describe the movements of the earth. Give the inclination of the year.

This is the eighth-grade final exam from 1895 in Salina, Kansas. This exam is taken from the documents on file at the Smokey Valley Genealogical Society and Library in Salina, KS and reprinted by the Salina Journal.

Notice that the exam took five hours to complete. It gives the saying "he only has an eighth grade education" a whole new meaning doesn't it?

Exercise:

Compare the above standard requirements for your eighth-grade graduation:

____

____

Monmouth County Results and the NYC Test Results

Test Scores of Graduating Seniors

The College Board's reasoning test for students graduating in 1999 in New Jersey showed that boys outscored girls in both verbal and math and that minority students trailed white students. Here are the average scores.

Monmouth County SAT Scores

Race or ethnicity	Verbal		Math	
	Male	Female	Male	Female
Asian/Pacific Islander	516	516	589	565
African American	428	429	438	419
American Indian/ Alaskan Native	476	458	493	462
Hispanic:				
Latin, South or Central American	455	432	475	432
Puerto Rican	438	434	454	426
Mexican or Mexican American	460	461	463	463
White	522	516	543	512
Other	496	490	516	487

Exercise:

Why the difference in scores?

____

____

____

____

NYC Test Results

Best Performing Schools			Worst Performing Schools		
Fourth Grade		%	**Fourth Grade**		%
Special Music School of America	Manhattan	100.0%	Benjamin Franklin	Bronx	5.9%
Mott Hall	Manhattan	100.0%	Mary McLeod Bethune	Manhattan	6.9%
Independence	Manhattan	98.0%	Hans Christian Anderson	Manhattan	7.2%
Alexander Graham Bell	Queens	98.0%	PS 340	Bronx	7.3%
North Hills School	Queens	97.0%	Lab School for Children	Bronx	8.0%
Manhattan New School	Manhattan	94.3%	PS 360	Bronx	10.2%
David Porter School	Queens	93.8%	Raphael Hernandez	Manhattan	10.6%
Douglaston School	Queens	93.3%	Eagle School	Bronx	11.5%
P.S. 159	Queens	93.3%	Little People	Bronx	11.5%
Lillie Devereux Blake	Manhattan	93.1%	St. Mary's Park	Bronx	11.7%
			Dumont	Brooklyn	11.7%
Eighth Grade			**Eighth Grade**		
Mamie Fay	Queens	100.0%			
Mott Hall	Manhattan	100.0%	Paul L. Dunbar	Bronx	0.0%
Crown School	Brooklyn	98.0%	Sunset Park Prep	Brooklyn	0.0%
NYC Lab School	Manhattan	98.0%	Acad.of Comm. Studies	Bronx	0.0%
Mark Twain	Brooklyn	97.0%	Mahalia Jackson	Brooklyn	0.3%
The Center School	Manhattan	94.3%	Dr. Charles R. Drew	Bronx	0.6%
Gateway to Health Services	Queens	93.8%	Sarah Garnet	Brooklyn	0.6%
Bay Acad. of Arts & Sciences	Brooklyn	93.3%	Henry Lou Gehrig	Bronx	1.1%
Park Slope Elementary	Brooklyn	93.3%	Gustave Straubenmuller	Manhattan	1.4%
Manhattan Acad. of Technology	Manhattan	93.1%	Benjamin Cardozza	Queens	1.4%
			Dr. Betty Shabazz	Brooklyn	1.5%

% = % of students that meet standards

Mandated School Curriculum, New Jersey Public Schools

The legislature and the state board have mandated the teaching of secure areas of study in all public schools as follows:

1. A two-year course in social studies, history of the United States, including materials on black history recommended by the commissioner, is required for all high school students:
   One-credit course, world history/culture
2. A course in health, safety and physical education, adapted to the ages and capabilities of the students. Every student must take the course unless excused by the school medical inspector as being physically incapable. The time devoted to the course in physical education must aggregate at least 2.5 hours per school week (one credit for a year).
3. Minimum course requirements for graduation from high school including and in addition to the requirements in one and two above, course requirements established pursuant to the T&E Law. These requirements include:
   a. One credit year of English for the year of enrollment, up to four credit years.
   b. Three credit years of mathematics.
   c. Two credit years of natural or physical science.
   d. One credit year of fine, practical and/or performing arts.
   e. One-half credit year of career exploration or development.

4. The study of community civics, geography, history and civics of New Jersey and the privileges and responsibilities of citizenship, in appropriate grades.
5. The nature of alcoholic drinks and narcotics and their effects on the human system in such manner as may be adapted to the age and understanding of the students and sufficiently emphasized in appropriate places in the curriculum.
6. Instruction in accident and fire prevention in appropriate grades and classes.
7. Instruction in the Constitution of the United States beginning no later than seventh grade.
8. A family life education program designed to develop an understanding of all facets of human development, sexuality and reproduction. The curriculum must be designed to strengthen family life, and must be implemented through a coordinated, sequential, elementary/secondary program.

In addition, each local board must develop minimum standards for high school graduation that must include the attainment of state-determined proficiency levels in reading and computation, and may also include demonstration of proficiencies other than those required by the state.

Students must meet the curriculum requirements through demonstration of mastery of statewide core and locally determined course proficiencies, in each of the preceding curriculum areas or through program completion procedures. This determination will be made by the district board of education.

The New Jersey Core Curriculum Content Standards

Because our schools need to produce both excellent thinkers and excellent doers, the New Jersey Core Curriculum Content Standards describe what students should know and be able to do in nine academic areas:

1. Visual and Performing Arts
2. Comprehensive Health and Physical Education
3. Language Arts Literacy
4. Mathematics
5. Science
6. Social studies
7. World Languages
8. Technological Literacy
9. Career Education and Consumer, Family and Life Skills

The last two standard areas replace the cross-content workplace readiness standards adopted in 1996.

The content standards themselves are concerned with the knowledge students should acquire in the skills they should develop in the course of their Pre-K–12 experience. They are broad outcome statements that provide the framework for ***strands*** and ***Cumulative Progress Indicators*** (**CPI's**).

Strands: Organized tools that help teachers locate specific content and skills. Under each strand is a number of CPIs at specific benchmark grades.

CPI: Provides the specific content or skills to be taught and are cumulative; that is, the progress indicators begin at the foundation or basic level and increase in complexity as a student matures, requiring more complex interaction with the content.

For a detailed scope and sequence of the New Jersey Core Curriculum Content Standards, please view www.state.nj.us/education. Current standards can be assessed through Academic and Professional Standards.

School Improvement Adequate Yearly Progress (AYP) Monitoring Categories

No Child Left Behind– Marker of:

- School accountability
- Flexibility and mobile control
- Options for parents
- Emphasis on teaching methods that are proven to work

Adequate Yearly Progress

Adequate Yearly Progress **(AYP)** refers to the growth needed in the proportion of students who achieve the state benchmarks of academic proficiency. Schools that do not make **AYP** for two years in a row are designated as "***in need of improvement***" and subject to a range of consequence.

95 Percent

Ninety-five percent is the required participation rate of students enrolled in each school and needs to be tested in order to achieve **AYP**.

Sanctions Process

Each school and district must complete an analysis of their assessment results and make adjustments based on the individual needs of the student population:

Year One: Student assessment results are analyzed to determine if the school meets **AYP** requirements. If the school does not meet **AYP**, this is considered the "***early warning year.***"

Year Two: Students are assessed and results are analyzed to determine if **AYP** has been achieved. In the second year that benchmarks have not been achieved, the school does not achieve **AYP**, and the school will be identified as "***in need of improvement***" at the beginning of the next school year. Schools identified as being "***in need of improvement***", must develop an improvement plan, and the parents must be notified and given the option to transfer their children to a higher performing school and district.

Year Three: If a school does not meet **AYP** for a third consecutive year, then supplemental educational services must be made available to low-income students at the school. In addition, school choice must continue to be offered and the improvement plan must be further developed.

Year Four: If a school does not meet **AYP** for four consecutive years, it is identified for "***corrective action***." Children can to continue to transfer to other schools or receive supplemental educational services. Additionally, the district and school are required to increase at least one, but not necessarily all of the following corrective actions:

- Replace the school staff that are relevant to the failure to make **AYP**.
- Institute a new curriculum, including appropriate professional development.
- Significantly decrease management authority at the school level.
- Appoint an outside expert to advise the school.
- Extend the school year or the school day for the school.
- Restructure the school's internal organizational structure.

Year Five: If a school does not make **AYP** for five consecutive years, it will be restructured. Children can continue to transfer to other schools or receive supplemental educational services.

School Category

Category I—*School in Need of Improvement*
School did not meet **AYP** and has an achievement gap of more than 25 percent in attaining standards in language arts or mathematics.

Category II—*Schools in Performance Monitoring*
Schools did not achieve **AYP;** however the schools have demonstrated the ability to make progress toward eliminating the achievement gap. If **AYP** is not met, the next academic year the school will enter Category I.

Category III—*Schools Approaching the Standards*
Schools have nearly achieved **AYP** with less than 5 percent of students having not achieved state standards in one content area. Schools are likely to meet standards; however, if not achieved in one school year, they will be placed in Category II.

Category IV— *Schools Receiving Conditional Approval*
These schools have achieved their designated **AYP** and are progressing toward meeting the state standards. However, they must be monitored for maintenance of achievement.

Category V—*Schools Receiving Full Approval*
These schools have met state standards in at least one of the prior two years in each subject area.

Category VI—*Schools Demonstrating Excellence*
These schools have always met or exceeded state standards and may be considered as exemplary models of success.

Preliminary List of Monmouth County Schools Not Meeting AYP

Asbury Park	Year 3 Status	Restructuring Assign New Principal Assign New Vice Principal Implement Block Schedule
Freehold Regional	Year 2 Status Hold	
Long Branch	Year 2 Status Hold	Reconfigure schools into small learning communities New administrators for new academy language arts, math, social studies/science facilitator Reassign 2/3 middle school staff Replace some staff Self-contain grade seven Adopt Connect Math Program
Red Bank Regional	Year 2 Status	
Monmouth Regional	Year 1 Status Hold	
Neptune Township	Year 1 Status	

AYP Sanctions Timeline for Implementation

Year 1 Status: *"Warning Year" status*

Student assessment results are analyzed and if the school meets AYP requirements. If the school does not meet the AYP requirements, this is considered the warning year.

Year 2 Status: *"School Choice" status*

Any of those schools that receive Title I funding must offer parents intradistrict school choice at another school that received **AYP** within the district. If the choice is not available in the district, either because there is only one school at that grade level in the district or because the other schools at the grade level are either already at capacity or did not make **AYP**, the school must offer supplemental educational services, such as tutoring, and develop and implement a school improvement plan.

Year 3 status: *"Supplemental Educational Services" status*

Schools that miss **AYP** for three years in a row are now in the third level of **AYP** sanctions. If they receive Title I funding, they are required to offer parents intradistrict choice, if feasible, and supplemental educational services such as tutoring, using twenty percent of the Title I money they receive. The school must also create a school improvement plan.

Year 4 status: *"Corrective Action" status.*

Any of those schools which receive federal Title I funding must allot twenty percent of their Title I funds for parental options, such as intra-district school choice, if feasible, and supplemental educational services such as tutoring, complete or update a school improvement plan, undergo a comprehensive review, and take other corrective actions.

Year 5 status: *"Restructuring" status.*

These schools now face more severe federal sanctions, as administrators must begin planning for restructuring and for the improvement of the restructuring plan in the 2007–2008 school year, should the school miss the **AYP** proficiency targets next year. Under **NCLB** rules, restructuring requires the imposition of an alternative governance arrangement for the school. In New Jersey, this could involve major operational or governance changes within the school. These changes may include the replacement of all or most of the school staff deemed relevant to the school's inability to make progress, or the reopening of the school as a charter school. Department of Education officials are already working with the year 5 schools to help them create and implement a blueprint for change and to identify their responsibilities and options under **NCLB** rules. All of the schools have been visited by Department of Education sponsored **CAPA** (Collaborative Assessment and Planning for Achievement) teams, which help identify obstacles in student achievement and develop customized solutions to the school's problems.

Year 6 status: *"Most Serious" status*

Schools that have not made **AYP** for six consecutive years are now in the process of implementing restructuring plans that have been submitted to the Department of Education for approval.

Commissioner Comment on the AYP

"While we have been supportive of the federal attempt to quantify accountability, it is important for schools, parents and the public to understand that the New Jersey Department of Education does not regard **AYP** as the only measurement of student achievement or progress," said Commissioner of Education Lucille E. Davies. "We have very high expectations and very high standards here, and while we're making progress, there is still a great deal to be done if we are able to prepare our children to compete in the twenty-first century," she said.

The Changing Faces of American Schools

American schools are meeting new challenges and opportunities with the increasing demands to be accountable for the education of all students. In the past, schools have addressed the needs of a dominant culture with a vision of America as a "melting pot". Today, however, American culture can be described as a "salad bowl". Numerous responses to this shift by local, state and federal education mandates have identified a wide expanse of programs and opportunities to meet the needs of the increasingly diverse student populations they serve. Issues related to urban education, the atypical learner, inclusion, adolescent learners, diverse ethnic values and needs, English language learners **(ELL, ESL)** preschool and early education, family structures and the like have created the need for differentiated programs and services and as a result, have redefined what it means to receive an education in America.

State and local school boards required to meet program mandates for a thorough and efficient education are often challenged to develop and fund such programs. In response to schools' limited successes, in educating a diverse student population, alternative public education choices have emerged, such as voucher systems, charter schools, magnet programs, small schools, and high school campus designs.

Exercise:

1. What does the research say about these alternative approaches to learning?

___

2. How have these programs and opportunities met student needs?

___

3. What programs are being offered through local Monmouth County schools?

___

4. How have local school districts diversified?

___

5. How have they succeeded?

____
____
____

6. What challenges remain?

____
____
____

Academic Performance HSPA (2004–2005)

Student Type	Total enrolled/ Tested	Proficiency Adv. Proficiency Language Arts %	Proficiency Adv. Proficiency Math %
African American	13,578 / 13,297	61.4 / 5.7	41.9 / 6.8
Asian Pacific Islander	6,647 / 6,635	57.4 / 31.8	36.0 / 53.9
American Indian Native	121 / 119	68.9 / 11.8	47.5 / 17.8
Hispanic	12,738 / 12,581	61.5 / 6.7	48.5 / 10.0
White	57,410 / 57,090	66.1 / 25.3	50.1 / 35.7
Student with a disability	13,841 / 13,490	43.0 / 3.5	27.1 / 5.5

Other Board Policies

A board may elect to establish a sexual assault prevention program in accordance with guidelines established by the department of education.

The board may provide, by contract and appropriate funds, for the support and maintenance of existing museum facilities and services for the use and benefit of students.

Appropriate exercises are to be held on the last day of school before Lincoln's and Washington's birthdays, Memorial Day, Columbus Day, Veterans Day, Thanksgiving Day, and such other patriotic holidays as are established by law.

Appropriate exercises for Flag Day are to be held in every public school on June 14 of every year.

Arbor Day is to be observed in all public schools with appropriate programs prepared by the superintendent of schools.

Commodore John Barry Day is to be observed in the public school on September 13, or the nearest school day if the 13th occurs on a weekend, with appropriate exercises as prescribed by the commissioner.

Every board must display a United States flag on or near the school building during school hours and have a flag in each assembly and classroom.

The board must require the students to salute the flag and pledge the oath of allegiance on every school day. Children with conscientious scruples against such pledge and salute, and children of accredited representatives of foreign governments may not be required to make the pledge and salute.

Exercise:

What other exercises should schools hold and why?

Chapter Notes & Additional Information:

Chapter 6:

Financing Schools

Chapter Topics:

A School Budget Description and Impact

Public schools are financed through federal, state and local sources. The budget plan directing the allocation of resources and the future financial operations of school district incorporates a strategy to be employed by the district to achieve legally intended missions, goals and objectives. Budget plans are prepared for each program and service offered. Money is then allocated to each area as directed by the mission statement and academic plans. The complete accounting of how the budget is spent and the sources of income are placed in funding lines, recorded and accounted for each year. A proposed budget is presented to the Commissioner of Education by January 15th each year for the following year. Upon approval, the district board of education then prepares the budget for the ensuing year on or before the first Tuesday in March. A public hearing follows between the first Tuesday in March and March 18th. The budget is voted on at the April election.

A site-based budget is a plan intended to provide individual schools within the district the opportunity to decide on money allocations based on their particular needs. Each school allocates monies to specific programs and then submits the plan to central administration where the separate school budgets are consolidated and presented to the superintendent of schools. Site-based budgeting has the advantage of individual school control over allocation and spending. In addition, it is a way of assuring proper distribution of funds to all schools within the district.

Funding Schools

Recent state superior court decisions have said that school systems are not providing an ***equal education*** for all children because their ways of funding are "***not fair***." There are several ways of funding schools, such as the state income or sales taxes, lotteries and property tax. On average, approximately 5 to 10 percent of the monies to finance schools come from the federal government, with the rest shared between the state and local school districts.

The trend, however, has been for an increase in state revenues and a decrease in federal and local shares.

School year	Federal percent	State percent	Local percent
1920	0.3	16.5	83.2
1950	2.9	39.8	57.3
1960	4.4	39.1	56.6
1970	8.0	39.4	52.1
1980	9.8	46.8	43.4
1987	6.4	49.8	43.9
1995	9.0	47.0	44.0
1998–1999	3.7	41.3	54.9
2002–2004	3.7	42.4	54.9
2004–2006	3.7	42.3	54.9

Education is primarily a state and local responsibility in the United States. It is the states and communities, as well as public and private organizations of all kinds, that establish schools and colleges, develop criteria, and determine requirements for enrollment and graduation. The structure of education finance in America reflects this predominant state and local role. Of an estimated $909 billion dollars being spent nationwide on education at all levels for school year 2004–2005, about 90 percent came from the state, local, and private sources.

That means the federal contribution to national education expenditures is about 10 percent. This 10 percent includes educational expenditures not only from the Department of Education, but also from other federal agencies, such as the Department of Health and Human Services' Head Start program and the Department of Agriculture's School Lunch program. Subtract these other dollars, and the Department of Education is left with less than 8 percent of total education spending. The Department of Education's $71.5 billion appropriation, by the way, is about 2.9 percent of the federal government's nearly $2.5 trillion dollar budget for fiscal year 2005.

Exercise:

Explain the changes in the percentages.

____

____

The Property Tax

Property taxes are annual assessments that property owners pay based on the estimated value of their property. The assessing process works as follows:

1. The ***market value*** (the price property could sell for) is determined (reevaluation done on a periodic basis—10 years in N.J.)
2. a certain percentage of that amount is calculated according to a local tax index to determine the ***assessed value*** of the property, and
3. a ***local tax rate*** is applied to the assessed value.

Sample Property Tax: Middletown, New Jersey

	Rate per $100	Amount of Tax
County Tax	0.560	$1,722.56
District School Budget Tax	2.260	$6,951.76
Municipal Tax	0.686	$2,110.14
Municipal Open Space Tax	0.020	$61.52
County Open Space Tax	0.032	$98.43
Garbage District Tax	0.146	$449.10
2006 Total Tax	3.704	$11,393.51

Property taxes have become one of the focuses of public controversy about school financing, and those controversies include the following circumstances:

1. Property tax increases usually require public votes and people do not like to vote themselves more taxes.
2. Widespread continuing increases have led citizens to believe that they are taxed too much.
3. Over recent years, the proportion of property owners who have school-age children has dropped dramatically, while the proportion of those living on fixed incomes has risen.
4. Citizens in general have developed a widespread distrust for politicians, including those who raise taxes and fund schools.

Exercise:

What is the local tax rate in your town?

Town: ______________________________

Tax Rate: ______________________________

School: ______________________________

Municipal: ______________________________

Imbalance in New Jersey Tax System

An expert on state tax policy has described New Jersey's tax systems as "***out of balance***."

"New Jersey is in a much better fiscal position than most other states" with "a stronger than average tax base, but less than average spending needs." noted Dr. Harold A. Hovey, president of the State Policy Research Inc. of Hilton Head, S.C. "However," he added, "the state's reliance on local property taxes is 16 percent higher than the nation as a whole."

The report showed that per capita education spending by state government is below the national average, with New Jersey ranking 38th among the 50 states. New Jersey funds cover only 39.3 percent of school spending, versus a national average of 48.7 percent. Consequently, local property taxes have had to shoulder the primary burden.

Current Issues Affecting School Funding

New Jersey is facing the ***highest property tax*** in the country. Although several issues are in state legislature to address the costs to New Jersey citizens, discussions on public school funding, especially the cost of Abbott funding, has been highlighted as one area in which to consider change.

Consider this: 45 percent of the state's local tax revenue is raised from property taxes, compared with an average of about 30 percent for the rest of the nation. The owner of a modest home in New Jersey pays $6,000 a year or more in property taxes.

One measure addressing the high cost of living in New Jersey is to reconsider how schools are funded. Currently, legislative gains have considered changing the state funding formula for state aid to school districts, encouraging the consolidation of school districts and municipal services and giving county school superintendents greater power to control spending by school districts. Of these suggested changes, local districts and mayors are adamant about letting go of local district control. They argue that although consolidation is tempting, it does have hidden costs.

Some concerning questions are:

- How might two districts combine if one is operating successfully and the other is in need of improvement?
- Who would carry the burden to fund these changes?

Another issue questions how school districts with uniquely different education needs come together to provide efficient education for all children.

Adding to the complex issue of funding schools, New Jersey is reconsidering how children who are at risk for failure can receive an adequate education. In a recent report of misappropriated school spending, a damaging report on the Abbott district reveals that numerous problems in Camden, Newark, Jersey City and Paterson exist. These districts were the first of the 31 so-called Abbott districts to be audited under an order by the New Jersey Supreme Court. These school districts are among the state's poorest and have received $35 billion in state aid since the State Supreme Court ruled, 10 years ago, that the poorest urban districts should be given the resources to spend as much on their students as the wealthiest suburban districts do. Violations included keeping personnel on the payroll years after they have been deceased, inefficient use of funds for flowers, unnecessary trips and hidden administrative expenses. Damaging reports from these districts call attention to the high cost of education and the concern for wasteful management. In recent months, a growing number of critics have called for changes to the school financing system, saying it has wasted millions of dollars in the Abbott districts while shortchanging others. Lucille E. Davy, the Education Commissioner, stated that "in all honesty, when you look at some of the expenditures of money, there are people making poor judgments about the public money."

Exercise:

1. ***What issues must be addressed concerning school funding?***

2. ***How does funding for state and federal mandated programs such as IDEA affect local school budgets?***

Governor Corzine's Tax Proposal Plan

Recently, the NJEA president's message addressed Governor Corzine's tax proposal plan to control credit and caps.

- In an attempt to provide significant credit to property tax payers, Governor Corzine proposed to issue strong caps on school budgets currently proposed to be limited to 4 percent.

- The state is ignoring the problem of inadequately funded school budgets.

- Property tax increases are not the best response to slashed state aid, but schools were able to maintain high standards and program opportunities for children.

- With hard property tax caps, districts will have no funds to address emergencies, salary and benefit costs, program costs and especially special education, or to hire the best teachers.

- Support for early education needs for children is at greater risk than school failure.

- What alternative revenue stream will be created if the state curtails revenues from property taxes to fund education?

A-8/S-49 Countywide School Districting Plan

Governor Corzine proposed countywide school districts as a way to consolidate schools and address duplicate services. In response to this proposal, the New Jersey School Boards Association (njsba.org) called attention to the risks involved in this proposal:

- Giving a politically appointed state official sweeping power over the local school district budgets
- Eliminating savings that school districts have already achieved
- Affecting school district grade organizations and boundaries

By concentrating power at the county level, the county superintendent bureaucracy can actually cost taxpayers more. For example, it could negate achievements in the areas of staffing, purchases and negotiations that have taken place at the local level.

NJSBA opposes for the following reasons:

- Neither voters nor local school boards would have a voice in authorizing the pilot county school district.
- It could potentially cut existing educational services.
- The inability of local school districts in the pilot county would be unable to return to local governments if the experiment fails.

School Health Benefit Negotiation

Currently school boards have had no negotiation rights for health benefits when school unions come to the table. The cost of health benefits can be quite a burden to smaller school districts whose budgets are already overtaxed. The New Jersey School Boards Association considers that if school boards could negotiate with unions over the cost of benefits, millions of tax dollars could be saved every year. The ability to bargain over aspects of health benefits, however, is not available to school boards that provide their employees coverage through the New Jersey State Health Benefits Program **(SHBP)**, explained **NJSBA** lobbyist Barbara M. Horl in testimony to the Joint Committee on Public Employee Benefits Reform.

- Almost 40 percent of New Jersey's school districts use the state plan.

- State regulations preclude these districts from negotiating levels of deductibles, copayments, employee contributions to premium, placement of new employees, less costly managed care systems and other aspects of coverage.
- The best cost-savings solution would be to give **SHBP**-member districts the ability to negotiate provisions to control health benefit costs. Because of huge increases in premiums since the mid-1990s and the plan's rigid structure, 218 school districts have left the **SHBP** and gone with private health insurance.

Other Restrictions

- The largest chunk of taxpayer-funding for schools, approximately 75 percent, is spent on salaries and employee benefits.

- Health coverage represents the most rapidly escalating employment cost.

Increased Competition

- Some school districts are forced by the market to remain in the SHBP because private carriers will not accept them or the high costs would be prohibitive.

- Granting **SHBP**-member school districts the ability to negotiate aspects of health coverage would make the state plan more competitive with private carriers therefore attracting school districts back into the state program.

Exercise:

1. ***How would negotiated health benefits affect teachers and school staff?***

____

____

2. ***What effect would be placed on teacher salaries?***

____

____

3. ***What affect would it have on the teachers' desire to remain in the field?***

____

____

4. ***What are other concerns?***

____

____

Monmouth County District's per Student Regular Education Facts and Figures 2005–2006 Totals

District	Budget per Student	State Aid (%)	Federal Aid (%)	Local Tax Support (%)	% of Classified Students	Median Admin. Salary	Median Teacher Salary
Asbury Park	18,893	81	8	6	15.6	94,156	50,975
Belmar	10,251	14	3	65	11.7	93,825	48,600
Brielle	9,250	5	2	92	8	88,583	44,920
Colts Neck	10,144	8	1	88	10.6	94,297	47,470
Deal Borough	11,866	6	1	71	11.2	125,863	38,409
Eatontown	12,106	23	6	68	15.7	117,900	61,630
Fair Haven	8,834	4	1	84	14.1	94,195	54,240
Farmingdale	13,120	36	2	59	13.1	64,458	65,259
Freehold Twp.	9,317	9	2	85	11	108,440	47,480
Hazlet	10,327	28	2	66	13.2	107,329	46,615
Holmdel	10,771	6	1	90	9	111,033	56,660
Howell	10,240	34	2	60	14	108,671	46,425
Long Branch	9,420	63	4	31	11.1	108,606	46,235
Little Silver	10,660	5	1	89	11.7	95,000	43,300
Manalapan/ Englishtown Regional	9,325	30	3	63	10.6	86,135	48,585
Manasquan	10,102	5	1	47 (34 tuition)	11.3	113,457	49,700
Matawan	9,279	16	2	80	9.9	109,617	49,455
Aberdeen	11,124	20	2	75	7.5	110,891	54,190
Middletown	10,342	16	2	79	14.3	116,800	56,985
Millstone	8,485	16	11	77	13.3	121,712	45,850
Mon. Beach	10,108	6	2	87	4.4	80,632	50,213
Neptune City	9,251	23	3	65	10.1	98,900	43,875
Ocean Twp.	13,056	16	2	77	11	106,904	57,265
Oceanport	8,745	7	2	84	10.3	98,962	44,465
Rumson	10,235	4	1	84	14.1	94,195	54,240
Sea Girt	13,738	5	2	90	6.6	115,321	52,836
Shrewsbury	10,175	6	1	91	12.5	93,920	47,580
Spring Lake	13,023	7	2	90	10.9	80,800	49,350
Spring Lake Hts.	9,854	7	2	90	10.9	80,800	49,350
Tinton Falls	11,353	17	3	72	11.2	96,262	47,090
Wall	10,484	10	1	81	14.1	111,629	44,328
W. Long Branch	9,420	7	2	87	10.8	107,474	43,000

New Jersey Schools Fast Facts

1. There are 2,422 schools within 592 functioning districts.
2. In addition to elementary, secondary and middle schools, there are 51 charter schools.
3. 111,256 teachers educate more than 1.3 million students.
4. Of the 86,000 students graduating each year, nearly 85 percent plan to continue their education.
5. On average, teachers make over $58,000.00 per year, whereas administrators and supervisors are over $105,000, and superintendents make $142,000 on average.

District Rating in Monmouth County

(A = Poorest J = Wealthiest)

Asbury Park City	A	Matawan-Aberdeen Regional	FG
Atlantic Highlands Boro	GH	Middletown Twp.	GH
Avon Boro	I	Millstone Twp.	I
Belmar Boro	DE	Monmouth Beach Boro	I
Bradley Beach Boro	CD	Monmouth Regional	GH
Brielle Boro	GH	Neptune City	CD
Colts Neck Twp.	I	Neptune Twp.	CD
Deal Boro	GH	Ocean Twp.	FG
Eatontown Boro	FG	Oceanport Boro	GH
Fair Haven Boro	I	Red Bank Boro	CD
Farmingdale Boro	DE	Red Bank Regional	FG
Freehold Boro	B	Roosevelt Boro	GH
Freehold Regional	GH	Rumson Boro	J
Freehold Twp.	GH	Rumson-Fair Haven Reg.	J
Hazlet Twp.	DE	Sea Bright Boro	FG
Henry Hudson Regional	DE	Sea Girt Boro	I
Highlands Boro	CD	Shore Regional	GH
Holmdel Twp.	I	Shrewsbury Boro	I
Howell Twp.	FG	South Belmar	CD
Keansburg Boro	A	Spring Lake Boro	I
Keyport Boro	CD	Spring Lake Heights	FG
Little Siver Boro	J	Tinton Falls	GH
Long Branch City	B	Union Beach	CD
Manalapan-Englishtown Reg.	GH	Upper Freehold Regional	GH
Manasquan Boro	GH	Wall Twp.	GH
Marlboro Twp.	I	West Long Branch Boro	FG

The DFGs were calculated using the following six variables that are closely related to SES:

1. Percent of adults with no high school diploma.
2. Percent of adults with some college education.
3. Occupational status
4. Unemployment rate
5. Percent of individuals in poverty
6. Median family income

2006–2007 State Aid, Excluding Debt Service

	District of Asbury Park (A)	Middletown (GH)	Rumsom-Fair Haven Regional (J)
County	Monmouth	Monmouth	Monmouth
Total State Aid Payment 2005–2006	$58,709,576	$19,341,547	$586,769
Core Curriculum Aid	$26,194,617	$0	$0
Supp. Core Curriculum Aid	$1,256,722	$0	$0
Education Opportunity Aid	$20,035,703	$0	$129135
Transportation Aid	$498,157	$3,127,720	$337531
Special Education Aid	$4,776,450	$6,481,044	$0
Early Childhood Ed. Aid	$3,160,320	$0	$0
Demonstrably Effective Program Aid	$1,644,068	$0	$0
Stabilization Aid	$0	$6,709,865	$0
Consolidated Aid	$388,848	$1,144,380	$62,233
Additional Formula Aid	$0	$563,346	$15,902
Other Aids[4]	$172,720	$2,070,869	$98,816
Total State Aid Payment 2006-2007	$58,127,605	$20,097,224	$643,617
Dollar Increase/Decrease from 2005-2006	$-58,4971	$755,677	$56,848
% Change in State Aid	-1.0%	3.9%	9.7%
% Change Net Budget	-.09%	0.6%	0.4%

Notes:

[4] Other Aids are Bilingual, County Vocational, F.T. Post-Sec Voc., Instructional Supplemental Aid, Abbott Bordered District Aid, School Choice, Above Average Enrollment Growth, Help Aid and S. Stabilization /Regional Incentive.

Percent of School Districts Classified as Successful, by District Factor Group

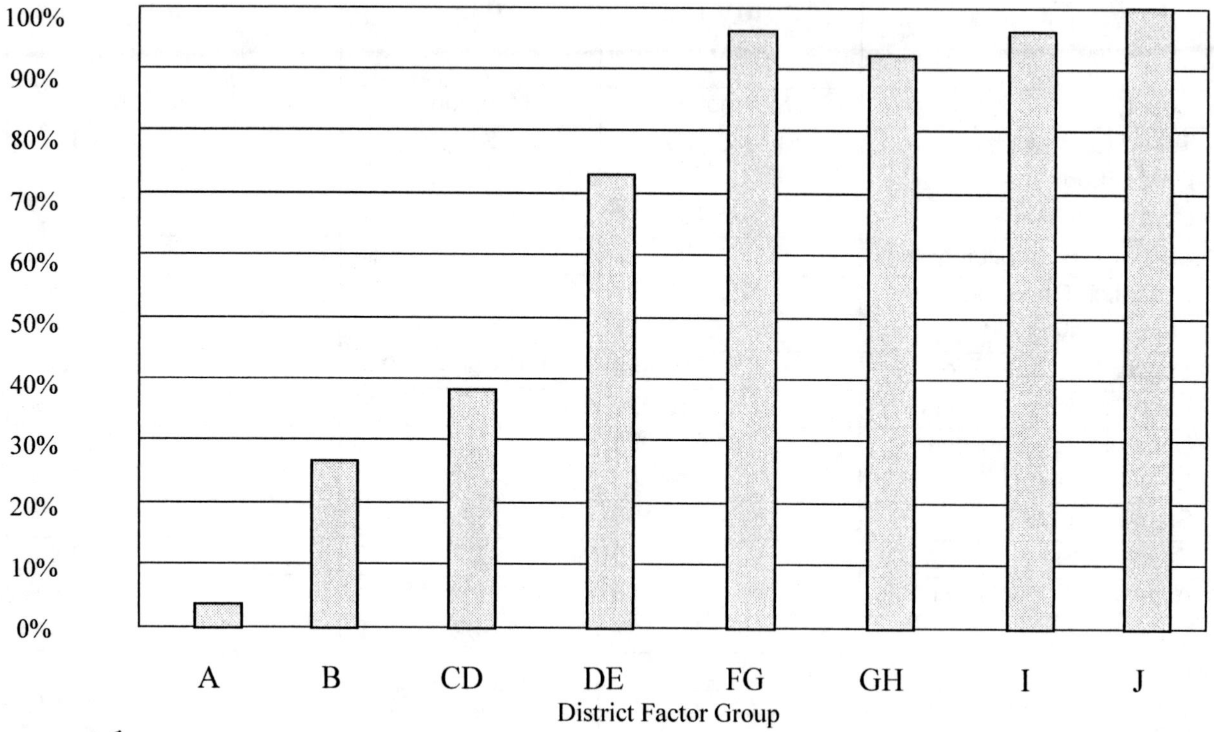

Exercise:

What trends can be derived from the above graph?

What accounts for the differences among school outcomes?

Equal Educational Opportunity

Serrano v. Priest

In *Serrano v. Priest*, the California Supreme Court was called on to determine whether the California public school financing system, with its substantial dependence on local property taxes, violated the Fourteenth Amendment. In a six-to-one decision in 1971, the court held that heavy reliance on unequal local property taxes "makes the quality of a child's education a function of the wealth of his or her parents and neighbors." Furthermore, the court declared: "Districts with small tax basis simply cannot levy taxes at a rate sufficient to produce the revenue that our affluent districts produce with a minimum effort."

At the time of the *Serrano v. Priest* decision, the Baldwin Park School District for example, spent $577 per student, whereas the Beverly Hills District spent $1,232 per student. Yet the tax rate in Baldwin Park of $5.48 was more than double of the $2.38 in Beverly Hills. The discrepancy was caused by the difference in wealth between the two districts. Beverly Hills had $50,885 of assessed valuation per child; Baldwin Park had only $3,706 validation per child, a ratio of 13 to 1. The inequalities resulting from the property tax are at least twofold. The tax is oftentimes inequitably applied to the taxpayer, and in poor districts, the tax frequently results in unequal opportunities for education.

Officially, the California Supreme Court ruled that the system of school financing in California was unconstitutional, but did not forbid the use of property taxes.

Robinson v. Cahill 1973 N.J.62.7 (473)
Abbott v. Burke 1990 and 1994 NJ.

The first of several New Jersey Supreme Court decisions took place in 1973 (Robinson v. Cahill) declaring that New Jersey's financing systems of education was unconstitutional, it did not provide for a "***thorough and efficient***" education. New Jersey had to find a new way of equalizing education.

The legislature's response to the ***Robinson v. Cahill*** decision was the Public School Education Act of 1975. In enacting this statue, the legislature declared its intention to fulfill the constitution mandate by:

- Defining the overall goal of a thorough and efficient system of free public schools.
- Establishing guidelines and monitoring procedures to ensure progress toward thorough and efficient education goals.
- Establishing a funding structure to ensure adequate financial resources to implement a thorough and efficient public school system.

In New Jersey, the court held that an "***efficient***" system was one that prepared every student to be a citizen and a competitor in the marketplace. According to the court, "This record proves what we all suspect: that if the children of poorer districts went to school today in richer ones, educationally, they would be a lot better off. ***Everything in this record confirms what we know; that the children of poorer districts need that advantage much more than other children. And what everyone knows is that, as children, the only reason they do not get the advantage is that they were born in a poor district.***"

Exercise:

Do you agree or disagree with the last statement? Explain your reasons.

____

____

____

____

State Aid

State education funds are usually provided to local school districts in the form of ***state aid***, which is distributed in two ways:

General Aid ***Categorical Aid***

General aid is given to school districts as a single large amount, and the local district has wide latitude in determining how it is spent. Often it is provided through a ***foundation*** program formula, whereby the state bonds are matched by a certain percentage of local taxes to provide a per student amount of money that is considered to be the foundation level (minimum amount) needed to educate each child adequately. Local districts that can afford to do so usually provide additional revenues beyond the matching money from their own sources to increase funds above the foundation level. General aid funds are supposed to finance relatively equal levels of education for each student across all school districts in a state.

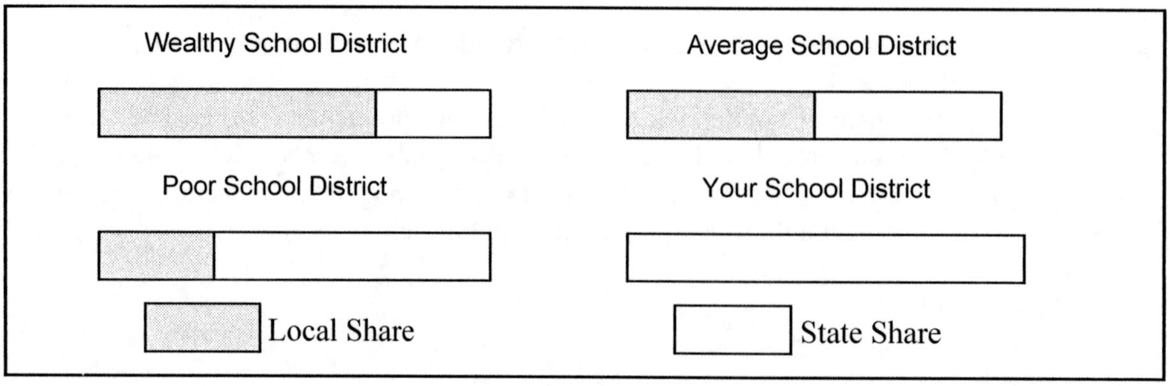

Under the "T & E Law" funding for public schools is a responsibility shared jointly by the state and local school districts. Because local districts are compelled to rely on local property taxes to meet their share of the obligation, the law provides for two types of state aid which attempts to equalize, to some extent, the resources available for education regardless of the amount of taxable property within the community: current expense equalization aid and capital outlay and debt service equalization aid.

Both types of aid are computed under complex formulas set out by statute that, in general, provided for greater state aid to those districts that have less property wealth available for local taxation. The formula also provides for greater state aid to those districts that have a higher expenditure level per student, up to a state support limit. Funds spent by a district beyond the state support limit did not trigger any corresponding increase in state aid. The formula also contains a provision that guarantees a minimum level of current expense equalization aid for districts with greater property wealth available for taxation.

The statute also provides ***categorical programs aid,*** which supplies additional state funding to help districts meet the extra costs of special education classes and other classes and services, including bilingual education, compensatory education, approved local vocational education, private school tuition, and supplementary and speech instruction. The amount of categorical programs aid received by each district depends on the number of students being provided special services and on a weighting factor for each type of handicap or for the type of other special class or service.

New Jersey Education Budget

Over 406 million dollars are proposed for the year 2006–2007 budget for Monmouth County schools. This figure does not include parity, grants and other sources of funding available to local districts. In categorical aid the state budget provides for the following for Monmouth County schools:

- **Core Curriculum Standards** aid: over $155 million
- **Supplemental Curriculum Standards** aid: over $11 million
- **Special Education**: over $67 million
- **Early Childhood Program** aid: over $14 million
- **Student Transportation** aid: over $26 million
- **Demonstrably Effective Program** aid: over $8 million
- **Parity Remedy (Abbott funding)** aid: over $17.8 million
- **Stabilization Aid**: over $21.6 million
- **Other aid programs including Bilingual, County Vocational, Distance Learning, Awards, Incentives and School Choice** aid: over $16.4 million

Aid variations by districts related to the following:

- Abbott funding
- Budget construction
- Capital expenditures
- Federal programs support
- Special education needs
- Local tax support basis
- Other local needs

Sample Illustration of Budget

The state determines budget lines.

Budgets above the Box. If a budget is defeated, the municipal governing body may cut the entire amount of the increase plus 2 percent of the prior year levy with adjustments for enrollment growth or reduction.

Cuts of amounts above the box cannot be appealed. If the cuts reduce the budget to an amount inside the box, that part of the cut that is inside the box may be appealed to the Commissioner or Education.

Budgets in the Box. If a budget is defeated, any cuts made by the municipal governing body may be appealed to the Commissioner or Education.

Budgets below the Box. If a budget is defeated, any cuts made by the municipal governing body are automatically reviewed by the Commissioner or Education with the "burden of proof" on the municipality.

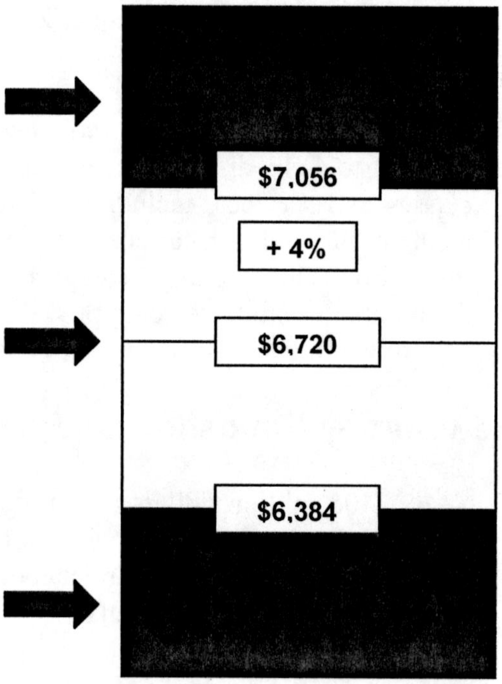

Exercise:

What other needs would your district add?

____

____

____

____

____

____

____

The current district budget can be adjusted by the Statutory Growth Limitations Budget Adjustment. In effect, this adjustment overrides any cap limitations set on budgets by allowing districts to apply to the state for additional funds that support unusual or unexpected financial demands, such as capital needs, additional special program needs and special education needs. With the new Spending Growth Cap Law recently passed, local districts can now apply for and receive funding above current needs, then bank the balance of awarded funds for future use.

Special Students/Classifications

Each board of education, according to rules prescribed by the commissioner, must identify and provide services for any child between ages of 3 and 21 residing in the district and enrolled in public or nonpublic schools of this state, who cannot be properly accommodated through the school programs usually provided because of handicaps. Programs and services may be provided by a district board of education, at their option, to students below the age of 3 and above the age of 21.

At a minimum, however, each board must provide information to parents of handicapped children below the age of three regarding services and programs available through other state, county or local agencies that may prevent their handicap from becoming more debilitating.

Each child between the ages of 3 and 21, who is identified as eligible for special education and/or related services, must have or be classified under one of the following categories:

- Mental Retardation
- Orthopedic Handicap
- Communications Handicap
- Visual Handicap
- Neurological Handicap
- Perpetual Handicap
- Chronic Illness
- Emotional Disturbance
- Social Maladjustment
- Auditory Handicap
- Autistic
- Multiple Handicaps
- Preschool Handicap

This determination is accomplished through procedures prescribed by the commissioner and proved by the state board.

The category of mentally retarded children is further divided by statute into three subcategories:

- Educable mentally retarded children
- Trainable mentally retarded children
- Children eligible for day training

Exercise:

What limitations do you feel should be placed on schools?

Spending Caps

Some states restrict the amount of money that can be raised via the local property tax. The state will only allow a certain percentage increase based on such factors as inflation.

Exercise:

1. ***Explain how this may hinder the quality of schooling.***

2. ***Explain how this policy may protect property owner.***

Questions Concerning Your Schools

1. What is the school's educational philosophy or mission?
2. How is your child doing in the school? Is he or she meeting the grade level expectations?
3. How is a student's progress monitored, in addition to grades?
4. How does the school ensure that all students are being challenged?
5. How does the school monitor teachers' performance and help them grow?
6. What steps are taken to include students classified with disabilities in the general education setting?
7. What are the school's greatest accomplishments?
8. How does the school use technology to improve learning?
9. In addition to teaching academic skills, what steps are taken to ensure that students are taught to be good thinkers and good citizens?
10. On any topic, especially about your child: "What can I do to help?"

Top Five SAT Scores

Monmouth County		
School	**Score**	**State Rank**
High Technology H.S.	**2038**	**1**
Communications H.S.	**1891**	**5**
Marine Academy of Science and Technology	**1870**	**6**
Academy of Allied Health	**1856**	**8**
Holmdel H.S.	**1764**	**13**
Ocean County		
Point Pleasant Beach H.S.	**1605**	**70**
Toms River East H.S.	**1519**	**135**
Toms River North H.S	**1509**	**143**
Point Pleasant H.S.	**1506**	**145**
Toms River South H.S.	**1502**	**149**
*** Your High School**		

Profile: University High School, Newark

Grades 7–12: 565 Children
Average Class Size: 20
Percent of Students in AP Classes: 24 percent
Percent Going to College: 83 percent

Language Arts: 93% passing (17% Advanced)
Math: 93% passing (33% Advanced)
Science: 98% passing (36% Advanced)

Urban Gem:

★ Scored as a selective magnet school in the 1960's, University is just one of five urban schools to gain three stars and the only one to get three stars for both its high school and middle school scores.

★ Senior seminars include Latina and Africana studies, women in literature, the U.S. Constitution and a methods class for future teachers.

★ "It's our mission: not only to do your craft, but to impact your community." —Roger Leon, Principal.

Profile: Bayberry School, Watchung

Grades Pre-K–4: 403 Children
Average Class Size: 17

Language Arts: 99% passing (14% Advanced)
Math: 99% passing (69% Advanced)
Science: 96% passing (47% Advanced)

Excellence on the Hill:

★ Already lofty, overall language arts and math passing rates each jumped more than 5 percent last year.

★ Students in the Bayberry Community Service Club provide help to food banks and sent care packages to soldiers overseas.

★ "There is not a teacher who shuts their door; we all work together, that is how it is here." —Mary Nunn, Principal.

Profile: Troy Hills Elementary School, Troy Hills

Grades K–5: 319 Children
Average Class Size: 19

Language Arts: 96% passing (8% Advanced)
Math: 96% passing (44% Advanced)
Science: 94% passing (54% Advanced)

Something Special:

★ Improved at least five points on its language arts, math and science pass rate, and on its advanced pass rates in math and science.

★ Each month stresses a different character trait, with students recognized for kindness, for showing respect, and so on.

★ A former music teacher, Principal Renee Brandler plays clarinet with the school band.

Chapter Notes & Additional Information:

Personal Thoughts & Drawings

Chapter 7:

Negligence, Defamation, Educational Malpractice

Chapter Topics:

Negligence Generalizations
Negligence Incidents
Areas of Concern
Defenses against Negligence
Negligence Illustrations
Defamation of Character
Defamation Illustrations
Intentional Infliction of Emotional Distress
Education Malpractice
Education Malpractice Illustrations
Negligence Exercises

233-pound roll of paper falls on and kills 4th grader

A fourth grade pupil sent on an errand by her teacher was killed by a 233-pound roll of art paper that fell on her head. "Christina, 10, and a classmate were sent by a teacher at Liberty Elementary School to a school garage Monday to return a 2-pound roll of paper," Liberty County Sheriff Don said.

The heavier, 8-foot-long roll was standing upright against a wall, and her classmate moved it.

Christina's mother, Barbara, questioned why school officials allowed the children in the garage without supervision.

Definitions of Negligence

Tort Liability of Teachers: A tort is a private or civil wrong that does not flow from breach of contract and that result in loss or damage to an individual or to his property. Perhaps the most common torts are negligence causing personal injury, trespass on property belonging to another, maintenance of a nuisance, and defamation of character.

Negligence

Negligence has been defined as conduct involving unreasonable danger to others that should be recognized by a reasonably prudent person. The courts require teachers to exercise a greater degree of care to protect pupils from injury than they require of the ordinary person. Perhaps it would be more accurate to say that the standard of conduct demanded of a teacher is that of the "***reasonably prudent teacher***."

Criteria for Establishing Negligence

Liability for negligence rests on three factors: (1) a duty to act so as to protect others from unnecessary risks, (2) the failure to so act, and (3) the injury of another **causing** loss or damage as the result of such failure to act. A teacher may be liable either for an act that a *reasonably prudent teacher* should have realized involved an unreasonable risk of injury to another or for failure to do an act that the teacher was under a duty to do for the protection of another.

The major criterion used by the courts in determining negligence is the ability to foresee; that is, should the defendant as a reasonably prudent teacher have foreseen the possible harmful consequences of his or her action or lack of action, and did he or she regard these consequences? If the answer of the court is in the affirmative, liability for negligence exists.

Defenses against Negligence

A number of legal defenses against negligence that relieve the teacher of liability have been rather clearly defined by the courts. The first and most common defense is, of course, a denial that any negligence exists. The person bringing suit (the plaintiff) must prove negligence by proving that the conduct of the defendant fell below the standard of reasonable prudence.

1. **Contributory Negligence:** In most states an individual is relieved of liability contributing to his own injury, and proof by the plaintiff that he has done so is known as contributory negligence.

2. **Proximate Cause:** Casual connection is a major factor considered by the courts in assessing whether negligence exists; there must be an unbroken "chain of causation" between the negligence of the teacher and the resultant pupil injury. In other words, the negligence of the defendant must be the proximate cause of the injury. A "break" in the chain of causation that results from the intervening act of a third party, for example, may mean that the court will conclude that the proximate cause of the injury was not the negligent conduct of the defendant and thus relieve the defendant of liability.

3. **Assumption of Risk:** An adult who knowingly engages in a dangerous occupation or activity normally is considered by the courts to have assumed the risk of the occupation. Except in the case of gross negligence of an employer or any other person, who may not recover any compensation if they should be injured. This is known as the doctrine of the assumption of risk. Except in the cases of athletic injuries, in which the student and the student's parents know that the activity may be physically hazardous, this doctrine is seldom used as a successful defense in cases involving the schools.

4. **Act of God:** An occurrence that is caused by nature or other natural event that could not be predicted based on current circumstances or conditions causing bodily harm.

Standard of Care

An examination of the cases and commentaries disclosed that three basic duties arise from the teacher–student relationship: (1) the duty to supervise, (2) the duty to exercise good judgment, and (3) the duty to instruct as to correct procedures, particularly (but not exclusively) when potentially hazardous conditions or instrumentalities are present.

Negligence Generalizations

- Schools will not be held liable when they use adequate preparation and supervision that meet or exceed local or nationally accepted standards.
- Schools will be held liable for injuries received during regular school events resulting from "the school's" failure to provide a reasonably safe environment, failure to warn participants of known hazards, to remove dangers where possible, to properly instruct, or to provide supervisors appropriate for the type of activity and age of the students.
- Schools will not be held liable when they have no way of knowing of danger or preventing an accident and can't be held liable for lack of supervision just because it happened. (Note: Duty does not mandate a constant surveillance of each student at every moment; however, it does necessitate removal of known dangers.)
- Schools will not be held liable for maintaining a playground unless it can be demonstrated that the playground was maintained in a way that it presented a hazard.

Each year thousands of students are injured in school and related activities. All activities that the schools sponsor or sanction leave them responsible for the welfare of the participating children. Whether it be on the playground, field trip, school bus, athletic field, hallway, or classroom, the teachers and the school are responsible.

Exercise:

Questions to ask for potential negligence cases:

Activity ________________

Was the activity overtly dangerous?________________

Was there adequate supervision? ________________

Was proper safety equipment being used? ________________

Was there adequate preparation for the activity? ________________

Were safety factors and rules explained properly? ________________

Were there a safe number of participants? ________________

Were the safety rules enforced? ________________

Negligence or Accidents

Chemical prompts exodus

The discovery of an explosive chemical forced the cancellation of classes and athletic events at a high school in Maine.

Students and faculty evacuated the high school after a consultant brought to the school to train teachers in the disposal of hazardous materials discovered two old cans of ethyl ether in a storage room.

The unopened cans showed an expiration date of 1985, and if jostled could have exploded with the force of two sticks of dynamite, said the assistant principal.

Officials decided to "err on the side of caution" and send the students home. The chemical is commonly used in science experiments, and exposure to sunlight over time can increase its chances of exploding.

The assistant principal said a retired science teacher may have left the chemical behind.

Soccer accident kills schoolboy

A high school soccer player died of a brain hemorrhage after a collision during practice, authorities here said today. John Doe, who would have been 17 years old Tuesday, died Saturday during a Smith Catholic High School scrimmage when he was bumped by another player while picking up a ball as a goalkeeper.

Players and coaches at the school said the contact was minimal.

Suit Filed in death of student

Jane Doe was taking a biology course at Jones College last spring when she unwittingly drank a toxic solution during an experiment. Four days later, she died, a tragedy that months of investigation have failed to fully explain.

Ms. Doe was part of a 27 student anatomy and physiology class at Jones College. As part of a urine test experiment, she drank what was supposed to be a simple saline solution. Instead, what she swallowed was isotonic buffered saline containing the toxic preservative sodium azide.

Teen impaled by javelin at track meet

A 15-year-old high school student survived a freak accident shortly before 5 p.m. yesterday when a javelin impaled him in the throat during a track meet, police said.

John Doe was struck during a warm-up period before a scheduled track meet between Smith and a team from Jones High School. The javelin that struck Doe was apparently an errant warm-up throw by a member of the Jones team, witnesses said. Doe had just finished setting up cones to mark the boundaries of the javelin-throwing area when he walked away from the throwing zone with two teammates.

Doe, who is manager of the track team, said he was about to get ready to start marking throws when he heard a shout of warning. He said he was standing about 130 feet from the throwing areas. Doe said he was conscious from the time he was impaled by the 8-foot aluminum javelin until he was taken into the operating room about 1 ½ hours later.

Boy, 11, killed in accident on school ski trip

An eleven-year old boy from Jones Township was killed in a skiing accident over the weekend while on a day trip with classmates, said school officials and family members.

John Doe, a sixth grader at the Jones Intermediate School, was skiing on a mountain in Pennsylvania's Poconos on Saturday afternoon when he fell off the slope and slid headfirst into a rock, said his mother.

The boy had tried skiing for the first time just a week earlier. The accident raises questions about the safety of such school trips.

"It's next to impossible to supervise such trips," the superintendent of schools said. "You have 150 students. Some are going up. Some are coming down. It's physically impossible."

Fifth graders sickened by sampling cocaine

Fourteen youngsters got sick when a fifth grader brought what was believed to be cocaine to school yesterday and shared it with classmates, authorities said.

The 11- and 12-year-old children ingested the substance at an elementary school when a student passed it around the classroom, said Pat, a spokesman for the Los Angeles School District.

Pat said it was cocaine, but another police officer said it was listed as an unknown substance until laboratory analysis could be completed.

Three boys apparently drowned on an overnight camping trip

Scuba divers and policing boats battling rapid currents yesterday to search the muddy creek for the bodies of three Jones grade school boys who apparently drowned while on an overnight camping trip at a teacher's house.

Classmates said the missing boys are the third group to go on an overnight trip to the teacher's house.

The police said the accident happened Tuesday as four boys were wading in the wake in a rural section of the Jones County community about five miles south of Smithville. The trouble apparently happened when the boys suddenly hit a deep spot with a rapid current.

Falling table kills boy; second fatality in two months

A seven-year-old boy is the second in two months to be killed at a suburban school by a falling portable table.

John Doe, a first-grade student at Jones Elementary School was killed Tuesday when a folding table fell on his head. Doe had been helping at about 3:15 P.M. He was helping adults clean up after a fund-raising event in the gymnasium. The table was a large one, resembling a ping-pong table that folded in the middle.

The death closely paralleled an April 6 incident in which a falling table killed John Smith, 9, of Jones. He had been helping an eighteen-year-old youth put the table away when it fell on his head at Jones school.

Four-year-old is left in an empty school bus

A four-year-old boy was stuck inside a school bus for almost three hours when he was apparently left behind after the route was completed.

The child was reported missing to the police by his family on Monday evening when his bus failed to drop him off at home after preschool. After a frantic search, the child's grandmother found him inside the bus, which had been parked for the evening in the parking lot of United Progress, which administers the Head Start program that he attends.

The grandmother told a newspaper she could see the outline of a person inside one of the four buses parked at a lot, and sitting there on the steps of the bus was the boy. The grandmother used her cane to pry the doors of the bus open. Her grandson was cold and had wet his pants. "He didn't talk to me," she said. "He didn't talk until he got home, but he hugged me tight." The bus driver and the escort in the bus were dismissed.

Suit in player's death

The family of a high school sophomore who died after a football practice has sued the school district, charging violations of the league regulations on hot weather workouts and medical emergencies. The student, 16, died from heart and kidney failure brought on by dehydration and heat exhaustion on the first practice at the high school, according to the federal lawsuit. The family is seeking unspecified monetary damages. The superintendent said that he had not yet seen the lawsuit, but the district had found no wrongdoing.

Cheerleader has plenty of courage

University cheerleader John Doe, paralyzed from the neck down while performing a routine last week, said yesterday that he had no regrets. Doe, captain of the cheerleading squad for two years, damaged his spine when he landed on his neck after a flip from a minitrampoline during a school scrimmage. Use of the minitrampoline in three-tier pyramids has been banned at UK in the wake of Doe's injury and the death of a state cheerleader, who died when she fell from atop a pyramid.

Doe said that he actually did one and a half flips instead of the single flip he had planned. He tended to overrotate as he did a front flip off the minitrampoline, so that he landed on the back of his neck because he did not come down squarely on his feet.

Areas of Concern

1. **Classroom activities:** Normally a teacher is not responsible for the injuries occurring to pupils off the school grounds or after school hours. Under certain circumstances, however, the teacher may be held liable, because ***teachers apparently have the responsibility of warning students about the dangerous practices that arise from of classroom activities.***

2. **Playground:** Playground or outdoor athletic activities are probably inherently more physically dangerous than most classroom activities. Teachers who are charged with the responsibility for such outdoor activities ***should therefore make certain that pupils are warned against unreasonable hazards and should supervise these activities very carefully.***

3. **Errands and Field Trips:** When you become a teacher, you probably should avoid having students run errands off the school grounds except in cases of real emergencies. Two areas of possible liability exist: (1) injury to the students themselves, in which case a court might be called on to determine whether a reasonably prudent teacher would send a child on such an errand, and (2) injury or damage done by the student to a third party or to that person's property, in which case a court might hold that the student was acting as the agent of the teacher and that the teacher was liable.

4. **Paraprofessionals/Substitutes:** Teachers are held to higher standards of care for the supervision of young people in their charge than the person on the street would be. A similar standard of care is expected for those who assist or substitute for teachers; however, liability is shared because teachers and administrators also are responsible for informing and training paraprofessionals and others who work in the school setting. This includes cafeteria workers, custodians, secretaries and other school employees. Volunteers also fall into this category. To limit tort liability school officials must do the following:

    - Develop relevant policies and procedures to manage volunteers.
    - Maintain adequate and appropriate liability insurance.
    - Develop descriptions of responsibilities for volunteers.
    - Sufficiently screen volunteers.
    - Provide orientation and training for volunteers.
    - Adequately supervise volunteers.

(*Legal Basis*, ***A Handbook for Educators,*** Phi Delta Kappan Educational Foundation, 1998)

Notes:

Exercise:

List the precautions and steps to provide a safe field trip environment.

1. ____
____
2. ____
____
3. ____
____
4. ____
____
5. ____
____

You should keep in mind that a signed parental permission slip does not relieve the teacher of liability, because any individual (even a parent) may not sign away the right of another to sue. However, parental permission slips at least inform parents about the proposed field trip, and they might be used as evidence of reasonable prudence on the part of the teacher. Strangely, perhaps, most of the lawsuits arising from the injury to students on school field trips have been brought against the industrial plants in which the injuries occurred. Whether the student was legally a licensee for any invitee has been significant in these cases. A licensee can be defined as one who visits the premises of another for his or her own benefit; an invitee visits the premises of another for the benefit of the owner or for the benefit of both the invitee and the owner. Although a plant owner owes a normal degree of care to protect a licensee from harm, the owner owes a much bigger degree of care to an invitee.

Negligence Illustrations: Guilty

The boxing match

In a physical education class the instructor told two students to box three rounds. No prior instruction took place before the match, and one student received a cerebral hemorrhage. The court ruled that the teacher was negligent for failing to warn the students of the dangers in boxing and for not providing instruction on the activity.

Lack of gym shoes

A young boy slipped in the gymnasium as the result of not wearing gym shoes, resulting in the loss of two teeth. The youngster had been instructed to play in stocking feet.

The rolling log

On the beaches of Oregon, youngsters on a class trip were playing on a log on the beach. A large wave swept up on the shore, moving the log. One child fell off toward the seaside. The water then receded, and the log rolled over the child, causing injury. The teacher pleaded that it was impossible to foresee the action of the wave and therefore she could not guard against such an action. The court ruled, however, that it was foreseeable and pointed out that occurrences such as this have happened often on the Oregon coast.

Spilled spaghetti sauce

A high school student slipped on spaghetti sauce in the school lunchroom. The school was held liable because they failed to take reasonable care to protect the student against every hazard, resulting in unreasonable risk or harm.

Negligence Exercise

Girl's death spurs closer look at the playground

A housing authority official will examine the monkey bars from which 8-year-old Sharon fell, hit her head and died the next day. Residents have questioned the safety of the play area since Sharon's death.

Sharon was swinging from the monkey bars—about 8 feet off the ground—while her mother was at work. One witness said she lost her balance and hit her head on an adjacent concrete wall. She felt fine until the next day.

Today's playgrounds are safer, cleaner and less prone to lawsuits. Nationally more than 200,000 children are seriously injured each year. The most common injury is broken bones, but for younger children almost 60 percent of the injuries involve the face and the brain. Safety changes include:

- Rubber surfaces or other soft ground materials
- Fencing around swing sets
- Use of boxy, colorful, climbing structures
- Removal of sandboxes
- Removal of tunnels and other visually obstructive equipment
- Replacing wading pools with sprinklers
- Removal of seesaws

Exercise:

1. The playground—Write safety rules for a typical primary school playground:

Merry-go–round: (Explain why it has been removed from the playground.)

____

____

Slides:

____

____

Swings:

____

____

Jungle gym:

____

____

Horizontal ladder:

____

____

Pedal toys/Developmental playground:

____

____

2. ***Write ground rules for the playground (e.g., check all equipment).***

____

____

3. ***The chemistry/industrial arts lab: List safety rules.***

____

____

4. ***Field trips: Explain precautions to take on a field trip to Sandy Hook.***

____

____

5. ***Reflect on your school experiences and write about a student injured in a school-related activity.***

Incident: ________________ Grade level: _________ Place: ________________

____

____

6. ***List dangerous games/activities played in physical education. Why?***

____

____

7. ***What are possible dangers in an art room?***

____

____

Defamation of Character

Another tort for which teachers occasionally are sued is defamation of character, which may be defined as damage to a person's reputation through communication involving ridicule, disgrace, contempt or hatred. Written defamation is known as libel, and spoken defamation is known as slander.

Teachers are involved in possible liability for ***defamation of character*** in such activities as writing letters of recommendation to or talking to prospective employers or college representatives about students, entering comments on student records, making comments to parents or to other teachers about students, or making public or newspaper statements concerning students.

1. **Truth as a defense:** In many states truth is a defense against defamation of character lawsuits. Should the person against whom a lawsuit is brought be able to prove the truth of the statement, no liability exists in these states. In other states (and the number appears to be growing), truth is not a full defense unless it can be shown that spoken or written publication of the defamation material was made without malice or with good intentions in justifiable ends.

2. **Privilege as a defense:** In many instances the law excuses the publication of defamatory material under the doctrines of absolute privilege.

Absolute privilege is based on the proposition that in some cases persons must be completely free to speak their mind without fear of reprisals in the form of lawsuits for libel or slander. Absolute privilege is extended to comments by judges in court proceedings, statements by legislators during legislative sessions, and comments by certain executive officers of government in the exercise of their duties. Absolute privilege is not usually extended to school personnel as a defense against defamation.

Qualified (or conditional) ***privilege***, on the other hand, is frequently used as a defense by school personnel against whom a suit is brought for defamation. Qualified privilege rests on the assumption by the courts that certain information should be given to certain individuals or agencies in the protection of the interests of the individuals, of the agencies, or of society as a whole. The existence of qualified privilege depends on the reason that exists to communicate the information. If the person to whom defamatory information is communicated has a valid reason to receive such information, the communicator may be protected by qualified privilege.

In the case of statements that are defamatory on their face, the plaintiff has to prove only that they were false and is not required to show injury. The amount of damages can vary depending on whether the statements were made maliciously.

The Supreme Court's decision in the case of ***The New York Times*** *v. Sullivan* was that public figures and public officials can be awarded damages only if they can prove that the statements were made with malice. To prove malice, the defendant must have made the statements either knowing that they were false or with reckless disregard for whether they were true or false

Generalizations Concerning Defamation

Statements made about students (written or spoken) should accurately describe relevant, observable behavior rather than making derogatory remarks about students.

Statements should reflect facts versus opinions and gross generalizations. Statements should be communicated only to interested parties (those who have a **need to know**).

Pitka Case

Fairbanks Publishing Company newspaper headline: "North Pole Teacher Fights Board; Territorial Police Called to Expel Fired Schoolmarm, Dispute at Outlying Community Finds Teacher Defying School Board: She is Arrested for Disorderly Conduct."

Elizabeth Pitka resigned her position, but a few days later she changed her mind and the school board agreed with her withdrawal of resignation. On October 7 she wrote the board and stated she would like to resign 30 days from October 7. She received a letter on October 18 stating that they voted to relieve her of her duties as a teacher effective October 18. She ignored this letter and another advising her not to enter school property. She still returned to the school and the school board had her arrested for disturbing the peace. (Fischer, Schmid & Kelly. ***Teachers and the Law***, New York: Longman, 1981.)

Disposition: The Alaska Supreme Court ruled that the teacher was libeled. To be found libelous, the statements must be unambiguous as to leave only one interpretation. The court found that "fights," "fired" and "police called to expel" damaged her professional competency.

Exercise:

Explain this ruling:

Gay alumnus sues high school

A gay former student is suing a county high school for allegedly failing to respond to his complaints of antigay harassment by other students. He charged that students shoved him, spit on him, and frequently taunted him calling him "faggot" and other disparaging remarks. The student charged that official's violated his civil rights by failing to invoke the school's anti-discrimination policy. The school officials deny the charge.

Board hears about hazing

Hazing practices have increased tremendously in one school district. Some incidents reported are: one student being held upside down by his ankles to shake change out of his pockets; a freshman girl ordered to prepare a lap dance for a senior boy in the school and to whisper sexual suggestions in his ear; and a soccer player, pummeled and bruised as part of the pre-practice hazing ritual. Students are getting punched and others are forced to bring in extra money. The administration is upset with these actions and the lack of supervision and security at the high school level. Kids don't report because they're afraid of the repercussions.

Wrestlers to get money to settle libel lawsuit

The former publisher of the ***Home News*** of E. Brunswick has agreed to pay high school wrestlers $110,000 to settle a libel lawsuit filed after an obscene phrase appeared in a story about their match.

The phrase, which appeared in a March 14, 1992, story, explicitly stated that John Doe was performing oral sex while in a wrestling hold with his opponent.

The phrase was inserted into the story by a veteran sports desk editor who took dictation from a reporter by phone, said the ***Home News*** attorney. That editor resigned the day the story appeared in the paper.

The paper which was then called ***The Central New Jersey's Home News*** was later bought out by its current owner, ***Asbury Park Press, Inc.*** The paper's editor published an apology the following day, calling the language, "inappropriate, unprofessional and inexcusable."

John Doe went on to win the New Jersey State Interscholastic Athletic Association's Wrestling Tournament in Atlantic City the weekend after the article appeared, but his lawyer told the ***Home News*** that the victory was soured by the incident.

"The proudest day of his life turned out to be a source of incredible embarrassment for him," said the attorney. ***Asbury Park Press***, October 10, 1994.

Defamation Illustrations

John Doe, who was a high school teacher for Smith County, published a long, sarcastic letter in the local newspaper about the way his superintendent and the school board raised and spent school funds. Doe's letter detailed his objection to the "excessive" athletic expenditures by school officials who were then allegedly unable to pay teachers' salaries. He also wrote that "taxpayers were really taken to the cleaners" by those who built one of the local schools, and he criticized the "***totalitarianism teachers live in***" at the high school.

Angered by the publication of the letter, the board of education charged that it contained false and misleading statements, "damaged the professional reputations" of school administrators and the board, and was "detrimental to the efficient operation and administration of the schools." Doe argued that his letter should be protected by his right of free speech, but an Illinois court ruled against him. Because Doe held a position as a teacher, the state court wrote that he "is no more entitled to harm the schools by speech than by incompetence."

Intentional Infliction of Emotional Distress

Definition: ***Conduct that "exceeds all bounds tolerated by a decent society— that is calculated to cause and does cause serious emotional distress."***

Usually emotional distress is related to some physical injury (not just mental); however, many states have ruled that physical injury is not necessary for intentional infliction of emotional distress, but for negligent infliction of emotional distress, physical injury is needed.

In disciplining teachers, teachers have the obligation not to unduly embarrass students. Such activities as wearing dunce caps, having them don unusual clothes, or painting their faces might be construed as ***causing emotional distress***. A teacher can isolate students, remove them from the body of students (not out of view), criticize them in front of their peers, but only in an appropriate manner.

In *Phyllis P. v. Superior Court* (228 California Reporter), an 8-year-old girl was raped repeatedly by a 13-year-old boy over a four-month period, both en route and on school grounds, during which time the girl's principal, teacher and school psychologist all knew of the assault but did not notify the girl's mother.

The courts held for the mother (***severe emotional distress***) in that the school failed to guard against the reasonably foreseeable potential emotional distress of the mother by not informing her. The school was also found negligent in failing to handle the student's case in a ***reasonable*** and ***prudent manner***.

Exercise:

Using the definition of emotional distress, list three teacher actions that may lead to emotional distress.

1. ____

____

2. ____

____

3. ____

____

Sexual harassment in class is ruled school's liability

WASHINGTON, May 24— School districts can be liable for damages under federal law for failing to stop a student from subjecting another to severe and pervasive sexual harassment, the Supreme Court ruled today.

The 5-to-4 decision, with a majority opinion by justice Sandra Day O'Connor, found the court bitterly divided over the appropriate role for federal law in the classroom. The ruling opened school districts to liability for sexual harassment by students on essentially the same grounds that a Supreme Court decision a year ago set for liability when teachers harass students.

What Justice O'Connor, the author of both decisions, described today as a statutory weapon against behavior so severe that it impairs a victim's ability to learn was labeled by Justice Anthony M. Kennedy's angry dissent as an unwarranted federal intrusion into "day-to-day classroom logistics and interactions," a judicial overreaction to "the routine problems of adolescence."

In her opinion, Justice O'Connell emphasized that "damages are not available for simple acts of teasing and name calling among schoolchildren" but rather for behavior "so severe, pervasive and objectively offensive that it denies its victims the equal access to education" guaranteed under Title IX of the Education Amendments 1972. School officials must have known of the harassment and, acting with "deliberate indifference" failed to take reasonable steps to solve it, she said.

The case was brought by the mother of a girl who, as a fifth grader in Forsyth, GA, complained that she had been subjected to months of sexual advances, taunting and unwanted touching of her breasts and genital area by a boy who was eventually charged and convicted in juvenile court of sexual battery against her. For example, the girl said the boy had put a doorstop in his pants and acted in a sexually suggestive manner toward her in a gym class.

Teachers and school administrators refused to respond to complaints brought by the mother, AD, and by her daughter, L, who sat next to the boy in class and kept asking to have her seat changed. Unable to concentrate in school, her grades dropped and she wrote a suicide note.

Two allegedly humiliated by teacher

A former substitute teacher has been charged with endangering two students after he allegedly wrapped one boy in masking tape and butcher paper in his classroom, and egged on other students to tape up another youth.

In one instance, authorities said, students taped the second boy to a chair, and in another, were told to give him a "swirly"—a dunking in a flushing toilet. The dunking wasn't carried out.

The teacher was a permanent substitute in the high school until he was fired when the allegations were brought to the school officials' attention. The victims were two freshmen boys, one, 14, and the other 15.

The accused is charged with two counts of endangerment and one of criminal restraint for the alleged taping and wrapping of the 15-year-old. Several students involved were punished with in-school suspension.

Exercise:

1. ***Describe or cite how teachers/coaches have verbally abused their "charges."***

____

____

____

2. ***How can coaches be monitored to prevent such types of behavior?***

____

____

____

Malpractice

Surgery takes off wrong foot

A man who went into surgery to have his right foot amputated awoke to learn the wrong foot was gone. The patient, in his mid 50s, was told of the blunder while he was in the recovery room. The man's leg was severed midway between the ankle and knee, a hospital spokesman said. He did not know if the surgery team made an attempt to reattach the limb, and said patient confidentiality concerns and his wishes prevented him from naming those involved and providing other details. The hospital was investigating the mistake.

Educational Malpractice

Definition: ***Failure to perform duties as expected. The student is injured academically because of negligent actions on the part of school educators. The courts have ruled that graduation from high school is a property right and a right under freedom!***

Exercise:

1. ***What are some other duties and responsibilities of the school for the education of its students?***

____

____

____

2. ***Who is responsible for student learning?***

____

____

____

There have been three cases involving educational malpractice suits. As you read each, list the key factors in making your decision for or against the school.

Peter W. Doe v. San Francisco Unified School District (60 Cal. App. 3d. 814.31 California Reporter)

In 1973, Peter W. Doe, a high school graduate with fifth-grade reading ability, sued the San Francisco School District for failing to provide him with adequate instruction in basic skills. A district intelligence test showed that Peter had at least an average IQ, and when Peter's mother asked about her son's academic progress, she was assured by teachers and administrators that he was performing at or near grade level. The State of California Constitution guarantees that students will be educated to minimal (eighth grade) level of achievement. Peter received satisfactory grades on his report cards but was unable to do simple mathematics. Peter charged that the school district had negligently assigned him to classes with unqualified instructors, placed him in inappropriate reading groups, failed to inform his parents about his educational problems, and advanced him through grades without his acquiring the knowledge required. Peter also claimed that the school owed him a "***duty to care***" and was required to fulfill that duty by following certain professional standards that would have prevented negligence on the part of his teachers in the school.

Exercise:

How did Peter "slip through the school system"?

Hoffman vs. Board of Education of the City of New York (410N.Y.S. 2d. 874.31 July 1978)

Danny Hoffman had a severe speech defect when he started kindergarten in 1956. At age 4 years and 10 months, Danny was given the Merit Palmer Test indicating above-average ability, but the results were never presented to his mother or made available to the school until he was 19 years old.

When the school psychologists gave him an intelligence test at age 6 that was primarily verbal, Danny scored 74, one point below normal, and he was placed in a class for Children with Retarded Mental Development (**CRMD)**. The school psychologist noted in his report that Danny "***obviously understands more than he is able to communicate*** ... and should be reevaluated within a two-year period so that a more accurate estimation of its abilities can be made."

When eight years old, Danny was given a reading readiness test that placed him in the top 10 perent of the nation's children indicating high potential for reading, but Danny remained in classes for the retarded for 11 years and was not retested until 1969, when he scored 94 percent, placing him in the normal range of intelligence. Danny had gone through a special vocational program and was given the IQ tests as required by Social Security to verify disability.

Danny sued the school board for negligence in failing to reevaluate him after two years and for keeping him in the **CRMD** classes, causing him diminished intellectual growth and psychological injury. Danny sued for damages and redress (to force the school board to correct the problem).

Exercise:

1. ***Should Danny win/lose his lawsuit against the Board of Education? Why?***

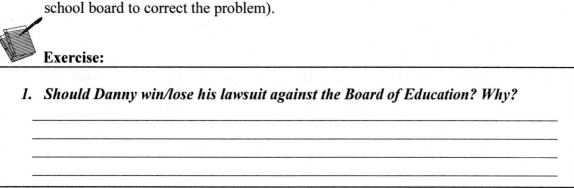

2. ***What are damages?***

3. ***What is redress?***

In the prior two cases the courts ruled in favor of the defendants.

The basis for dismissal was based on the argument that although there is "one standard of care," the educators will not be held responsible, that is, the science of pedagogy (the profession or function of a teacher) is fraught with inconsistencies and theories, and achievement in school is influenced by a lot of factors. In essence, the court shouldn't second-guess the professionals.

However, in the Hoffman case, Danny was awarded $750,000, but it was reduced to $500,000.00 and then dismissed on appeal. It had become apparent to the courts and the school system that the likelihood of a successful malpractice case was very close unless significant changes were made in the school system.

The results of these and similar cases was the enactment of minimal standards for graduation. Students must demonstrate competencies for progression through the grades and graduation.

Exercise:

1. ***Why are there minimum standards required for the graduation in New Jersey, i.e., HSPA (High School Proficiency Assessment)?***

2. ***What purpose might the ESPA (Elementary School Proficiency Assessment) and GEPA (Grade Eight Proficiency Assessment) serve?***

Chapter Exercises:

School hit with lawsuit over dodgeball safety

The high-energy schoolyard game of dodge bowl is getting tossed around a New York courtroom, where questions are being raised about whether it's just too dangerous for young children to play. A New York state Appellate Division panel refused to dismiss a lawsuit that claims a school wronged a 7-year-old girl who broke her elbow while playing dodgeball. State and national officials say what makes the case unique is that the lawsuit doesn't fault the school for supervision—but for allowing children that young to play at all. The new challenge comes as the game is flourishing as a trendy adult activity; the obsession was the comic focus of the movie starring Ben Stiller. But the game also is being targeted as unfair, exclusionary and war-like for school-age youngsters. Some schools in Maine, Maryland, New York, Virginia, Texas, Massachusetts and Utah have banned dodge-ball or its variations including war-ball, monster ball and kill ball.

"Dodgeball is not an appropriate activity for K-12 school physical education programs," according to the National Association for Sport and Physical Education, a nonprofit professional organization of 20,000 physical education teachers professors, coaches, athletic directors and trainers. The version included several balls and no safety or protection zone to run from the thrown balls.

The student became entangled with another child and fell, breaking her elbow. Her lawyer said the injury required surgery and there is a continuing concern her injured arm might not grow as long as her other arm because the growth plate may have been affected.

The judges wrote: "While there are no established standards of age for dodgeball, it is recognized as a potentially dangerous activity and has been banned by several school districts in New York and elsewhere."

Exercise:

1. ***List rules for dodge ball.***

2. ***List reasons why dodge-ball is a "potentially dangerous activity."***

Lesbian sues school district over harassment

All she ever wanted was an education. Instead, the teen-ager said she got a daily lesson in humiliation from her classmates who called her names, threw bottles at her, urinating in her backpack and pushed her down a flight of stairs. The student, 18, is a lesbian. She was when she started high school in 2001 and when she left after nearly three years of what her mother called "a living nightmare." Lambda Legal, a national gay rights organization, filed suit charging that school officials knew about the abuse and systematically ignored it.

The lawsuit is the first in New Jersey, asking for injury to determine monetary damages for antigay harassment in schools, which is illegal under the state's civil rights laws.

"It is an atrocity that school officials would ignore laws in NJ, which are touted as being the most comprehensive non-discrimination laws on the books," a Lambda staff attorney said.

The superintendent said the school code of conduct explicitly bans harassment based on various factors, including sexual orientation, and requires principles to report all harassment.

Last year, the New Jersey Division of Civil Rights ordered the regional school district to pay $50,000.00 to a boy who was slapped, punched and taunted by classmates who thought he was gay. The district was also fined $10,000.00 and ordered to upgrade its policies.

The suit said the abuse began in 2001 when she was in ninth grade. She was not the only gay or lesbian student at the high school, but was the only one "***outted***" by one of her classmates. The classmates were identified as a small cluster of males and females who called her names and threw bottles and food at her in the cafeteria. She and her mother complained several times, but "school officials took no effective measures in response."

In the spring of ninth grade, her backpack was stolen. It was found in one of the boys bathrooms, covered with urine. Soon after that, her locker was broken into and belongings scattered around the school hallway, spat on and damaged. She complained and was again told nothing could be done. "Instead school administrators charged her for the books that had been destroyed," the complaint stated.

When she was in tenth grade, the abuse became physical, culminating when students, who were not identified, pushed her down a flight of stairs. Her mother continued to beg for help from school authorities, but without success. By her junior year she was so upset that counselor at the local YMCA intervened with school administrators. The school placed her on home instruction for the rest of the year.

The suit seeks compensatory damages for physical and emotional pain and suffering. It also seeks an order forcing the school to implement better antidiscrimination policies.

Exercise:

1. ***What actions as a parent would you have taken to prevent the harassment?***

2. ***What is your "school code of conduct?"***

Coaches pledge caution after ruling

High school coaches said this week's 1.5-million jury award stemming from a coach's verbal abuse will force them to watch what they say and do more closely than ever.

"Just listening to this makes you kind of say to yourself. What did I say that was not too smart or could be construed differently?" said a basketball and softball coach.

"I think this might make us reflect on how we say things to people. You never know how your tone of voice might be construed."

J and her father claimed in their civil lawsuit that a coach verbally abused her during the 1995–1996 season, while she was a member of the high school basketball team. The lawsuit also claimed that she developed an eating disorder after the coach told her she needed to lose 10 lb. The county jury ruled in the student's favor, ending a four-month trial.

"Sometimes we, as coaches, don't understand the impact of our words on these kids," said a football and girls basketball coach.

"Think back to when you were 15 and how much emphasis you put on your coaches' words. Sometimes there's something that you think is just a throwaway comment, but they latch onto it like glue," the coach said.

Besides the award given to his daughter, the father was awarded $100,000 because the jury found that he was unfairly barred from speaking at a school board meeting.

Exercise:

1. ***Describe or cite how teachers/coaches have verbally abused their "charges."***

2. ***How can coaches be monitored to prevent such types of behavior?***

Chapter Notes & Additional Information:

Personal Thoughts & Drawings

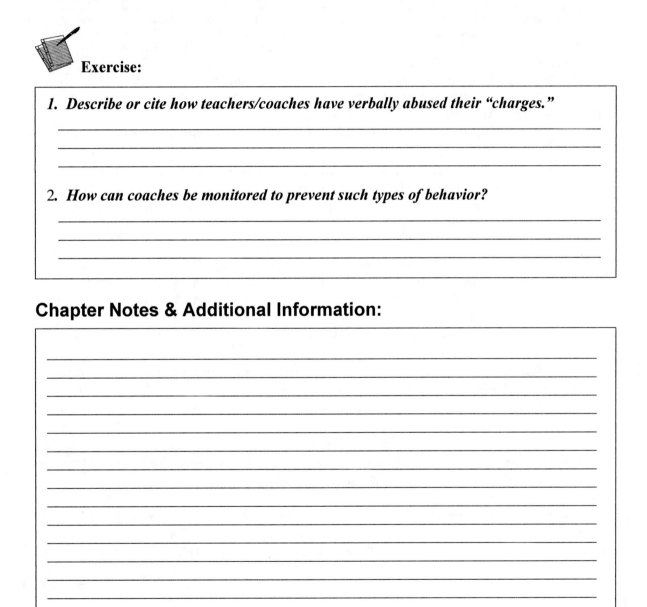

Chapter 8:

Corporal Punishment

Chapter Topics:

Corporal Punishment

Definition: New Jersey Statute 18A:6-1—Corporal Punishment of Students

No person employed or engaged in a school or educational institution, whether public or private, shall inflict or cause to be inflicted corporal punishment on a student attending such school or institutions; but any such person may, within the scope of his employment, use and apply such amounts of force as is reasonable and necessary:

1. to quell a disturbance, threatening physical injury to others:
2. to obtain possession of weapons or other dangerous objects on the person within the control of a student;
3. for the purposes of self-defense; and
4. for the protection of persons and property:

and such acts or any of them will not be construed to constitute corporal punishment within the meaning and intent of this section. Every resolution, by-law, rule, ordinance, or other act or authority permitting or authorizing corporal punishment to be inflicted on a student attending a school or educational institution will be void.

Corporal punishment of students has been prohibited in New Jersey since 1867, and in 1938, the Commissioner or Education defined corporal punishment as ***"any punishment causing, or intending to cause bodily pain and suffering."***

Diocese fires nun in threat to student

An assistant principal at a school, described by one parent as an "old-school nun," was fired after allegedly threatening to knock a student's teeth out. A 69-year-old nun, who was the school's disciplinearian, was relieved of her teaching duties nearly a month after allegedly threatening the sixth-grader, said the director of communications for the diocese.

The student's father filed a complaint with the town police the day he said the nun threatened his 11-year-old son. The nun told the police, "You won't have any teeth in your mouth," because of his attitude, according to the police report. The father said yesterday that the nun made the alleged threat when his son went down the wrong flight of stairs. The father said his son is an alter boy, a star player on the basketball team, and is not a troublemaker or a wise guy.

Exercise:

Did the nun commit corporal punishment? Why or why not?

Supreme Court Ruling

In 1977 the U.S. Supreme Court ruled on and finally resolved many of the issues related to corporal punishment (*Ingraham v. Wright,* 1977). The opinion established that states may ***constitutionally*** authorize corporal punishment without prior hearing or notice and without consent by the students' parents and may, as a matter of policy, elect to prohibit or limit the use of corporal punishment. It also held that corporal punishment is not in violation of the Eighth Amendment (cruel and unusual punishment).

The United States Supreme Court stated that due to the openness of the schools and community awareness, the safeguards of the Eighth Amendment do not apply to school children.

Exercise:

Explain why corporal punishment does not apply to schoolchildren.

Factors in Corporal Punishment Cases

The ***reasonableness*** of the corporal punishment administered is usually a major factor in determining the liability of the teacher. The courts normally will assume that corporal punishment that results in permanent injury is with malice, which usually means with wicked motives or in anger, but is also likely to be considered ***unreasonable***. An Alabama court has listed certain guidelines that the courts tend to follow in determining whether corporal punishment is reasonable;

"In determining the reasonableness of the punishment or the extent of malice, proper matters of consideration are the instrument used and the nature of the offense committed by the child and other attendant circumstances," (***Suits v. Glover***, 71 So.2d 49 1954).

The legality of corporal punishment of school students, perhaps more than any other aspect of student punishment, depends on the circumstances. What might be considered reasonable corporal punishment for a child of a certain age or sex might be considered unreasonable for another child of a different age or sex.

In addition, the size of the student and the suitability of the instrument and force applied, as well as the degree of punishment in relation to the infraction, are also taken into consideration in corporal punishment cases.

Exercise:

What might be considered "reasonable" circumstances?

____

____

____

____

Corporal Punishment by States

States that Forbid Corporal Punishment

New Jersey	1867	Virginia	1989
Massachusetts	1971	North Dakota	1989
Hawaii	1973	Oregon	1989
Rhode Island	1975	Minnesota	1989
Maine	1975	Indiana	1989
New Hampshire	1975	Connecticut	1989
Vermont	1984	Alaska	1989
New York	1985	South Dakota	1990
California	1987	Utah	1992
Nebraska	1988		
Wisconsin	1988	(Under federal jurisdiction: the District of Columbia, Puerto Rico, and overseas military bases)	
Michigan	1988		

Three million children will be paddled or spanked in school in the name of learning each year according to the USDE. It estimates that 30,000 schoolchildren are physically injured each year because of corporal punishment.

Exercise:

List, without using names, schools or incidents in school (public or private) where you suspect corporal punishment had been administered.

1. ______________________________
2. ______________________________
3. ______________________________
4. ______________________________
5. ______________________________

Editorial: Breaking the Hickory Stick

Congress is considering a Teacher Liability Protection Act, sponsored by President Bush, that is likely to increase the number of paddlings in the states and school districts where corporal punishment is still legal. The practice of corporal punishment in schools is most prevalent where a fundamentalist belief in the Bible is the strongest.

- All the major educational associations, including the American Federation of Teachers and the National Education Association, have argued that this act is unnecessary because teachers are already protected by insurance through their school districts and professional groups.

- In states where such acts have been passed, like Texas, more than 80,000 students are paddled annually. This is a highly increased rate of corporal punishment over states that have not passed the Teacher Liabilities Protection Act.

- A survey of ***Parents Magazine*** reveals that 55 percent of parents disapprove of paddling, 38 percent approve and 7 percent are not sure.

- Parents in southern states have a 53 percent approval rate.

- A national poll of teachers reveals 48 percent oppose corporal punishment, 41 percent approve it, and 11 percent are unsure.

- In a statewide study in Louisiana of teacher perceptions of the use of corporal punishment, 75 percent perceived it to be legal, legitimate and effective as a process of student management. In addition, 63 percent of administrators state that they would not support legislation to abolish corporal punishment in Louisiana.

Exercise:

1. ***Should teachers be sued for assault and battery for child abuse where corporal punishment is reasonable punishment?***

2. ***If corporal punishment was legal in New Jersey, what is reasonable punishment?***

Corporal Punishment Incidents

- A first grader was given three swats with a paddle because she circled instead of underlining a word in the reading lesson. (Ohio)
- First graders have been tied up and their mouths taped. (West Virginia)
- Seventeen honor students were given six blows on the buttocks for skipping class one day. (North Carolina)
- Any 11-year-old boy sneaked into the girl's bathroom and was forced to remove his trousers and don a red dress and parade around the school while the teacher ridiculed him. (Arizona)
- An 11-year-old girl was caught chewing gum in class and the teacher spanked her and allowed the entire class to come up and hit her on the buttocks with a paddle. (Michigan)
- An eight-year-old boy was hit 17 times with a paddle. (Texas)
- A 12-year-old girl had scars on her leg after receiving blows from the principal. The male teacher lifted her upside down while the female principal held her legs. (New Mexico)
- Twenty-two grade-schoolers were paddled for neglecting to bring water colors to art class. "It wasn't corporal punishment but a love tap." (Texas)
- Fourth- and fifth-graders were required to carry bricks in their hands or around their necks if they repeatedly forgot to take supplies from one class to another. (Texas)
- "Parents say kids were "guinea pigs" in a treatment of learning disabilities." The program involves squeezing students skulls, pressing fingers into eye sockets, thumbs

shoved into roofs of mouths. These treatments were given by chiropractors in an attempt to cure dyslexia, epilepsy, etc." (California)

- A 13-year-old boy was locked in a cafeteria closet for three school days for fighting. The boy was kept in a 4ft. x 5ft. closet from 8:25 A.M. to 2:45 P.M., and meals were served to him and he had to urinate in a bottle. (Oklahoma)

- Three sixth-graders who received scores below 80 on a math exam received paddling from their fellow students. The teacher said that those who scored above 80 would be rewarded with a day of free work if they punish the lowest scores by paddling them. (Wyoming)

- To quell seventh-grade students, the teacher (substitute) cast a voodoo spell on the class by shaking and chanting, throwing ritual powder on them and warning that their houses would burn down. (New Jersey)

- In New Jersey, teachers have been found guilty of slapping, shaking, throwing objects at students, placing students in headlocks and grabbing students by the neck, hair, or ears.

Self-Defense or Corporal Punishment?

Exercise:

A female social studies teacher was walking in the hall when a student came up behind and "goosed" her. In a fluid motion, she turned and swung a book she was holding and hit the student on the side of the head, knocking him to the floor.

Reflex actions are considered appropriate self-defense, whereas thought-out responses are not considered so in cases where there is no real danger of repeated assault.

Was it a reflex action or corporal punishment? Why?

____

____

Self-defense should be no greater than is necessary to repel the attack. A teacher was involved in a bathroom altercation with a club-wielding student who was intent on using the club. The teacher ran from the scene into the parking lot where he got a gun from his car and used it to fend off the student. When the student with the club came toward the teacher, the teacher brandished a gun to ward off the students attack.

Was it a reflex action or corporal punishment? Why?

____

____

As a teacher was talking to another teacher, a 14-year-old boy struck a light blow to the teacher's back. He was told to go to his classroom; he turned and fired a rubber band from 2 ft. away into the teachers face and then ran from the teacher into the assigned classroom. About ten minutes later, the teacher went into the classroom, pulled him into another room and punched him several times.

Was it a reflex action or corporal punishment? Why?

Corporal Punishment Decisions

- In North Carolina, an appeals court ruled that it is legal as long as reasonable force is used and ***no lasting injury*** is caused (six whacks with a paddle).

- In Texas, the court upheld punishment and stated that it violates due process only if it is arbitrary or capricious or an inhumane and shocking abuse of power (three swats).

Exercise:

1. Define arbitrary.

2. Define capricious.

- In Virginia, U.S. District Court ruled in favor of a teacher who punished a girl by piercing her upper arm with a pin. The court stated that the conduct was ***not*** malicious or sadistic as to give rise to the deprivation of the constitutionally protected right to be free from physical intrusion of the person.

Exercise:

What is your opinion? Why?

- In Louisiana, a student was thrown against a locker. The court ruled in favor of the school, saying they did not believe the injury was severe.

Exercise:

What do you believe would be considered a severe injury?

Teachers have been dismissed for the following reasons in various states:

- Spanking students while in an intoxicated state.
- Slamming students' heads against walls and tearing shirts to enforce instructions as an attention-getting device.
- Using a cattle prod on students, unless their name was placed on the blackboard under "cowards list."
- Pushing a child against a blackboard and a bookcase with such force that the boy struck his head (excessive force).
- In a basketball game, a student pushed a teacher from behind, and the teacher reacted by striking the student with a fist, causing him to lose a tooth (unfit to teach).
- A principal warned a 13-year-old boy to stop fighting by whacking him on the buttocks.
- A football coach struck a seventh-grade player in the helmet, knocking him to the ground and then grabbed his facemask after the student had difficulty mastering a blocking assignment. The student spent several days in the hospital recovery room. The coach pleaded his actions were instructional and were used to encourage the child to perform better.

Exercise:

A classroom teacher punished students who failed a spelling test by:

a. Doing ten minutes of exercise.
b. Sitting at their desks with a log over their heads to reflect on mistakes.
c. Writing each misspelled word correctly 100 times.
d. Wearing a letter F for failure throughout the day.

What is your choice? _______ ***Why?***

Corporal Punishment Articles

Charge: Teacher Put Student in Box

A teacher charged with taping an unruly student's mouth and sealing him in a box has a history of similar behaviors, police said. She once taped another child's mouth and threatened to feed him to a snake.

Holly, 26, who works with the emotionally disabled students, was reassigned from her teaching job and charged with aggravated child abuse. She was freed on $2,500 bond.

Her only comment was that she did nothing wrong, police said.

She allegedly put the six-year-old boy in a cardboard box on September 16 at an elementary school, but the incident was not disclosed to police until several days later. Police then found out about the case involving a second child.

"We received a complaint late last night from another parent that her son had his mouth taped and was told he would be fed to a snake if he was not quiet."

New Teacher Charged in Student's Mass Beating

A teacher was placed on administration leave yesterday after being charged with assault for allegedly ordering first-grade students to beat a child while she held him.

Allison, 25, was arrested and released on her own recognizance. The alleged beating victim was treated at a hospital for minor head injuries.

"She is a new teacher," said the school system spokesperson.

Student Lodges Criminal Complaint

A vocational and technical high school student signed a criminal complaint yesterday against his soccer coach for allegedly assaulting him during a dispute over a team jersey.

Darwin, 18, told police that the high school's assistant boys' soccer coach David, 37 grabbed him by the throat and then pushed him to the floor in a school locker room around 5:30 P.M. in front of the team and other coaches.

The judge also will consider a complaint filed by William last week against the assistant coach, claiming that he was assaulted by him. William was not injured and told police that the assistant coach "bumped him in the chest."

Exercise:

Are coaches held to different standards than teachers concerning corporal punishment?

Shop Teacher Accused of Using Electric Shock

A high school teacher was suspended after being accused of using electric shocks to discipline a student. The shop teacher forced a sophomore to hold a spark plug in one hand and a piece of metal connected to an electric current in the other, according to a federal lawsuit filed by the student's mother. The lawsuit charges the teacher caused three volts of electricity to course through the boy's body. The final shock was an alleged 30-second jolt.

A teacher for more than 15 years, he declined to comment. The teacher had been suspended and faces a hearing on whether he should be fired. The lawyer for the school said school officials were unaware the teacher was using electric shock. The lawsuit claims he had been using the punishment for many years.

Parent Claims Teacher Tapes Students to Wall and Desk

A teacher has resigned after being accused of disciplining two sixth-grade students by taping them to a desk and to a wall with masking tape, police and school officials said. The principal said the teacher told him he used masking tape on the students because they were misbehaving and that he said he used the same technique on other students.

"It is a ridiculous form of discipline, don't you think?" said the principal who recommended that the teacher be fired.

Alex, 11 said his head was taped to a desk.

"I did not like it," Alex said. He said it made him "feel like a prisoner."

Teacher Arrested After "Joke"

A teacher at a public school was arrested yesterday after an investigation of a complaint that he hung a five-year-old boy in the closet by his belt last Thursday, the police said.

The teacher, Jason, 24, who teaches music, was said to be playing a practical joke on another teacher, the police said. The child hung from a coat hook for three or four minutes and was not harmed, the police said. The teacher, who is in his second year of teaching, faces misdemeanor charges of reckless endangerment and endangering the welfare of a child and has been placed on administrative duty.

High School Teacher Held in Severing of a Student's Finger

A science teacher for the last 25 years was arrested today and charged with assault for slamming the door to his classroom on the finger of a 14-year-old Haitian student, an act that led to the severing of the boy's middle finger, the police said.

The teacher is being charged with second-degree reckless assault, a felony with a penalty of six years in prison. The police said the teacher told them that he hoped his arrest would shed some light on problems at the school, where he teaches a science class to 23 Haitian students, most of whom do not speak English.

About 1:45 PM on Thursday, the police said, the teacher was teaching a science class to 23 Haitian students when one began to misbehave. The teacher allegedly forced the student to leave the classroom by pushing him out the classroom door. "The teacher told the student to get out of the room for disciplinary reasons," said a detective. "The student was in the doorway with his schoolbag when the teacher slammed the door on him and severed his finger."

The detective said a school custodian who witnessed the incident rushed to the boy's aid. The student was taken by ambulance to the hospital, where doctors tried unsuccessfully to reattach the finger, the middle one on his left hand. The police said they had interviewed several Haitian students who said they had witnessed the teacher using force on classmates.

"The class is made up of 23 Haitian students, ranging in ages from 13 to 17, most do not speak English," said the detective. "The bizarre thing is, the teacher does not speak Creole," the detective added. "According to him the school will not give him an aide who speaks Creole to assist because of budgetary reasons. When the kids need to be disciplined, he often sends them out of the room. He tells them to get out of the room and go down to the principal's office or cafeteria."

Coaches: A Double Standard?

A high school student told a municipal court judge yesterday his coach grabbed his face mask and "violently jerked it back and forth" during a football game last November. The student, sixteen, said the coach met him near the 10-yd. line after the student had failed to stop an opposing player from scoring a touchdown.

He grabbed my facemask and was leading me off the field," the student said. "He was yelling and cursing at me. He let me go and when I got a little in front of him, he grabbed my shoulder pads and spun me around and grabbed my facemask again. He started violently jerking it from side to side. I had to move my head to keep my neck from being hurt."

The boy's father filed a citizen's complaint in municipal court, charging the coach with simple assault, a disorderly person's offense, shortly after the game. The father, who took the stand before his son, told the judge he was in the stands during the game, about 150 yd. from where the incident took place, and he saw the coach meet his son at the 10- or 15-yard line and began yelling at him.

"He was gesturing with his hands outstretched and looked like he was screaming," the father said. "I could not hear what was said. My son continued to walk. When he got a few steps ahead of the coach, the coach put his hand on my son's shoulder pad and spun him around. The coach grabbed my son's facemask and pushed the mask up and down and sideways."

The father testified he has viewed about 100 games and seen the coach do the same thing to other players "about three or four times."

Exercise:

Cite similar incidents where coaches have used excessive "force" to discipline athletes.

____

____

____

____

Substitute teacher accused of choking boy with string

A police officer arrested a substitute teacher in the alleged assault of a seven-year-old boy. The teacher is accused of slipping a string around the child's neck and drawing it tight because the boy had not done his homework. The teacher was fired by the school district and police charged him with aggravated assault following the incident. A public school's spokeswoman confirmed the incident happened to the second-grader at an after-school program and said the teacher was terminated immediately.

"The district has issued an apology and let the family know that students' safety is their first priority," said the director of communications. The substitute teacher reportedly told the boy that he was going to strangle him if he did not do his homework. When the boy did not, he had the boy stand on a chair, he then took the string, attached to the ceiling light and tightened it around the boy's neck and released it.

The spokesman said the boy left the classroom and was seen by a school secretary putting water on his bruised neck. The boy's aunt said her nephew is still in pain and frightened by what happened to him. I do not want another teacher to do something similar to another student," said the aunt. "I want the parents to be alert about what is going on at school with their kids."

The director of communications said substitutes go through rigorous background checks, including obtaining fingerprints before they are allowed into the classroom. She said that the teacher underwent the same evaluation and that there were no incidents involving him on file.

Teacher Accused of Ordering Attack on Student

An investigation is underway into charges that a Newark kindergarten teacher ordered her young charges to punch a classmate who tore up her lesson plan. The tenured teacher has been suspended and the injured child is being kept out of school by his fearful mother.

If the charges prove valid, the teacher faces a range of possible consequences, including being brought up on tenure charges or termination. A spokesman for the school district said, "Our mission is to ensure that children have a safe environment in which to learn and in which teachers can teach. We intend to make sure that our mission takes hold throughout the district. An incident like this will not be tolerated anywhere in the school district."

Hazing Alleged at Camp

A thirteen-year-old boy attended a football summer camp at a Staten Island college last month to improve his knowledge of the game and to impress his coach enough to make the program. But when the boy's mother saw his shaved blond head and sunken eyes, and the fresh cuts and bruises, she suspected her son had been subjected to something more brutal than football.

That is how the boy's lawyers describe things when they announced plans to sue the school, the board of education and the college, claiming that supervisors from both entities failed to stop four days of hazing by upperclassmen who waged a campaign of physical and psychological torment against the boy and other incoming freshmen attending camp.

Bus Driver Refuses to Take Kids Home

A substitute bus driver found a new way to punish rowdy eleven- and twelve-year-olds. He refused to take them home.

The driver cursed at about eight children from a middle school, and then dropped them off Friday at an industrial park one mile from their homes when they refused to behave, school officials said.

One boy called his mother who drove him and a friend home. Parents conceded their kids may have gone overboard, but where outraged.

School officials filed an internal report on the driver, whose name was not released and recommended that he not handle any of their bus routes.

Girl Who Attacked Teacher Gets Prison

A high school girl got two and one half to seven years in prison for bashing her pregnant teacher in the head with a hammer.

Jay, sixteen, attacked her teacher in a classroom last April, hitting her twice with a carpenter's hammer. The girl told police she was angry because the teacher had gone to her parents about her poor grades, causing her to miss the prom.

The teacher who suffered a fractured skull said that she has almost fully recovered and that her baby, now three months old is fine. She has returned to teaching in another school. Jay pleaded guilty to assault and the judge ordered psychiatric counseling.

Chapter Notes & Additional Information:

Personal Thoughts & Drawings

Chapter 9:

Discipline

Chapter Topics:

School Discipline	**Enforcing School Rules**
Various Discipline Techniques	**Does it Work?**
Assertive Discipline	**Discipline That Doesn't Work**
Classroom Rules	**Discipline in Headlines**
"To put it another way..."	**Creative Discipline**

School Discipline

School discipline is one of the most serious problems facing teenagers and the educational system as a whole. Statistics indicate that 3 percent of teachers and students in urban schools are attacked each month. Close to 17,000 students per month experience injuries requiring medical attention.

There are over 2 million suspensions per year and countless instructional hours used to handle behavior problems. The U.S. Department of Education reported recently that 6,300 students were expelled for carrying firearms, 58 percent handguns, 7 percent rifles or shotguns, and 35 percent other weapons, including bombs and grenades.

A well-managed classroom will minimize the negative behavior but will not eliminate all incidents. Actions may be necessary to maintain a conducive learning environment.

Discipline is defined in various ways and may include both prevention and remediation: enforcement of rules to maintain a learning environment, or punishment to correct.

For our purposes, discipline will be defined as ***"an action designed to correct inappropriate behavior."*** It may be construed to be punishment, but remember, you didn't do the inappropriate behavior, and the student took that action. The consequences of the "action" were clearly stated, and the "lack of control" by the student caused the active discipline.

Food fighters miss graduation

Despite last-minute appeals to the New Jersey Commissioner of Education, high school students involved in a food fight last month were barred from participating in Monday's graduation ceremony. An Administrative Law Judge denied the students' appeal Monday before the ceremony.

Racial slur near teacher's home

A black teacher, who tried to stop a food fight at a high school, woke up on the morning of graduation, to find a racial slur spray painted on the street in front of her house and her mailbox blown up.

Authorities are investigating Monday's vandalism as a bias crime and are trying to determine if it was related to the fight at school.

The teacher learned a food fight was planned when she found two girls eating lunch in a bathroom to avoid getting caught in the melee. She went to the cafeteria to stop the fighting and found other teachers and administrators there who had also learned what the students planned.

Authorities declined to release the teacher's name because she was the victim of a crime. Eleven students were suspended following the food fight. Eight seniors involved were barred from participating in Monday's graduation ceremony, and a few other students' skipped graduation to show support for their friends.

Zero tolerance for chaos

A cafeteria food fight isn't child's play. Neither is vandalism when a mailbox is blown up and racist graffiti is scrawled on the street. School officials and police are giving the two recent incidents the serious attention they deserve.

Some parents have dismissed the food fight at the high school as nothing more than a youthful exuberance. Sorry, but students pelting each other with ketchup packets, water bottles and soda cans went too far. It was flat out dangerous. Students and teachers slipped and fell. Students in wheelchairs were caught in the crossfire. "It showed total disrespect for the teachers and created an unsafe environment in the school."

School administrators came down hard on the students involved, suspending eleven from afterschool activities. The eight who are seniors were barred from participating in the graduation Monday. The state commissioner of education wisely turned down the appeal by three seniors to be allowed to walk with their classmates.

The administrator's tough stance on the food fight was well warranted. Officials need to deliver a stern message that chaos will not be tolerated in school buildings.

The home vandalism is no less disturbing. A black teacher who tried to stop the food fight found her mailbox destroyed and a racial slur painted on the street in front of her house the morning of graduation. It is being treated as a bias crime.

Exercise:

What form of discipline would prevent like or similar behaviors?

____

____

____

____

Various Discipline Techniques

A wide range of techniques can be used to maintain order in the classroom, including behavior modification, problem solving, confrontation, nonconfrontation and assertive discipline.

Assertive Discipline

Lee Cantor developed an approach to discipline based on teachers' assertiveness. The approach calls on teachers to establish firm, clear guidelines for student behavior and to follow through with consequences for misbehavior. Cantor comments on how he arrived at the ideas behind assertive discipline:

> I found that, above all, the master teachers were assertive; that is, they taught students how to behave. They established clear rules for the classroom, they communicated those rules to the students and they taught students how to follow them.

Assertive discipline requires teachers to do the following:

- Make it clear that they will not tolerate anyone preventing them from teaching, stopping learning or doing anything else that is not in the best interest of the class, the individual, or the teacher.
- Instruct students clearly and in specific terms about what behaviors are desired and what behaviors are not tolerated.
- Plan positive and negative consequences for predetermined, acceptable or unacceptable behavior.
- Plan positive reinforcement for compliance. Reinforcement includes: verbal acknowledgments, notes, free time for talking, and of course, tokens that can be exchanged for appropriate rewards.
- Plan a sequence of steps to punish noncompliance. These range from writing a youngster's name on the board to sending the student to the principal's office.

Classroom Rules

- Maintain the respect and dignity of the learner.
- Correct the student in private instead of in public.
- Respond to the incident calmly and fairly.
- Target the causes, not just a specific incident.
- Involve the class in making the rules.
- Keep the rules short and to the point.
- Phrase rules, where possible, in a positive way. ("Sit quietly while working" instead of "Don't talk to your neighbors.")
- Remind the class of the rules at times other than when someone has misbehaved.
- Make different sets of rules for various activities.
- Let children know when different rules apply (work/play).
- Post rules in a conspicuous place, and review regularly.
- Keep a sheet on your desk and record the number of times you review rules with the class.

Exercise:

Clarify, with examples, the following guidelines:

a. Maintain the respect and dignity of the learner.

____

____

b. Correct the student in private instead of in public.

____

____

c. Respond to the incident calmly and fairly.

____

____

d. Target the causes, not just a specific incident.

____

____

e. Involve the class in making the rules.

____

____

f. Keep the rules short and to the point.

____

____

g. Phrase rules, where possible, in a positive way. ("Sit quietly while working" instead of "Don't talk to your neighbors.")

____

____

h. Remind the class of the rules at times other than when someone has misbehaved.

____

____

i. Make different sets of rules for various activities.

____

____

j. Let children know when different rules apply (work/play).

____

____

k. Post rules in a conspicuous place, and review regularly.

____

____

l. Keep a sheet on your desk and record the number of times you review rules with the class.

____

____

"To put it another way…"

- ***Holding and communicating high expectations for student learning and behavior.*** Through the personal warmth and encouragement they express to students, and the classroom requirements they establish, effective manager/teachers make sure that students know they are expected to learn well and behave appropriately.

- ***Establishing and clearly teaching classroom rules and procedures.*** Effective managers teach behavioral rules and classroom routines in much the same way as they teach instructional content, and they review these frequently at the beginning of the school year and periodically thereafter. Classroom rules are posted in every classroom.

- ***Specifying consequences and their relationship to student behavior.*** Effective managers are careful to explain the connection between students' misbehavior and teacher-imposed sanctions. This connection, too, is taught and reviewed as needed.

- ***Enforcing classroom rules promptly, consistently, and equitably***. Effective managers respond quickly to misbehavior, respond in the same way at different times, and impose consistent sanctions regardless of the gender, race, or other personal characteristics of misbehaving students.

- ***Sharing with students the responsibility for classroom management***. Effective managers work to inculcate in students a sense of belonging in self-discipline, rather than viewing discipline as something imposed from the outside.

- ***Maintaining a brisk pace for instruction and making smooth transitions between activities.*** Effective managers keep things moving in the classrooms, which increases learning as well as reducing the likelihood of misbehavior.

- ***Monitoring classroom activities and providing feedback and reinforcement.*** Effective managers observe and comment on student behavior, and they reinforce appropriate behavior through the provision of verbal, symbolic and tangible rewards.

The use of cooperative learning structures can increase student test engagement, acquaint students with the benefits of working together, and ease the tensions that sometimes arise among racial/ethnic groups. All are related to reductions in the incidence of misbehavior.

The work of other researchers has also revealed that it is beneficial for teachers to use humor to hold students interest, to reduce classroom tensions and to remove distracting materials such as athletic equipment or art materials that encourage inattention or destruction. Research on well-disciplined schools indicate that a student-centered environment incorporating teacher/student, problem-solving activities, as well as activities to promote students' self-esteem and a sense of belonging, is more effective in reducing behavior problems than punishment. Findings indicate that, rather than relying on power and enforcing punitive models of behavior control, decision-making power is shared, and so a school climate in which everyone wants to achieve some discipline is maintained.

Enforcing School Rules

Yes, even in school environments with excellent preventive discipline, problems still rise and must be addressed. Of the many practices in use, which ones have researchers identified as effective in remedying of school discipline problems? Not surprisingly, the answer depends on the severity of the problems. For the discipline issues faced by most schools, research supports the use of the following practices, many of which are applicable at either the schoolwide or classroom levels.

Researchers have found punishment to be an effective method of remedying individual misbehavior and, therefore, improving school order if the punishment is:

- Commensurate with the offense committed.

- Perceived by the student as punishment. Punishment can sometimes be too light, or even unintentionally reinforcing to students. Effective, frequently used punishments include depriving students of privileges, mobility, or the company of friends.

- Delivered with support. Students often need encouragement to improve their behavior and assistance in learning how to do so.

Does it Work?

Expectations are that once you've administered the discipline, it will solve the problem. It may, if the behavior is not a long-term problem (a student who has been constantly disruptive). For more serious (unusual behavior) problems, an assertive approach will eliminate the behavior.

Discipline That Doesn't Work

It is important for educators to be aware of the strategies research has shown to be ineffective. This knowledge can assist teachers in planning local programs. Unfortunately, some of these practices continue to be used unwisely. Ineffective practices include:

- ***Vague or unenforceable rules.*** The importance of clear rules becomes obvious when observing, as researchers have, the ineffectiveness of "rules" such as, "Be in the right place at the right time."

- ***Teachers ignoring misconduct.*** Both student behavior and attitudes are adversely affective when teachers ignore violations of school or classroom rules

- ***Ambiguous or inconsistent teacher response to misbehavior.*** When teachers are inconsistent in their enforcement of rules or when they react in inappropriate ways (such as lowering students' grades in response to misbehavior), classroom discipline is generally poor.

- ***Punishment that excessive or delivered without support or encouragement for improving behavior.*** Among the kinds of punishment that produce particularly negative student attitudes is public punishment.

- ***Corporal punishment.*** Most of the literature on corporal punishment is unrelated to research on effectiveness.

Discipline in Headlines

Girl may be expelled for nail clipper knife

Pensacola, Fla.: Administrators yesterday recommended the expulsion of a fifteen year old girl for taking to school a nail clipper with a 2-inch knife.

Ms. D, a sophomore, said she thought the attention was simply for cleaning fingernails. A panel of other principals sided with the Pensacola High School principal, who wants Ms. D expelled for a year under a zero-tolerance policy on weapons.

First grader uses a gun to threaten teacher

Bushnell, Fla.: A first grader has been expelled from school until next fall for firing a handgun on school grounds, and then threatening to shoot a teacher who scolded her.

No injuries resulted from the shooting by the unidentified 6-year old boy. During a field trip, a teacher had scolded the boy for misbehaving and he threatened to shoot her. It was then that the teacher found a gun in the boy's jacket and learned that he had earlier fired it on into the ground outside the school.

The school board ordered that the boy be tutored for the rest of the school year and undergo a psychological evaluation before returning next fall.

His parents said school officials have rejected their earlier request that the child receive a psychological evaluation, saying his misbehavior was not serious enough.

Pleas from a hell of a classroom

SOMEBODY HELP!

A desperate Bronx teacher fired off an anonymous letter to the city council describing hellish conditions of a violent middle school.

"Words cannot describe the nonsense and the abuse that has to be put up with just to stand in these classes," the exasperated teacher wrote. "Forget about teaching."

The short but startling letter read aloud during today's city hearing on student safety reveals how unruly kids make it impossible for other children to learn.

Judge won't reinstate boy suspended for "foul mouth"

Newark: A 13-year old boy booted from a Regional High School in Newton turned his suspension into a federal case. But, a judge yesterday refused to reinstate him.

Attorney E.G. charged that R. W.'s constitutional rights to due process of the law were violated when he was suspended for insubordination and foul language.

U.S. District Judge D., however, called the teenager, "a foul mouthed, undisciplined, young man" and ruled that it would be inappropriate to send the eighth grader back to school.

A school attorney welcomed the judge's decision, calling the complaint "totally frivolous."

The incident began when a teacher complained that R.W. had called her a "bitch", and refused to take his hat off unless ordered by the principal.

After lunch, R. W. said he and a friend were going to recess when another teacher ordered him into the auditorium, where recess was being held due to poor weather.

The teacher, Mrs. J., hit him in the jaw with a notebook as she pointed him toward the auditorium doors, R.W. said.

"I said, 'If you ever hit me again, I'll (expletive) punch you in the face," R.W. said in an affidavit.

In a telephone interview, R.W. maintained that; the teacher hit him, that it may have been accidental, that he was not hurt and said it was OK to use foul language with teachers who don't respect him.

Mrs. B., for her part, categorically denied any wrongdoing.

"I did not touch R.W." she said in an affidavit. Judge D. showed little sympathy for the boy and said a three-day suspension would not harm him.

"His conduct was inexcusable and the school cannot tolerate it'" Judge D. said. "Mr. G., tell them to start behaving himself...You just don't behave like that in eighth grade."

Is kindergarten suspension fair?

After a 5-year old was suspended for striking a teacher during gym class, relatives of the kindergarten student have criticized the school district for what they feel is unfair punishment.

"I can't believe it," said her mother. "How can they suspend a kindergarten student for something this minor?"

The student was in gym class when she became upset about a decision to exclude her from playtime because of a disciplinary problem. She then slapped her gym teacher on the leg, her mother said.

The child was suspended and returned to school after relatives met with the school's child/student team.

"Nobody, but nobody messes with my grandkids," said the grandmother. She said her granddaughter should have been punished for doing something wrong, but suspension was ridiculous.

According to the school handbook of people conduct:

"Any pupil who commits an assault... upon a board member, teacher, administrator or any employee of the Board of Education, shall be suspended from school immediately."

Under this policy, which was based on state codes, suspension in this type of case is mandatory, the superintendent said.

The Director of Controversies and Disputes for the state Department of Education said it appears that the school's policy is based on the state education statute covering suspension for assaulting a teacher or other school employee and appears written in a "mandatory mode."

Creative Discipline

Although school systems have established discipline codes, it might be useful to look to some alternatives.

Ninth grader faces a fine for profanity

When 14-year-old C called a girl a "fat cow" and screamed a profanity at school, teachers didn't take the matter into their own hands, they went to the police.

Now the ninth grader faces a pretrial hearing on two misdemeanors, disorderly conduct citations. The charges, on the level of parking tickets, carry fines totaling $164.

"I wouldn't mind if they gave him pops, made him run around the track, put him in detention," said the mother, herself a middle school teacher. "But it's wrong that it has gone to the police and become a legal matter."

School and police officials said C isn't the first of the high school students to be cited for offensive or vulgar language.

School policy allows both the girl who was taunted and the teacher who overheard C scream the profanity during a flag-football game, to go the police, an official said.

The school superintendent defended his school's willingness to allow the legal system to handle matters that are typically handled at school.

"If you come to my school and you start cussing, you are going to have to pay for that. It may include various options within the district and outside the district because you are also breaking laws."

While C isn't the first student ticketed under this law, he apparently is the first to fight it. The American Civil Liberties Union is representing him.

"His conduct is so clearly not legal," said the ACLU regional director. "It's an abuse of power to prosecute this kid."

Bad-conduct policies provoke parents

A school policy intended to dissuade students from bad behavior by threatening their involvement in after-school activities has drawn the ire of parents who say the district is overstepping its authority.

"Our contention is: we have no problem with that if the child gets in trouble in school, or on school property, or to school function, but if it concerns what the child does at home, off school grounds or when school is out, that should be the responsibility of the parents," said JC.. "That, to me, is grossly overstepping the bounds and taking rights away from the child and the parent."

The Board of Education president said the policy is intended to discourage underage drinking, drug use, crime and other inappropriate behavior. The policy applies to any student who "brings notoriety" to the school or to his or her peers because of illegal or inappropriate behavior.

"If participating in extra-curricular activities... are of significant importance to students then the potential for sacrificing those activities will have some meaning to the students."

JC said he and other parents learned of the policy when their children brought home forms for them to sign before the students could play sports and take part in after school activities. He and other parents will attend tonight's Board of Education meeting to discuss the issue.

While the board seems to agree on the focus of the policy, Mr. B. said there are questions among board members as to whether it will be in effect year-round or just during the school year.

Mr. B. also recognized there are several issues remaining about how the policy should be implemented, including more structured guidelines as to what the punishment would be and who makes a determination.

"A lot is going to be discussed," he said. "What we are finding out is that the broad language, although it is perhaps intentionally broad, may in turn create other problems because it doesn't cover every scenario."

Useful student discipline

Getting suspended from school is supposed to be a punishment. But for many kids, a couple of days out of school is anything but. They get a chance to hang out at home or go shopping or hit the streets instead of being stuck in high school.

That is why some states use suspension programs with a difference: suspended students sweep out buses, stock food pantries' shelves or perform other community services. New Jersey school administrators are talking about starting community service suspensions here, and it is an excellent idea.

Ten schools throughout the state are working with the New Jersey Education Department and the Rutgers Center for Applied Psychology to offer the volunteering effort beginning in the fall. The University of Medicine and Dentistry is starting a similar program with another group of schools.

Other schools, including North Carolina and Indiana, have found such programs work well, offering the potential of combining a dose of humility with what can be a positive learning experience.

Combining these two goals requires a bit of skill. The "job assignment" should help dissuade the offending student from fighting, skipping class, or other bad behavior that got him in trouble. But administrators don't want to sour the students on the positive aspects of community service.

One promising idea being discussed by parents and administrators from districts such as South Hunterdon Regional is to hold service hours on Saturday. Everyone would win if a student came away thinking, "I didn't want spend my Saturday helping at the animal shelter, but the work itself is okay."

A few concerns must be addressed. Someone must supervise students at the bus garage or cleaning up the riverbank. A substitute teacher my fill the bill nicely, at minimal cost to taxpayers, and schools must be alert to potential liability issues. Districts already have insurance to cover students on off-campus field trips and the like, but the student and the program must be right for each other. Community service isn't appropriate for the few teens who might be a danger to themselves or to others.

Parents also have an important role. They must approve the service assignment, and they can reinforce the practical lessons that basic shores can teach.

Community service suspendsions won't be right for all districts. Larger schools have enough students to make in-school suspension practical, but smaller districts, like South Hunterdon, which has some 350 students in grades 7-12, often don't have the staff for in-house programs.

For South Hunterdon, and in many other districts, community services is an idea that can provide a positive aspect to suspensions that might otherwise be nothing more than unscheduled vacations for students at risk.

The return of school uniforms

In the following selection JP describes a mandatory uniform policy adopted by a California school district in 1994. Since the policy went into effect, JP noted, the number of assaults, fights, and suspension in the school district has dropped dramatically.

Uniforms reduce undesirable behavior because they put students in the right frame of mind to learn, writes JP. Uniforms also makes intruders easy to identify and reduces student violence associated with the wearing of gang colors, she points out. Though some students and parents have complained of the added expense and the monotony of the uniform policy, JP explains that most have embraced school uniforms as a positive measure to increase school safety. She also reports that other school districts across and U.S. are implementing or considering similar policies. JP is an assistant editor for a magazine.

School Uniforms Continued

Ms. L has been feeling especially proud lately. And she has a president to thank. In the State of the Union address in 1996, the president praised student uniforms as a way to promote safety and discipline in public schools. Ms. L, the principal of a middle school, felt a particular satisfaction in the endorsement.

"Everybody is looking for answers, and here is a district that is doing something that is working," she said. Since 1994, the 83,000-student system has required its elementary and middle school students to dress in uniform fashion. It was the first public school district in the nation to do so

The president may have had this California school system in mind when, in his speech, he challenged public schools to mandate uniforms, "if it meant that teenagers

(would) stop killing each other over designer jackets."
Since the mandatory uniform policy was launched in 56 elementary and 14 middle schools here in fall 1994, violence and discipline problems have decreased dramatically, the survey by the district shows.

From the year before uniforms were required, 1993–94, to 1995 assault and battery cases in grades K–8 have dropped 34 percent. Physical fights between students have dropped by 51 percent and there were 32 percent fewer suspensions.

Though each school in the district can choose its own uniform, most students are required to wear black or blue pants, skirts, or shorts with white shirts. Nearly 60,000 K–8 students are affected by this policy.

Parents have the option of excusing their children from the requirement, but so far only 500 parents have filled out petitions to exempt their children, according to a spokesman for the district.

Dressing for success

"It's about dressing for success," said Ms. M., who said she wears a school uniform as a gesture of solidarity with her students. She has a selection of bright red blazers in her home closet.

Not one parent at the middle school has opted out of the plan in 1996, and a quick look around the campus at the unbroken stream of red, white and black shows that students are largely compliant. But there are a few exceptions.

In February, 1996, when Ms. M. darted down the hall between classes, the former coach was scanning the crowds.

"Tuck in that shirt," she called up to one disheveled teenager who was slouching against a locker. She looked disparagingly at another whose sweater was clearly purple, not red.

In addition to choosing uniform colors, each of the district's schools is allowed to choose the fabric and style of dress. One elementary school requires its pupils to wear ties, and few others prefer plaid, but most stick with black or blue and white.

Notes:

Ideas & Drawings:

Exercise: "Situations"

Situation One: "Missing Money"

Setting:	Classroom
Time:	End of a class.
Persons:	Bev, Carol and Eileen (three of your students) and the rest of the class.
Backgrounds:	Bev is a pleasant, hardworking pupil who has never been in trouble. Carol has exhibited behavior problems many times in the past. In fact, you have caught her cheating and lying on two different occasions. Eileen is quiet, yet does not do her schoolwork.
Circumstances:	All of your students have been engaging in activities that require a great deal of movement around the room. Bev has just walked over to you and said, "My money is missing from my wallet." You ask, "Are you sure you had the money when you came in?" She says, "Yes."
Situation:	You stop the class activity and say, "Bev is missing some money. Does anyone have anything to say?" Someone shouts out, "Carol took it!" Then Carol says, "Oh, no, I didn't. I saw Eileen take it." Eileen looks shocked.

1. What is your first reaction?

____

____

____

2. Other options?

____

____

____

3. If no one confesses, what will you do? Say?

____

____

____

4. Your long-term solution:

____

____

____

Situation Two: "Restroom Caper"

Setting: A hallway in your school near the students' restrooms
Time: Lunch hour
Persons: Four students from the school

Background: Your school has been plagued by acts of vandalism lately. Last week your principal asked faculty members to keep an extra sharp eye out for vandals. Three teachers per day have been assigned just to walk the halls during lunch. Today is your day to walk.

Circumstances: You are walking alone down a hallway at the far end of your building. No one else is nearby, and all is quiet. Suddenly, you hear a loud crash coming from one of the student restrooms and some muffled cheering.

Situation: You cautiously open the restroom door. Inside you find four very guilty looking students, who appear to be shocked by your intrusion. One of the stall walls has been pulled from the restroom wall and is lying on the floor.
You say, "OK, let me have your names."
The four say, "No way!"
So you say, "OK, Come with me then." Again they refuse.

1. What is your reaction?

____
____
____

2. Other options?

____
____
____

3. What will you say to the four students?

____
____
____

4. If the students were to physically threaten you, what would you do?

____
____
____

Situation Three: "Vocabulary"

Setting: Your classroom
Time: Near the end of a class.
Persons: Sean (one of your students) and the rest of your class

Background: Sean has been a severe behavior problem. He's been suspended from school before for hitting other students, kicking a teacher and smashing windows. He is a big fellow and most students and quite a few teachers are afraid of him.

Circumstances: You've only had a few minor problems with Sean. Today, however, he seems quite irritated. You have been ignoring him and have not even pushed him to do any work.

Situation: You're handing back tests that your class did yesterday. Sean got a score of 38. One of the student asks you what the highest test score was, and you say, "The highest was 96 in the lowest was 38."
Sean says softly, but loud enough so that everyone can hear, "Why you #x@##)$!"
You look at Sean and say, "Do not ever say that again!"
He jumps out of his seat with teeth clenched, fists raised and starts walking toward you.

1. What is your first reaction?

____

____

____

2. Other options?

____

____

____

3. How will you prevent this in the future?

____

____

____

4. If you need help, how would you get it?

____

____

____

Situation Four: "Affection"

Setting:	Your classroom
Time:	Mid-lesson
Persons:	Ana and Joe (Junior High)
Circumstances:	Students are working in pairs on a report
Situation:	Students are basically on task except for Ana and Joe, who seem to be more engrossed in each other than the report. Ana is constantly nudging and fawning over Joe, who responds in kind to the attention. The rest of the class is well aware of the display.

1. What is your first reaction?

2. Other options?

3. How do you explain to Ana and Joe that this behavior is not acceptable in class?

4. Your long-term solution:

Thoughts & Ideas:

Situation Five: "*Your* Corporal Punishment Situation"

Setting: ______________________________
Time: ______________________________
Persons: ______________________________

Circumstances: ______________________________
____
____
____

Situation: ______________________________
____
____
____

1. What was the teacher's reaction?
____
____
____

2. How did students respond?
____
____
____

3. What might you have done in similar circumstances as the teacher/coach?
____
____
____

Chapter Notes and Additional Information:

____
____
____
____
____
____
____
____
____
____

Chapter 10:

Classroom Management

Chapter Topics:

Maintain Control in the Classroom
Who is in Control?
Things I Can't Control
School Policies and Administration
Weather
Students (Numbers and Availability)
Parents/Guardians
Classroom
Taking Control
General Recommendations for Making Decisions
Classroom Rules
The Classroom
The Physical Environment
Safety
Seating
Dress and Grooming
Time Management
Day-to-Day Lessons
Transitions
Smooth Transitions
Distinctive Times
Entering the Classroom
Exiting the Classroom
Students Rights
Student Responsibilities
Teacher Rights and Responsibilities
Code of Conduct
School Behaviors
Student Dress Code
Cafeteria Rules
Consequences for Infractions
Assemblies
Books and Equipment
Field Trips
Fire Drills
Hall Passes
Toys
Telephone Usage
Appendix: Rules Explanation
Appendix: Classroom Arrangement

Classroom management has varied definitions, but on the whole***, it indicates the activities by a teacher to establish order and engage students' cooperation while maintaining an environment in which teaching and learning can take place.***

Key principles that have come forth from the literature in managing the classroom are:

- Monitoring student behavior (recognizing potential problems)
- Communicating clear expectations
- Keeping students engaged
- Less time in transition
- Clear directions
- Anticipating problems and disruptions
- Preventive vs. reactive
- Building a caring climate
- Encouragement of student responsibility
- Being flexible to new "events"
- Taking time to establish routines and procedures
- Behaviors vs. student
- Meaningful academic tasks and activities
- Teaching desirable behaviors to students
- Utilizing active learning

Maintain Control in the Classroom

The greatest fear of teachers is control of the classroom, or in educational parlance, classroom management. Loss of control in the classroom stems from many possibilities but almost always leads to teacher and student frustration. Self-doubt on the part of the teacher grows as the classroom disintegrates into students controlling the class. This control of the classroom by students can be convert or overt, as in defiance of a teacher's request. This chapter will help you understand the values and knowledge necessary to manage your classroom.

Exercise:

The Worst-Case Scenario of Classroom Management:

Think back to your schooling or teaching career and identify the worst teaching/learning situation that you've experienced. Be specific as to what the problems were (e.g., students shouting out, students picking on other students, failure to listen to the teacher, cursing, and disrupting).

Grade: __________ Subject: ____________ Number of Students: ___________
Time of Day: _________ Day: ____________ Place: ______________________

1. ***Did the same student(s) cause the problems for all the other teachers?***

   Yes __________ No __________

2. ***If no, explain why not.***

   ____
   ____
   ____

3. ***If yes, explain who was responsible for order in the classroom.***

   ____
   ____
   ____

4. ***Describe the best-managed classroom and the reasons why!***

   ____
   ____
   ____

Who is in Control?

The first step in having good classroom management skills is an attitude that it is *your* classroom. You are the professional, certified teacher, having had classes in education, and psychology. Start by stating, "This is my classroom. I may allow you (students) to make decisions, but only after I see that you can ***(observe)*** expected behavior."

You are not a teacher to become a friend or buddy to your students, but to teach them! Too many teachers allow the need to be liked (loved) by their students to get in the way of their responsibility of managing the classroom. Students will like, love you only after they respect you, that is seeing what you are expected to do—***teach.*** All students want to learn. They all may not be ready to learn, but have the drive and need to grow. This cannot and will not take place in classrooms that are "governed" by the students. (This can happen, but with mature students and a strong teacher lead.)

Control of the classroom is an ***attitude, belief, philosophy***, a choice that is in your sphere of influence. If you don't believe that you are capable or have the power, then all is lost—find a new career. But, first reflect on your students and their behavior with other teachers. Do they have the same "behavior" with other teachers they are in contact with? Are they a disruptive problem in class? When are they at their best? Chances are that students learn the behaviors that are expected of them as they move from teacher to teacher and make their adjustments. The question becomes: What types of classroom management style will work for me? None will, unless you believe that you have control of the classroom.

Things I Can't Control

It is important to recognize the elements of teaching that you have little or no control over for your personal sanity. Once you recognize that fact, your teaching will improve and the less self-flagellation you will suffer. As soon as this takes place, students will recognize that they too must realize that ***they don't have control over you.***

Note that students come from different home environments, cultures and economic conditions and make changes to adjust in a common setting. From class to class each day, the students adjust their behaviors as to what they can do, what they can control and what they cannot. This is dependent on the teacher and the teacher's dynamics of classroom management.

Believe that the students can adjust and change. Don't expect immediate changes in behavior, but look for small increments of positive behaviors.

Home Environment—Pertains to living conditions both physical and mental.

- Parental values for education
- Moral values (religious, personal, societal)
- Adequate food and shelter
- Materials to support living

You may have little control over all of the preceding, but you may be able to supplement or assist in their attainment.

With the aid of the faculty association and the Board of Education, school administrators design and develop before and after-school programs for study, academics, safe haven, nutrition supplements and enrichment. This helps develop a school with a positive environment from the preschool hours to after-school hours and evening activities which may include library, gym and art.

School Policies and Administration

The school is governed by the Board of Education and its established policies. The administration is there to interpret and enforce rules and regulations. Often, dress codes, behavior and manners are loosely enforced. This is when you can establish your presence within the classroom. On a larger scale, the faculty association can lobby for changes via the Board of Education.

Weather

We have absolutely no control over the weather. It will affect both you and your students mentally and physically. Those sunny days, dreary days, cloudy days, snow days, freezing cold days and humid days will challenge the best of teachers. Anticipate and plan activities (lessons) that are different from the normal routine, but still teach. Don't let the outside elements (weather) dictate your mental state or the state of your students.

Students (Numbers and Ability)

You are asked to teach a given number of students with varying ranges in their academic achievement and ability. You cannot say, "I can't teach that many!" or, "They are academically behind. It's impossible!" As far as numbers go, think about the whole group and plan independent strategies. Not all students have to be taught the same thing at the same time, nor do they have to be taught the exact same concepts. See the parts of the whole and work with each part to form the whole.

Abilities and achievement levels of the students will change with good instruction. Utilize peer teaching, creative projects and interest groups to allow student success. Less teacher-directed time is generally needed for the more gifted, but clear direction and focus are necessary for all levels.

Parents/Guardians

Constant and specific communication will help alleviate problems arising from attitudes, behaviors and expectations. Clearly state at the outset what the expected behaviors are in the school, and in your classroom. Have a standard, written policy of handling incidents to head off irate parents. Use witnesses as part of procedures whenever possible. Keep supervisors informed on a regular basis of suspected problems and solutions.

Classroom

Most likely your classroom will not change (***size and space***); however, the interior and how it's arranged is up to you. Even if you share, go to a different classroom and take time to rearrange it to the way that best suits your strategies. Safety and health features of the classroom should all be reported and addressed by the administration (legal aspects). Put your personal touch on each classroom, even if it means bringing a paper flower with you each day.

Taking Control

Control means that you know what choices you have to make in the course of teaching. Making choices and decisions are what all teachers do. Better teachers, those in control, make better choices.

There are three basic styles of classroom management (decision-making):

Authoritative—the teacher makes a high degree of decisions

Democratic—shared decision-making process between the teacher and students

Laissez-faire—students are given a high degree of decision-making power.

Think of choices or decisions as your "***right,***" and student choices as "***privileges***". The difference is that a right is "given" but can be revoked under extreme circumstances, and a privilege is earned and can be revoked. ***Classroom management starts with what and who makes the decisions in the classroom.*** Teachers can make, share and abdicate their "*right*" to make decisions in the classroom. In all cases they are responsible for the final decisions.

The choices ("***rights***") for all teachers (save the exceptions) are as follows:

- Classroom
- Physical Environment
- Seating
- Time Management
- Teaching Strategies
- Dress and Grooming
- Transitions: Entering/Exiting/Within

General Recommendations for Making Decisions

1. For a beginning or experienced teacher who has "***control problems,***" ***utilize the authoritative approach.*** It is easier to allow choices than take them back. Observe the students to see how they respond to expected behaviors.

2. ***Try out new approaches*** with the smaller, well-behaved class versus a larger class or those with behavior problems. Work in choices with materials with which you are familiar and use them in small blocks of time.

3. ***Know what your alternatives are*** and the possible result of selection. (i.e. If putting students in groups, realize that some students may not carry their responsibility.)

4. Not all students will have or make the same choices, nor do they have to be involved with the same activity. Remember, choices are a "***privilege,***" not a "***right.***"

5. ***Guide*** students' choices; model their behavior; give examples and consequences; limit decision making at the onset.

6. **Anticipate! Anticipate!** Think what possibly can happen, go wrong, foul up or not work. **Don't assume. Be prepared!** Have alternatives and responses ready.

Classroom Rules

These rules are specific to your classroom and generally fall under the larger school rubric. Ensure that rules are discussed, illustrated, and hard copies are sent home to parents. The rules should be posted clearly and explained during the first week and restart of school.

Along with the rules, the consequences and sequence for misbehavior should be explained. The behavior consequences are also sent home to parents. Fairness is critical to the application of punishment, and when deviated from the norm, it should be explained to the class.

1. Manners Rule: Set a positive tone for your classroom. It reflects not just one idea but an attitude of how we interact as social beings. The following are areas that are generally reflected within this rule.

Names:

a. You are always Mr., Mrs., Ms., never by the first name.
b. Adults are always addressed in a formal way. Janitors, cafeteria and staff are all addressed in this way.
c. Students will utilize first names and not last names or nicknames (only if accepted).

d. Address your students by first name or Mr. P. or Mrs. A.
e. Name-calling and teasing are not permitted and should be addressed at once!

Movement: Entering, leaving, passing rooms and areas in the school also reflect a discipline.

a. Always walk, unless instructed to do otherwise (gym class, without pushing, shoving and cutting in line).
b. Utilize the rules of the road; exit classrooms and walk on the right side.
c. Always say "Excuse me" when you wish to pass a person or walk faster.
d. Wait in line in a courteous fashion, keeping your hands to yourself and speaking in a quiet manner if allowed.

2. Be Prepared: Help students to understand their responsibilities in the learning process. Consequences of not being prepared should be included in the hard copy to parents and guardians.

Materials: Paper, books, supplies are in readiness for lessons. Establish a routine as to when pencils are to be sharpened and supplies are gathered. This is not to be done during lessons.

Homework: Each lesson should reflect some practices or prep for the next class. It should be meaningful and addressed each day. Routines to collect and review written homework are vital for students to see its importance.

Reading: The practice of reading is an essential part of preparation for the lessons. To ensure students read the assigned materials, call on them to explain, clarify and write answers on the board. Surprise them with pop quizzes. They shouldn't escape this process if you are diligently utilizing the readings.

The Classroom

Your first obligation is to ensure a safe physical and emotional environment in which students can learn. A safe physical environment ***means that you have eliminated physical hazards and elements that may be injurious to students.*** The emotional environment is the ***tone of the classroom with respect to how learning takes place***. Is there a supportive atmosphere? Do students feel safe from other students, both physically and emotionally? Does ridicule, bothering or teasing, isolate some students from the rest of the class?

The Physical Environment

Safe classrooms are welcoming and supportive. Your task is to ensure that students feel good about being in that environment. Is it pleasurable and fun to be in this classroom? Does it feel, smell and look good? Is your classroom inviting?

Guidelines for a Safe, Happy and Healthy Classroom:

- Keep your classroom clean and neat.
- Keep your classroom orderly and organized.
- Keep your classroom cheerful. Use bright colors.
- Keep your desk clutter free. Set an example for your students.
- Bulletin boards should reflect student work. Display projects and new material. Keep them current.
- Involve students in decorating the classroom and bulletin boards.
- Post the "Classroom rules" clearly and in view of all.
- Ensure students are clean and use sanitary measures in class and prior to leaving.
- Use nature to add to your classroom. Plant flowers as student projects.
- Music (classical) is a way of introducing new concepts and can provide a pleasant background.
- Change is always a surprise!
- Add soft furniture, chairs, cushions and rugs for extra comfort.
- Isolate a space for silent reading that is quiet, comfortable and easily accessible for added pleasure.

Safety

Your physical and mental obligation is to ensure that your classroom is a physically safe environment for students. Prior to starting or conducting lessons, check to see if floors and surfaces are clear of debris, all equipment is safe to operate, chemicals and toxic materials are locked in cabinets, and safety rules are posted and enforced.

Your second obligation for a safe environment is that students are protected from mental and psychological anguish: bullying, teasing, sexual harassment and so forth. Your classroom rules should clarify this, and such behavior should not be tolerated. Legally, the school and you can be sued if charges can be proved.

Seating

There are many ways of arranging seating, and it generally depends on the number of students and the type of instruction that takes place. Some guidelines for the classroom are:

- Students have clear view for instructional purposes.

- Students have easy access to materials and school supplies.
- Students have space to work by themselves without being pestered (grouping may encourage this practice).
- Distracting elements are in back or out of view of students (animals, windows, and aquariums)
- Teacher has a clear view and access to all students—make corridors for ease of access.
- Change students' seating as needed.
- Have independent seating, time-out or late arrival seating that does not interfere with class routine.

When organizing the classroom for various teaching methods (demonstration, discussions, groups or laboratories), reflect on the following aspects:

- Duration of activity and transition time.
- Movement from one activity, flow to another.
- Number of students per activity.
- Makeup of activity groupings.
- Working with others is a privilege, not a right!
- Each lesson may setup or prepare for the next (i.e., lecture, discussion for laboratory experiments). Room is arranged prior to activity.

The choice is whether to assign or not to assign seating, and if so, how. Structure allows students a freedom of knowing what their limits are, and arranged seating at the outset gives this security. General guidelines are for seating arrangements:

- Assign seating at the outset of school, unit, major theme or project
- By assigning seating, learning student names will become much easier
- Different activities require movement and change of seating structure. (Be clear as to how this will take place (assign responsibility for moving desks, chairs and persons in groups)
- Do not group desks or chairs together on the outset until you know how well students have learned appropriate behaviors for group instruction and personal space.
- Have desks and seats for latecomers and students who have difficulty working in groups in a place that will not disturb flow of lessons.
- Allow students to select seating after they have demonstrated appropriate behavior.

Dress and Grooming

All schools have a dress or grooming code. Private school "codes" are usually more conservative and clearly spelled out. Public schools may run the gamut from very conservative (uniforms) to ultraliberal (fashion statements). Know the limits of your school. Ask very specific questions as to the interpretation of items.

The enforcement of the dress and grooming codes will generally vary from teacher to teacher. The code is there to help you maintain a conductive educational, nondistracting learning environment! ***You can't control what other teachers do, but you can in your classroom.***

You will be challenged. Students will test you to see how far they can go in their expressions of the "***first amendment right***". So be ready to act. Some guidelines to prevent the crisis of clothing pressures are:

- Discuss the dress code the first or second day of class and give examples.
- Be more conservative or liberal, if allowed, to create your own dress code.
- Stop little challenges as soon as they appear, (shirts not tucked in, the amount of exposed skin, and unacceptable "print" on clothing or skin)
- Have extra shirts, sweaters, etc. available for quick cover-ups.
- Don't debate the code with students in front of the whole class, take them aside.
- ***Maintain your own professional dress. Model behavior and actions.***
- Discuss how clothes and hygiene affect feelings, learning, life and success (especially with junior and high school students.)

Time Management

With a well-organized daily plan, many of the "management" problems can be eliminated. Wasted time in the classroom, disorganization, and lack of clarity allow and encourage student challenges. Think of the daily plan as a road map taking you to a specific destination. Plan for all possible contingencies, including breaks.

Routines are important, but may vary day to day and week to week. They do not have to be the same; however, the entering and exiting (transitions) and behaviors are constant.

Too often, the time allotted doesn't include enough to complete the planned activity. In planning, be realistic about which objectives can be covered and how long the strategy to process this will take. Included in that timeframe are the entry, explanation and exiting, (the transitions). The following are general guidelines for organizing your elementary classroom schedule.

Timeframe:	5–15 minutes	15–25 minutes	25+ minutes
Planned activity:	Explanations Lectures Media	Discussions Demonstrations	Projects Games Labs

Day-to-Day Lessons

Plan each day's lesson to set up the next day or days of activity. More time may be needed as the strategy and/or emphasis of lessons changes. Don't plan in isolation. Mondays may be a preparation day or startup if students are not prepared for the activity.

Transitions

Making transitions from activity to activity, whether within the classroom or outside the classroom, need to be smooth and as trouble free as possible. It is best to teach the students to behave properly as early on as possible during the school year in order to acquire smooth transitions for the rest of the year.

Listed are some suggestions to make that transition easier on everyone.

1. **Provide a warning**—Let the students know before the end of an activity that it will be ending in five minutes. Remind them again at one minute so that all students are prepared in advance and can finish what they are working on. A timer with a bell works wonderfully in this instance.

2. **Be specific**—Use proper time frames. Make sure you end an activity in five minutes if you say five minutes, not ten minutes later. This will keep students on time and give them a sense of time.

3. **Set specific routines**—Instruct the students on how to put their materials away, and sit at their desks quietly when they are prepared to start the next activity. Have students remain quiet when lining up to proceed to the hallway.

4. **Wind Down**—End each activity in a calm manner, so the students are not over stimulated when the activity ends.

5. **Positive recognition**—Acknowledge positive behavior in students who make transitions smooth and trouble free. The other students will want positive recognition also and will behave in a more positive manner.

6. **Daily routines**—Remind students in the beginning of the day when activities or specials will occur, so there are no surprises.

7. **Quiet**—Wait until the entire class is quiet and listening before transitions can occur.

8. **Reminders**—Remind students of proper behavior before transitions occur.

9. **Organization**—Line up the students single file or two by two, with an assigned line leader for the students to follow.

10. **Positive attitude**—Begin and end each activity with a positive attitude so that students look forward to each activity.

Smooth Transitions

It is important to keep a classroom running smoothly from activity to activity. Wait until the entire class is quiet and attentive before instructing them on making a transition. Instructions should be clear and direct. Write any important information on the board if the transition is difficult and confusing. Carefully monitor all transitions as they are occurring and make appropriate changes.

Distinctive Times

Besides transitions, the following are distinctive times that require a teacher to organize carefully:

- The beginning of the class period
- The last period of the day (particularly Friday)
- The few minutes just before lunch
- The day before a big event or holiday
- The beginning of a period following a rally, school assembly, or fire drill
- The time before, during, and after report cards are distributed

Entering the Classroom

The first impressions people get when they see your classroom is how they will judge you as a teacher. Is your classroom neat, clean and organized? Does your classroom give off a warm, caring attitude? Is your classroom bright and cheerful?

Using good organizational skills combined with creativity, color and the students work will help your classroom be more inviting and comfortable for the students and their parents/guardians. Have separate areas for each activity, such as a quiet corner for reading or a designated art area.

Greet students at the door of your classroom by name. Say, "How are you today, Samantha?", or "It is nice to see your smile, John." Be the last one into the classroom after all of the students are welcomed into the room.

Exiting the Classroom

As with entering the classroom, make sure the room is neat, clean and organized when you exit each day. Do not allow students to leave areas otherwise. Remind students of all homework assignments, tests, projects or activities in the near future. This will help students to remember what they need for home study. After the classroom is tidy, move to the exit and excuse your class with a cheerful exit. "Enjoy the rest of your day", "Have a great weekend," or "Until we meet again."

Exercise:

1. ***Describe the "worst" teacher-managed classroom. Cite specific examples and teacher reactions.***

Grade: _______________ Subject: __________________

Incident: ____
Teacher Reaction: ____

Incident: ____
Teacher Reaction: ____

How would you have handled either of the above?

____
____

2. ***Describe the <u>best</u> teacher- managed classroom. Cite specific examples and teacher reactions.***

Grade _______________ Subject __________________

Incident: ____
Teacher Reaction: ____

Incident: ____
Teacher Reaction: ____

Why was the "best" teacher successful and the "worst" not successful?

Best:____
____
____
____

Worst: ____
____
____
____

Student Rights

Schools are committed to safeguarding the rights given to all students under state and federal law. In addition to those rights, all students have the right to the following:

- A safe, healthy, orderly and civil school environment.
- Take part in all district activities on an equal basis regardless of age, race, religion, color, natural origin, gender, sexual orientation or disability.
- Present their version of the relevant events to school personnel authorized to impose a disciplinary penalty as in connection with the imposition of the penalty.
- Access school rules and, when necessary, receive an explanation of those rules from personnel.
- Address the board of education on the same terms as any citizen.

Student Responsibilities

All students have the responsibility to:

- Contribute to maintaining a safe and orderly school environment that is conducive to learning.
- Show respect to other persons and to property.
- Be familiar with and abide by all academic policies, rules and regulations.
- Attend school every day (unless they are legally excused), and be in class, on time, and prepared to learn.
- Work to the best of their ability in all academic and extracurricular pursuits and strive toward their highest level of achievement.
- React to direction given by teachers, administrators, and other school personnel in a respectful, positive manner.
- Utilize anger management strategies to support a positive learning environment.
- Ask questions when they do not understand.
- Seek help in solving problems that might lead to discipline.
- Accept responsibility for their actions.
- Conduct themselves as representatives of the district when participating in or attending school-sponsored extracurricular events and to hold themselves to the highest standards of conduct, demeanor, and sportsmanship.
- Make constructive contributions to their school and report objectively the circumstances of school-related issues.
- Utilize time management techniques to balance academic and extracurricular responsibilities.

Teacher Rights and Responsibilities

All district teachers are expected and encouraged to:

- Promote a safe, orderly and stimulating school environment that supports active teaching and learning.
- Maintain a climate of mutual respect and dignity, which will strengthen students' self-concept and promote confidence to learn.
- Be prepared to teach.
- Demonstrate interest in teaching and concern for student achievement.
- Know school policies, rules, and academic department policies, and enforce them in a fair and consistent manner.
- Communicate to students and parents:

    a. Course objectives and requirements
    b. Marking/grading procedures
    c. Assignment deadlines
    d. Expectations for students
    e. Classroom discipline plan

- Communicate regularly with students, parents and other teachers concerning growth and achievement.
- Provide the educational environment necessary for students to develop time management skills.

Code of Conduct

The Code of Conduct is designed to protect the rights of the total school community. It reflects the school's desire to further student development of desirable character traits, self, and the acceptance of responsibility for one's actions.

Students are expected to follow the school rules and be on their best behavior at all times. Such things as common courtesy, respect for the rights and property of others, a neat appearance, friendly communication and the completion of all assigned work, will foster a rewarding and enjoyable school experience. Students who find it difficult to comply with these expectations will ultimately find it difficult to succeed and will be unable to cope with day-to-day activities.

To this end students should:

- Act respectful and courteous toward peers and adults.
- Respect the rights and property of other people in the school.
- Use reasonable means to solve disputes. (Fighting is an unacceptable method.)
- Respect and care for school property.
- Report promptly to class. Be prepared with the required material for learning.

- Follow individual classroom rules and procedures.
- Move quickly and in an orderly manner in the corridors.
- Refrain from the use of profanity or other unacceptable forms of communication.
- Refrain from the use, distribution, or possession of drugs, alcohol, tobacco, and other controlled substances.
- Remain on school grounds or designated areas.
- Refrain from chewing gum.
- Eat only in designated areas.
- Refrain from inappropriate displays of affection.
- Dress in an appropriate manner. Shirts or other articles of clothing that display inappropriate language and/or slogans will not be permitted.
- Leave at home items that will interfere with the learning process such as a skateboard, MP3 player, CD player, iPod, electronic game or any other toy.
- Bring no weapon or object that is designed as or can be used as a weapon.
- Stay after school only when directly supervised by a staff member.
- Participate in all field trips and school activities.

School Behaviors

Student Dress Code

1. **General rules**:
   a. Students are expected to be clean and well groomed in their appearance.
   b. Students are expected to avoid extremes in appearance that are so disruptive or distracting that the reaction of other students is beyond normal control.
   c. Dress or grooming that jeopardizes the health or safety of the student or of other students or is injurious to school property will not be tolerated.

2. **Prohibited clothing and articles:** ***(The following garments and articles of clothing are prohibited in school and at school-sponsored activities.)***

- Any revealing clothing is not permitted.
- Tops must extend to the waist and meet the waistband of pants, skirts, and shorts. Clothing must cover the entire front and back of the student.
- Pants, skirts, and shorts must be worn in such a manner that no undergarments are visible.
- Tube tops, tank tops, halter tops, half shirts and short shorts are not permitted. Shorts must extend past fingertips of hands placed at the sides of students.
- Proper and safe footwear (no slippers, thongs, sandals or open-toed shoes) is required at all times. Students may not go barefooted. Footwear must be worn at all times.
- Bandannas, hats and other headwear are not to be worn or carried in the building. Students should place all headwear in their cubbies (lockers) at the beginning of

each school day. Hats may be worn to school but are not to be worn in the building.

- Coats, jackets, or outerwear are not permitted to be worn in the building. These items must be kept in the students' cubbies (lockers).
- Cellular phones and/or paging devices are not permitted.
- Slogans or pictures that promote drugs, alcohol, obscenities, or ethnic violence cannot appear on clothing or property.
- Patches and emblems, which might distract other students, may not be placed on clothing, backpacks, book bags, purses or other belongings.
- Pants, skirts, shirts and/or shorts with letters, words, numbers, designs, or pictures that are distracting to other students may not be worn. More specifically, jeans and sweatpants with phrases such as "naughty girl," "princess," or pictures of lips on the buttocks or any other region are not permitted to be worn by students.
- Clothing or jewelry that could cause injury to any student or damage to school property is not to be worn (i.e., spiked bracelets, choke chains, dog collars, or sharp body jewelry).

Cafeteria Rules

The aim regarding the cafeteria is to provide students with a pleasant dining atmosphere. This requires appropriate student behavior. As soon as students enter the cafeteria, they are expected to adhere to the following rules. In the event students do not adhere to these rules, the consequences that follow will be imposed.

- Students must be seated at all times.
- Every student is responsible for cleaning up his/her own garbage.
- Students may not throw food for any reason.
- Students must walk while entering the line for food and may not cut or engage in horseplay while in line.
- Other rules as determined by School Administration.

In addition, students should be aware that no food is to be taken out of the cafeteria unless the student had been given permission to do so by a cafeteria supervisor. Oftentimes exceptions to this rule are made when students are receiving extra help from a teacher, working on a project or school event, making up schoolwork, or serving lunch detention.

Consequences for Cafeteria Infractions

If a student does not follow one or more of the rules listed pertaining to expected cafeteria behavior, a cafeteria supervisor will change the student's seat for an extended period of time after meeting with the student to identify and discuss the inappropriate behavior. If a change in behavior is not observed after these steps have occurred, the student will be referred ***directly*** to the administration. At that point, the administration will deal directly with the student. It is up to the administration's discretion on how to deal with the severity of the instance, with detention or other harsh action.

Assemblies

Assemblies will occur at various times throughout the school year. When attending assemblies, students will be accompanied and supervised by teachers. Students are also expected to proceed to and from assemblies in an orderly fashion with a minimum amount of noise. Audience members are to commend assembly participants through applause. There should be no whistling, booing, or excessive noise made during assemblies. Students who choose not to demonstrate proper behavior will lose the privilege of attending assemblies. Constant talking during assemblies will not be tolerated.

Books and Equipment

Students are responsible for the care of all books, equipment, and materials that are assigned or loaned to them during the school year. Textbooks are to be kept covered so they can be returned with a minimum amount of wear or damage. Students should examine their textbooks carefully when they receive them. They should call their teacher's attention to any marks or ripped pages so that they are not held responsible for previous damage. Fines will be levied at the end of the school year for any marks, ripped pages, or any other additional damages infracted by students. With respect to textbooks, parents and students should be aware that depending on the amount of damage, fine amounts may be levied for the replacement cost of the damaged book. Lost textbooks will result in fine amounts of the replacement cost of the lost textbook. Parents and students should also be aware that final report cards and standardized test scores will be withheld until payment is received for all fines.

Field Trips

A field trip is an optional activity, which enhances or expands the educational programs at the school by providing an experience not available in the traditional classroom setting. In order to attend a field trip, students must provide school officials with permission slip signed by a parent or guardian. Parent/Guardian notes will not be accepted in lieu of permission slips. As for conduct, students may be denied the privilege of attending a field trip if their behavior shows a negative pattern. If parents decide not to give their child permission to attend the field trip, their child is expected to be in school for the entire day. Teachers will develop appropriate lessons for each student remaining behind. Students and parents should also be aware that the code of conduct extends to field trips.

Fire Drills

New Jersey state law requires schools to conduct fire drills. Every classroom must post fire drill procedures as well as a map of fire drill escape routes. During a fire drill, students should walk quickly, silently, and in a single file line from the classroom.

While outside, students should stand quietly and wait for the signal to return to the building. After the signal has sounded, students should return to their classrooms in an orderly fashion. Students should be aware of alternate routes to evacuate the building in the event designated escape routes are blocked.

Hall Passes (Bathroom, Nurse and Office/Guidance)

All students ***must*** have a hall pass if they leave their classroom during class time.

1. Bathroom

If a student needs to use the bathroom while in class, the student must obtain permission to do so from the teacher, sign the classroom log, and take the classroom hall pass to the bathroom. Students should be aware that they are permitted to use the bathroom when classes change as long as they are on time to their next class.

2. Nurse

Students who wish to visit the nurse must have a pass from a school official except in the case of a true emergency. Any student who feels he/she cannot remain in school for any reason should receive a pass from his/her teacher and report directly to the nurse. Students are not permitted to telephone parents to request transportation from school.

3. Office/Guidance

With respect to the office and guidance, students may make an appointment to speak with office staff or request to see their guidance counselors at any time for assistance. To arrange a guidance appointment, students should complete a guidance appointment form. Guidance/Office appointment forms are available in the guidance offices, main office, and the nurse's office.

Toys (Laser Pointers/ Pens)

Certain personal belongings are considered to be disruptive to the learning process. Articles of this nature (including toys, technical devices, etc.) are not permitted in the school and will be confiscated by school officials if students are handling or using them. Once a school official has confiscated a toy or disruptive article, it will be handed over to the administration. The first time this occurs, the article will be returned to the student at the end of the school day. The second incident will result in the article being returned on the last day of the school year.

In addition, laser pointers/pens are dangerous and can cause eyesight damage. Therefore, students are not permitted to have laser pointer/pens in school, on the school bus or on school property. School officials will confiscate laser pointers/pens if students are handling or using them. Once an official has confiscated a laser pointer/pen, it will be turned over to the administration and not returned until the end of the school year.

Telephone Usage

Students are not permitted to use the main office or guidance office telephones to call parents unless the student is experiencing a true emergency. Students will not be allowed to call parents to bring in homework, class projects/materials, gym clothes, field trip permission slips, physical forms, progress reports, or other school materials/forms that the student is responsible for bringing to and from school himself/herself. Part of the school experience includes encouraging students to fulfill their responsibilities with respect to this issue.

When a student uses the telephone to call a parent and must be summoned to the office to pick up items delivered by a parent, the announcement is a disruption to other students in the class. The student being called to the office is also missing valuable instructional time. To that end, we expect parents to respect this rule and refrain from calling school officials with messages for students unless it is an emergency. Students should also be aware that they are not permitted to use the school's pay phones without the permission of the administration.

Chapter Notes & Additional Information:

Personal Thought & Drawings

Appendix: Rules Explanation

RULE 1: RESPECT AND BE POLITE TO ALL PEOPLE.

Teaching students to be polite and respectful to everyone, not only those who enter the classroom, but those outside the classroom as well, is extremely important. Teaching students not only to respect others but to respect themselves is the key to having a safe, comforting environment for students. The behavior shown by the student in the class reflects greatly on the teacher and his or her ability.

Respect—*to take notice of; to regard with special attention; to regard as worthy of special consideration; hence; to care for; to heed.*

Polite—*Behaving in a way that is socially correct and shows awareness of and caring for other people's feelings.*

- Elders, teachers, class assistants, staff members and parents are to be given respect and polite behavior both inside and outside the classroom.
- Peers, including classmates, friends and other students who enter the classroom, are to be treated with respect and admirable behavior.
- Property, including all items belonging to the teacher or other students in the classroom, should be treated with care. Any items of value should be placed in a special area designated as such and should not be handled by the students unless properly supervised.
- When addressing younger students, (K–3), make sure that all rules and procedures are written clearly and simply and understood by the students. It is advisable to also include why each rule is important to follow.

The following are some examples on how to be polite and respectful.

- Students will raise their hand to speak.
- Everyone must keep their hands, feet and objects to themselves. Hitting, fighting, biting and pulling hair are not acceptable behaviors.
- Everyone will share.
- Everyone will be polite to all who enter the room.
- Everyone will listen when the teacher or a classmate is speaking. This will show others that what they have to say is important.
- When students speak or talk about others, use of any negative language or negative connotations toward each other is not allowed.
- Everyone will call each other by their proper name or an appropriate nickname agreed to by both parties.

RULE 2: BE PROMPT AND PREPARED.

Being prompt and prepared is not only important at that beginning of the day, it is also important throughout the day. Having assignments turned in on time, being prepared for class, and having the appropriate materials ready for class are all part of being prompt and prepared. Establishing good work habits early in the school year will help establish routines that will keep you organized throughout the year

Prompt—*Done immediately, done at once without delay, quick to act; ready, punctual.*

Prepared—T*o make or get something ready for something that will happen in the future.*

The following are some examples on how to be prompt and prepared:

- Be in the classroom and prepared to start the day when the bell rings.
- Students should have the proper equipment necessary each day including paper, pens, pencils, crayons, markers, books or any other equipment to teacher deems necessary.
- Have all schoolwork, classroom assignments and projects completed and turned in to the teacher in the time allowed.
- All assignments should be neat with no smudges, smears, holes, rips or tears and placed in the appropriate location.
- All late assignments will be graded per the penalty decided by classroom procedure depending on how late the assignment is.
- Students should hand in assignments that they feel they have given their best effort in completing. Assignments may have the guidance of the parents, ***but not be completed by the parent.*** Parents need to allow their children to learn and be creative which will greatly improve their self-esteem.
- Students should start their school day well rested, well fed and mentally ready to start the day. An average of eight hours per night of sleep, a well-balanced breakfast and establishing good hygiene procedures are essential in providing a healthy environment. Students who are undernourished, tired or ill will not perform their best.
- Follow all classroom directions and procedures.
- Discuss classroom procedure for students who are absent to make up the work and what timeframe it needs to be turned in.

RULE 3: LISTEN QUIETLY WHILE OTHERS ARE SPEAKING.

It is important to learn how to be a good listener. Having a classroom of students who are respectful to others and are not disrupting the classroom will promote a more successful learning environment.

Listen—*To give attention to someone or something in order to hear them.*

The following are some examples of different ways to learn how to listen:

- Conduct classroom activities that involve listening and respecting others while speaking. Games such as "Telephone" reinforce listening skills.
- Ask the students to repeat what the speaker has said and comment on what they heard.
- Teach the students to be respectful to others and understand that what others say is important.
- Initiate classroom policies to have students raise their hands or sit quietly and wait to be called on. Do not acknowledge students who are disrespectful to others.
- Realize that sometimes students who act out are doing so to receive attention, not just positive attention. This type of behavior may need to be addressed separately.
- Encourage activities where students stand in front of the room and speak to the class. This will enable students to feel important and understand the feelings others have when they are in the front of the room.
- Encourage positive feedback.

RULE 4: OBEY ALL SCHOOL RULES.

Establishing your classroom rules, settings and procedures early in the school year, is a time-saving strategy that sets routines that are helpful for teachers and students. This will help students focus on the work ahead and creates a less-stressful, peaceful environment. Setting acceptable procedures in the classroom helps students to understand what is expected of them right from the start.

Obey—*To act according to what you have been asked order to do by someone in authority; to behave according to a role law or instruction.*

Rule—*An accepted principle or instruction that states the way things are or should be done, and tells you what you are allowed or are not allowed to do.*

Behavior—*To act in a particular way or to be good by acting in a way society approves.*

Responsibility—*Having good judgment and the ability to act correctly and make decisions on your own.*

- Classroom rules can be discussed and decided on by both the teachers and students giving everyone a hand in understanding and following procedures.
- Rules and regulations should be well defined and easily understood by everyone in the classroom. This will result in less confusion and a well-managed classroom.
- Rules and regulations are followed by everyone (special circumstances and disabilities may need to be considered). Students should understand that they need to take responsibility for all of their actions.

- Classroom rules can be posted in the classroom for all to see, to read and to remember.
- Warnings for the misbehavior can be issued while learning rules for a limited timeframe to allow all an adjustment period.
- Consequences for students who break the rules should be well defined before the incident occurs. This will allow all students to understand the consequences they face when they break a rule.
- Good behavior should be acknowledged and rewarded. Positive reinforcement is a powerful tool that gives students self-esteem and pride in themselves. Physical rewards such as stickers, snacks and small toys can be used, but in limited quantity.
- All rules will apply inside and outside of the classroom and on school property.
- All procedures will be followed in the classroom when the teacher is absent and a substitute teacher is in the room.
- All parents should be aware of the rules in case they are called in to discuss a child's actions and/or behavior. This can be done in the form of a note from the teacher, information from administration, or a classroom handbook. Parents may be asked to sign a form saying that they read and understand classroom procedures and will abide by them. Any questions should be directed to the teacher or administration.

Appendix: Classroom Arrangement

There are many important ideas to discuss on classroom arrangement. Furniture, equipment, supplies, ventilation, safety, and spatial issues are top concerns. All items that are used in any classroom should be sturdy, nontoxic, easily movable, well made with no sharp edges or visible sharp hardware, and child sized for children (K–2).

Furniture

- All storage furniture should be easily washable and removable to enable teachers to rid the classroom of germs, unwanted marks, labels or stickers.
- Any furniture that is easy to tip over should be safely secured to walls. This includes bookcases, large cabinets and storage bins.
- Children should have a place to be able to store their belongings, such as a cubby, hooks to hang jackets or sweaters, or cabinets that are easily accessible and extremely durable.
- Desks should have a washable, smooth writing surface and enough inside storage for books and all other necessary materials required by the teacher.

Equipment

All equipment in the classroom should be:

- Easily storable when not in use.
- Easily accessible to children at all times without the help of the teacher (Rulers, pencils, crayons, markers, erasers and paper).
- Safety equipment should be readily available (Eye protection for science, smocks for art).
- Sports or recess equipment should be well maintained to prevent injury.

Supplies

All school supplies to be used by children should be high-quality, safe, nontoxic products. It is usually a better idea to go with name brand products instead of generic; they usually last longer and are of better quality.

Many schools require the children to bring in their own products for classroom use. These children are usually given a list prior to the school's start of what is required by each specific teacher.

Classroom Ventilation

All rooms in the school including classrooms, bathrooms, libraries, cafeteria, gymnasium, offices and resource rooms should be properly ventilated with windows, fans, heat or central ventilation systems. This will enable the children to receive proper ventilation throughout the school year. Children who are overheated, cold, or in a room with no ventilation will not perform at their best and may become ill. If at any time a child becomes ill from poor classroom ventilation, please report the problem to the administration immediately.

Be advised when using the following items, that they may have strong or toxic odors:

- Dry erase markers
- Permanent markers
- Paints
- Play dough
- Glue/paste
- Chemicals used in science laboratories
- Cleaners and deodorizers

Safety

Although there are many safety issues to be considered in a classroom environment, the following will only touch on safety in classroom arrangement.

- Keep all walkways clear and free of debris.
- Anchor all heavy furniture items to the wall.
- Do not overload bookcases and storage units.
- Do not block doorways or windows.
- Make sure heating systems are not blocked or covered.
- Use nonslip pads under rugs if floors are heavily waxed.
- Do not overload electrical outlets.
- Allow each child clear, unobstructed access to his or her chair and desk.
- Hold frequent fire drills so children are comfortable with this procedure and are prepared in an emergency.

Other Classroom Arrangement Ideas

Each teacher has their own classroom arrangement that is comfortable to them. Listed are some ideas on how to use classroom space effectively.

- Become inspired, think creatively. Steer away from the traditional alphabetical order seating.
- Allow students to sit in clusters of four or five when doing small-group instruction.
- When teaching unit lessons, maintain the same seating, as some students learn better from association. (Students remember where they were when they learned a specific lesson.)
- Decorate the classroom with student's artwork instead of teacher oriented items. This will give the children a feeling of satisfaction and pride in their classroom.
- Arrange the classroom in a way that shows *your philosophy on teaching* environment.

- Arrange the desks to provide clear and safe traffic patterns.
- Keep active areas separate from quiet areas to avoid distraction. Locate the teacher's desk in the area that enables the teacher to monitor all areas of the classroom with no blind spots.
- Use nonskid mats under carpets and rugs on slippery surfaces to avoid injury.
- Arrange a room on graph paper before physically moving furniture. This will save time, energy and muscle power.
- As a teacher, sit in a student's desk to get their eye view of the classroom arrangement. Rearrange anything that is distracting or intrusive to the learning process.

Early connections add these ideas:

- If computers are in the classroom, place them in areas that encourage their integration in class activities. Allow computers to be visible to all.
- Avoid areas with food, liquid or chalk dust as these can be harmful to the computer.
- Make sure all wires to computers are safely secured.
- Arrange classroom to avoid glare from the sun through windows.
- Providing areas where two or three students can work together in a comfortable, spacious area.

Other ideas to consider:

- In younger classrooms provide a carpeted area for comfortable silent reading or game-playing activities.
- Arrange the desks in a large U-shaped area where everyone is visible to everyone else. The center of the U can be used for class speakers, oral presentations or dancing.
- Arrange the classroom so genders are not separated or secluded.
- Allow the students easy accessibility to all supplies in the classroom.
- Arrange a quiet area for one-on-one, student–teacher conversation.

Classroom Arrangement

Each teacher has their own classroom arrangement that is comfortable to them. Listed are some ideas on how to use classroom space effectively.

- Peak learning system advises (http;//www.peaklearn.com)
- Become inspired, think creatively. Steer away from the traditional alphabetical order seating.
- When working on different lessons, arrange desks in different ways for use by the children.

Behavior Description Sheet I

____ Disrespect
____ Talking during a lesson
____ Talking out of turn
____ Throwing objects in class
____ Touching or hitting
____ Not returning a behavior sheet
____ Disrupting class
____ Inappropriately out of seat
____ Enter/leave classroom noisily
____ Inappropriate hallway behavior
____ Other

1. Describe the nature of the situation or problem.

____
____
____

2. Why did you choose this behavior?

____
____
____

3. How did your behavior affect others?

____
____
____

4. What will happen if you continue to act this way?

____
____
____

5. Let's solve the problem. What can we do to reach a solution we can both live with?

____
____
____
____
____

Student's signature: ______________________ Date: ____________

Teacher signature: ______________________ Date: ____________

Parent signature: ______________________ Date: ____________

Behavior Description Sheet II

Teacher's name: ______________________________ Date: __________________________

Student's name: ____

Place: ____

The following rule(s) has not been followed:

____ Show respect to others in all areas
____ Be prepared for all classes (includes assignments, books, folders, homework planners, notebooks, pencils, pens and paper.)
____ All work must be completed according to directions and handed in on time.
____ Candy and gum are prohibited during class time.
____ Show respect for learning. (Be quiet in class and halls, raise hand to speak, be an attentive listener)
____ Other: ____

Teacher's signature: ____

Student's signature: ____

Parent's signature: ____

Explanation (Teacher):

____
____
____
____
____

Explanation (Student):

____
____
____
____
____

Response (Parent):

____
____
____
____
____

Chapter 11:

Student Rights

Chapter Topics:

The Bill of Rights	Grades and Discipline
Teacher, Student and the Constitution	Schools Look at Lockers, Shirts, Etc.
Amendments	Flag Salute
Dress Codes	Dress and Grooming
Parameters for Student's Rights	Student Publications
Prechapter Exercises	Freedom of Association
Major U.S. Supreme Court Decisions	Participation in Extracurricular Activities
Suspensions and Expulsions	Pregnant Students
Zero Tolerance	Dissection Issues
Handicapped Children Act	Religion
IDEA-2004	Community Service
Discipline and IDEA	

The Bill of Rights

The Bill of Rights offers a wonderful vehicle for the educational institutions to help students understand and respect what living in a democracy means. But too often, students fail to grasp the nuances of the Constitution. They may have cursory (basic) knowledge of the document, but no working definition of its powers. Or if they do, it may be a gross generalization of its application. The courts have balanced the need for the schools to conduct classes in a safe and orderly fashion, yet still granting that students have constitutional rights. Schools are expected to administer with fairness and reasonableness.

This chapter offers a series of significant court cases illustrative of potential conflicts along with parameters for maintaining student rights. However, a cautionary word: ***You have no rights unless you and your supporters are willing to preserve those rights.***

The Teacher, the Student, and the Constitution

Selected provisions of the U.S. Constitution

Amendment I

Congress shall make no law respecting an establishment of religion, or prohibiting the free exercise thereof, or abridging the freedom of speech, or of the press; or the right of the people peaceably to assemble, and to petition the Government for a redress of grievances.

Amendment IV

The right of the people to be secure in their persons, houses, papers, and effects, against unreasonable searches and seizures, shall not be violated, and no Warrants shall issue, but upon probable cause, supported by Oath or affirmation, and particularly describing the place to be searched, and the persons or things to be seized.

Amendment V

No person shall be held to answer for a capital, or otherwise infamous crime, unless on a presentment or indictment of a Grand Jury, except in cases arising in the land or naval forces, or in the Militia, when in actual service, in time of war or public danger; nor shall any person be subject for the same offense to be twice put in jeopardy of life and limb; nor shall be compelled in any criminal case to be a witness against himself, nor be deprived of life, liberty, or property, without due process of law; nor shall private property be taken for public use, without just compensation.

Amendment IX

The enumeration in the Constitution, of certain rights, shall not be construed to deny or disparage others retained by the people.

Amendment X

The powers not delegated to the United States by the Constitution, nor prohibited by it to the States, are reserved to the States respectively, or to the people.

Amendment XIV

Section 1—All persons born or naturalized in the United States, and subject to the jurisdiction thereof, are citizens of the United States and of the state wherein they reside. No State shall make or enforce any law which shall abridge the privileges or immunities of citizens of the United States; nor shall any State deprive any person of life, liberty, or property, without due process of law; nor deny to any person within its jurisdiction the equal protection of the laws.

Exercise:

Under what conditions may schools suspend your right of freedom of expression?

Dress Codes and a Student's Right to Free Speech

"So who was Jefferson Davis?" the reporter asked.

He was talking with Jane Doe, an 11th grader from a high school, who was home Tuesday, suspended from the high school for wearing a Confederate flag T-shirt.

"I've heard the name," she says, "but I am not sure."
Silence. OK. Tough question. Let's move on.
"General Ulysses Grant: Did he fight for the North or for the South?"
"The South," she says.
"General William Sherman?"
"I am not sure," she says.
"What happened at Gettysburg?"
"I'll have to read about that."
"What happened at the Appomattox Court House, Virginia?"
"I do not know about it," she says.

Doe contended she wore Confederate T-shirts to school to celebrate her heritage, not to offend people.

"It is about the Civil War and stuff," she says. "It's like the South, and the Southern heritage."

Is it possible to honor a heritage, even if one is extremely fuzzy on the details?

The vice principal at the high school said the decision to suspend Jane for wearing the T-shirt had more to do with avoiding unnecessary rumbles in school than censoring or modifying student opinions.

"Somebody asked me what I would do if a student showed up with a picture of Robert E. Lee or Jefferson Davis on a T-shirt," the vice principal said. "And I said that would be fine. I would do nothing. Nobody would know who they were."
"Only articles of clothing that could be disruptive or cause a safety problem at school would be banned on campus."
"It is all about students saying. 'You can't tell me what to wear,'" the vice principal said. "That is the bottom line."

Exercise:

List three issues surrounding this case.

1. ______________________________
2. ______________________________
3. ______________________________

General Parameters for Student Rights

The following are reasonable guidelines to consider prior to taking any action that may deprive students of their basic constitutional rights.

1. The school may restrict/prohibit rights when there is evidence of:
    - Indecent or offensive speech
    - Destruction of school property
    - Disregard for school authority
    - Material and substantial destruction of school order
2. Due process must be given in all cases when rights are denied (may be removed from school property immediately if there is a danger to oneself or others, rights issued at a later date).
3. All rules, regulations and policies must conform to standards that do not violate constitutional law.
4. Banning of clothing, cell phones, etc., only after sufficient evidence of disruption, improper use or distraction occurs.
5. The school has a legal obligation to maintain and protect the ***health, safety*** and ***welfare*** of all students.

Examples of various court rulings include the following:

- Pregnant and married students have the same rights as all other students attending public schools and may not be prohibited from attending.
- Harassment, if so severe, pervasive and objectively offensive that it denies the student equal educational opportunity. It is against the law.
- If corporal punishment is allowed (state law), it must not be inflicted with such force as to be considered ***malicious, excessively cruel*** or ***unusual***.
- Rules and policies pertaining to punishment should be published and disseminated to parents and students.
- School searches may be conducted by school officials if there is reasonable suspicion. When outside agencies are brought in, probable cause ***must*** be established.
- Dressing and grooming codes are generally supported by the courts if they are reasonable.
- Materials such as school newspapers and magazines may be reviewed by school officials, but not subject to broad censorship. Evidence must be given as proof that the distribution or content will create a material and substantial disruption.
- Students may protest and demonstrate as long as it does not disrupt an orderly and peaceful learning environment.
- Freedom of expression rights cannot be banned simply because it causes discomfort.
- Metal detectors and surveillance cameras may be used when there is evidence of a serious threat to the student body.
- Arbitrary searches of persons and places are ***illegal*** if not justified as reasonable.

Prechapter Exercise:

For each item clarify your choice. **Y = Yes N = No U = Undecided**
CR = Conditions or Reasons

As a student in a public school you can:

______ 1. Participate in religious activities on school property.
CR: ______________________________
______ 2. Wear religious related clothing to school.
CR: ______________________________
______ 3. Abstain from certain curricular activities based on religious or philosophical beliefs.
CR: ______________________________
______ 4. Study religion as part of the curriculum.
CR: ______________________________
______ 5. Unilaterally express your opinion on controversial issues in the classroom or on school property.
CR: ______________________________
______ 6. Use obscene gestures and language when expressing opinions.
CR: ______________________________
______ 7. Wear clothing that is expressive but not distracting or that can cause disruption.
CR: ______________________________
______ 8. Wear open-toed shoes, clogs, spike heels, taps or shoe points.
CR: ______________________________
______ 9. Wear clothing that is a representative style of celebrities (Michael Jackson).
CR: ______________________________
______ 10. Wear pink hair, Mohawk haircut or a shaved head.
CR: ______________________________
______ 11. Participate in extracurricular activities.
CR: ______________________________
______ 12. Date a teacher in your school.
CR: ______________________________
______ 13. Attend school as a married student.
CR: ______________________________
______ 14. Attend school as an unwed mother.
CR: ______________________________
______ 15. Attend school as a pregnant married woman.
CR: ______________________________
______ 16. Belong to an honor society and be pregnant or have had an abortion.
CR: ______________________________
______ 17. Play sports on the opposite-sex team.
CR: ______________________________
______ 18. Have the right to see school records.
CR: ______________________________

_____ 19. Write to the school paper on a controversial issue.
CR: ____

_____ 20. Not be suspended or expelled if you are handicapped.
CR: ____

_____ 21. Not have your locker or desk searched without your permission.
CR: ____

_____ 22. Refuse to stand or salute the flag.
CR: ____

_____ 23. Belong to a secret fraternity, sorority or club formed by school students.
CR: ____

_____ 24. Distribute an underground newspaper on school property.
CR: ____

_____ 25. Be stopped from displays of affection.
CR: ____

_____ 26. Be banned from attending graduation ceremonies for not agreeing to wear proper attire.
CR: ____

_____ 27. Be withheld from receiving your diploma for disciplinary reasons, even though you completed all requirements.
CR: ____

_____ 28. Be filmed by surveillance cameras to prevent damage of school property and drug use by students.
CR: ____

_____ 29. Be banned from attending school if you're a divorced teenager who has not completed your graduation requirements.
CR: ____

_____ 30. Play punk rock as part of a school band.
CR: ____

_____ 31. Wear very tight-fitting clothes when running track and field.
CR: ____

_____ 32. Refuse to dissect a frog, cat or other animal.
CR: ____

_____ 33. Bow your head in silent prayer.
CR: ____

_____ 34. Use obscene gestures in a speech class.
CR: ____

Major U.S. Supreme Court Decisions Reflecting Student Rights

The ***Brown v. Board of Education*** of Topeka, Kansas case in 1954 became the landmark decision in addressing segregation, but it also raised additional concerns about students' constitutional rights. The issue of segregation of public schools had been raised several times in the courts over the years, but the plaintiffs had lost based on the precedent of "***separate but equal***" established in the ***Plessy v. Ferguson*** case in 1896. The Supreme Court ruled that separate facilities and services were constitutional and did not violate the Equal Protection Clause of the Fourteenth Amendment. It is interesting to note that the case referred to transportation, not public education.

Brown et al. v. Board of Education of Topeka; ***Briggs et al. v. Elliott et al.***; ***Davis v. County School Board of Prince Edward County***, Virginia et al. (Summary). Class actions originating in the four states of Kansas, South Carolina, Virginia and Delaware, by which minor Negro plaintiffs sought to obtain admission to public schools on a nonsegregated basis. On direct appeals by plaintiffs from adverse decisions in the United States District Courts, District of Kansas, Eastern District of South Carolina, and Eastern District of Virginia, and on grant of certiorari after decision favorable to plaintiffs in the Supreme Court of Delaware, the U.S. Supreme Court, Mr. Chief Justice Warren, held that ***segregation of children in public schools solely on the basis of race, even though the physical facilities and other tangible factors may be equal,*** deprives the children of the minority group of equal educational opportunities, in contravention of the Equal Protection Clause of the Fourteenth Amendment.

Segregation of white and colored children in public schools has a detrimental effect on the colored children. The impact is greater when it has the sanction of the law; for the policy of segregating the races is usually interpreted as denoting the inferiority of the Negro group. A sense of inferiority affects the motivation of a child to learn. Segregation with the sanction of law, therefore, has a tendency to retard the educational and mental development of Negro children and to deprive them of some of the benefits they would receive in a racially integrated school system.

Interpretation:

The case was won on the issue of the Fourteenth Amendment (Equal Protection Act). Prior to this juncture, the courts agreed that the amendment did not apply to public schools, but Chief Justice Warren stated that the Fourteenth Amendment must be considered in light of current facts and conditions and not those of 1896 when the amendment was adopted. In essence, the court looked on the Constitution as a "***living document***" and not one that is fixed and closed to new interpretation.

Busing as an attempt to achieve desegregation is based on ***Brown vs. the Board of Education*** (1954) and subsequent cases.

- In several cases the Supreme Court ruled that segregation caused by locality violates constitutional rights. The Supreme Court gives power to district courts to uphold desegregation efforts should school districts fail to devise effective remedies. With the Denver case, minority students included black and Hispanic populations.
- Plans for busing are an attempt to desegregate school districts. Students may be required to attend schools outside their neighborhood or in nonadjoining zones to achieve desegregation. Other provisions include constitutionally ordered teacher assignment to achieve faculty desegregation. School construction and abandonment patterns may not

perpetuate or reestablish a dual system. Racial quotas used by the court are acceptable when devising a desegregation plan. Once desegregation is achieved, the school boards will ***not*** be required to make yearly adjustments in the racial composition of the student body.

- In 1991 in a 5 to 3 holding, the Supreme Curt ruled that desegregation decrees are not intended to remain in effect in perpetuity. If the board of education made a significant showing of constitutional compliance, the district court should decide whether the district has complied in good faith with the desegregation decree and whether the vestiges of past de jure desegregation had been eliminated to the extent practical.

Exercise:

Define these key terms and phrases:

Segregation:

Desegregation:

Separate but equal:

De facto: simple existence:

De jure: by law:

Busing:

1. ***Does desegregation serve the purpose of providing equalized education? (Placing minority students within a majority population.)***

2. ***In California, recent census reports revealed the majority is now the Hispanic population and the previous majority Caucasian population has fallen below that level. What are your thoughts on this matter?***

Tinker vs. Des Moines

The *Tinker* and the *Goss* decisions were also significant in securing constitutional rights of students. Prior to these two decisions, schools operated in a very conservative manner under ***"in loco parentis"*** (in place of parent) regarding students rights. Resulting from these actions was the knowledge that students had not left their constitutional rights on the "***doorstep***" when they entered school—that they did have freedom of speech and due process. However, the court decisions also demonstrates that rights are not absolute, but are governed or tempered by the schools' responsibility to go about their business in a safe and orderly fashion.

John F. Tinker and Mary Beth Tinker, Minors v. Des Moines Independent Community School District (Summary)

Action against the school district, its board of directors and certain administrative officials and teachers to recover nominal damages and obtain an injunction against enforcement of a regulation promulgated by principals of schools prohibiting the wearing of black armbands by students while on school facilities. The U.S. Supreme Court, Mr. Justice Fortas, held that, in absence of demonstration of any facts that might reasonably have led school authorities to forecast substantial disruption of, or material interference with, school activities or any showing that disturbances or disorders on school premises in fact occurred when students wore black armbands on their sleeves to exhibit their disapproval of Vietnam hostilities, regulation prohibiting wearing armbands to school and providing for suspension of any student refusing to remove such was an ***unconstitutional denial of students' rights of expression of opinion.***

Interpretation:

In December 1965, a group of students wanted to protest and publicize their opposition to the war in Vietnam and support for a truce by wearing black armbands during the holiday season and by fasting on December 16 and New Year's Eve.

When the school officials became aware of these actions, they adopted a policy that any students wearing armbands to school would be suspended if they refused to take them off. Students were allowed to wear political and symbolic statements, including the Iron Cross. ***The order was specifically aimed at the wearing of armbands in protest of the Vietnam War.***

The court stated that unless the "***speech***" was "***materially and substantially***" interfering with school operation, the students were entitled to freedom of expression. School officials did not possess absolute authority over their students, and students, in school or out, are persons under the Constitution.

Exercise:

How many limitations may be placed on freedom of speech?

Norvall Goss et al. vs. Eileen Lopez et al. (Summary)

An Ohio statute empowered the principal of an Ohio public school to suspend a student for misconduct for up to 10 days or to expel him; in either case, the principal must notify the students' parents within 24 hours and state the reasons for his action. In the class action brought by Ohio Southern District of Ohio, the named plaintiffs alleged that they had been suspended from public high school in Columbus, Ohio, for up to 10 days without a hearing; the action was brought against the Columbus Board of Education and various administrators of the school system for deprivation of constitutional rights. The complaint sought a declaration that the statue was unconstitutional in that it permitted public school administrators to deprive plaintiffs of their rights to an education without a hearing of any kind, in violation of the procedural due process clause of the Fourteenth Amendment, and also sought to enjoin the public school officials from issuing further suspension pursuant to the statute and to require them to remove references to the past suspensions from the records of the students in question. A three-judge District Court granted the relief sought by plaintiffs.

On direct appeal, the U.S. Supreme Court affirmed. In an opinion by Justice White expressing the view of five members of the court, it was held that the Ohio statue, in so far as it permitted up to 10 days suspension without notice or hearing, either before or after the suspension, violated the due process clause and that each suspension was therefore invalid.

Interpretation:

Two students, Lopez and Crone, at Central High School and McGuffey Junior High, were suspended without a hearing. Lopez was a bystander when a disturbance took place in the lunchroom, and property damage occurred. He and 75 other students were suspended.

At the different school, Crone was at a demonstration and was arrested, not formally charged, and then was released. Prior to school the next day, she was notified that she had been suspended for 10 days.

There is no indication or evidence that a hearing was held in either case.

The Fourteenth Amendment forbids the state to deprive any person of life, liberty or property without due process of law. The students' right to an education is viewed as "***property***," and the possible damage to one's good name, reputation, honor or integrity is an arbitrary deprivation of liberty.

The Court ruled that students must be protected from the arbitrary removal from school and allowed the minimum due process.

For ***short-term*** suspensions of 10 days or less, a student must be given oral or written notice of charges against him or her, an explanation of evidence, and the opportunity to respond if he or she denies the charges.

For suspensions of more than 10 days or expulsion, a formal hearing is required, including:

- Notification of charges against him or her
- Names of adverse witnesses
- Copies of statements and affidavits of such witnesses
- The opportunity to testify
- The opportunity to present witnesses and evidence in defense
- The opportunity to cross-examine adverse witnesses
- The opportunity to be represented by counsel

When a student possesses a danger to persons or property, or when he or she presents an ongoing threat or destruction of the academic process, he or she can be removed immediately and given a hearing when practical.

Exercise:

Why are students given a "cursory" hearing in suspension of 10 days or less?

____

____

____

____

Suspensions and Expulsions

Definition: ***Suspension refers to the temporary denial of a student's right to attend school.***

New Jersey statutes provide for education to any person over 5 and under 21 years of age. They also require compulsory education for children between the ages of 6 and 16.

Exercise:

List reasons for suspension at your previous high school:

1. ______________________________
2. ______________________________
3. ______________________________

Explain why suspensions are necessary to school life.

____
____
____
____

Describe or explain what your view of "in-school suspension" would be.

____
____
____
____

Definition: ***Expulsion refers to the permanent denial of the student's right to attend school.***

The New York City Board of Education's new policy requires the expulsion of students for certain violations of school safety rules and allows local school superintendents the discretion to oust students for other violations.

Expulsion is mandatory for these actions:

- Bringing a gun to school.
- Injuring someone with any other weapon, including a knife, razor, switchblade, box cutter, billy club, bomb, or baseball bat.

Expulsion is at the superintendent's discretion in these cases:

- Possession or use of a controlled substance, such as a tranquilizer or a narcotic without a doctor's authorization.
- Engaging in intimidation, coercion or extortion.
- Engaging in physical sexual aggression.
- Behavior that creates a substantial risk of injury or results in injuries, such as starting a riot or committing arson.
- Possession, use or sale of illegal drugs or alcohol.

- Possession of a weapon, such as a knife, razor, switchblade, box cutter, billy club, bomb, or baseball bat.
- Using force or trying to injure school personnel or students.

First grader uses a gun to threaten teacher

A first grader has been expelled from school until next fall for firing a handgun on school grounds and threatening to shoot a teacher who scolded him.

No injuries resulted from the shooting by the unidentified six-year-old boy, which occurred outside the cafeteria of the school in a town about 50 miles south of Jacksonville.

During a field trip later that day, the teachers scolded the boy for misbehaving and he threatened to shoot her, the authorities said. It was then that the teacher found the gun in the boy's jacket and learned that he had earlier fired it into the ground outside the school.

The boy's parents told school officials that the child had apparently got the gun by stacking stereo speakers and furniture to reach atop a 7 ft. cabinet. He found bullets elsewhere and loaded the gun himself, they said.

On Tuesday, the school board ordered that the boy be tutored for the rest of the school year and undergo a psychological evaluation before returning the next fall.

His parents said school officials had rejected their earlier request that the child receive a psychological evaluation, saying his behavior was not severe enough.

Exercise:

Were the parents responsible? Why or why not?

Zero Tolerance

Many schools across the United States have begun to initiate a "***zero-tolerance***" policy in relation to the use of drugs, threats and weapons.

Exercise:

1. Define "Zero Tolerance":

2. List events or reasons that have caused this dramatic shift in policy.

Girl may be expelled for nail-clipper knife

Administrators yesterday recommended the expulsion of a 15-year-old girl for taking to school a nail-clipper with the 2 in. knife. The sophomore said she thought the attachment was for cleaning fingernails.

A panel of other principals sided with the principal, who wants her expelled for a year under a zero-tolerance policy on weapons.

Arrest of girl, 5, was a way to get her help, the school says

A five-year-old girl was booked, fingerprinted and questioned in county jail on allegations that she assaulted a 51-year-old school counselor. Her parents were shocked to know that they even took her mug shot. The girl who is average size and weight for a kindergartner has a history of "out of control" rages. The officials said that they asked for a warrant as a way to get the girl help. This is not the only recent case. A 6-year-old was arrested and taken in handcuffs from his kindergarten class after he was charged with battery on school workers and a sheriff's deputy. The boy was sentenced to stay at home until the charges are resolved.

Six students suspended over Web site threats

Six eighth graders were suspended for posting threatening statements on a Web site against fellow middle school students, the school superintendent said yesterday.

The six are believed to be the only ones responsible for the site, which police began investigating last week, the superintendent said.

Four of the students received 10-day suspensions, two got 5-day suspensions and thus can return to school today. A county prosecutor said yesterday that no charges have been filed, but the investigation was continuing.

Exercise:

How has the use of computers in both home and school affected the teaching/learning process?

Positive:

It is easy to access information

Negative:

A variety of "adult" materials are available

Notes:

Flag-covered Cannon Ends Yearbook Dispute

A school has decided to allow a senior to pose in the yearbook perched on a cannon, as long as the barrel is draped by the American flag.

The compromise was reached, ending a month-long battle over the photograph of the student. The administrator of the school had rejected the photograph because it violated their "zero-tolerance" policy on weapons.

School policy prohibits images of guns, knives or other weapons on shirts, hats or in pictures. More than 100 students walked out of the class on November 3 to protest the ban on the photograph, leading to 50 suspensions. The new photograph, taken outside a Veterans of Foreign Wars post, shows the student atop 155-mm howitzer with a flat covering the barrel.

The student enlisted in the army earlier this year.

"It is basically the same picture, she is still wearing her Army shirt," said her mother. "My daughter got what she wanted. I am glad that it is over."

Public Law 94-142

Prior to Public Law 94-142, two important court decisions set the stage for this law's enactment. The first was ***Mills v. Board of Education,*** 1972 in Washington, DC. The school system suspended and expelled handicapped children as a practice. Nearly 22,000 more were classified, and 18,000 of those were not given programs aiding their special education needs. The school system pleaded not enough funds, which the court rejected, forcing the system to address the needs of the handicapped.

The second case, ***PAAC v. Commonwealth of Pennsylvania***, 1972, dealt with the practice of excluding children who were certified by a psychologist as "uneducable and untrainable."

PAAC sued on the following basis.

Fourteenth Amendment

- The action violated due process—notice for hearing was not given to parents.
- Denied equal protection under the assumption that the children were uneducable without rational basis of fact.
- The Pennsylvania State Constitution provides for education for all children.

The findings for the plaintiff in the preceding cases led the way for the Public Law 94-142.

The Education for all Handicapped Children Act of 1975 (Public Law 94-142)

The Congress finds that:

1. There are more than 8 million handicapped children in the United States today.
2. The special education needs of such children are not being fully met.
3. More than half of the handicapped children in the United States do not receive appropriate educational services which would enable them to have full equality of opportunity.

4. One million of the handicapped children in the United States are excluded entirely from the public school system and will not go through the educational process with their peers.
5. There are many handicapped children throughout the United States participating in regular school programs whose handicap prevent them from having a successful educational experience because their handicaps are undetected.
6. Because of the lack of adequate services within the public school system, families are often forced to find services outside the public school system, often at great distance from their residence and at their own expense.
7. Developments in the training of teachers and in diagnostic and instructional procedures and methods have advanced to the point that, given appropriate funding, state and local educational agencies can and will provide effective special education and related services to meet the needs of handicapped children.
8. State and local educational agencies have a responsibility to provide education for all handicapped children, but present financial resources are inadequate to meet the special educational needs of handicapped children.
9. It is in the national interest that the federal government passes state and local efforts to provide programs to meet the educational needs of handicapped children in order to assure equal protection of the law.

It is the purpose of this act to ensure that all handicapped children have available to them, within that time period specified in section 612(2) (B), a free appropriate public education that emphasizes special education and related services designed to meet their unique needs, to ensure that the rights of handicapped children and their parents or guardians are protected, to assist states and localities to provide for the education of all handicapped children, and to assess and ensure effectiveness of efforts to educate handicapped children.

121A.5 Handicapped Children

As used in this part, the term "***handicapped children***" means those children evaluated in accordance with 121a.530-121a.534 as being mentally retarded, hard of hearing, deaf, speech impaired, visually handicapped, seriously or emotionally disturbed, orthopedically impaired, other impaired, deaf-blind, multihandicapped or as having specific learning disabilities, who because of those impairments need special education and related services.

IDEA-2004

Individuals with Disabilities Education Improvement Act

Since the inception of Public Law 94-142, there have been several interpretations of its meaning and intent. From additional court cases, IDEA-2004 was created to ensure a continuity of response by school systems.

Some key aspects of the act are:

- **Equal protection**: All children, regardless of handicap, are entitled to a free appropriate education. States must provide the same rights and benefits to students who are classified as to those without disability.

- **Least Restrictive Environment:** Education is delivered in settings that best meet the needs of the students in as close to the normal education setting as possible.

- **Parent Consent:** Written permission is needed for all testing, evaluation and change in status/services.

- **Individualized Education Program (IEP):** An IEP is to be developed for each student with a disability and include:
  a. current levels of performance
  b. annual goals
  c. extent and participation in general education programs
  d. beginning dates and anticipated duration of service
  e. evaluation methods

  Participants in IEP planning are to include at least one special and general educator, a representative of the local education agency, ***an evaluation specialist, related-service specialist*** and ***parents.***

Discipline and IDEA

There are no provisions in the **IDEA** that specifically referred to discipline. Even so, discipline sanctions that are applied to students with disabilities are sometimes the source of litigation.

- The Supreme Court ruled that special education students cannot be expelled for disciplinary reasons if their misconduct is a manifestation of their disability. However, special education students may be temporarily suspended and are subject to other normal disciplinary sanctions.

- If expelled for reasons other than their disability, students do not give up their right to an education.

- The **IDEA** is not designed to protect disruptive students and as such the student must demonstrate that educators reasonably knew of the disability prior to disciplinary actions.

Disabled Girl Loses Fight on Prom

A judge ruled against a 15-year-old mentally handicapped girl who sued school officials for barring her from the high school prom because she isn't in the ninth grade. The eighth grader had claimed the district's requirements that students attending the prom at the high school be at least in the ninth grade was discriminatory.

She has a developmental handicap of borderline mental retardation and was held back to the first grade. Many students for her age are in the ninth grade.

But the United States District Court Judge said she was barred from the high school prom because of her grade level, not her disability. In his ruling, the judge said that she may attend dances for seventh and eighth graders and can go to the prom when she is in the ninth grade. He said there was no evidence the policy was adopted to discriminate against students with disabilities. The student said the decision was unfair.

"I'd just feel mad," she said. She was invited to the prom by her boyfriend, a junior. Her legal guardian also criticized the rule. "It is unfair to her," she said. "They take these handicapped kids and put their faces in the dirt, and that's where they keep them.

Grades and Discipline

In the past, grades have been used as a means to discipline students. The lowering of grades to punish student behavior, poor citizenship, or attitude was fairly common in educational circles. However, the courts have held that as a general rule, behavior and academics are to be treated separately. When it does become an issue, the burden of proof is on the student to demonstrate that the reason for lowering the grade was illegitimate and not related to the quality of work.

In New Jersey, the Commission has ruled that the board may impart penalties for unjustifiable tardiness, truancy and other unexplained absences, but may not penalize students who have been suspended by not allowing them the opportunity to make up missed work. In general, grades may not be used to serve disciplinary purposes.

Exercise:

Cite a personal educational experience where you felt your grade was lowered for disciplinary reasons (no names).

____

____

____

Oftentimes, diplomas have been withheld as punishment for violation of a school rule, but once again, the courts see the diploma and school rules as separate issues. The diploma is a symbol and recognition of academic achievement and not a reward for good behavior. Therefore, each should be treated according to established and legitimate criteria (e.g., discipline code, grading or policy).

Exercise:

Explain the difference between a right and a privilege.

Right:

____

____

Privilege:

____

____

Schools Look Hard at Lockers, Shirts, Bags and Manners

School searches

Although the Fourth Amendment to the U.S. Constitution protects individuals from unwarranted searches and seizures, it does allow for more leeway to school officers in conducting searches than it does to law enforcement officers. Operating under the "***in loco parentis***" powers, along with their responsibilities for "***duty to protect and care***" they have to the right to conduct searches and seize contraband on reasonable suspicion without judicial warrant.

In ***New Jersey vs. T.L.O.94 331***, the U.S. Supreme Court rejected the argument that school officials are prohibited from searches of students under the Fourth Amendment, and that searches may be held if there is reasonable suspicion—of infractions of rules. Justice White stated that the search is appropriate when a school official has reasonable grounds to suspect that the search will turn up evidence that the student is in violation of the law or school rules; and the search must be reasonably related to the circumstances that prompted the search.

The court also stated that the search must not be excessively intrusive in regard to the age and sex of the student and the nature of the infraction.

Twenty-three Strip Searched at School

Twenty-three third-graders were strip searched by a teacher and a crossing guard looking for about $20.00 that one student had reported stolen.

"The children were taken to separate closets and told to drop their pants," a Union County prosecutor said.

The woman crossing guard examined the girls while a male teacher examined the boys," he said.

"A tremendous error of judgment does not go into the criminal realm unless there is evidence of sexual gratification from touching," he said.

"An initial review by the State Division of Youth and Services found nothing of a sexual nature of or during the incident," he said.

Gun Found in Locker of a Fifth-grader

An 11-year-old student at an elementary school faces expulsion and was charged with weapons possession after a 0.380-caliber automatic handgun was found in his locker.

Neither police nor school officials would reveal how or where the fifth-grader obtained the weapon, stating yesterday that they could not comment on specifics while the incident remains under investigation.

The discovery of the weapon Tuesday in the locker was not released beyond the immediate community until a parent called the news media yesterday.

Exercise:

Describe either a search that took place at your school or circumstances under which a search could be conducted by a school official.

Flag Salute

"I pledge allegiance
to the flag
of the United States of America,
and to the Republic
for which it stands;
one nation, under God,
indivisible,
with liberty and justice for all."

The U.S. Supreme Court ruled in ***West Virginia Board of Education v. Barnette,*** 319 U.S. C24, 1943, that requiring students who have a conscientious objection to salute the flag is unconstitutional.

> "We think the actions of the local authorities in compelling the flag salute and pledge transcends constitutional limitations on their power…and invades the sphere of intellect and spirit which it is the purpose of the First Amendment to our Constitution to reserve from all official control."

The court considered freedom of religion to be a fundamental or preferred right versus an ***ordinary freedom.*** These freedoms can only be restricted if the government has a legitimate end and chooses reasonable means. The state must show a compelling need before a right is restricted.

In the State of New Jersey, all students must salute the U.S. flag, and repeat the pledge except those students who have "***conscientious scruples***" against the salute or pledge

(***Holden v. Elizabeth Board of Education***, 46 N. J. 281). Those students who object may sit quietly throughout the pledge.

Dress and Grooming

Pelletreau v. Board of Education, Borough of New Milford, 1967 S.L.D. 45. "It can hardly be disputed that school authorities are vested with the power to regulate student appearance in instances where it is, or threatens to become, so extreme as to be the obvious cause of indiscipline and destruction of the school program. Boards of education have a responsibility… to provide and maintain conditions under which learning can take place most effectively"

The *Pelletreau* ruling stated that a board may not act unreasonably or capriciously in adopting a dress code and may not promulgate a code designed to produce conformity among students, or which intends to impart its standards of good taste. Hair length and style can be regulated, but the guidelines must have a ***"legitimate purpose."***

The Commissioner of New Jersey also stated that participation in "***extracurricular activities***" must be open to all and selection be based on talent, and eligibility rules/limits not include hairstyle or length…unless it can be shown that such styles create disorder, present a clear danger to that student or fellow participants, or are detrimental to good health and hygiene. (***Harris, Sudra, Bromwell v. Board of Education, Township of Franklin City,*** 1970 S.L. D. 331). The courts in general have upheld dress codes as long as they are reasonable, clear and apply to maintaining discipline, order, safety and hygiene. In terms of hairstyling, "***grooming***," the courts are less restrictive in that a student may change clothes once they are away from school but it is more difficult to change hair at will.

Exercise:

Describe the dress code from your high school.

Explain or list reasons for having a dress code that is conservative or liberal.

School Says Hair Color is No Way to Wear Green

Two students were ousted from school for letting Saint Patrick's Day go to their heads. Fifth-graders showed up at an elementary school on Saint Patrick's Day with green hair and were sent home. A fourth-grade girl also was sent home for green streaks in her blond hair. Green is not a neutral color and it doesn't take much to distract a child from learning," said the principal of the school.

Girl changes lipstick, but it is not enough

A girl was turned away from school after she tried wearing purple lipstick to class. The school asked her to change her black lipstick, but did not agree with her new choice color. Her stepmother said the girl attempted suicide after the incident and had to be taken to a mental health facility. The parents felt the purple lipstick was a compromise but the school did not agree stating it still was a disturbing factor and did not represent a significant change in color.

School to rule on religious garb

A school that discouraged the wearing of satanic T-shirts is trying to decide whether to extend the policy to all religious messages.

That does not sit well with an eighth-grade student, whose wardrobe includes T-shirts with the slogans, "Pray Hard," "It's a God Thing" and "Jesus."

"I have been wearing these T-shirts since the sixth grade and nobody has said anything until now," she said.

The issue arose a couple of weeks ago when students who wore shirts with satanic themes were asked by school officials to leave them at home. Those students then asked that classmates not wear T-shirts with Christian sayings. The principal said she formed a panel of 13 students from all sides of the issue, plus a couple of administrators to study the issue.

Exercise:

What are the issues in the last article?

Rastafarian Garb OK'd

The parents of Rastafarian children have sued the school district from banning admission of their children based on their hair and clothing. School officials state dress code violations against ***"extreme"*** hairstyles and said that head coverings may conceal dangerous weapons.

A settlement was reached allowing the students to attend the school with their dreadlocks and their head coverings, which must match school uniform colors. The parties also agreed to allow the school to inspect the head coverings daily for contraband.

Exercise:

What is the compromise?

School May Ban Dixie Flag

A high school is considering banning students from wearing the Confederate flag on clothing after two white students were suspended for distributing racist jokes they found on the Internet, the superintendent of schools said.

About 15 of the 1,200 students at a high school had occasionally worn the Confederate flag on T-shirts and other clothes, said the district superintendent. He said students are entitled to free expression.

"However, if that thing is warn in conjunction with other acts or things... It raises it to another level where it becomes harassing and intimidating."

He said the suspensions last week were related to the Confederate flag.

Superior Court Test for Obscenity

- It must appeal to prurient or lustful interest of minors.
- It must describe sexual content in a way that is potentially offensive to community standards.
- Taken as a whole, it must lack serious literacy, artistic, political or scientific value.

Student Publications Return

The ***Tinker v. Des Moines*** Supreme Court decision reaffirmed and is the basis for much debate concerning the rights of students in both publication and distribution of literature and censorship. The courts have been consistent in ruling that schools do not have the authority to control student expressions that come under the aegis of the schools. (***Shanley v. Northeast Independent School District***, 462 F. 2nd 960 (5th circulation), 1972.

Mark Shanley and four classmates distributed an underground newspaper, ***Awakening***, that discussed subject matter such as drug laws and birth control. The paper did not use school resources and was distributed off school property before and after school hours. The paper caused no apparent school disruption, but was not published with school approval, as required by policy. The students were suspended.

Exercise:

Key points from the discussion were:

1. There is a significant difference between the freedom of speech of students in a public school and adults on a public street.

Why? ____

____

2. It is not necessarily unconstitutional to require materials for distribution to students to be reviewed by schools officials… as long as it does not interfere with the content of any publication in an unconstitutional manner and is not unreasonably onerous.

Why?____

3. Expression by students can be prohibited if it materially and substantially interferes with school functions or with rights of teachers, students or administrators.

What rights?____

4. Expression by students cannot be prohibited solely because other persons (students, parents or teachers) disagree with its content.

Explain :____

5. Expression by students may be subjected to prior screening under clear and reasonable regulations.

What might be a reasonable regulation? ____

Hazelwood School District v. Kuhlmeier

In the ***Hazelwood School District v. Kuhlmeier*** decision (484, U.S. 620) where a principal withheld material from the school newspaper (experiences with pregnancy and the impact of divorce on a student), the courts ruled in favor of the school. The court clarified its meaning of the scope of school experience activities.

Plays, newspapers, art exhibits may be considered part of the curriculum, regardless of where they occur in the school.

Schools can exercise editorial control for legitimate pedagogical reasons, articles that are ungrammatical, poorly written, prejudicial, vulgar or unsuitable for immature persons.

A school should be able to disassociate itself from students' speech that might be perceived to support drug use, unsafe sex, amoral behavior and the like.

Student speech or writing in school-sponsored activities allows for more school control than does students' personal speech (e.g., wearing armbands).

Burke

The ***Burke,*** 1970 S.L.P. 319, decision stated very explicitly that any policy that would restrict publication and circulation on school property to materials prepared under school sponsorship and supervision is an unlawful restraint on students' First Amendment rights.

Censorship of School Newspaper Opposed

Ms. S. got the telephone call within minutes of the United States Supreme Court's decision on free speech in a case involving a high school.

Could the principal of the Missouri school stop the student newspaper from printing a story about AIDS?

"If I had gotten the call 30 minutes earlier, I could have said, "No." As it was, I had to say, "Yes, the story could be censored," Ms. S. said. Now Ms. S. is on the board of directors of the National Student Press Law Center and is a journalism teacher in high school. Others are pushing for a bill that would help preserve that situation in New Jersey.

Ms. S. testified before the Assembly Education Committee yesterday on behalf of a bill (A557) that would guarantee students freedom of speech. The bill, which was held for further debate is sponsored by an assemblywoman and an assemblyman.

The bill calls for each school board in consultation with the newspaper staff and students to develop a code of publication guidelines. Only material that is "obscene, libelous or slanderous (or that) disrupts class work, involves substantial disorder or invades the rights of others, could be prohibited. Stories that are merely about controversial topics cannot be banned.

The bill applies to school publications, regardless of whether they are financially supported by the school, and also applies to such activities as wearing buttons or badges.

If the bill is passed, New Jersey would become the fourth state with such a law. A state can pass a law granting more rights than those detained by the Supreme Court, but cannot pass a law that is more restrictive than the Supreme Court allows.

Board considers restricting Chaucer tales

"The Canterbury Tales," that staple of English literature, is off limits to high school seniors during a debate over whether it's too raunchy for the classroom.

Parents and students have quietly complained that portions of Geoffrey Chaucer's fourteenth-century classic are too racy. As a result, a school board told the teachers to stop discussing the tales in their English classes while the board reviews the textbook.

The board principal says the issue is about education, not censorship.

Portions of *"The Canterbury Tales"* undoubtedly will be approved, he said, but the board must make sure sensitive material is handled appropriately.

Exercise:

What does "sensitive material is being handled appropriately" mean?

Student Sues for Censoring Articles

A 14-year-old student backed by the American Civil Liberties Union is suing his school district after administrators removed two of his movie reviews from a school newspaper because the film had R ratings.

The ACLU filed a lawsuit in Superior Court against officials at a high school for refusing to publish the student's reviews of *Mississippi Burning* and *Rain Man*. The suit contends the school violated the constitutional right of free speech and challenges a 1988 U.S. Supreme Court ruling on a case giving school officials broad censorship powers.

The suit asks the court to find that school officials acted arbitrarily and unreasonably in pulling the reviews. It also seeks an injunction requiring the school to publish the reviews in the next edition of the school paper, and provide legal fees.

"It is an important case because it will address the extent that administration can censor students," said the ACLU's legal director.

"The articles are not controversial."

ACLU officials said the suit was filed in superior court rather than in federal court because New Jersey has a liberal freedom of speech clause.

The boy, an eighth grader at the time, said he was shocked when school officials removed his reviews the day before the "Pioneer Press" was published.

"I was really surprised they would do anything like that," he said. "There was nothing offensive in the actual reviews. I hope that we win so that this won't happen anywhere again. We should not be judged by our age, but by our ideas and our own selves."

The boy's mother actually brought the suit on behalf of her youngest child, but she says he was the driving force behind the litigation.

"He was quite offended that the action was taken. He's always been an activist." The boy said he had not decided yet if he wants to become a journalist or a politician, but he said the legal battle will not discourage him from seeking a journalism career.

"I will probably be more drawn to it," he said.

Freedom of Association

In the ***Bradford v. Board of Education*** (Ct. App. Cal.1912) decision, otherwise known as the Mana Club decision, the courts upheld the right to bar secret fraternities in public schools.

The Mana Club was originally a secret society with handshakes, rituals and Greek letters, but after going public and eliminating the "***secrets,***" it was still not allowed to function, although its constitution stated objectives of literature, charity and democracy. Ultimately the court found that the club had a different purpose than what was in the stated objectives.

Secret organizations are prohibited when they:

- Derive their membership principally from public schools
- Use a selection process designed to create membership composed of the social elite
- Try to maintain class segregation and distinction by self-perpetuation, rushing, pledging, and admitting a select few of the total student body.

Every fraternity, sorority or secret society or organization that is composed in part or all of public school students and that seeks to organize itself by taking in student members on the basis of decision of the organization's membership rather than from the free choice of any students who are otherwise qualified to fill the special aims of the organization, has been disclosed by law to be "inimical" to the good of the school system and the democratic principles and ideals of public education in the public good (N.J.S.A.18A:42-6).

Court Orders Florida School to Allow Gay Student Group

A lesbian student, who, in the face of taunts and commendation, sued for the right to establish a gay-straight alliance at her school, received an early graduation gift yesterday: a federal judge ruled that the club can begin meeting on campus immediately.

"I am really happy," the senior said. "I do not know if it will end all of the harassment at school, but at least other students will have someone to talk to, which is something I did not have." She said she intends to call her first campus meeting within two weeks.

The 12 page order by the U.S. District judge does not end the student's lawsuit against the school board, but allows the club to gather at the high school while the litigation proceeds. Still, the order, which says the student has a "substantial likelihood" of proving her case, all but guarantees the board will have to follow the lead of hundreds of schools across the nations, including more than 100 in Florida, that already sponsor school-based gay-straight alliances.

Founded in Massachusetts in 1980, the club's aim was to end harassment and promote tolerance of gay students.

The order rejected the board's argument that gay-straight alliances are "sex-based" clubs that would violate the district's abstinence policy and endanger the well-being of students by exposing them to obscene and sexually explicit material.

Rather, the order says, the board failed to show the purpose of the club was anything other than what the student and other members say it would be in their proposed charter: "to provide a safe, supportive environment for students and to promote tolerance and acceptance of one another, regardless of sexual orientation."

Exercise:

What are the criteria for the organization of school clubs or groups?

Participation in Extracurricular Activities

A 16-year-old female was prevented from trying out for the junior varsity football team by a state regulation that prohibited mixed competition in basketball, boxing, football, ice hockey, rugby and wrestling. The student sued and the court held that the regulation denied females equal protection of the law, because the law assumed that all females were physically incapable of competing safely with males in contact sports. The regulation was struck down because the role did not sufficiently relate to the state's objective of ensuring safe competition.

In another case, the district rule prohibited girls from wrestling on the all-boys team. At trials, the district introduced evidence that girls are not as fast or strong as boys and girls' muscle power output was less than the boys and, thus, the girls were far more likely to be injured than boys. The court held for the girl and stated that no evidence had been put forth regarding the strength, speed, or muscle power of the girl in this case. (***Lantz v. Ambach***, 670 F. supp. 663 (S.D.N.Y. 1983).

Exercise:

A high school boy wants to participate on the girls' field hockey team, but rules limit field hockey to girls only.

1. ***What is your comment on this ruling?***

2. ***Why do you think girls/boys are allowed to participate in each other's activities?***

Vol. 20 USC, 1681-Education Amendment of 1972, Title IX, Section 901 of Title IX:

No person in the United States shall, on the basis of sex, be excluded from participation in, be denied the benefits of, or be subjected to discrimination under any education program or activity receiving federal assistance.

The regulation does allow for separate teams for both sexes (including contact sports), and where there is not enough demand for separate teams, girls may try out for boys' teams.

Exercise:

What arguments were raised to prevent participation of girls on boys' teams?

All-girls School May Violate Rights of Boys, Officials Say

The experimental all-girls public academy that opened last fall appears to violate civil rights laws by discriminating against boys, but a compromise could keep it open. federal education officers said yesterday.

The school chancellor, however, balked at any suggestion of concessions and hinted that he would be willing to go to court to defend the school.

The federal education officials did not issue a formal finding of violation against the school yesterday or order it to close. Instead, they asked the Board of Education to begin negotiations on a possible solution: either arranging to admit boys to the school, or establish a separate program near the campus for boys only. But a spokesman for the chancellor said he did not intend to support either option.

"I am confident that strong legal grounds support the continued operation of this school and believe a final ruling alternately will be issued in its favor," said the chancellor in a statement.

The chancellor had been a strong advocate of the school, which admitted 55 seventh-grade girls last September and this month, expanded its roster to 165 girls in grades seven through nine. The school is scheduled to expand to grades ten through twelve.

The preliminary finding by the U.S. Department of Education's Office of Civil Rights was conveyed yesterday in a series of telephone calls to the school board lawyer's as well as to the civil rights advocates who were challenging the single-sex school as a violation of the Title IX prohibition against sex discrimination.

Pregnant Students

The courts have held that married students and pregnant students do not give up their rights to an education.

- Rules involving pregnant students violate their Fourteenth Amendment rights of equal protection. The rules are arbitrary and capricious and therefore are in violation of the students' right of due process.

- If rules are reasonable and necessary to protect the health, safety and welfare of the student, they are justified and the court will uphold them.

- The fact that a girl is unwed and pregnant is not sufficient reason to deny her attendance at a public school. Unless it is found after a fair and due process hearing that she is lacking in moral character and that her presence in school will "***taint the education of other students***," she may be barred.

- Federal monies shall not be prohibited to any student nor shall the student be barred from its education program, or activity, including any class or extracurricular activity on the basis of student pregnancy, childbirth, false pregnancy, termination of pregnancy, or recovery therefrom, unless the student voluntarily requests to participate in a separate program.

Pregnant Cheerleaders Bring Turmoil

As a pink and crimson sky slowly faded along the horizon, the stadium lights came up over the prairie on Friday night and the football team charged onto the grass. But, three varsity cheerleaders were not there to greet them, because they had been ordered by the school board to stay off the field. They are all pregnant.

Whispers and arguments also swirled around another girl, the fourth of the school's fifteen cheerleaders to be discovered pregnant this fall. She had an abortion and with no medical reason to prevent her from resuming cheerleading, school officials allowed her back on the squad.

Among the boys watching the game, observations on the whole matter varied widely, from the notion that the boys were 50 percent of the problem and ought to be responsible to the idea that if the girls got pregnant, tough.

At its meeting a few days before the board grappled with the issues of pregnant school officers for the first time. It voted six to one to forbid male or female students in an elected position, which includes the cheerleaders, from keeping their posts if they are pregnant or if they have children.

Pregnant Pitcher Forced to Walk Due to Publicity

When the parents of a teenage daughter told them she was pregnant, they had a tough choice to make. The decision involved their daughter's delivery—from the pitcher's mound.

The 17-year-old senior was five months pregnant and starting to show. But she was the star pitcher on her school softball team and determined to play.

"She's a great softball pitcher and she wanted to play even though she's pregnant," her mother said. "Sure, she made a mistake, but she's a good kid and she's been pitching since she was eight years old."

They consulted with school officials and found there is no prohibition against pregnant athletes participating providing they are academically eligible and have a doctor's permission. But not everyone is happy about her playing, including some her teammates.

The family doctor was skeptical at first, but came around after being told that the girl trains year-round, her mother said. They also went to an obstetrics and gynecology clinic, where all three physicians cleared her to play.

Woman's Ousted Backed

A federal judge refused to reinstate a woman into a school honors club that kicked her out after she became pregnant.

A U.S. District Judge ruled the case was moot because there is no longer a National Honor Society chapter at the high school. However, he rejected arguments that the dismissal was discriminatory.

The student's lawyer had argued that because a woman's sexual activities are readily apparent when she becomes pregnant, the dismissal was discriminatory.

He wrote the student, now 23, was dismissed because of premarital sex, not because she had a child out of wedlock.

In dismissing her from the club, the school's faculty council said she failed to uphold requirements of character and leadership.

Exercise:

The presence of pregnant girls or married students in schools disrupts educational activities, and they should be excluded from school and activities.

Explain why or why not. ______________________________

____

____

Dissection

Sophomore Awaits Ruling on Dissection

An administrative law judge is expected to decide today whether a high school sophomore will be exempted from dissecting animals, a requirement of a biology course.

The 15-year-old student asked the judge to allow alternative materials and lessons to be counted toward her biology grade instead of some of the laboratory exercises normally required. She is a vegetarian and only wears cotton clothing and refused to participate in an assignment that entailed handling preserved animal parts and she said she will not participate when the class dissects worms, frogs and fetal pigs later this year. She said the assignments violate her religious and moral beliefs.

"I did not think this would be any huge thing to ask for."

The American Civil Liberties Union filed a petition with the State Department of Education in support. ACLU officials went to the Education Commissioner to prevent the school district from penalizing the student for her refusal to dissect animals. But officials and the school district said the student had plenty of warning that course requirements would not be changed to accommodate her beliefs and stood by the decision to fail her on any assignment she refused to complete.

"By state statute, the school boards make decisions regarding curriculum," said the attorney for the regional Board of Education.

Assembly Clears Bill to Give Students Alternatives to Dissecting an Animal

New Jersey public school students who cannot stomach dissecting a pig, frog, rodent or cat would be allowed to opt out under a bill approved by the assembly. The bill would require schools to provide alternative education projects for students in kindergarten through 12th grade who choose not to participate in dissecting or capturing an animal or experimenting on it. The students would not be penalized with a lower grade.

Under the bill, an alternative project could include videotapes, models, films, books, computers, "or any other tools which provide an alternative method for obtaining and testing the knowledge..." Schools would be required to notify students and their parents at the beginning of each school year of the right to declined to participate. Within two weeks of the receipt of the notice, students or their parents would have to notify the school if they want an alternative lesson.

And assemblyman is a co-sponsor of the legislation. He said virtually all legislators received complaints from students or their parents about the requirement to dissect animals when they do not need the experience to further their education or feel they can learn the lesson another way. He said some students object for religious reasons or dislike dissecting a cat, for example, when they have one at home.

"They feel why sacrifice an animal when they feel they are not learning much and will not major in biology," the assemblyman said. A spokesman for the Department of Education said there is nothing in science or biology curriculum standards that mandate a student dissected an animal. He said dissecting is encouraged as a practice, but that some schools do offer alternatives.

Exercise:

Should students without religious beliefs or other prominent beliefs be required to participate in dissection? Why? Why not?

____

____

____

Religion

Student Gridder Sacked in Pregame Prayer Suit

A high school football player and his family lost the first round in their suit against Christian prayers at football games and other public school activities, hours before he kicked the winning point for his team.

A high school senior and his family, who are Jewish, objected specifically to the mention of Jesus Christ in prayers at football games and other extracurricular activities. They also alleged in the suit filed Thursday that the school officials promoted Christian organizations and activities and say a biology teacher refusal to mention evolution for religious reasons

But Friday afternoon the U.S. District judge refused to issue a preliminary injunction to halt the pregame prayer.

At the game that night, an associate pastor at the church in this Bible Belt town, prayed for the safety of players "in Jesus' name" just before the kickoff at the high school. With the score tied fourteen to fourteen, the Jewish boy kicked the game-winning extra point.

Explaining his refusal, the judge said the purpose of the preliminary injunction is to preserve the status quo but that granting one in this case would have done just the opposite.

In addition, the judge ruled the Jewish family failed to prove irreparable harm from the prayer Friday night, and also did not prove that they would likely prevail when the merits of the case are decided.

Exercise:

List arguments for and against this case.

For:

Against:

School Board Retracts Ruling on Jewish Star

A school board has reserved a decision that prevented a Jewish boy from wearing a Star of David pendant because the six pointed star is sometimes used as a gang symbol.

"When we made the decision last week, it was based on information from the security officers only," the school board president said after Monday's vote. "But we realize that it infringed on freedom of religious expression, and that freedom supersedes the safety issue."

Girl Fights Schools Praying Tradition

A girl testified that she was stunned after moving to a suburb when she saw her classmates in seventh-grade physical education class link hands in prayer.

"I was just not used to having to pray," said the girl, who along with her parents filed a lawsuit seeking to prohibit prayer in the school district.

"I really did not like it, but since I was in a new school, I did not want to start anything. I just wanted to be accepted," she said.

Lawyers representing her and her parents asked a district judge on Tuesday to the issue an injunction prohibiting religious activities in the school.

The practice is a violation of constitutional guarantees of free speech and separation of church and state, the ACLU argued. The lawsuit claims prayers were said at pep rallies, on buses after games, and after daily practices.

District officials testified that Christian prayers have been a part of sports and other school activities for more than two decades.

The testimony of the girl and her parents was reported Monday and read in court Tuesday by ACLU lawyer to protect their identities. The girl said she bowed her head in prayer until her father told her that she did not have to participate.

After one game in the seventh grade, she testified, as she stood behind her kneeling teammates at center court, while they recited the Lord's Prayer, a spectator yelled, "Why isn't she praying? Isn't she Christian?"

The school district maintains that the prayers are student initiated and do not interfere with the right to free speech. The girl said prayers were used at the prompting of coach.

Community Service

Students may be assigned community service without violating the rights of the student or that of his or her parents.

In a 1983 civil rights action, the right to assign community service was challenged as a violation of the Thirteenth Amendment. The parents of a boy allege that the community service program requiring the student to do 40 hours of service during high school constituted involuntary servitude. The court disagreed stating that the rights of the student and his parents were not violated. The parent had a right to remove the student from that school district to transfer to another district, a private school, or participate in home schooling to avoid taking part in the program. Community service was also upheld in elsewhere when the Fourth Amendment affirmed the judgment of the school district that it did not violate the Thirteenth and Fourteenth Amendment rights of the student and the parent.

Exercise:

Discuss this as a form of discipline or a part of a curriculum.

____

____

____

____

Chapter Notes & Additional Information:

____

____

____

____

____

____

____

Chapter 12:

Teacher Rights

Chapter Topics:

In viewing teacher rights, two factors must be considered:

1. ***The teacher (person) and his or her rights as a citizen of the United States***
2. ***The adjustment of those rights as required by the occupation. (i.e., the teaching profession)***

Because of the unique nature of schooling and its responsibilities (in place of parents), the school has a duty to care for and protect the student, and certain accommodations are made in the rights of those who served in this capacity. Teachers, therefore, may not have the same degree of ***"rights"*** as do laypersons.

This chapter will explore some of the adjustments (and the reasons for them) that you may experience in the teaching profession concerning your rights.

Illustrations of Court Cases

The Constitution does guarantee you those rights as a U.S. citizen, but the courts also have weighed your personal rights versus the rights of the students and institutions of schooling. In essence, there are limitations placed on your rights, and as a teacher you should be fully aware of your actions in relation to those possibilities.

In the case of ***Pickering v. Board of Education*** (1968), the U.S. Supreme Court established reference points for standards that may be applied when questions of violation of constitutional rights (speech) arise.

Marvin Pickering was a high school teacher from Will County, Illinois, who published a long sarcastic letter in the local newspaper about the way his superintendent and school board raised and spent school funds. Pickering's letter detailed his objection to the ***"excessive"*** athletic expenditures by school officials who were then allegedly unable to pay teachers' salaries. He also wrote that "***taxpayers were really taken to the***

cleaners" by those who built one of the local schools. And he criticized the ***"totalitarianism teachers live in"*** at the high school.

Angered by the publication of the letter, the board of education charged that it contained false and misleading statements, ***"damaged the professional reputations"*** of school administrators and the board and was ***"detrimental to the efficient operation and administration of the schools."*** Pickering argued that his letter should be protected by his right of free speech, but an Illinois court ruled against him. Because Pickering held a position as teacher, the state court wrote that he ***"is no more entitled to harm the schools by speech than by incompetence."***

Translation:

The U.S. Supreme Court ruled in favor of Pickering, balancing the rights of the individual (teacher) in commenting on issues of public concern and the interests of the employer and the performance of their responsibilities. The court found that one, his remarks were not made with malice or reckless disregard of the truth; and, two, the remarks also did not damage his relationship with his immediate supervisor. In essence the Court stated that a teacher has a right to speak out on public issues as long his statements reflect an honest attempt to tell the truth and the remarks do not affect the ability of the school to continue its business.

The standards for dismissal in use of ***"speech"*** are:

1. Disruption of superior–subordinate relationship
2. Breach of loyalty or confidentiality
3. General disruption of public service
4. Indication of unfitness from content of the statement
5. Failure to comply with established grievance procedure

Exercise:

What is your translation of the Pickering case?

____

____

____

____

The following are general guidelines that may be used when constitutional rights are brought into question:

1) The courts will set aside the issue of constitutional rights and view other issues for dismissal before for looking at the ***"violation."*** If dismissal is warranted, observant of the constitutional issue, the plaintiff's case is dismissed.
2) Circumstances of the situation help determine ***where and how*** your rights are limited.
3) ***"Balancing test"***— Courts will balance the teacher's rights to academic freedom against legitimate interest of the community.
4) You have a right to present scholarly nonpornographic material to your class. Factors to be considered when using ***"questionable"*** material:
   a) Age/grade of students
   b) Context of material
   c) Curriculum guidelines
   d) Community standards
5) You can't disobey a direct order unless it is deemed to be unreasonable.
6) You cannot use the classroom as a forum to voice your personal, philosophical, or religious views that are completely irrelevant to the subject being taught.
7) Your freedom of speech may be restricted only when it materially and substantially interferes with the requirements of appropriate discipline in the operation of the school.
8) Your appearance is appropriate as long as it does not impair the education process.
9) You may conduct your personal life as you wish, as long as it does not affect your ability to teach—or does not violate community standards.
10) You may ***"associate"*** with various groups and participate in political activities as long as they do not materially and substantially interfere with the efficiency and discipline in the operation of the school.

Exercise:

1. Write a dress code for teachers.

____

____

____

____

2. Write your guidelines for conduct of personal affairs.

____

____

____

____

1915 Rules for Teachers

1. You will not to marry during the term of your contract.
2. You are not to keep company with men.
3. You must be home between the hours of 8:00 P.M. and 6:00 A.M. unless attending a school function.
4. You may not loiter downtown in ice cream stores.
5. You may not travel beyond the city limits unless you have the permission of the chairman of the board.
6. You may not ride in a carriage or automobile with any man unless he is your father or brother.
7. You may not smoke cigarettes.
8. You may not dress in bright colors.
9. You may, under no circumstances, dye your hair.
10. You must wear at least two (2) petticoats.
11. Your dress must not be shorter than 2 inches above the ankle.
12. To keep the schoolroom neat and clean, you must:
    a. sweep the floor at least once daily
    b. scrub the floor at least once a week with hot, soapy water,
    c. clean the blackboards at least once a day, and
    d. start the fire at 7:00 A.M. so the room will be warm by 8:00 A.M.

Exercise:

Draw a parallel between the 1915 rules and today's teaching standards.

Sex

Exercise:

Can you answer the following questions?

1. Where do we possibly get the term ***"hooker"?***
2. Can you give a substitute phrase for ***troilism***?
3. In Victorian days, what was the love that dared not to speak its name?
4. How does a ***frotteur*** get his kicks?
5. What is a ***catamite***?
6. Explain the difference between an ***incubus*** and a ***succubus***?

7. What does the prefix "***homo-***" mean in ***"homosexual"?***
8. In which position was the French President Félix Faure when he died in 1899?
9. The Biblical term "***onamism***" has what meaning?
10. Which well-known English author and member of the Parliament wrote the following description of the female anatomy, titled ***"Lines on a Book Borrowed from the Ship's Doctor?"***

The portions of a woman would appeal to man's depravity

Are conducted with considerable care,

And what appears to you and me to be a simple cavity,

Is really quite an elaborate affair.

And doctors who have bothered to examine these phenomena

On numerous experimental dames

Have searched the lower regions of the feminine abdomen
And given them delightful Latin names.

There's the vulva, the vagina, and the jolly perineum,
And the hymen which is sometimes found in brides.

And lots of other gadgets you would love it if you could see 'em—

The clitoris and God knows what besides.

So isn't it a pity, when the common people chatter of these mysteries to which I have referred,

That they use for such a sweet and delicate a matter

Such a very short and unattractive word?

Exercise:

1. ***In what class course would you use this material? Why?***

2. ***At what level or grade would you use this material? Why?***

3. ***Describe the objective or purposes of using this material.***

Remarks!

High School Track Coach Resigns Over a Klan Remark

A high school track coach resigned for telling a black student he'd send the KKK for a visit if she didn't join his team.

"It wasn't an appropriate remark. As a result, he has resigned his position. He explained that he made it one way and it was received another," said the superintendent of the school district.

The coach, who is white, stepped down and is also the mayor of the town and a retired teacher.

The 15-year-old student's father said the coach made the remark after she said she wanted to remain a cheerleader instead of joining the track team.

The coach said, "If you don't go out for track, I am going to send the Klu Klux Klan up to your front lawn."

Florida High School Teacher Critical of Jews, Disabled

School officials reprimanded a teacher who used inflammatory literature that criticized Jews and the disabled as part of the tenth-grade honors class homework assignment.

The teacher apologized to the 25 students in her high school English class and received a written reprimand for poor judgment and insensitivity.

The principal said, "This is not something that is a part of our curriculum."

He said the teacher brought in the worksheet from outside the school system, and he had not been aware that she planned to distribute it in class last week.

Coach Suspended Over Ethnic Slurs

A rural school district threatened with the loss of state financing has avoided that penalty by suspending, for at least five years, a coach accused of using derogatory racial terms with black and American Indian students.

The agreement between the school district and the State Department of Education also stipulates that the coach undertake a "culture awareness program," paid for by the district and approved by the state department.

The accusation against the coach, made by parents over a period of five years, included allegation that he used terms like "Tonto" and " wagon burner," in dealing with Indian students, and "jungle bunnies" and "tootsie rolls" with black students.

Under the terms of the agreement the basketball and football coach will continue teaching science and physical education at a nearby elementary school. But the district has now placed a notice of unprofessional conduct in the coach's file, a move that would be a necessary first step to a suspension or dismissal from his teaching post.

Teacher Loses Her Job for Talking About Jesus

A teacher has been fired for leading her class of 11- and 12-year olds in prayer and talk about "Jesus Our Savior." The untenured bilingual teacher violated separate church and state rights. The prayer occurred after one of her sixth-grade students accidentally drowned. The teacher said she asked the students whether they wanted to talk about God. She gave them the option to participate or to use the computer or read a book. All of the children chose to stay for the conversation.

Exercise:

1. ***What is your opinion about these situations?***

____

____

2. Were the teachers within their rights making such comments? Explain your position.

Tenure

Definition: ***A system of school employment in which educators, having served a probationary period, retain their positions indefinitely, unless they are dismissed for legally specified reasons through clearly established procedures. Tenure is commonly referred to as fair dismissal procedure, day in court, or due process.***

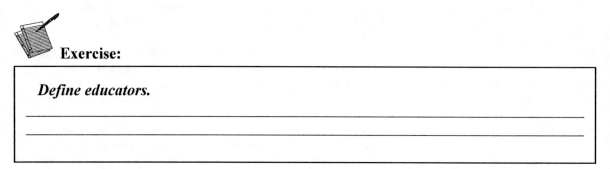

Exercise:

Define educators.

Not all states have tenure, and the length of service to obtain tenure varies, with approximately two-thirds of the states having some form of tenure laws. In lieu of tenure, some states will, after a probationary period, grant multiyear contracts to school personnel. In the state of New Jersey, tenure is granted via **NJSA 18A: 28.5** as follows:

A. three consecutive calendar years, or any shorter period which may be fixed by the employing board for such purpose; or
B. three consecutive academic years, together with employment at the beginning of the next succeeding academic year; or
C. the equivalent of more than three academic years within a period of any four consecutive years.

Zimmerman v. Board of Education of Newark, 183A. 2d 25 (NJ 1962)

Zimmerman was not given a fourth year contract after three years of employment and therefore was denied tenure. He pleaded that his employment under these annual contracts entitled him tenure. That court ruled that a teacher retained salary on a contract basis during probationary employment and is not guaranteed a fourth-year contract.

No teaching staff member may acquire tenure in any position unless he is the holder of an appropriate certificate, and unless he is, or until he becomes, a citizen of the United States (**NJSA 18A: 283 & 284**).

Tenure for superintendents and administrative principles was eliminated via P.L. 1881, Ch267 in August of 1991.

Exercise:

Clarification of Tenure:

Rationale for Tenure

The broad purpose of teacher tenure is to safeguard education personnel from enforced yielding to patronage, political correctness, religious views, and capricious actions of those charged with administration of school affairs. It is to provide teachers with a modicum of security (employment) free from unreasonable dismissal and interference.

Prior to tenure, teachers had been dismissed for reasons such as:

- Expressing political views
- Nonsupport of board of education candidates
- Teaching style
- Criticism of supervisors
- Religious views and positions
- Economics
- "Teaching the truth"
- "Curriculum creativity"
- Other:

Exercise:

1. ***Select any of the above, and justify the dismissal of a tenured teacher.***

2. Should tenure rights be changed? Explain your reasons.

____

____

Dismissal of a Tenured Teacher (NJSA 18A:6-10):

No person shall be dismissed or reduced in compensation,

A. if he is or shall be under tenure of office, position or employment during good behavior and efficiency in the public school system of the states, or
B. if he is or shall be under tenure of office, position or employment during good behavior and efficiency as a supervisor, teacher or in any other teaching capacity in the Marie H. Katzenbach School for the Deaf or in any other educational institution conducted under the supervision of the commissioner, ***except for inefficiency, incapacity, unbecoming conduct, or other just cause*** (clarified later in this chapter) and then only after the hearing held pursuant to this subarticle, by the commissioner or a person appointed by him to act in his behalf, after a written charge or charges, of the cause or causes of complaint shall have been preferred against such person, signed by the person or persons making the same, who may or may not be a member or members of the board of education, and filed and proceeded upon as in this subarticle provided.

Nothing in this section shall prevent the reduction of the number of any such persons holding such offices, positions or employment under the conditions and with effect provided by law.

Generalization: Whether a teacher is tenured or not, he or she cannot be dismissed for exercising his rights as guaranteed by the U.S. Constitution.

A teacher cannot be dismissed if the reasons are patently arbitrary, wholly unsupported in fact, or based on the violation of an unannounced policy.[5]

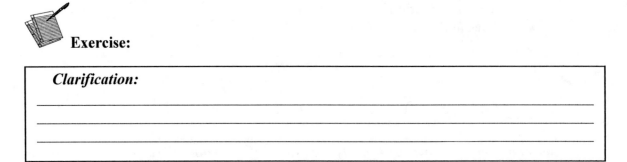

Exercise:

Clarification:

____

____

____

[5] *Rinaldo v. Dryer*, I.M.E 2d37 (Mass., 1936), at 38
Gotti & Gottu, *The Teacher and the Law*, West Nyack, NY: Parker Publishers, 1972.

Inefficiency, Incapacity, Unbecoming Conduct; Other Just Causes

Dismissal of a tenured teacher in the State of New Jersey will fall into one of the previous categories. The most common grounds for dismissal in the United States are:[6]

1. Incompetence
2. Immorality
3. Insubordination
4. Physical or mental disability
5. Unfitness or inadequate performance
6. Services are no longer needed due to decrease in students, courses, positions or school
7. Conviction for a felony or crime involving ***moral turpitude***
8. Failure to show moral improvement in professional growth and training
9. Any cause that constitutes grounds for revocation of teaching certificate

Exercise:

Define moral turpitude:

____

____

Inefficiency: The inability of teachers who cannot perform the duties required by contract. It also reflects a ***pattern of behavior*** and not isolated incidents.

Inefficiency is sometimes referred to as ***incompetence***.

The following are examples of grounds for dismissal under inefficiency:

- Lack of knowledge about subject
- Poor record keeping
- Little technical knowledge and skill
- Poor teaching methods
- Poor discipline
- Mistreatment of students

[6] ***Beebe v. Haslett Public Schools,*** 239 M.W. 2d 724 (Mich., app 1976) direct or implied order, reasonable in nature and given by and with proper authority. The person in question must willfully and deliberately defy school authority or viable school rules. The rules, however, must be clear, and the school must show the teacher was acting deliberately and/or defiantly.

Exercise:

Describe your "idea" of poor teaching methods.

Incapacity: This generally refers to the teacher's inability to perform his or her duties because of physical and/or mental illness.

- Excessive use of drugs and alcohol
- Poor hearing or eyesight
- Mental impairment
- Other: ______________________________

Unbecoming Conduct: This is sometimes referred to as ***immorality***—conduct that violates the community standards and/or the welfare of the school community. In many cases, the immorality must have a direct relation to fitness in the classroom or functions within the school.

Possible examples of unbecoming conduct are:

- Improper relationship with student or students
- Conviction for a felony
- Extreme violation of community values
- Using the classroom forum for personal views
- Cheating on an exam, certification or application
- "Improper" remarks in the classroom
- Excessive drinking

Exercise:

Explain what might be construed as violation of community values.

Other Just Cause: This category involves any grounds put forth by the school in good faith that are not arbitrary, emotional, unreasonable or irrelevant to the school's task of building up and maintaining an ***efficient*** school system. The teacher's actions must bear a reasonable relationship to fitness or capacity to discharge the duties of the teaching profession.

Insubordination is often cited as grounds for dismissal under "other just cause" and is defined as constant or continued intentional refusal to obey a direct or implied order, reasonable in nature and given by and with proper authority. The person in question must willfully and deliberately defy a school authority or viable school rules. The rules, however, must be clear, and the school must show the teacher was acting deliberately and/or defiantly.

Exercise:

1. ***What would constitute insubordination?***

2. ***Write an unreasonable rule for dress, grooming or classroom behavior.***

Dismissal Procedure: Tenured Employee

18A:6-11. Written charges; written statement of evidence; filing; statement of position by employee; certification of determination; notice

Any charge made against any employee of a board of education under tenure during good behavior and efficiency shall be filed with the secretary of the board in writing, and a written statement of evidence under oath to support such charge shall be presented to the board. The board of education shall forthwith provide such employee with a copy of the charge, a copy of the statement with the evidence and an opportunity to submit a written statement of position and a written statement of evidence under oath with respect thereto. After consideration of the charge, statement of position and statements of evidence presented to it, the board shall determine by majority vote of its full membership whether there is probable cause to credit the evidence in support of the charge and whether such charge, if credited, is sufficient to warrant dismissal or reduction of salary. The board of education shall forthwith notify the employee against whom the charge has been made of its determination, personally or by certified mail directed to his last known address. In the event the board finds that such probable cause exists and that the charge, if credited, is sufficient to warrant a dismissal or reduction of salary, then it shall forward such a charge to the commissioner for a hearing pursuant to **N.J.S.1 8A:6-16**, together with a certificate of such determination. Provided, however, that if the charge is inefficiency, prior to making its determination as to certification, the board shall provide the employee with written notification to the alleged inefficiency, specifying the nature, and allow at least 90 days in which to correct or overcome inefficiency. The consideration and actions of the board shall not take place at a public meeting.

18A:6-13. Dismissal of charge for failure of determination by board

If the board does not make such that determination within 45 days after receipt of the written charge, or within 45 days after the expiration of the time for correction of the inefficiency, if the charge is inefficiency, the charge shall be deemed to be dismissed and no further proceeding or action shall be taken thereon.

18A:6-14. Suspension upon certification of charge; compensation; and reinstatement

Upon certification of any charge to the commissioner, the board may suspend the person against whom such charge is made, with or without pay, but if the determination of the charge by the Commissioner of Education is not made within 120 calendar days after certification of the charges, excluding all delays which are granted at the request of such person, then the full salary (except for said 120 days) of such person shall be paid beginning on the one-hundred twenty-first day until such determination is made. Should the charge be dismissed, the person shall be reinstated immediately with full pay from the first day of such suspension. But should the charge be dismissed and the suspension be continued during an appeal therefrom, then the full pay or salary of such person shall continue until the determination of the appeal. However, the board of education shall deduct from said full pay or salary any sums received by such employee or officers by way of pay or salary from any substituted employment assumed during such period of suspension. Should the charge be sustained on the original hearing or an appeal therefrom, and should such appeal from the same, then the suspension may be continued unless and until such determination is reversed, in which event he shall be reinstated immediately with full pay as of the time of such suspension.

18A:6-16. Proceeding before commissioner hearing;

Upon receipt that such a charge and certification, or of a charge lawfully made to him, the commissioner or the person appointed to act in his behalf in the proceedings shall examine the charges and certification and if he is of the opinion that they are not sufficient to warrant dismissal or reduction in salary of the person charged, he shall dismiss the same and notify said person accordingly. If, however, he shall determine that such charge is sufficient to warrant dismissal or reduction in salary of the person charged, he shall conduct a hearing thereon within a 60-day period after the receipt thereof upon reasonable notice to all parties in interest.

18A:27-10. Non-tenure teaching staff member; offer of employment for next succeeding year or notice of termination before April 30

On or before April 30 each year, every board of education in this State shall give to each non-tenure teaching staff member continuously employed by it since the preceding September 30 either:

a. a written offer of a contract for employment for the next succeeding year providing for at least the same terms and conditions of employment but with such increases in salary as may be required by law or policies of the board of education; or
b. a written notice that such employment will not be offered.

18A: 27-3.2. Teaching staff member; notice of termination; statement of reasons; request; written answer

Any teaching staff member receiving notice that a teaching contract for this succeeding school year will not be offered may, within fifteen days thereafter, request in writing a statement of the reasons for such non-employment which shall be given to the teaching staff member in writing within 30 days after the receipt of such request.

Interpretation:

Teacher may also on request be granted a nonadversary hearing before the board of education to plead for his reemployment.

Exercise:

Explain nonadversary.

____

Withholding Salary Increments

18A: 29-14. Withholding increments; causes; notice of appeals

Any board of education may withhold, for inefficiency or other good cause, the employment increment, or the adjustment increment, or both, of any member in any year by a recorded roll call majority vote of the full membership of the board of education. It shall be the duty of the board of education, within ten days, to give written notice of such action, together with the reason therefore, to the member concerned. The member may appeal from such action to the commissioner under rules prescribed by him. The commissioner shall consider such appeal and shall either affirm the action of the board of education or direct that the increment or increments be paid. The commissioner may designate an assistant commissioner of education to act for him in his place and with his powers on such appeals. It shall not be mandatory on the board of education to pay any such denied increment in any future year as an adjustment increment.

The burden of proving the unreasonableness is on the teacher.

Withholding of a teacher's salary increment does not constitute a continuing violation; the fact that the teacher will always lag one step behind was not attributed to a new violation each year, but to the effect of an earlier employment decision, one that was protected by a regulatory period of limitations for bringing actions to protest.

***North Plainfield Education Association On Behalf of Koumjian v. Board of Education of Borough of North Plainfield, Somerset County*, 96 N.J. 587, 476 A. 2d 1245 (1984).**

Criminal History

18A:6-7.1. Criminal history record; employee in regular contact with pupils; grounds for disqualification for employment; exception

A facility, center, school or school system under the supervision of the Department of Education and board of education which cares for, or is involved in the education of children under the age of eighteen shall not employee or contract for the services of any teaching staff member or substitute teacher, teacher aide, child study team member, school physician, school nurse, custodian, school secretary, or clerical worker or any other person serving in a position which involves regular contact with students except individuals serving as school bus drivers unless the employer has first determined, consistent with the requirements and standards of this act, that no criminal history record information exists on file in the State Bureau of Investigation, Identity Division, or the State Bureau of Identification which would disqualify that individual from being employed or utilized in such capacity or position.

This section shall not apply to any individual who provides services on a voluntary basis. An individual other than a school bus driver shall be disqualified from employment or service under this act if the individual's criminal history record check reveals a record of conviction of any of the following crimes and offenses:

A. In New Jersey, any crime or disorderly persons offense:
   1. bearing on or involving sexual offense or child molestation as set forth in **N.J.S.2C:14-1** et seq.; or

2. endangering the welfare of children or incompetents, as set forth in **N.J.S.2C: 24-4** and **N.J.S.2C 247**; or

B. a crime or offense involving the manufacture, transportation, sale, possession, or habitual use of a "***controlled dangerous substance***" as defined in the "***New Jersey Controlled Dangerous Substances Act,***" **P.L. 1970, c.226 (C.24:21-1 et seq.)**;or

1. a crime or offense involving the use of force or the threat of force to or on a person or property including: armed robbery, aggravated assaults, kidnapping, arson, manslaughter and murder; or

2. a simple assault involving the use of force which results in bodily injury; or in any other state or jurisdiction, a conviction involving conduct which, if committed in New Jersey, would constitute any of the crimes or disorderly persons offenses described in this section of this act.

C. Notwithstanding the provisions of this section, an individual shall not be disqualified from employment or service under this act on the basis of any conviction disclosed by a criminal record performed pursuant to this act if the individual has affirmatively demonstrated to the Commissioner of Education clear and ***convincing evidence of his or her rehabilitation***. In determining whether an individual has affirmatively demonstrated rehabilitation, the following factors shall be considered:

1. The nature and responsibility of the position that the convicted individual would hold
2. The nature and seriousness of the offense
3. The circumstances under which the offense occurred
4. The date of the offense
5. The age of the individual when the offense was committed
6. Whether the offense was an isolated or repeated incident
7. Any social conditions that may have contributed to the offense
8. Any evidence of rehabilitation, including good conduct in prison or in the community, counseling or psychiatric treatment received, acquisition of additional or vocational schooling, successful participation in correctional work-release programs, or the recommendation of persons who have had the individual under their supervision.

18A:6-4.13. Nonpublic schools; final candidates for employment for position which involves regular contact with students; criminal history records check

Any nonpublic school may require all final candidates for employment as a teacher, substitute teacher, teacher aid, a school physician, school nurse, custodian, maintenance worker, bus driver, security guard, secretary or clerical worker or for any other position which involves regular contact with students, to demonstrate that no criminal history record information exists on file in the Federal Bureau of Investigation, Identification Division, State Bureau of Identification which would disqualify that individual from employment in the public schools of this state pursuant to the provisions of **P.L 1986, c.116(C.18A:6-7.1 et seq.).** Applications of this requirement by a nonpublic school shall be consistent and nondiscriminatory among candidates.

As used in this act, "***nonpublic school***" means elementary or secondary school within the state, other than a public school, offering education in grades K–12 or any combination thereof, wherein a child may legally fulfill compulsory school attendance requirements.

Illustration of Grounds for Dismissal

Delivery by tenured teacher, who served as president of teachers' bargaining agency, of orientation day speech which referred to dismissal of two nontenured teachers, superintendent's involvement in local politics, removal of books from an English curriculum and dearth of black faculty, which describes school system as a snake pit for young teachers and the superintendent as a villain, which suggested that nontenured teachers refrain from criticism until they obtain tenure, which described the school district hiring practices as callous economic gesture and which spoke generally against school administration and in particular, against superintendent warranted her dismissal from employment.
Pietrunti v. Board of Education of Brick Township, 128 N.J. Super 149,319 A2d 262 (A.D. 1974) certiorari denied 95 S. Ct. 640, 419 U.S. 1057 42 L.Ed.2d 654 certification denied 65 N.J. 573 325 a.2d 707.

Action of tenured teacher, who served as president of teachers' bargaining association, in sending letters to faculty members urging them not to comply with request of superintendent of schools to answer a questionnaire regarding the intentions of individual faculty members with respect to returning to teaching employment in ensuing year was an usurpation of essential function of township board of education, despite teacher's contention that there was no specific statutory authority for the solicitation of such information by superintendent. Id.

Unfitness to remain teacher may be demonstrated by a single incident if sufficiently flagrant. In re ***Fulcomer***, 93 N.J. Super. 404, 226 A, 2d 30 (A.D. 1967).

Where, after local superintendent has interrogated a school teacher who has raised Fifth Amendment in refusing to testify before a congressional committee as to membership in Communist Party, it appears that such teacher is currently member of Communist Party or subject to its ideologies and disciplines, that he has contumaciously or frivolously refused to answer before congressional committee, or he has willfully refused to answer pertinent questions fairly submitted by administrative superiors, such teacher may be discharged.

Laba v. Board of Education of Newark, 23 N.J. 364, 129 A.2d 273 (1957).

Removal of a school principal for inefficiency, incapacity or conduct unbecoming a principal should be easy and prompt within the school law.

Redcay v. State Board of Education, 130 N.J.L. 369, 33 A.2d 120(1943) affirmed 131 N.J.L. 326, 36 A 2d 428.

Evidence sustained finding of board of education that teacher was guilty of misrepresentation and fraud in making of application for loan and that thereby teacher was guilty of conduct unbecoming a teacher, justifying teacher's dismissal.

Smith v. Carty, 120 N.J.L. 335, 199A. 12 (1938).

Female public school teacher under tenure was not subject to dismissal on ground that she was married.

School District of Wildwood v. State Board of Education, 116 N.J.L 572, 185 A. 664 (1936).

That public school teacher employed under general contract, and entitled to indefinite tenure, was detailed to teach special class later merged with general students, did not warrant dismissal of such teacher for reasons of economy, while other teachers not entitled to indefinite tenure were retained under employment.

Seidel v. Board of Education of Ventnor City, 110 N.J.L. 31, 164 A. 901 (1933) affirmed 111 N.J.L. 240, 168 A. 297.

Conduct by a teacher in hitting the hands of student with a ruler with no physical harm resulting for disciplinary purpose, even though constituting corporal punishment did not warrant forfeiture of tenure rights.

School District of Borough of Red Bank v. Williams, 3 N.J.A.R. 237 (1981).

Incapacity, Grounds for Dismissal

Although school teacher was mentally and physically fit to perform her duties as a teacher, where no school district would employ her because of her transsexual status and feared effect that might have on students, she might be called on to teach, and where she was dismissed due to incapacity due to potential psychological harm to her students, teacher was incapacitated both for tenure and pension purposes.

Matter of Grossman, 127 N.J. Super 13, 316 A.2d 39 (A.D. 1974).

Tenure teacher with 17 years' experience may be dismissed from his position where the evidence overwhelmingly demonstrates lack of classroom control and incapacity to teach in an assigned area despite of many years of experience.

Board of Education Lawrence Township v. Lester Helmus, 2 N.J.A.R. 334 (1980).

Unbecoming Conduct, Grounds for Dismissal

Each act considered by Commissioner of Education deciding whether tenured, public high school teacher engaged in unbecoming conduct did not need to be proved by residuum of competent evidence, whether in each of the 11 acts charged was viewed as unbecoming conduct, as corroborative evidence that one or more acts were unbecoming conduct, or only as examples of course of unbecoming conduct, so long as combined probative force of relevant hearsay and competent evidence sustained Commissioner's ultimate finding of unbecoming conduct.

Matter of Tenure Hearing of Cowan, 541 A.2dl298, **224** N.J. Super. **737** (A.D 1988).

Where judgment of conviction for being a disorderly person was the only evidence on the print, state board of education could not find "unbecoming conduct" that would have warranted dismissal of tenured high school teacher in the absence of a residuum of legally confident evidence.

Matter of Tanelli, 194 N.J. Super. **492,477** A.2d 394 (A.D. 1984) certification denied 99 N.J. 181 491 A.2d 686.

Teacher's dismissal by a five to four vote of board for conduct unbecoming teacher after charge were preferred that questions that he had refused to answer in fitness hearing related to past Communist beliefs and affiliations were pertinent and that his refusal to reply impeded fair inquiry to determine whether he was presently subject to Communist ideology could not stand where two controlling votes were based on invalid grounds that a board member would not like such "type of person" to teach his children and that "moral issue" compelled vote for dismissal.

Lowenstein v. Newark Board of Education. 35 N.J. 94,171 A.2d 265 (1961).

The teacher had been acquitted in New York courts of forgery and kindred offenses and did not preclude subsequent dismissal of teacher by board of education for conduct unbecoming a teacher, since acquittal on criminal charge is merely an adjudication that proof was insufficient to overcome all reasonable doubt of guilt of the accused while the rule in all other cases that law is less exacting.

Smith v. Carty, 120 N.J.L. 335, 199A. 12 (1938).

Insubordination, Grounds for Dismissal

Evidence warranted dismissal of principal of county girls' vocational school for acts of insubordination and in excess of authority.

Harrison v. State Board of Education, 134 N.J.L. 502 48 A.2d 579 (1946).

It was contended that the prosecutrix could not be guilty of insubordination and dismissed pending her appeal from the order of transfer to teach in another grade to the State Commissioner of Education. This point was not well taken. She could have taken up the work in the school to which she was transferred under protest pending her appeal. Such a course would not have prejudiced her appeal. She chose to assume in her actions that the transfer was illegal. In this she acted at her peril. If the transfer was legal it necessarily follows that she was guilty of insubordination in refusing to obey the order, and that the board was justified, after charges had been preferred and notice given to hear the case, to order a dismissal if it chose so to act.

***Cheeseman v. Gloucester City*, 1** N.J. Misc. 318 (1953).

Evidence sustained decision of the state board of education that transfer of the prosecutor from one school to another was legal and that she was guilty of insubordination and properly dismissed as a teacher.

18A:6-10 Dismissal and reduction in compensation of persons under tenure in public school system.

Unbecoming Conduct, Grounds for Dismissal

Evidence was sufficient to find tenured physical education teacher guilty of conduct unbecoming a teacher and improper sexual contact toward students for improperly touching female students and exposing his genitals during class, warranting dismissal.

***In the Matter of the Tenure Hearing of David Borrelli*, 91,** N.J.A.R.2d 77 (EDU).

Insubordination, Grounds for Dismissal

Evidence was sufficient to find tenured teacher ineffective and insubordinate with respect to failure to provide required lesson plans, rejection of assistance from school administration, and failure to take corrective action, warranting dismissal from employment.

Township of Teaneck, Bergen County v. Wilburn, 91 N.J.A.R.2d 48 (EDU)

18A:6-14. Suspension under certificate of charge; Compensation; reinstatement compensation.

Tenured employee of local school may be suspended without pay only if indicated or if tenure charges have been preferred and certified to Commissioner of Education.

Slater v. Board of Education of Ramapo Indian Hills Regional High School District, 237 N.J. Super. 424, 568, A.2d 109 (A.D. 1989).

18A:6-18. Dismissal, reduction and compensation of persons under tenure in schools and institutions of higher learning.

Determination of State Board of Education reversing decision of Commissioner of Education and holding that appropriate penalty to be imposed on teacher for conduct unbecoming a teacher was forfeiture of six months' salary and loss of salary increments for two school years was not arbitrary, capricious or unreasonable and did not lack full support in evidence, and thus, decision would be affirmed.

Matter of Tenure Hearing of Tyler, 236, N.J. Super. 478, 566 A.2d 229 (A.D. 1989) certification denied 121 N.J. 615, 538 A.2d 315.

Expungement of Records

Public school guidance counselor, who had been convicted of child abuse 19 years ago, was entitled to explanation of records of conviction, after he successfully completed probationary sentence and had since led a law abiding life, even though order for expungement would not preserve availability of criminal records for inquiries by public school systems.

Application of V.S., 258 N.J. Super. 348, 609 A.2d 530 (L. 1992).

Rehabilitation, demonstration of

School custodian was properly disqualified from employment for three separate drug-related convictions and failed to prove rehabilitation by clear and convincing evidence, where he engaged in a continuing pattern of drug offenses which escalated over time, and had not received professional counseling for psychiatric treatment.

***Hall v. New Jersey State Department of Education*, 191 N.J.A.R.2d 46 (EDU).**

Teacher disqualified from employment for conviction of assaulting his wife sufficiently demonstrated rehabilitation, where marital discord and alcohol abuse giving rise to incident have been resolved by divorce and treatment for alcoholism.

Golinski v. New Jersey Department of Education, 91 N.J.A.R.2d 36 (EDU).

School custodian convicted of aggravated arson for setting a fire in a residential building for insurance purposes did not demonstrate sufficient rehabilitation to be qualified for school employment, not withstanding his good conduct during incarceration and parole, given short time since custodian's release from prison and position of trust in which his job placed him.

Miller v. New Jersey Department of Education, 91 N.J.A.R.2d 15 (EDU).

Substitute teacher disqualified from employment for disorderly conduct conviction more than 10 years earlier, demonstrated rehabilitation by clear and convincing evidence based on her personal and educational accomplishments and testimony of her colleagues.

Saunders v. Board of Education, 91 N.J.A.R.2d 12 (EDU).

Board of Education security officer disqualified from employment for conviction of possession of marijuana did not demonstrate his rehabilitation by clear and convincing evidence, where only 16 months have passed since conviction.

Armond v. New Jersey Department of Education, 91 N.J.A.R.2d 1 (EDU).

Newspaper Headlines

Teacher loses job despite drug acquittal

The local Teacher of the Year cannot have her job back despite her acquittal on charges of growing marijuana in her backyard because she knew her husband smoked pot, the school superintendent said yesterday.

The teacher was fired after her arrest on charges that she helped her husband grow marijuana in a vine-covered greenhouse. She could have received up to 11 years in prison but was found innocent by a jury Wednesday. She was fired for immorality for allowing her husband to use marijuana. The county School Board did not consider whether she was involved in possessing or growing marijuana. The Teacher of the Year said yesterday she is appealing her dismissal to the State Board of Education.

Teacher without tie loses job

A high school mathematics teacher who repeatedly defied a new dress code requiring him to wear a tie was fired last night. The Board of Education voted to fire the teacher for insubordination, accepting a recommendation of the school superintendent.

"First of all, we'll file the necessary papers for appeal," the teacher said.

The 46-year-old teacher, who owns a farm and a body shop, said he expected to be fired. He had already been suspended three times for not wearing a tie, and the dispute engendered considerable controversy in his county.

Teacher seized on steroid charges

A biology teacher also served as a head football trainer for a football team.

A former high school teacher, who also was the school's head football trainer has been arrested and charged with possession of steroids and hypodermic needles.

Ex-teacher gets seven years for storing drugs in school

A former special education teacher has been sentenced to seven years in jail on charges that she stashed 2 ounces of cocaine in her schoolroom supply closet.

Faculty endorses ban on student-faculty sex

University faculty members yesterday endorsed a compromise proposal that bans sexual relations between instructors and students they teach.

The faculty senate voted 31 to 4 for a ban instead of a strict prohibition against all sex between students and faculty that one committee advocated. The board of advisors, which sets policy at the school, will make the final decision.

Exercise:

Why such policies?

"Bandmaster cited in student sex case"

The former band director of a high school was indicted yesterday on sexual assault charges stemming from allegations that he had affairs with two of his students, one last year and one three years ago.

The indictment charges him with one count of sexual assault, two counts of criminal sexual contact and one count of endangering the welfare of a child. He was suspended from his duties as band director at the beginning of the school year. During the 1990–91 school year, he developed a relationship with another female student, age 17, which resulted in acts constituting criminal sexual content.

"Educator accused of child abuse"

Prosecutors in a child molestation case said they plan to show the national founder of a magazine and known educator has a history of molesting children. A motion filed Monday in a superior court said that the history involves 10 boys and young men as far back as 1969, said the district court attorney.

The teacher was indicted in September for allegedly molesting a 10-year-old boy at his cabin. He denied the charges, saying the allegation was made "to take advantage of his visibility."

In 1966 he founded a magazine published by his English students about old-time ways. Over the years, the project has resulted in best-selling books, a play, a movie, musical recordings and innovation approaches to education.

Teacher says he had sex with student

A 33-year-old teacher pleads guilty to sexual assault. The high school English teacher admitted in superior court yesterday that he had sex with a 16-year-old female with whom he said he had formed a "loving and caring relationship."

He taught the girl both as a freshman and last year when she was a sophomore. The two begin passing notes during the school day, and that developed into a relationship, he testified yesterday. The teacher admitted to having sexual relations with the girl at her house, and at two motels.

Critics say some coaches are overzealous

A football player was in pain as he was considering skipping football practice in September. So the coach gave him a couple of over-the-counter pain relievers. From that point on, the coach's days were numbered.

"Well, without thinking, totally stupid on my part, I said, 'Why don't you take what I take for my knee? '" the former football coach stated an interview.

"My intent was to help the kid...The next thing I know I'm being contacted by school officials saying I gave illicit drugs to students."

In the end, after 30 years of coaching football in high school and college, the physical education teacher relinquished his coaching position, and the ownership school board withheld part of his pay increase for next year.

School officials charge girls' coach with misconduct

A suspended high school teacher has been charged with nine counts of misconduct, including charges he served alcohol to high school girls and fell asleep beside two of them after a party.

"It's clearly conduct unbecoming a teacher," the superintendent of schools said. "It's serious enough to strongly recommend he be terminated."

Disciplinary action has also been recommended against eight other teachers as result of the probe.

In December, the suspended teacher forged a parent signature on a written excuse for a female student who was late for school.

In February, female high school students and male and female adults attended a party at the teacher's home, where alcohol was consumed by several students.

At the same party, he fell asleep in bed "between two of the female students."

In March, he bought alcoholic beverages at a bar for two minors."

Life skills class draws fire

The name of the class is Dynamic Living Skills. But when students at this summer school course were asked to place a condom over a banana as part of the sex education lecture, one mother thought the lesson was too dynamic for high school freshman.

She accused the district of failing to fulfill its responsibilities under state law to inform parents about the sex education curriculum and give them an opportunity to pull their children out of the lecture.

Some board members agreed and directed school officials to make it clear to both parents and children when information on reproduction will be discussed and to emphasize that they can skip such lessons.

Math professor adds a dress

A mathematics instructor finally decided to stop pretending to his students, so he came to class this week dressed as a woman.

He is a 58-year-old father of 10 who teaches at a junior college. He revealed that he is a transvestite.

"I accept what I am," he said. "I just decided I needed to quit living a lie."

This summer, with the support of his wife, the teacher decided to come out and began dressing full time in women's clothes. He even attended his 40th high school reunion in a dress.

"I have known about it all the time we have been together," said his wife. "I'm glad the hiding, the worrying and the concern for his mental health are over. This is the person she is."

Administrators at the school said that he can continue to teach as long as his lifestyle does not interfere with his duties. The biggest challenge has been which bathroom he should use. The problem was solved by putting an interior sliding bolt in the men's bathroom.

High school teacher suspended for starring in 100 porn flicks

A high school teacher was placed on leave after officials learned he produced and starred in more than 100 pornographic videos.

There was no indication that students were involved in the videos. "It was unclear what rules the teacher broke, except for using poor judgment," said the superintendent. The teacher is on leave pending investigation.

"Our immediate concern was to get him out of the classroom and away from students," said chair of the school committee. "We expect our teachers to maintain character that is an example for young people."

Officials would not identify the teacher or his department, except to say that he taught at the regional high school for at least 10 years. There are 4,584 students in the district.

A newspaper reported that the school learned of the videos from a resident who saw one at a video store. The tapes were released as "B____'s Videos," and the latest was produced in August.

"His name is all over the box," the superintendent said. "It is not a covert thing."

Five teachers suspended after movie incident

Five high school teachers have been suspended for three days without pay for watching an X-rated movie *Valley Girls* in the library while students were in assembly.

"A librarian, a math teacher, a science teacher and two physical education teachers at a high school watched the movie on a school-owned videocassette player in February," said the superintendent. The movie depicts modern-day California teenagers coping with peer pressures and using slang expresses such as "gag me with a spoon," "grody to the max," fer sher," "tubular," "tripindicular" and "like, totally awesome."

Teacher convicted of hate

A former teacher was convicted of promoting hatred yesterday for teaching students at a rural high school that Jews had hatched conspiracies for hundreds of years to gain control of the world. He was fined $2,640 at the conclusion of the jury trial. He could have drawn up to two years in prison and has 30 days to appeal.

He said outside the court that the verdict did not surprise him and he does not think he got a fair trial—"But no one who's convicted ever feels like they got a fair trial."

Seventeen of his students testified in the trial. They said the teacher taught them the Jews were evil and bent on destroying Christianity.

Teacher who gave out data on gays will retire

A high school English teacher who gave students literature about "the medical consequences" of homosexuality has agreed to leave the school.

The teacher denied hating homosexuals. He said yesterday that he sought to counter a presentation the week before by a homosexual man. He said literature he borrowed from Christian groups sought to discuss health risks such as AIDS.

"It is not that you hate homosexuals, but there are medical consequences to homosexual acts," he said.

Educator's raise withheld; sick days cited

A high school Board of Education has voted unanimously to withhold a $3,600 raise for a supervisor of the department. The board said at its meeting Wednesday night that he had taken an excessive number of unapproved sick days. The teacher contended during Wednesday's meeting that the action was retribution for his opposition to a planned reorganization that he said is inequitable and assigns him a heavier workload than other supervisors.

"He took 35 sick days this school year without furnishing the requisite note from a physician," the school principal said. He said that the supervisor had missed 98.5 days over the last four years, "essentially a half year of school."

Freedom of speech protects teacher

An Administrative Law Judge has ruled that a high school English teacher suspended two years ago for making racist remarks on a radio talk show was exercising his constitutional right of free speech and should be reinstated.

The judge made a preliminary ruling that a teacher for more than twenty years should not have been suspended for "conduct unbecoming a teacher" following his telephone call to a radio show in January of 1992.

In the telephone call, the teacher who identified himself by his first name—objected to being pressed by a supervisor to include African authors in his American Literature class during Black History Month. The teacher also referred to a banner in the school that read "200 Years of United States History, 2,000 Years of African History." "In 200 years we went to the moon," the teacher said. "After 2,000 years, they're still over there urinating in their drinking and bathing water."

Ironically the judge based much of his decision on an April court decision that reinstated another teacher to his position as chairman of the Black Studies department at a college. The judge found that the teacher's case was similar, in that both are tenured teachers who were removed from their positions following controversial statements. There was no evidence that either man's remarks interfered with the operation of the schools, the judge noted.

Teacher gives up her job to compete in marathon

When a teacher was told she would not be given time off to run in the Boston marathon, she had to make a decision.

She chose the jog over the job.

A special education teacher said she would quit her tenured $40,000 job five days before the marathon in April.

That's a Monday and her contract forbids taking personal days on Mondays, Fridays or around school vacations.

The teacher did manage to run a marathon last year, after school officials agree she had traded a day's pay for the time off. But the teacher told the district it was a onetime request. When the 35-year-old resident decided to ask officials for time off again this year she was turned down.

Teacher admits fondling students

A high school teacher accused of having sex with three female students admitted yesterday he touched their buttocks during school hours.

The guilty plea—to a single count of official misconduct—will cost him his teaching certificate and possibly up to 364 days in the county jail.

"He is precluded from teaching," the assistant prosecutor said afterward.

"Our primary concern was eliminating the possibility of that happening again."

"The fact that the incident happened during times he was supposed to be teaching brings it under official misconduct," the assistant prosecutor said.

Teacher loves her body; the school doesn't

A teacher who undressed in front of her adult class to spice up a lesson has resigned under pressure—despite protests from her students.

School officials at a high school in Sweden, accepted the teachers resignation saying "Teachers are not allowed to strip during class."

The teacher was teaching a group of unemployed women how important it is to love their own bodies. To drive home the point, the mother of five undressed.

School district is sued for using slave game

The parents of an 11-year-old Black student have sued his school district for using a computer gaming class called "Freedom!" in which players take on the role of enslaved southern blacks trying to escape.

Players start off as a illiterate and are referred to as "boy" as they try to gain the educational skills necessary to head to the North, according to the federal lawsuit filed by his parents.

"He was hurt that people were making fun of the characters in the game," they said." It was very condescending to him as a black. He woke up crying at night."

"Freedom!" was deleted from school district computers last year after complaints from his and other parents. The software company pulled it off the market in 1993 and said it instructed school districts to destroy any copies they have.

Teacher not hired back due to drug possession

A teacher who admitted to authorities that he had possessed marijuana will not be returning to his job this fall.

In a 6 to 3 vote that came during a three-and-a-half-hour closed-door session, the Regional Board of Education decided not to reinstate a health/physical education teacher. It also voted to ask the State Education Commissioner to revoke the teacher's tenure for "conduct unbecoming of a teacher."

He was also the high school's wrestling coach and had been on suspension since last summer, when he and another teacher were arrested and charged with possession of marijuana.

Trial to begin for principal in abuse reporting case

A municipal trial will begin against a school administrator who failed to report an act of child abuse. The principal of an elementary school received a summons in connections to allegations that a former janitor had sexually assaulted a nine-year-old student. The janitor pleaded guilty to the charge and is serving a 10-year sentence.

Exercise:

Write a series of guidelines to protect students from happenings of the previous headlines.

(Ex: Valley Girls: You are always on the job especially when at school.)

1. ______________________________
2. ______________________________
3. ______________________________
4. ______________________________
5. ______________________________
6. ______________________________
7. ______________________________
8. ______________________________
9. ______________________________
10. ______________________________

Name: ______________________ Date: __________________ Class: _____________

Legal Exercise

Teachers have been dismissed in the following cases. You are to decide if their dismissal was appropriate or not. All of the teachers were dismissed under tenure for one or more of the following reasons: ***incapacity, unbecoming conduct, inefficiency, and other just causes.***

In making your decision, consider the following principles:

Constitutional rights
Community values
Reasonableness
Limitation of rights
Academic freedom
Obligations of school; duty to protect and care

Scoring—Decide the cases based on the following measures: (place the appropriate letters alongside the statement.)

ND—Should not be dismissed
D—Should be dismissed
U—Undecided, depending circumstances

1. D Roy case: Teacher dismissed for failing to fill out an eight-page form; would leave class if evaluated by accreditation team; continuing intentional refusal to obey a direct or implied order, reasonable in nature, and given by/with proper authority.
2. D Teacher refused to go back to classroom until after he had a cup of coffee and checked mailbox.
3. ND Blunt case: Teacher taught for 25 years with appropriate evaluations, received negative evaluation in 1968–1969; said to be incompetent, poor planning, handwriting, grammar, and refused assistance.
4. ND Teacher had difficulty hearing; vile and obscene language used in class.
5. D Teacher hospitalized for mental illness twice.
6. U Teacher distributed questionnaire during school hours that asked students whether they favored his retention as a teacher.
7. D Teacher used classroom to support a certain candidate running for superintendent of schools.
8. D Teacher refused to follow plan of instruction after it had been in operation for one year.
9. U Teacher fined for hit-and- run accident.
10. ND Physical education teacher, female, 42 years old, 225lb., 5ft. 7in., was dismissed for not serving as a model of health and vigor.
11. U Biology teacher emphasized sex education and mental health in his course.

12. ND Civics teacher taught unit on race relations, responded to question, didn't oppose interracial marriage.
13. D Three students (Lat. Arts, F.L., L.A.) distributed materials about rock festival "Woodstock" to any student who wanted them (positive view on drugs, sexual freedom and vulgar language).
14. D Math teacher told his class that army recruits had no right to be on campus and to push them, throw apples at them and make them feel unwanted.
15. UD High school English teacher used article, "*Young and Old*" from *Atlantic Monthly* which contained the word "motherf_____" several times.
16. D Fifth-grade teacher told two girls in class who used the "f____ word" to write the word 1,000 times.
17. D Economics teacher allowed and encouraged students to determine course topics and materials, discussed conflicts, school policies and rules.
18. D English teacher refused to comply with schools teaching methods and philosophies.
19. D A teacher, a Jehovah's Witness, would not teach subjects having to do with love of country, the flag, or other patriotic matters.
20. D A teacher, a member of the Worldwide Church of God, requested and was denied certain days off for religious holidays and despite the denial took off 31 days between 1971 and 1975.
21. ND An English teacher wore a black armband to class protesting the Vietnam War.
22. ND West Virginia school employees dismissed for failure to support a board of education member.
23. UD Teacher whose contract was not renewed because of his sideburns and beard said the policy violated his rights.
24. D French teacher refused to stop wearing "short skirts."
25. ND Teacher who had a homosexual affair with another teacher was dismissed for immoral behavior.
26. ND An unmarried teacher became pregnant during the school year.
27. D A teacher played strip poker with a high school student.
28. D A college teacher who was in a car with a female student sped away and was arrested after 100mph chase.
29. D A high school teacher who proposed to spank a female student was perceived as making a sexual advance.
30. D A teacher engaged in "horseplay" with several female students, tickling and using sexually suggestive dialogue.
31. D A high school band instructor made remarks about virginity and premarital sex in his college class.
32. D A 12th-grade speech teacher held discussions concerning a house of prostitution, size of penis and intercourse with a cow.
33. ND Female teacher of eighth-grade spelling class answered the question, "What is a queer?"

Answer Key: 1D, 2D, 3D, 4D, 5D, 6D, 7D, 8D, 9UD, 10ND, 11D, 12ND, 13D, 14D, 15UD, 16D, 17D, 18D, 19D, 20D, 21ND, 22ND, 23UD, 24D, 25ND, 26ND, 27D, 28UD, 29D, 30D, 31D, 32D, 33ND

Exercise:

Explain your reasoning for the following numbers from the previous exercise:

1. ____
____

4. ____
____

10. ____
____

15. ____
____

21. ____
____

25. ____
____

Defamation of Character Cases

Letters of Recommendation and Personal Files

1. ____ Statement to board of education: "He is not a fit person to teach in any school. He is no good as a teacher and he will not teach in this school another year. He plays in the band for dances and then goes to sleep in the classroom during school hours."
2. ____ Teachers statement that a principal allows students to "pet" in the hallways.
3. ____ Teacher wrote about student that he "was ruined by tobacco and whiskey."
4. ____ Teacher talking in the teacher lounge reflected on a students "loose character and way with girls."

(All of these statements are considered libelous.)

Name: ______________________________ Date: ______________ Class: ________________

New Jersey Teacher Rights Quiz

Read each of the following statement and decide whether each statement is true or false.

1. ____ A teacher who has achieved tenure status in one school district does not lose that status if he/she accepts a job teaching in a different school district.
2. ____ All 50 states have tenure laws.
3. ____ A teacher obtains tenure in New Jersey after three full years of teaching in a school district
4. ____ No one may supervise, direct, administer or teach in the public schools of New Jersey unless he/she is properly licensed by the New Jersey Department of Education.
5. ____ Nontenured teachers are entitled to receive reasons for nonrenewal of their teaching contract.
6. ____ A school board is not required to supply a teacher with legal counsel if he/she is sued for inaction resulting from the discharge of his/her duties.
7. ____ Teachers in New Jersey may never use physical force with students.
8. ____ No teacher can be required to teach on a public holiday.
9. ____ Teachers must reside in the school district where they live.
10. ____ The school district may require an annual physical examination of its teachers.
11. ____ A teacher has the right to be a member of the school board in the district where he/she is employed as a teacher.
12. ____ A school board may not inquire as to a teacher's religion.
13. ____ A teacher must be granted leave for military service (with continued retiring credit paid for by his board) and for field training (with pay) if he/she is in the reserves or National Guard.
14. ____ Students must submit to the authority of the teacher and comply with school rules.
15. ____ All teachers who are members of the pension fund must retire within one year after reaching the age of 70.
16. ____ All teachers must join the pension fund.
17. ____ In addition to his/her pension, a New Jersey teacher also receives Social Security benefits when he/she retires.
18. ____ Every school district must give a teacher 10 days of cumulative sick leave per year.

Answer key: 1F, 2F, 3F (3 yrs. and 1 day), 4T, 5T, 6F, 7F, 8T, 9F, 10T, 11F, 12T, 13T, 14T, 15F, 16T, 17T, 18T

Ripped from the Headlines

- Harassed student's case in top court; suit charges Toms River Regional schools did not prevent bullying.
- Kearney student moves to sue district; he cites harassment after challenging teacher's preaching.
- Harry Potter wins a round; the Georgia Board of Education voted to reject a mother's petition to remove from library shelves the best-selling books by J. K. Rowling.
- District to address teachers complaints; teen who burned swastikas marched in graduation.
- Real-life lesson when he returns as a she; a middle school teacher changes gender.
- Teacher charged with bias; Long Island teacher is denied tenure and is suing for discrimination because she is rumored to be a witch.
- Board suspends Waretown teacher; underage drinking charges are reason, she made alcoholic beverages available at a party at her home.
- School driving teacher fired over DWI arrests.
- Georgia school system ordered to remove evolution warnings (in biology textbook, "evolution theory, not a fact").
- Mother of a slain girl, 14, suing school district over truancies; failed to tell her of daughter's truancies.
- Florida school officials reprimanded a teacher who used inflammatory literature that criticized Jews and disabled as part of a 10th grade bias class homework assignment.

Other Headlines:

Date: ____
Headline: ____

Date: ____
Headline: ____

Date: ____
Headline: ____

Chapter Notes & Additional Information:

Personal Thoughts & Drawings

On Becoming a Teacher

Some Important Things You'll Need to Know and Use

Part II

Strategies and Techniques For Successful Teaching

New Beginnings

Dr. Frank Paoni
Brookdale Community College

KENDALL/HUNT PUBLISHING COMPANY
4050 Westmark Drive Dubuque, Iowa 52002

Copyright © 1995, 1999, 2002, 2007 by Kendall/Hunt Publishing Company

ISBN 978-0-7872-4778-2

All rights reserved. No part of this publication may be reproduced, stored in a retrieval system, or transmitted, in any form by any means, electronic, mechanical, photocopying, recording, or otherwise, without prior, written permission of the copyright owner.

Printed in the United States of America
10 9 8 7 6 5 4 3 2 1

DEDICATION

This book is dedicated to all of the students who believe that they can make a positive difference in children's lives.

ACKNOWLEDGEMENTS

To Cynthia Kriparos for typing, editing and tweaking this manuscript.

To my colleagues, Joe, Art, Ave, Mary Ellen and Eileen, for their continuing support.

TABLE OF CONTENTS

Appendices

TABLE OF CONTENTS

PREFACE

On Becoming a Teacher was written to assist teachers and future teachers in the process of teaching more effectively. It is the author's believe that all teachers desire to improve and become what is commonly called a "master teacher. A master teacher is one who is able to make the correct decisions that impact upon the teaching/learning process through a series of planned exercises throughout the text. Examples of concepts are provided to give the viewer a clearer focus of the intended exercise purpose.

The text works not only as a book of information, but also as a workbook that reflects the semester's effort. But before a teacher can make those decisions, he must be able to understand his alternatives and the consequences of those choices upon the learning environment.

This book is designed to assist the teacher in better understanding his role in the decision making process. To start you off in the role of making decisions, let's design a children's museum.

Exercise

If money was not a factor, describe a museum you would build at your school for children. Describe your concept:

____

____

____

____

____

____

____

P.S. Give it a theme.

REFLECTIONS

A new idea is a rare thing. It is easier to adapt an old idea rather than create a new one. When a new idea appears, those with intelligence recognize it, develop it, and bring it to fruition.

It takes no intelligence to react negatively toward a new idea. It is just a reflex action of those with no imagination to create an idea.

Ingenuity Creates,
Reactionism Negates

M.K.P.

Chapter 1: Defining Teaching

Let us look at two decisions that are operational in both the preschool and collegiate teachings selections of curriculum and teaching strategies.

Chapter Topics:

Definition	**Steps in Decision Making**
Teaching Decisions	

***Definition:* Teaching is a cumulative chain of decision making—deciding among known choices.** The absence of decisions about various aspects of a lesson also reflects decision making—a decision not to make decisions about some aspects of the lesson.

The one universal among all teachers is that they all make ***decisions*** about the teaching/learning process. Each decision they make impacts differently on the learner and in turn determines the success or failure of the lesson. The student is most affected by the teacher's decisions or lack of decisions. The student is asked to recall information, sit in a particular place, follow an established set of rules, read certain materials and respond in a given manner. Every time a decision is made, conditions change for the student and new demands are placed on him.

The premise of this book is based on the theory that ***all*** teachers are basically the same, and they make the same category of decisions. Each teacher, whether teaching at the collegiate, secondary, primary or preschool level, is involved in an ***identical*** decision making process. To explore this theory—all teachers make the same category of decisions—let us look at the decisions that are operational in the teaching process.

Exercise:

1. List the subjects that are taught at collegiate and preschool levels.

College		Preschool	
________	________	________	________
________	________	________	________
________	________	________	________

2. List the strategies used at collegiate and preschool levels.

College		Preschool	
________	________	________	________
________	________	________	________
________	________	________	________

Following are the larger categories of decisions to make with examples of some decisions within each. (Note: Each decision leads to another decision.)

Teaching Decisions

Discipline (How to control students)

1. Student behavior code
2. Types of discipline
3. Standards for discipline
4. Punishment

Physical Environment (How should the room be arranged?)

1. Arrangement of furniture
2. Available materials and equipment
3. Room decorations, bulletin boards and exhibits
4. Learning centers and laboratories

Curriculum (What is taught)

1. The subjects
2. The emphasis and time given to subjects and topics
3. Expected outcomes: ***Cognitive, Affective*** and ***Psychomotor***
4. Coordination of subjects with other levels

Teaching Methods (How subject is taught)

1. Types of planning: unit, lesson, weekly, daily
2. Teaching strategies used

Measurement (How to assess student learning)

1. How often to measure: weekly, unit or semester
2. What to measure
3. Devices used: tests, reports, types of questions and team projects
4. Emphasis, pen instrument

Evaluation (What are the standards?)

1. Types of grades or reporting (A, B, C, percentage, pass or fail)
2. Norms used
3. How often and when

Motivation and Reinforcement (How students are encouraged to learn)

1. Intrinsic
2. Extrinsic
3. Feedback ratio
4. Humanistic/behaviorism

Books and Materials (Types of print and nonprint media)

1. Nonprint: TV, films, tapes, CDs, DVDs and computers.
2. Print: text, supplement, newspapers, booklets and periodicals
3. Reading levels and availability

Psycho/Socio Environment (Atmosphere of classroom)

1. Teachers attitude and posture toward students
2. Freedoms or responsibilities of students
3. Decision making: teachers, students or a combination of both

---

Communication (Exploring process)

1. Vocabulary
2. Length and complexity
3. Concrete or abstractness of statements
4. Illustrations

Steps in Decision Making

Do all teachers make these ***categories*** of decisions? The answer is, obviously, yes; they consciously or subconsciously do make the decisions. Does that mean that all teachers are identical? No. Each teacher makes a series of decisions within each of the categories. An example of this is that each teacher decides what the best, or the most appropriate, methods of measuring student progress. The college teacher may use essay tests or term reports, while the primary grade teacher may use projects or objective tests as a means of measurement. Then again, they both may use the same measures geared to their particular level. Another example may be the selection of teaching methods. At graduate school the instructor may use the lecture method for an hour for more, but at the primary level, for only 5 to 10 minutes.

The ***critical, or most important***, aspect about teachers making decisions is not the decision itself but ***how*** decisions are made. Each time a teacher makes a decision it impacts directly on the teaching/learning environment. Each results in a ***different*** set of consequences. The ***consequences*** of the decision are, in essence, the determining factor of whether learning has been impacted favorably or not. The decisions a teacher makes will determine the quality of teacher he or she will become. The master teacher makes the "**right**" decisions; the poor teacher makes the "**wrong**" decisions. The question then is how to make the right decision concerning the teaching/learning process. Let us now consider the steps in the decision making process:

- **Each teacher makes decisions.**
- **Each teacher makes the same types (categories) of decisions.**
- **Each decision has alternatives.**
- **Each decision has consequences.**
- **Each decision affects the learning process differently.**
- **Each student's behavior is a result of a teacher's decisions.**

As stated previously, the decisions a teacher makes directly affect the students. It is, therefore, necessary for teachers to know how to make decisions. The following formula for making decisions isn't foolproof, but, it does provide a model for thinking:

- **Step 1: See the need to make a decision.**
- **Step 2: Identify the alternatives or choices.**
- **Step 3: Identify the consequences or results of each alternative.**
- **Step 4: Assess the consequences in terms of objectives.**
- **Step 5: Make a decision**

Exercise:

Using the steps in the decision making process:

1. List alternative ways of testing. Ex: essay

a.______________________ d.______________________

b.______________________ e.______________________

c.______________________ f.______________________

2. Using Step 3, list possible consequences. (All essays must be written in complete sentences.)

Summary

Teaching is primarily a decision making process. All teachers are basically the same in that they all make the same types of decisions. Each decision a teacher selects has different consequences for learning. The key to making good choices is to know the alternatives and their consequences in relationship to the objectives.

References:

Mosston, Muska. *Teaching Physical Education.* Columbus, OH: Charles E. Merrill Publishing Co., 1966.

Eggleston, John. *Teacher Decision-Making in the Classroom.* London: Rutledge and Keegan Paul, 1979.

Chapter Notes & Additional Information:

Chapter 2:

Teaching Excellence

Definition of Teaching Excellence

Those who go beyond the expected; those who create excitement for their subjects; those who share a part of themselves, those who take risks.
Frank Paoni

Chapter Topics:

Introduction
What the Research Says
Characteristics of Good Teaching
Excellent Professor
What Makes an Outstanding Teacher
Helpful Hints
Other Hints

Introduction

What makes an excellent teacher? Certainly we know that super teachers make better decisions than other teachers, but are there a series of characteristics common to excellent teachers?

We know that there are different styles: philosophy is a method of teaching, and they may differ dramatically in their approach. Some teachers may be quiet and settled, while others are very dramatic, or may be highly structured versus loosely organized.

Our perceptions of teachers also differ, even when we look at the same teachers at the same time. One person may rate the instructor as outstanding while other evaluations will vary from good, average, to the worst teacher I've ever had.

Are all of these assessments correct, or are we looking for different criteria for excellence?

Exercise:

1. ***Describe the very best teacher that you've ever had.***

2. ***Describe the very worst teacher that you've ever had.***

What the Research Says

Crawford and Bradshaw (1968) asked their students to describe their most effective college teacher, and the four most frequently mentioned characteristics were: ***thorough knowledge of subject matter; well-planned and organized lectures; enthusiastic, energetic, lively interest in teaching; and student oriented, friendly, willingness to help students.*** The following is a list of characteristics compiled by other researchers on college students' views of outstanding teachers.

Characteristics of Good Teaching

Bousfield
- Fairness
- Mastery of subject
- Interesting presentation of material
- Well-organized material
- Clearness of exposition
- Interest in students
- Helpfulness
- Ability to direct discussion
- Sincerity
- Keenness of intellect

Clinton
- Knowledge of subject matter
- Pleasing personality
- Neatness in appearance and work
- Fairness
- Kind and sympathetic
- Keen sense of humor
- Interest in profession
- Interesting presentation
- Alertness and broad mindedness
- Knowledge of methods

Deshpande, et al.
- Motivation
- Rapport
- Structure
- Clarity
- Content mastery
- Overload (too much work)
- Evaluation procedure
- Use of teaching aids
- Instructional skills
- Teaching styles

French
- Interprets ideas clearly
- Develops students interest
- Develops skills of thinking
- Broadens interests
- Stresses important material
- Good pedagogical methods
- Motivate to do best work
- Knowledge of subject
- Conveys new viewpoints
- Clear explanations

Gadzella
- Knowledge of subject
- Interest in subject
- Flexibility
- Well-prepared
- Use of appropriate voca-bulary

Hildebrand
- Dynamic and energetic person
- Explains clearly
- Interesting presentation
- Enjoys teaching
- Interested students
- Friendly towards students
- Encourages class discussion
- Discusses other points of view

Pogue
- Knowledge of subject
- Fair evaluator
- Explains clearly

Exercise:

Select your five best traits of good teaching:

1. ______________________________
2. ______________________________
3. ______________________________
4. ______________________________
5. ______________________________

What Characterizes an Excellent Professor?

In a teaching and learning project, a committee of professors and administrators at Miami-Dade Community College set out to identify the ***"core of fundamental characteristics"*** that define classroom excellence for a faculty member. The committee members agreed that excellent professors (partial list, 16 out of 30):

1. Are enthusiastic about their work
2. Set challenging performance goals for themselves
3. Set challenging performance goals for students
4. Are committed to education as a profession
5. Project a positive attitude about students' ability to learn
6. Display behavior consistent with professional standards
7. See students as individuals operating in a broader perspective beyond the classroom
8. Treat students with respect
9. Are available to students
10. Listen attentively to what students say
11. Are responsive to student needs
12. Give corrective feedback promptly to students
13. Are fair in their valuations of students' progress
14. Present ideas clearly
15. Respect diverse talents
16. Create a climate conducive to learning

Perry (1969), as part of a study for the University of Toledo's Office of Institutional Research, examined ***faculty*** perceptions of effective teaching. Six characteristics led the list. They are:

1. **Be well prepared for class.**
2. **Demonstrate comprehensive subject knowledge.**
3. **Encourage intelligent, independent thought by students.**
4. **Motivate students to do their best.**
5. **Be fair and reasonable in evaluating students.**
6. **Be sincerely interested in the subject being taught.**

Student perceptions of effective teaching were examined by **Apple (1970)**, in a study completed by the Center for Research and Development in Higher Education at Berkeley. From the student's point of view, a good teacher:

1. **Is a dynamic and energetic person**
2. **Explains clearly**
3. **Has an interesting style of presentation**
4. **Seems to enjoy teaching**
5. **Has a genuine interest in students and is friendly toward them**
6. **Encourages class discussions**
7. **Discusses points of view other than his own**

Reactions:

____

Seldin (1975), in a study of 410 ***academic deans*** of good teaching, found an effective teacher:

1) **Is well prepared for class**
2) **Motivates students to do their best**
3) **Communicates effectively to the level of the students**
4) **Demonstrates comprehensive subject knowledge**
5) **Treats students with respect.**

Irby (1978) analyzed 16 studies dealing with students perceptions of teachers. He found a heavy cluster response on four points. They are:

1) **Organization/clarity**
2) **Enthusiasm/stimulation**
3) **Instructor knowledge**
4) **Group interaction skills**

In a review of studies going back to the beginning of this century, **Eble (1976)** noted ***"reasonably consistent findings about the earmarks of good teachings***." In a summary he says:

> Most studies stress knowledge and organization of subject matter, skills in instruction, and personal qualities and attitudes useful to working with students.
>
> If ***personal characteristics*** are emphasized in a particular study, good teachers will be singled out as those who are enthusiastic, energetic, approachable, open, concerned, and possessed a sense of humor.

If characteristics of mastering a subject matter and possessing teacher skills are emphasized, good teachers will be those who are masters of a subject, can organize and emphasize, can clarify ideas and point out relationships, can motivate students, can pose and elicit useful questions and examples, and are reasonable, imaginative and fair in managing the details of learning.

Developed by Miller (1972), many students, faculty and administrators would probably agree with this definition of good teaching:

A good teacher personifies enthusiasm for his students, the area of confidence, and life itself. He knows his subject, can explain it clearly, and is willing to do so in or out of class. Class periods are interesting and at times alive with excitement. He approaches his area of competence and his students with integrity that is neither stiff nor pompous, and his attitude and demeanor are more caught than taught.

What Makes an Outstanding Teacher?

Exercise: ***Explain each trait:***

Their descriptions of characteristics of the college instructor that they had rated "outstanding" covered a very wide range of personal and professional characteristics.	Now take a look at the "bottom five characteristics" which distinguish those teachers as "poor."
The top five characteristics:	***The bottom five characteristics:***
1. Knowledge of subject ____________________ ____________________	1. Dry, dull, cool, aloof, no personality ____________________ ____________________
2. Well organized ____________________ ____________________	2. Unorganized, not prepared ____________________ ____________________
3. Concerned about and responsive to students' needs ____________________ ____________________	3. Disinterested, uncaring, disrespectful toward students ____________________ ____________________
4. Enthusiasm for subject ____________________ ____________________	4. Not knowledgeable about subject ____________________ ____________________
5. Friendly and personable ____________________ ____________________	5. Unable to communicate effectively ____________________ ____________________

Helpful Hints

Excellent teachers do a lot of things right! They are consistent. They constantly evaluate their actions, and they have a lot of "tricks of the trade." Not all of them work for all students, but there is one or two for every class that will succeed.

Enjoy your teaching career.

Exercise:

Highlight your top choices.

It is important to know your audience at the beginning of the semester. Give out a "***Student Survey***" to be completed by all class members. Find out what their other responsibilities are: how many hours they are taking, if they are a parent, whether they work, and if so, how many hours a week. Ask each student to write three descriptions about themselves.

The **first class** sets the tone for the rest of the semester. Make sure that you keep students for the entire class period.

If possible, have students arrange chairs/desks in a horseshoe shape. This way everyone can be seen. Research supports the effectiveness of this type of seating arrangement.

Key Points:

____

____

Learn every **student's first name** as quickly as possible. Tell the students by what name and title you prefer to be called.

If a student misses more than two consecutive classes, you as a teacher should call him or her. Research supports this practice. It lets the student know that you are concerned and care about him.

Be aware that the **first five minutes** of any class period is the most important time. You must work to capture their interests and set the tone for the learning environment. At the beginning of each class period, announce your topic for the day and your objectives.

We all have "great moments" as teachers. Take time after a class to **analyze your great moment** so that they might happen more often!

Require one student/teacher conference during the semester. This can last for up to 30 minutes and can be scheduled around midterm.

Key Points:

____

____

Provide a small notepad on your office door so students can leave messages if you are not in.

Provide students with practice and rewards. Be creative in coming up with reward ideas. You'll be surprised at how favorably students react to even small rewards. Keep in mind that students' perceptions of information are different, based on their background experiences. The same information may need to be presented in a variety of ways. Keep in mind different learning styles!

If you are lecturing for a class, distribute an outline of your lecture notes, or put it on an overhead projector before class starts. This may assist students in organizing the material you are presenting.

Key Points:

____

____

Remember that we **are models** for our students. Enthusiasm generated by us for a subject will be transmitted to them.

Provide students with "***peripherals***" (positive thinking quotations). Write them on your syllabus or other handouts and tests.

Ask questions before selecting a respondent.

Provide "***wait time***" when you ask questions. Give the students time to think.

Key Points:

____

____

Try to address a question **to every** student during every class.

Rearrange groups for small-group activities often. Avoid the establishment of cliques.

Demand regular and punctual attendance **by a method such as this: put a few** questions on the board or overhead at the beginning of each class (a five minute writing exercise). Students hand in their answers at the end of the five minutes. All of these are added together for a test grade at the end of the semester.

Invite guest experts to discuss the application of your subject area in their work.

Key Points:

____

____

Reduce test anxiety by calling them **"inventories"** rather than tests or exams. A test is really an inventory of what the student has in relation to course knowledge.

Play soothing music as the students enter the class on a test day.

Incorporate an interview into an assignment. For example, in a radio, television, or film class, students could interview a local radio or television personality. Interviewing forces the student into an unusual learning situation.

Get to class before all the students arrive and be the last person to leave. If you have to miss a class, explain why and what you will do to make up the time and/or materials.

Key Points:

____

____

Maintain good eye contact with students. This is important in and out of class.

Vary your instructional techniques. (Lectures, debates, small-group activities and role-playing.)

If you require term paper, arrange for a library or Internet orientation for students.

Schedule the first test of the semester to cover a small unit of material. Students feel more comfortable once they get an idea what tests in each classroom are like.

Key Points:

____

____

Ask students to evaluate your tests at the end of the test or as a part of the next class.

Encourage students to feel free to ask questions. When you answer a question, make sure the student understands the answer. You might ask the student to repeat the answer in his or her own words.

When grading student papers, be sure to include positive comments. You might point out general errors by saying, "You could improve this paper by …"

Permit and encourage students **to bring** a friend to class.

Encourage study groups. (Students can learn from one another). Research shows that study groups assist students in and improving their understanding of course material.

Use the library reference desk for some of your old tests and quizzes. Tell students that they are available to assist their studying.

Team-teach a class with a fellow faculty member or switch classes a few times. Invite fellow faculty members as guest lecturers.

Invite reading/study skills/learning style experts to your classes to **talk to students.** Conduct learning styles inventory at the beginning of each course so that you know how your students learn best.

Key Points:

____

____

Integrate the arts into various content areas whenever possible. Aesthetics should be a facet of the college curriculum.

Notes:

____

____

____

____

*Other Hints:

- Let students make up their own test questions (provide guidelines and examples).
- Have students outline the chapter's key aspects and put them on the board. Have students work in pairs, not alone.
- Students review films, DVDs or provided samples. Write notes on board.
- Do readings in class, picking out descriptive parts. (You read first, then select or ask for volunteers.)
- Utilize political cartoons or comments in class to reflect on events and current times.
- Use writing to help students learn. Short, five-minute, written exercises can be incorporated daily. Writing helps students to organize their thoughts.
- Have yourself videotaped while you are teaching, then work on getting rid of those annoying habits you didn't even know you had!
- Every so often, send postcards to your students. Let them know that you have missed them in class if they have been absent. Let others know they are doing well in class.
- Let the students know that yours is a class where they can learn and have fun. Greet them from the first with such remarks as, "I'm glad to see you," and "I'm glad you are in this class," etc.

*Material from paper: *Active Learning Needs Active Instructors or Reach Out and Teach Someone!* **Ellen Marshall and Kathy McAuliffe**

- Have students respond to newspaper articles by writing a letter to the editor.
- Hold an amnesty day that allows students to turn in past-due work without penalty.
- Allow 3 X 5 crib notes for a test.
- Relate the arts (music, paintings or dance) to various subjects.
- Provide sample term papers/projects.
- Have students develop a portfolio for your class (notes, handouts, tests, films, projects, reports, etc.)
- Develop a laboratory exercise for your students, (e.g., for history, conduct interviews with personalities of the Civil War).
- Have students complete observation forms for various aspects of the course, (e.g.,Television and violence).
- Utilize case studies as an alternative to a test.
- Give trivia questions for each class (use for bonus points). Give a clue the previous day.
- Allow students to do different assignments as part of their grade.

Key Points:

____

____

Exercise:

List five new hints:

1. ______________________________
2. ______________________________
3. ______________________________
4. ______________________________
5. ______________________________

Chapter Notes & Additional Information:

Personal Thoughts & Drawings

Chapter 3:

Classifying Teaching Strategies

A teaching strategy is an organized means of presenting skills, knowledge, or values.

Chapter Topics:

Introduction	**Physical Dimension**
Educational Dimensions of Teaching Strategies	**Cognitive Dimension**
	Affective Dimension

Introduction

Teaching strategies (methods)[1] are a part of a system of actions intended to affect learning. The system is the complete educational process that encompasses those categories of decisions identified in chapter 1. Since teaching strategies represent anywhere from 60 to 85 percent of the instructors' and students' time, they are critical to the learning process.

Teaching strategies are not only important because of the amount of time devoted to them, but also ***for their intended nature—to give an opportunity for students to receive and interact with the information.*** No other decision that a teacher makes has such a profound impact on the student. Each strategy requires different forms of participation as well as thinking from the learner. Therefore, every method can be classified as to its educational requirements or dimensions.

Exercise:

Explain why teaching strategies are "neutral."

____

____

Educational Dimensions of Teaching Strategies

Teaching strategies have been classified several different ways according to factors such as student/teacher interaction, level of desired learning, subject specialty and grade level. The following classification of teaching methods is not absolute; it also offers as complete a view as possible of the strategy in terms of its educational impact. The strategies are first

[1] *The word "method", will be used synonymously with strategies throughout the text.

classified as to the level of physical activity. Then they are further categorized as to the cognitive and affective demands placed upon the student. The limitations of the classification schema are the following:

a. **There is no hierarchy of dimensions (one dimension is no less important than another).**
b. **The dimensions are artificially separated for the purposes of analysis.**
c. **Each method is given a classification that is representative of the largest degree of factors in the dimension.**

Physical Dimension

This dimension classifies teaching methods as to their level of physical activity. Every strategy has some physical activity; but there is a wide range in terms of the level of activity. Some strategies require the student to sit and write; others, to speak or demonstrate, all according to the purpose of the desired outcome of the strategy. The levels of these classifications are:

- ***Category I—Passive:*** The student is a passive recipient of the information via sight/sound or combination thereof. Little activity is expected of the student within this category of teaching strategies, other than sitting and writing. The strategies in the passive category provide the student with the necessary background of information to effectively participate in other categories of strategies. This level of activity allows the student to collect and organize his thoughts for future reference.

- ***Category II—Responsive:*** This category asks the student to do more than receive information. It requires them to physically respond to the data. The students respond to the instructor and the subject matter by sharing ideas, answering questions and asking questions. The responding strategies help to develop the higher powers of reasoning and critical analysis.

Examples of Physical Dimension Classification

Methods	***Classification***
Lecture:	***Passive*** (Students sit, listen and take notes. Sometimes a limited amount of questions are asked.)
Discussion:	***Responsive*** (Students answer questions, ask questions. Note taking may also be part of process.)
Games:	***Interactive*** (Students respond to data by playing, moving objects and role playing.).

The physical dimension of each strategy is only a means of identifying the level of physical activity and doesn't make judgments as to the worth or benefits of each strategy.

- ***Category II—Interactive:*** This category requires the student to do more than receive and respond orally to the information received. The student physically interacts with the data in some way, such as in a laboratory experiment, simulation game, demonstration, field trip, or sociodrama. The level of physical activity takes on a different dimension; the students are moving, doing, and applying the concepts.

Exercise:

1. Describe your most physically active class. Be specific (e.g., art class, creating a sculpture).

____
____
____
____

2. Describe your emotions (well-being) after the class.

____
____
____
____

Cognitive Dimension

The cognitive domain represents a means of classifying knowledge (ways of thinking) such as recall, applying or evaluating information. The following means of classifying knowledge provides a general formula for representing what cognitive skills are asked of the student via the teaching strategy. The two categories used in this classification of teaching strategies are:

- ***(Primary)*—Acquiring and Organizing**: Within this category the student receives and organizes the knowledge (information). The knowledge is categorized and translated into a meaningful matter for later recall and use. This primary cognitive category is necessary to give the student the essential background to effectively carry on the higher-order functions of the cognitive domain.
- ***(Secondary)*—Utilizing:** This category requires the student to put to use the information acquired by applying, analyzing, synthesizing or evaluating. Once the knowledge has been organized, the student is expected to use higher forms of thinking other than recall and memorization.

Examples of Cognitive Classification

Method	*Cognitive dimension*
Debate:	***Secondary*** (Students put data into action; must use incoming data to form arguments)
Television:	***Primary*** (Student is receiving and organizing information)
Drill:	***Primary*** (Student gives knowledge back to instructor in repetitious matter, very little higher-order thinking is conducted.)

Exercise:

1. Describe the class that demanded the most in the thinking process (math class, solving geometry formulas).

2. Describe the feelings you had after the class.

Affective Dimension

The affective classification refers to values, attitudes and feelings, and how an individual acquires a set of values. The two categories of the effective domain used in this model represent the initial awareness of values and the actual implementation of those values.

- **(*Primary*)—Attending and Receiving:** The student at this level is a willing listener to the message. He may respond by agreeing, asking questions, accepting, or expressing a value or feeling. There is little opportunity or expectation to organize or commit oneself to the values represented.
- **(*Secondary*)—Commitment:** The strategies that fall within this classification allow the student to demonstrate a form of conviction concerning the value(s). The commitment may be in the form of defending ones views, attempting to convince others, or using the values to guide their lives.

Notes:

Examples of Affective Classification

Method	*Affected Dimension*
Field trip*:*	***Primary*** (Student is observing, with possible dialogue, e.g., visit to nursing home).
Seminar:	***Secondary*** (Student has the opportunity to express his views, (e.g., the place of nursing homes in our society).
Panel*:*	***Primary*** (The student is not a panelist, but is part of the audience. Vice versa, it would be secondary.)

Exercise:

1. Describe the class that challenged your feelings or excited you the most.

2. Describe your feelings after the class.

Summary

The selection of a teaching method(s) is a vital decision in that 60 to 80 percent of the class time is spent on teaching methods. Teaching methods can be classified as to their educational dimensions which are representative of the requirements and potential outcomes of the method. The three educational dimensions are: ***Physical***, ***Cognitive*** and ***Affective.***

Chapter Notes & Additional Information:

Chapter 4: Active Learning

> ***All genuine learning is active, not passive. It involves the use of the mind, not just memory. It is a process of discovery in which the student is the main agent, not the teacher.***
> ***Mortimer Alder***

Chapter Topics:

- Definition
- Active Learning Guidelines
- Portraits of Active Learning
- Role-Playing
- College/High School Role-Playing
- Middle/Elementary Role-Playing
- Problem Solving
- College/High School Problem Solving
- Elementary Problem Solving
- Using Science/Mathematics
- College/High School Science/ Mathematics
- Elementary School Science/Mathematics
- Contests and Competitions
- Middle/High School Contests and Competitions
- Middle/High School Contests
- College/High School Contests and Competitions
- Example of Middle/High School Competition
- High School Competition
- Middle/High/College Competition
- Example of Elementary Competition
- Elementary School
- Examples of Elementary School Contests
- Contest and Competition Articles
- College Techniques
- High School Techniques
- Middle School Techniques
- Elementary Techniques
- Field Trips
- Volunteering
- Elements and Characteristics of Cooperative Learning

Definition: ***All genuine learning is active and not passive. It involves the use of the mind, not just memory. It is a process of discovery in which the student is the main agent, not the teacher.***

Exercise:

Find two creative ideas and write a topic sentence describing the essence of each idea.

1. Title:______________________________ Source: ________________________

____

2. Title:______________________________ Source: ________________________

____

Active Learning Guidelines:

- It should be a part of every subject matter.
- It has to be focused and purposeful.
- It has to relate to the task or objective.
- All students should be able to participate.
- Active learning is a part of every school day.
- Active learning is balanced with passive learning.
- Active learning can be in both a physical and cognitive form. Active learning can be done in classes of all sizes.
- Active learning can take place in all room environments. Active learning can be done in groups or by individuals.
- Active learning can be done in the following ways: having a discussion, role-playing, storytelling, playing a game, creating a simulation, conducting a laboratory, holding a workshop, inventing, researching, raising questions, answering higher order questions, problem solving, demonstrating, evaluating, creating, field trips, active reading and writing.

Exercise:

Describe your most active high school academic lesson (history, math or science).

____

____

____

____

____

Portraits of Active Learning

The classroom can be an exciting place and the following "***portraits***" allow us to think and create a new beginning for ourselves and for our students.

Role Playing

College/High School Role Playing

Teacher Acts out History Characters

A Princeton graduate strolls into a college classroom in Minnesota wearing a straw hat, full-length raccoon coat, spectacles, pullover sweater, plaid bow tie, and affected Boston accent. He is the personification of the roaring twenties with an eye for "Ford's, flappers and bathtub gin."

Amid the students' frequent outbursts of laughter, the professor engages in a lively dialogue about the world of April, 1929, expanding on Prohibition, the jazz clubs of Harlem and the politics of prosperity as embodied by President Herbert Hoover.

Throughout his two-semester American History class the professor dons both the costumes and personas of characters and lectures to students' to give greater clarity to the periods of history they represent.

"I try to develop the student's ability to think," he says. "These lectures are more than just information which will come flowing back (in tests)."

The interaction brings students into contact with history.

"Oftentimes, students will find it humorous to see me dress up, but then they get into the act, posing serious and difficult questions," he says.

Middle/Elementary School: Role-Playing

Glen Rock Pupil's Give Long John Silver His Day in Court

Billy Bones, the rum-soaked old sailor, returned from the grave to tell his side of the story. He sat on the witness stand explaining how he hid the treasure map in his old sea chest and how he got the black spot, the death notice, when he refused to turn the map over to Long John Silver's men.

An exasperated lawyer got up to cross-examine him. She turned to the jury: "How can you listen to the testimony of a drunk?"

She turned back to him: "Is it true you had alcohol problems?"

Bones admitted he took a bit of rum daily. The lawyer then accusingly pointed at a note card in his hands and asked why he used it for his answers.

"As I was an alcoholic my memory has failed me," he said.

"If it has failed you," the lawyer said triumphantly, "why should I believe you?

The accusations flew furiously, one after another, as seventh graders in Glen Rock last week put on trial Long John Silver, the infamous pirate with a parrot and a wooden leg in Robert Louis Stevenson's novel, *Treasure Island.* Silver was accused of piracy and four counts of murder.

Students in two of teacher Jane Doe's English classes took opposing sides in the trial, which replaced the traditional test on the book. As John Smith, who played Jim Hawkins, said, "If we did the book and the test, you'd forget the book in a month or so. If we do it this way, it's a lifetime experience."

Students acted out the parts of the four-member prosecution and defense teams and the witnesses for each side. They spent weeks trying to come up with answers for questions about their characters and building their cases. At last, Silver went on trial before a 12-member jury composed of school and town officials.

Right of Passage, Ellis-Style

Clutching their most valuable mementoes and dressed in clothes from their ancestors' homelands, the huddled mass of students trembled as they passed through America's golden doorway. Under one arm D. proudly carried masonry tools and rubles his grandfather brought to the U.S. when he left Russia in the early 1900s. D. was among 67 enthusiastic, fifth-grade students, who relived their ancestors' passage to this country, when they transformed several hallways and classrooms at an elementary school into a mini version of Ellis Island and the Great Hall.

"I didn't have a job, so I had to report to the detention center," said D., explaining how he and his classmates dramatized going through the entire immigration process, once they arrived at the international port.

The students visited Ellis Island's newly refurbished museum in September as part of the innovative social studies project. They have been studying the historical and cultural significance of the immigration process.

C., a fifth grade teacher, said the student simulation of the Ellis Island experience marked the end of a three-month project, which marked the celebration of their ethnic roots. JB, the school's principal, commended the faculty for contributing their personal experiences and making the school project an authentic one. He called the project a partnership, which enables parents to work closely with their children in researching their ethnic backgrounds.

"Our philosophy is to work in partnership with our parents," S. said, adding that many students also called relatives across the country to learn more about their immigration experiences.

Exercise:

Identify key elements in the preceding articles.

____

____

____

____

Problem Solving

College/High School Problem Solving

Required Readings in Accounting 101: Lessons in Taxation from a Spy Novel

The results in *The Ultimate Rip-off:* A Taxing Tale, a spy thriller that the author says has even captured the attention of some of his most unin-spired students.

The Ultimate Rip-off, which was published this year is about a corrupt I.R.S. Commissioner who joins forces with a coin making enterprise to steal $758 million in income tax revenue. Their goal is to finance the building of a neutron bomb.

Mass Wedding is Just a Dry Run

A mass wedding ceremony marked the beginning of life together in the classroom for 37 couples in a sociology course: Marriage and the Family. There were no wedding kisses, no tears and no champagne, but the teenage couples who pledged their "I do's" at an afternoon ceremony, were getting a glimpse of what the real thing might be like, nevertheless.

And though courses taken in high school or college may serve as an introduction, the two partners getting married must prepare together.

Students were paired together, engaged, randomly last week. They were assigned partners, rather than choosing them, so they could learn about a person they didn't know.

During the course, students will learn communication skills, problem solving, research and jobs, housing and planning and for their final assignment, each couple will have to solve a marital problem.

Elementary Problem Solving:

Inventive Students Prove Solution to Many Problems is "Elementary"

The problem fourth grader Amy saw was fairly simple: When her father practiced putting in the house she usually had to retrieve the golf ball from across the room.

A's solution was to outfit a putter with fishing reel and attach the ball with lightweight line. Thus, her father could putt and then reel in his own shots.

The invention, which Amy called "Exec-U-Putt," won a first place award for her age group in the Mini-Invention-Innovation Team Contest as part of the New Jersey Technology for Children Spring Conference.

For the invention contests, students had to develop a problem and begin keeping a journal to record their efforts, K. said. The problems ranged from the likelihood of planes to explode and burn during an emergency runway leading to developing a seat belt for dogs.

The students research the problems to see if there any solutions or remedies this thing. If they couldn't find any, they set out to solve the problem with a new invention or innovation, K. said.

The invention contest requires the children to think creatively to solve the problems they have encountered during the process, whether it's a design flaw or marketing question and it can also help the students start thinking about careers.

Exercise:

Identify key elements in the preceding articles.

____

____

____

____

____

Using Science/Mathematics

College/High School Science/Mathematics

Credit for "Ingenious" Questions about Chemistry; Newspapers as Course Assignments

A chemistry professor at Virginia Polytechnic Institute and State University encourages freshmen in his introductory course to pay attention by awarding extra credit to those students who ask "perceptive and ingenious" questions based on material covered in the class lectures".

Mr. B. says it is almost impossible to get freshmen to speak up in class, so he has them write out their questions and hand them in at the end of the period, or slip them under his office door.

Cal Poly Students are Making Aviation History

Engineering students at the California Polytechnic State University have made aviation history last week when their human powered helicopter lifted inches off of the ground in a two second flight.

After adjustments were made to the 100lb. helicopter, G. M. an engineering major who races on the U.S. cycling team, pedaled to lift the craft off the university's gymnasium floor.

The flight of the Da Vinci III, named for Leonardo, who had sketched a similar craft, makes it the first successful version of four models the students have built since 1981.

Elementary School Science/Mathematics

Wise Ideas Make Winners of Teachers

A third-grade teacher in Arizona put the multiplication tables to music. Fifth graders in an Idaho classroom can reel off the names of all 50 states in 30 seconds or less. Educators on an Indian reservation in Minnesota cut the dropout rate in half by adding Indian culture to the curriculum.

Those are among the 100 winning ideas in a contest sponsored by the National School Boards Association of ways to spark school improvement. The Association published a 35-page booklet called "100 Winning Curriculum Ideas."

A teacher says his original songs, "The Keys to Memorize" and "Learning My Times" get his pupils in the right frame of mind for practicing multiplication tables. When they get up to 12 times 12, they become Times Champs.

Another school in New Plymouth Idaho, a fifth-grade teacher teaches geography with the help of a "Motor Mouth Contest" in which the children get 30 seconds to name all the states.

Exercise:

Identify key elements in the preceding articles.

Contests and Competition

Middle/High School Contests and Competitions

Many high school and middle school graduating classes need to acquire community or public service hours in order to graduate. Listed below are ideas that can be held as charity events with the hours used for the community or public service hours needed. The proceeds can be used to help with the rising costs of educational equipment that will benefit the school.

Middle/High School Contests

- **All elementary school contests can be modified for younger students.**
- **Name That Tune**—a few notes are played each day of a specific tune and the students enter guesses on the name of the song. All correct guesses are gathered, and the winner is chosen and receives a gift card or other reward.
- **Build a Bridge**—see attached
- **Hill Climber**—see attached
- **Build a Parachute**—students are given instructions to create a parachute that will fall 15 feet, opens correctly and lands on a target.
- **CO_2 Dragster race** – students design and build a CO_2 dragster and race in the gym.
- **Pine Box Cars**—students will design, build and race pine box cars. An admission can be charged and proceeds donated to charity.
- **Catapult Contest**—see attached
- **Build a Hot Air Balloon**—similar to the parachute but build a hot air balloon instead.
- **Debate**—choose a topic and hold an in class or entire-grade debate
- **Computer Contest**—have the students design a new computer game.
- **Civics Contest**—see article review above.
- **Robotics Contest**—see previous review above
- **Essay Contest**—assign a specific topic and have students write an essay about the topic. The winning essays can be published in the school paper or local town paper.

Example of Middle/High School Competition

Bridge:

Description: This project is designed for students in middle or high school.
Team: 2–4 members
Approximate Time: 60-90 minutes per day for 1 week. Begin on the first day of the week and have the projects completed by the fifth day. Allow a

weekend for ample drying time and conduct the contest on the following, available day.

Competition:

The object of this project is to design and make a bridge that meets the requirements in order to win a bridge-building contract. The bridge that meets all the requirements and is the cheapest price will win 15 extra credit points added to their final grade.

A tie will be decided by a single coin toss with the first team to present their bridge choosing heads or tails.

If no bridges meet the requirements, the class will have three class periods to redesign and rebuild their bridges.

Requirements:

a. Students will work in teams of 2-4 members.
b. Six (1–1 ½ hour) class periods will be used for this project.
c. All work will be done in class using only the supplied materials. All bridges will be tested on the sixth class day.
d. **No** work on bridges will be done on that day or at home. Uncompleted projects will also be tested. ***Please allow for drying time.***
e. Bridge will be designed on paper and materials ordered. Only one order per team can be placed, so design carefully. **No** trading or borrowing from other teams.
f. The flat bridge area must be a minimum of 5 inches high off the ground. (**not** including rail height) Supports are not included in the height.
g. The bridge must be 12 inches long and include an on and an off ramp. The ramp lengths are **NOT** included in the 12-inch length requirement.
h. Bridge must be at least 3.5 inches wide, inside the rails.
i. Bridge must have a guardrail that runs the entire length of the bridge including the on and off ramps.
j. Bridge must hold a 2-lb. weight for a 1 minute period of time. Bridge must remain in original state for entire 1 minute.
k. A complete supply list and cost breakout will be supplied to the teacher. ***(Unused supplies must be added into the final price.)***

Supplies:

a. Thin popsicle sticks – 1 stick = $5,000.00
b. Fat popsicle stick – 1 stick - $8,000.00
c. Flat toothpick – 1 stick = $500.00
d. White tacky glue – FREE - will be supplied by teacher.

Once the design is completed and the order is made, the teams will receive their supplies in a bag supplied by the teacher so there are no conflicts. Supplies that are not used are still incorporated in the total price.

Project Evaluation: 200 Points Available

70 Points—Final design presentation, including supply list
20 Points—Bridge height
20 Points—Bridge length
20 Points—Bridge width
20 Points—Bridge holds 2-lb. weight
50 Points—Final bridge construction

High School Competition

Catapult:

The object of this project is to design and make a catapult that can throw a baseball-sized water balloon and hit a target 50 feet away. Three attempts will be judged. Points will be awarded for the closest hits to the target.

A tie will be decided by a single coin toss with the first team to present their catapult choosing heads or tails.

If no catapult meets the requirements, the class will have three class periods to redesign and rebuild their catapults.

Requirements:

a. Students will work in teams of three.
b. Ten class periods will be used for this project. All work will be done in class using only the supplied materials. All catapults will be tested on the eleventh class day. **No** work on catapults will be done on that day or at home. Uncompleted projects will also be tested.
c. Catapults will be designed on paper and material lists provided in written form.
d. The catapult must be a minimum of 18 inches high from bottom to top, not including throw bars.
e. Catapult should hold and throw a baseball-sized water balloon and hit a target 50 feet away. Three attempts will be judged. Points will be awarded for the closest hits to the target.
f. Any materials can be used to make the catapults. (wood, plastic, metal etc.).
g. Students must make their own catapults. (No premanufactured kits or items can be used).
h. No materials that are dangerous or unsafe can be used.

i. No power tools can be used in class. Screwdrivers, hammers and hand tools are allowed under supervision.
j. All teams will be supervised by an adult.
k. Safety equipment must be worn when necessary.

Once the design is completed and accepted by teacher, the students can gather materials and begin construction.

Project Evaluation:

50 Points—Design and Supply List
50 Points—Construction, Final Appearance (Match to Design)
25 points—Catapult works

1–25 points—Each for the three throws of the water balloon. Target marked out on the ground with points. Inner circle is 25 points, Next circle 15 points, Next circle 10 points and outer circle is 5 points. Misses receive 2 points as long as catapult launches more than 5 feet.

Middle/High/College Competition

Write It/Do It

Description: This event will test a competitor's ability to communicate with a colleague in writing.
Team: 2–6 members
Approximate time: 60 minutes

Competition:

Half of the team is shown an object, a system or an arrangement, built from blocks, science equipment, science materials, Tinker Toys, LEGOS, Constructs, K'NEX, Lincoln Logs, straws and pipe cleaners or any other inexpensive building materials.

Requirements:

a. The students will have 25 minutes to write a description of the object and how to make it. There will be no advantage to finishing early.
b. Only words and numbers may be used.
c. Symbols and diagrams are not allowed.
d. All abbreviations must be defined either at the beginning or when the abbreviation is first used.
e. The supervisor of the event will pass the description to the remaining team members who are in another room. They will then take the description an attempt to recreate the original object in 20 minutes.

Project Evaluation:

The team that builds the object nearest to the original design is declared the winner. A point will be given for each piece of material placed in the proper connection. No penalty will be assessed for parts that were not assembled. The use of diagrams or pictures will disqualify the team. The decisions of the judges are final. Time for the construction phase only may be used as a tiebreaker.

First—100 points
Second—80 points
Third—40 points

Elementary School Contests and Competitions

Many elementary schools frown on adding any type of contests to their curriculum. Everyone is a winner. There are no losers. The board of education feels that children need to be given encouragement and positive feedback instead of negative feedback or experiences (losing at a game or contest). On the other hand, life is not as kind and children need to learn to accept both the positive and accept the negative events life has to offer. A child can use a negative experience to learn from and possibly make a better choice in the future. As a teacher a Collier High School stated previously, "The students who made the most mistakes learned the most."

Examples of Elementary School Contests

- **Spelling Bee**—Spell age-appropriate words. The student who spells the most words correctly will win.
- **Mathematic Contest**—Same as a spelling bee, but using age-appropriate math problems.
- **Design a poster**—(environment, recycle or positive purpose). Display the posters in the halls of the school.
- **Reading**—Many businesses reward students for reading books in a specific time period. Lakewood Blue Claws give students free tickets to games when the student completes reading 10 age-appropriate books. Six Flags—Great Adventure will give discounts for students who complete 60 hours of age-appropriate reading.
- **Tabs for Time**—Students collect the tabs on soda cans and turn them in to Ronald McDonald House. They in turn give free rehab to their patients. The schools get recognized for their contributions.
- **Volleyball or any sporting tournament**—Entrance fees for teams and admissions charged can be donated to different charities.
- **Collect Food for Local Food Pantries—e**ach class collects cans for a month-to-month food drive contest. The food can be donated to local pantries. The winning classes can be rewarded with an ice cream or pizza party (usually paid for by the school PTA).

- **Box Tops for Education**—Students collect box top tabs that are located on many food products such as cereals, soups, cake mixes and cake icings. They are redeemed for $0.10 each for school supplies and needed equipment such as sports equipment for the classrooms, computer software, scanners, and any many other items. (For the past three years, an elementary school has collected over $5,000 each year and acquired many great items for their school, including digital cameras, scanners and sports equipment for each classroom.)
- **Star Student**—Students are rewarded tickets for good behavior by any staff member throughout the year. Each month all the tickets are gathered and a Star Student is picked for the month. The reward varied from books to gift certificates to Barnes and Noble.
- **Poetry contest**—Assign a specific topic for students to write about. Winning entries can be made into a book and distributed to students at the end of the year.
- **Hoops For Heart**—Each class of students is asked to have the students shoot 10 foul shots with a basketball. The top boy and girl from each class are chosen to compete against the other classes for a new basketball and gift card. These items are often donated from different business in the area that then donates money to children's charities in the winning students' names.

Contest and Competition Articles

High School

Much Ado About Shakespeare for Area High School Students

Many area high school students recently competed in a Shakespeare Competition sponsored by the Monmouth County chapter of the Union and BCC Performing Arts Department.

The event was offered to all high schools in the area. Each high school could enter two students who they felt could deliver a great Shakespearian monologue and a one of his sonnets. All three winning student's were first-time participants and thrilled to have been chosen as winners. The fun doesn't stop there though, all three will participate in the Monmouth Civic Chorus's "Sounds Like Shakespeare" and the first-place winner will move on to compete in the national competition. Winners also receive $200, $150 and $100 along with their title.

Robotics Team Tinkers Its Way to Rookie Award

The Jetson's had Rosie the housekeeper robot, the "Lost in Space" crew had "Robot" and now a high school is getting into the act by creating a robotics club. Little did they know that six months later, their first competition, the NJ FIRST-Robotics Competition, would be such a success. They will now compete in the championship event in Atlanta. FIRST (For Inspiration and Recognition of Science and Technology) is a non-profit organization that supports teamwork and professionalism. Each team in the competition had to design a robot that could complete a specific task. In this case, the robots had to take Nerf balls and put them into a high goal or two bottom goals. Each team was given a deadline in which to finish. The next goal for the club after their first win was to acquire the $10,000 entrance fees to be able to participate in two other competitions. Thanks to the generosity of Bristol-Meyers-Squibb, NASA, and enthusiastic parents and mentors, their goal was easily reached. Best of luck to the students of Allentown Robotics! For more information, visit them at www.usfirst.org.

New School Finds a New Use for Old Trees

The students at the New School in Holmdel were given a unique challenge. They were given a six-foot, artificial, tinsel tree and asked to do research and decorate the tree based on a given theme. The students were divided into groups, given their theme and put to work. They had to calculate the number of branches on each tree, graph information, and use mathematical calculations to show price increase and decrease before and after the holiday. Once that was complete, they had to research their subject and decorate their tree accordingly. The trees were then displayed for families in the courtyard. The students say they learned a lot about the environment, supply and demand and used great imagination in the creation of their unique trees. Children never cease to amaze!

New Winner in High School Civics Contest

West Windsor-Plainsboro North High School beat reigning champions East Brunswick High School by seven points in the We the People...The Citizen and the Constitution competition in Trenton. E.B. has been unbeatable in past years, not only winning the state level (17 of 18), but the past two national levels competitions as well. West Windsor's team studied hard and put in many extra hours that seem to have paid off as they head for the national competition with EB. Each team could hold up to 20 members for the five categories they would be judged on. The students are given four minutes to present a prepared statement and then asked questions on it for six minutes. The judges would review their performance and award points to see if the students could apply their knowledge. The judges also looked at whether each team understood their topic, applied reasoning, could supply supportive evidence for their statements, responded well to questions and participated in the questions. According to the national sponsors of the competition, students who participate in events such as this outperform adults by 28 percent and keep more abreast on current affairs, government policy and political affairs.

Stock Market Games Teach Serious Lessons

"Stocks reports are in" is not something usually heard in a classroom discussion, but it is a common thought when playing in the Stock Market Game. The game was started in 1977 and is available worldwide. Several high schools, middle schools and many technical schools, are taking ideas from the Stock Market Game and incorporating them into their classroom environments. The students are getting a feel that "economics is a vital part of life." says one high school teacher in CH High School in Marlboro. "My goal is to make them better citizens, to have them question everything. I want them to see through rhetoric... The kids that make the most mistakes are the ones that learn more."

Here is the way the game works. Each student is given a specific dollar amount in which to invest in the stock market. (Fictitiously, of course). For a set number of days the students are asked to play in the stock market, buying and selling stocks to see how the market works. At the end of the time period, the results are analyzed and the student who did the best will win. While many schools are adapting this idea to their curriculum, some are competing in the game nationwide. Teachers like JB at CH feel it is a great opportunity for kids to learn leadership skills, organization, negotiation and cooperation. It also teaches mathematical skills, economics, decision making skills and life lessons.

To get more information about competing in the Stock Market Game, you can access the web at www.smgww.org. Good Luck and happy investing!

Exercise:

Identify key elements in the preceding articles.

College Techniques

In "Failure 101" University of Houston Engineering Professors Offer an Innovative and Creative Approach to Design.

Walking into an engineering class at a University, a professor and his guests are greeted by students making the thumbs down gesture and singing out a chorus of "Boo's."

The professor, wearing a WWI combat helmet and a T-shirt that pictures a two-legged chair with the word "Failure" written above it, is pleased.

In this class, officially called "Innovative Designs for Civil Engineers", but known by students as "Failure 101," those are signs of approval and even affecttion.

Instead, Mr. M. and his students participate in brainstorming exercises, fantasy games, and what Mr. M. calls "design therapy," where students discuss and criticize each other's design projects.

During a class last semester, students shared with their classmates the two resumes that they were assigned to prepare: one, a list of 5 successes in their lives: the other, a list of five failures. Mr. M. had asked the students to think about the connections between the risks they have taken and the failures or successes they have experienced.

Ideas for the Classroom

A professor at a polytechnic institution has found a way to create a level playing field for the mix of science and humanity majors who enroll in his technical writing and editing courses. He makes them get down on the floor and play with Tinker Toys.

"I was having trouble getting a sufficiently easy subject for students without a heavy, science background to write about in a short piece," says the director of the master's program in technical communication.

So, he says, he divided the class into small groups of students, passed out fistfuls of Tinker Toys and told them to "develop a product with two main parts, name it, describe its function and write an assembly manual."

After the students recovered from their initial shock says Mr.C., they applied themselves to the project with "great fervor," creating helicopters, catapults, and other machines.

High School Techniques

Modern day colonists—Smith Township students reenact constitutional convention

With all the fervor of the founding fathers—and with a slight change or two in history—85 seventh and eighth graders reenacted the Constitutional Convention yesterday at a high school.

Students from the ten middle schools debated, discussed, caucused their way through the issues of representation and slavery.

Teachers and students involved in the event simulated the 1787 convention with tri-cornered hats, colonial-style garb, at least one fake accent adapted by a mock North Carolina delegate, John Doe, of Smith Township.

"You can understand what they went through that long hot summer," PB said after portraying an argumentative—for permission to remove white cotton wigs that began falling apart on a school bus ride to the mock convention.

The students themselves also defied history by altering the way the original constitution saw slavery. If they conventioneers hadn't run out of time, they would probably have voted to abolish slavery.

Middle School Techniques

Teacher Shops for Science

Sixty-six students at a middle school in Brooklyn are spending two class periods a week in stores along Brooklyn's Fifth Avenue. They are learning the practical applications of science in beauty salons, plumbing stores, ice-cream parlors and other businesses.

The students ask the shopkeepers about the specific techniques that apply in each business, keep a record of their observations and present a written report on their findings. A sixth-grade science teacher said that he thought of the project while looking out his classroom window at a pharmacy across the street. He decided to take his chemistry class there for a lecture. Walking home he noticed a variety of stores, he wondered if all of the shopkeepers and employees could work alongside his students, helping teach them about science and how it can be applied. The result was the program, which lasted six weeks.

"The unusual aspect of the project is the interaction between the kids in the community," Mr. W. said. "The premise is that science is everywhere."

Elementary Techniques

Social Studies - Mapping Your School

Kids will gain basic geography and math skills through this mapping activity. Divide your class into four groups and have each group be responsible for measuring either, the east, west, north or south side of your school building using tape measures you supply or that kids bring in from home. Students should also measure the individual rooms along their assigned side of the school. After they have done this, choose a scale and have all the groups draw the rooms to scale. Then, take their four drawings and connect them onto a larger paper to make a school map. Then see if you can get a copy of a small blueprint map or drawing of the school building from maintenance personnel to see how the students have come to measure accurately.

Volunteering

Pupils from Immaculate Visit Cerebral Palsy Center

Youngsters with cerebral palsy have a chance to reach out to other children through a pilot program started at the Cerebral palsy Treatment Center of Union County. The program involves voluntary visits to the Union Township Center by students from a school in Elizabeth.

A center nurse said the goal of the program is "to help bridge the gap between the disabled and the non-disabled population, by bringing them together."

Sixth-, seventh- and eighth-grade students from school will be helping the center's youngsters with their classroom work, accompanying them on field trips and participating in group activities such as cooking pizza.

Exercise:

Identify key elements in the preceding articles.

____

____

____

Elements and Characteristics of Cooperative Learning

Definition: ***"Cooperative Learning is an instructional technique that requires students to work together in small, fixed groups in a structured, learning task."***

Johnson and Johnson

All cooperative learning methods share the idea that students work together to learn, and are responsible for one another's learning, as well as their own.

Student Team Learning (STL) Methods, in addition to this idea, emphasize the use of team goals and team success, which can only be achieved if all members of the team learn the objectives being taught. That is, in Student Team Learning, the students' tasks are not to do something as a team, but to learn something as a team.

Three concepts are essential to all STL methods:

Team rewards
Individual Accountability
Equal Opportunity for Success

Team Rewards: Teams earn certificates or other team rewards if they achieve above a designated criteria.

Individual Accountability: The team's success depends on the individual learning of all team members. This focuses the activity of the team members on explaining concepts to one another and making sure that everyone on the team is ready for a quiz or other assessment that they will take ***without*** teammate help.

Equal Opportunities for Success: Students contribute to their teams by improving over their own past performances.

It is not enough to simply tell students to work together; they must have a reason to take one another's achievement seriously.

Student Team—Achievement Division (STD): Students are assigned to four-member learning teams, mixed in performance level, sex and ethnicity. The teacher presents a lesson, and then the students work within their teams to make sure that all team members have mastered the lesson. Finally, all students take individual quizzes on the material, at which time they may not help one another.

Teams–Games–Tournament (TGT): Uses the same teacher presentations and team work as in STD, but replaces the quizzes with weekly tournaments. In these, students compete with members of other teams to contribute points to their team scores. A ***"bumping"*** procedure changes table assignments to keep the competition fair. The winner at each tournament table brings the same number of points to his or her team, regardless of which table it is, which means, that this means that low achievers (competing with other low achievers) and high achievers (competing with other high achievers) have equal opportunities for success.

Team-Assisted Individualization (TAI): Team-Assisted Individualization combines cooperative learning with individualized instruction. TAI is specifically designed to teach mathematics to all students in grades 3 to 6 (or older students not ready for a full algebra course). In TAI, students enter an individualized sequence according to a placement test and then proceed at their own rates. In general, team members work on different units. Teammates check each other's work against answer sheets and help one another with any problems. Final unit tests are taken without teammate help and are scored by student monitors.

Because students take responsibility for checking each other's work and managing the flow of materials, the teacher can spend most of the class time presenting lessons to small groups of students drawn from the various teams, who are working at the same point in the mathematics sequence.

"Jigsaw" Method of Cooperative Learning: Students are assigned to six-member teams to work on academic material that has been broken into sections. For example, a biography might be divided into early life, first accomplishments, major setbacks, later life and impact on history, each team member lends to his or her section. Next, members of different teams, who have studied the same sections, meet in ***"expert groups"*** to discuss their sections. Then, the students return to their teams and take turns teaching their teammates about their sections. Because the only way students can learn sections other than their own, is to listen carefully to their teammates, they are motivated to support and show interest in one another's work.

The methods Johnson and Johnson have researched involve students working on assignment sheets in four- or five-member, heterogeneous groups. The groups hand in a single sheet and receive praise and rewards based on the group product. Their methods emphasize ***team-building activities*** before students begin working together and regular discussions within groups about how well they are working together.

Group Investigation Method: Students form their own two- to six-member groups. After choosing subtopics from a unit being studied by the entire class, the groups further break their subtopics into individual tasks and carry out the activities necessary to prepare group reports. Each group then makes a presentation or display to communicate its findings to the entire class.

Chapter Notes & Additional Information:

Chapter 5:

Strategies & The Classroom

By modifying various elements of the strategy, it can be made to accommodate the needs of the individual classroom.

Chapter Topics:

Introduction

Stated earlier was the premise that teachers of various levels and subjects can use the same array of methods. With a few exceptions, most methods can be used at any level or with any subject or discipline. By modifying various elements of the strategy it can be made to accommodate the needs of the individual classroom. Two important elements of strategies are ***time*** and ***content.***

Governing Principles for Time and Content

- **Each strategy has minimum and maximum limits.**
- **Each level establishes effective limits.**
- **Effectiveness of the strategy decreases beyond the stated limits.**
- **Limits are affected by age and abilities of students and subject.**

Time

Minimum — **Maximum**

Content

Simple — **Complex**

Concrete — **Abstract**

Elements of Change

Time: The time devoted toward the strategy can be decreased to effect the desired change. By decreasing the time of a lecture from one hour (maximum) to 10 minutes, it can be used in the kindergarten and first grades.

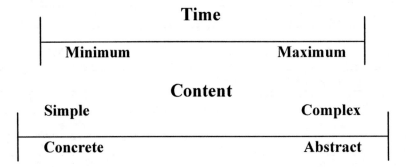

Through increasing the upper time limits of a strategy, it can be as detrimental as not devoting enough time to the strategy. A recitation that lasts for more than 25 minutes can destroy the benefits that may have been derived. Students become restless, bored and inattentive, knowing the limits have been surpassed. Conversely, not devoting enough time for a simulation game to allow for a thorough debriefing session can lessen the educational benefits of the strategy.

Each strategy should be conducted within its ***minimum*** and ***maximum*** time limits. The range provides enough flexibility to accommodate the teaching level and subject matter needs.

Content: The second element that can be used to modify a strategy for use on various teaching levels or subject is the content complexity. The complexity of the content that the strategy is presenting can be viewed from the following perspectives:

- **Is the content simple or complex?**
- **Is the content concrete or abstract?**
- **What levels of thinking are involved?**
- **How much material is to be learned?**
- **What is the emphasis on learning: facts, skills, concepts or values?**

Strategies that seem to be geared for particular age groups, such as the lecture, seminar, storytelling and research, can be modified to accommodate needs at other levels by increasing or decreasing the complexity and/or amount of material that is to be learned. Generally, rules for changing the amount or complexity of the subject are:

- **The lower grade levels; the more concrete and less abstract the material.**
- **The newer the subject; less instead of more material should be presented.**
- **The lower the level; less instead of more material should be presented.**
- **Discovery versus deductive learning; more time is needed.**

The use of basic common sense will dictate the amount and complexity of material that should be used with each strategy. However, there is always a tendency to give ***too*** much information at any given time without careful consideration to the preceding guidelines. It is better to learn something well and understand it fully, than to be introduced to several concepts without grasping their meaning.

Selecting the Teaching Strategy

A lesson and a unit are more likely to utilize more than one teaching method. The planning of the lessons/unit in terms of the strategies is an important factor in how much and what type of learning will take place. With the proper planning, there should be little reason to constantly repeat the same methods on a daily basis. Different strategies can be used to teach the same material and objectives without "endangering" the program.

One of the foremost decisions a teacher will make is that of selecting the strategies for the lessons. The choice of teaching methods will play a major part in the success of the teacher and students. The selection of the strategy is primarily a teacher decision; however, it can be ***shared*** with the students. This sharing of decisions, with guidance, encourages greater participation and responsibility from the students.

In order to make the appropriate choice of methods, it is necessary to first establish the criteria for selection. Several factors (criteria) should be observed prior to the selection of the strategy. The emphasis given to any particular factor(s) is dependent on the situation.

Notes:

The Criteria for Selection of Teaching Strategies

1. ***Subject:*** By the nature of the discipline, certain strategies may be appropriate or inappropriate. Physical education courses lend themselves to the use of demonstrations or drills, but are highly limited in terms of discussions and role-playing.

2. ***Learning Aims:*** What is the expected outcome of learning? Memorizing dates? Applying formulas? Demonstrating dance steps? Appreciation of classical music? The specific category of learning (cognitive, psychomotor or affective) as well as the range within each category should be identified.

3. ***Number of students:*** The number of students in a classroom limits the methods that can be utilized. With 15 students, it is inappropriate to give a formal lecture, and conversely, with 120 students, a discussion is not advised.

4. ***Environment:*** The physical limitations of the available facilities are a factor that needs to be considered in selection of methods. If the room has movable furniture versus fixed, it increases the number of strategies that can be utilized.

5. ***Time:*** How much time is available for instruction is an important consideration as well as the time of day. When classes are scheduled in one-hour blocks of

time, strategies such simulation games, discovery and learning are limited unless modified. During certain periods of the day, passive or active strategies should be accepted.

6. ***Previous lessons:*** The strategies used in prior lessons, as well as content, will influence the selection of a strategy. If you have lectured the previous lesson to introduce information, then a discussion or films would be appropriate. Constant use of the same strategy reduces the effectiveness of the strategy.

7. ***Teacher**:* The teacher's breadth of teaching strategies will affect his choice or limit them as well as his own personal preferences. Each teacher tends to favor strategies that he feels secure in using. Certainly a small mastery of methods confines one selection, but it is the obligation of each teacher to expand the range of teaching strategies.

8. ***Students:*** The students' experience and abilities (cognitive, affective and physical) are important considerations in selecting a strategy. If students do not have the necessary attention span, note taking and organizational abilities, then the lecture should not be used until those skills are developed. Student experience or interest will determine in part if a passive, active or receptive strategy is chosen. When a student has a high interest or experience in the subject, more strategies can be utilized than not.

In the actual selection process, the teacher should evaluate and weigh the criteria each time a strategy is to be selected.

Exercise:

Interview a teacher and ask the following questions:

1. How do you select a method?

____

____

2. What method seems to work best?

____

____

3. In a typical lesson, what is the most difficult aspect of planning (i.e., time, strategy, organization)?

____

____

4. What is your most creative idea?

___

___

5. Where do you look for new approaches?

___

___

6. When do you use a new idea?

___

___

7. What happens if the new idea succeeds/fails?

___

___

8. What motivates you to teach better?

___

___

Acquiring New Strategies

The problem of acquiring or using new strategies is not because of the lack of methods, but from other barriers. Some of the barriers that keep teachers from trying new teaching strategies are:

- ***Effort:*** Usually it is easier to teach a class as you've done in the past than to try something new. Effort is not so hard to overcome if you use the diagnostic information discussed earlier and are aware of the weaknesses in your teaching.

- ***Fear of Loss of Status:*** To most instructors the status of the teacher is a cherished reward for years of study. To be an authority that dispenses crumbs of wisdom to the multitudes of students is a very satisfying role. Trying a new technique may involve a threat to your status. If the new method fails, the students are likely to feel that you don't know what you're doing. Even if it works, it may mean some changes in your status. Permitting student participation means that more embarrassing questions are likely to be asked and that less emphasis will be placed on learning from the instructor. The instructor's leadership may be challenged by aggressive, intelligent students.

- ***Fear of Failure:*** Teachers who try new techniques are not likely to be skilled in its use and are likely to imagine consequences far more catastrophic than any that are likely to occur. In using new techniques, instructors may feel that they are losing control of the situation and that anything may happen.

- ***Fear of Unfavorable Reactions from Colleagues:*** Even when a new teaching method is successful, experimenting instructors are likely to feel they are deserting the tried-and-true academic traditions in order to curry student or administration favor.

Implementation

When and after a teacher has made the decision to use a new strategy or alter the old one, several steps should be implemented.

I. ***Diagnosis:*** Realistically analyze your methods in terms of their strengths and weaknesses.

This analysis can be done in several different ways:

a. ***Self Evaluation***
b. ***Peer Evaluation***
c. ***Supervisors Evaluation***
d. ***Student Evaluation***

It is suggested that whatever combination is used to make the assessment, an objective form be used to guide the process. It is recommended that the diagnostic process include:

- ***Strengths and weaknesses:*** Only major strengths and weaknesses are identified. Don't spend time looking at each technical skill of teaching; concentrate on major areas, lesson organization versus handwriting.
- ***Observation:*** When observation is part of the process, conduct the lesson in a class and subject where the instructor feels comfortable and confident. Don't cloud the diagnosis with discipline, content or environmentalist problems.

II. ***Prescription:*** Once the diagnosis has been completed, then a plan of improvement is to be designed. The plan should take into consideration the following:

- ***Be Realistic***: That the recommendations not attempt to change the whole teacher, but only specific concerns. Keep a realistic perspective as to what can be accomplished in a short period of time.
- ***Select Areas:*** Don't overwhelm yourself or instructor with a multitude of recommendations, but identify selected areas.
- ***Improvement:*** Concentrate on areas that will show the quickest and the easiest improvement. Build on the either a strength or a weakness where immediate positive changes will take place.
- ***Recommendations:*** Recommendations should be made along with specific sources (print and nonprint) of how they can be accomplished. The plan should outline in detail the steps that should be taken.

III. ***Implementation***: The process of putting into effect the recommended changes (plan), has many critical steps.

- ***Methods:*** Understand the new method or changes in the old method through reading, questioning and observing. The method, its organization and process should be thoroughly understood before an attempt is made to put it into practice. It is not expected that the method be mastered the first time used, but that the instructor has a working knowledge of its major characteristics.

- ***Setting:*** The setting for the instruction of a new strategy should be free from major concerns, such as student behavior problems and learning a new topic. Whenever possible the instruction of a new strategy should be with students who are not discipline problems, and with a subject topic that the teacher is thoroughly familiar. The added task of managing a class and learning new content will distract from the teachers effort in concentrating on the method.

- ***Practice!***: Before implementation, practice the method several times. Anticipate trouble spots, review critical statements, organize groups and plan sequence of activities. Don't attempt to ***utilize the method*** without reviewing and practicing the vital components several times.

Other Guidelines

- ***Colleagues:*** Work with another teacher(s) in learning new techniques. The support of colleagues will alleviate part of the fears in attempting something new.

- ***Approval:*** When deciding to use a radically different approach (not standard practice), seek administrative approval. Explain your reasons to administration, in as much detail as possible. Include who, what, when, where, why and how.

- ***Expectations:*** Keep expectations at a normal level. Try not to be overly optimistic or pessimistic in the implementation of a new strategy. The process, as a learning venture, is new to both the instructor and students and should be treated as the introduction of any new learning beset with all its problems and conditions.

Preparing the Students for New Strategies

One of learning's important concepts is that of ***readiness***. Readiness implies that the learner has at his command the necessary attributes (physical, psychological, social and intellectual) to acquire the "knowledge" at a given period of time. Part of the readiness is the preparation or establishment of a set for the learning. As stated in chapter 2, each strategy requires the student to perform, respond and interact differently. When a new skill is introduced, it should not be thrust upon students, but gradually introduced allowing students a period of adjustment.

The introduction of a new teaching method requires the same preparation as does other forms of learning. Much of the success in implementing a new method depends on the introduction of the students to the method.

- ***Have realistic expectations:*** Don't expect the students to respond the first time the method is introduced the same way as if they were experienced in the strategy. The students need time to grow with their role and expectations of the method as does the instructor in his presentation.

- ***Explain and Identify:*** Explain what part (role) they are expected to play in the strategy. Include both cognitive aspects (prior readings and knowledge) and the responsibilities of interaction. Identify any special skills or characteristics that are needed to effectively participate in the strategy.

- ***Special Skills:*** Special skills and characteristics should be taught prior to the introduction to the method. Don't compound the problem by attempting to teach three things at once: special skills, content and process (strategy).

- ***Prepare students ahead of time:*** Don't spring a new method on students without giving enough lead time to prepare them for their responsibilities. In most cases a day or two is all the lead time needed to make the initial preparation. In strategies such as field trips, observations and simulation games, a week or more may be required.

- ***Guidance:*** Guide and assist the students in their responsibilities throughout the process. Keep reminding and encouraging them about their roles both formally an informally. By stopping and reflecting (formally) upon the steps, procedures or roles, the teacher directs the attention of the whole class to the process.

Informally, the teacher may ***"comment"*** to the whole class, individuals or small groups, but doesn't stop the normal flow of the strategy. Assistance such as clarifying characters and role-playing, cueing students on what to look for in field trips or observations and suggesting questions one might ask as a discussion, are part of the process in guiding a student in a new teaching method. The behaviors ***(responsibilities)*** that are necessary for a student to function effectively in a teaching strategy are learned. They need to be reinforced and practiced if they are to be mastered.

Summary

Any strategy can be used at any grade level and discipline can be modified (content and time). There are minimum and maximum limits to each strategy. Selection of a teaching strategy is not a chance process but a very deliberate process in the analysis of several criteria.

When planning to implement a new strategy, care must be taken to prepare the students as well as oneself. The change of method requires a new role for both the students and the instructor.

References:

Hyman, Ronald. *Ways of Teacher*, 2nd ed. Philadelphia: J.B. Lippincott Company, 1974.

McKeochie, Wilbert. *Teaching Tips*, 7th ed. Lexington, MA: D.C. Heath and Company, 1978.

Chapter Notes & Additional Information:

Personal Thoughts & Drawings

Chapter 6:

Organization & Planning

Planning allows the teacher to visualize the sequence of activities that will take place over a period of time…

Chapter Topics:

Introduction	**Lesson Plan**
Steps in Planning Process	**Lesson Plan Categories & Explanations**
Unit Plans	**Sample Student Lesson Plan (Storm Chasers)**
Elements of the Unit Plan	

Introduction

Planning for teaching is another one of the ***myriad of technical skills*** all teachers must possess. Every master teacher has the ability to organize his course, unit or lesson so it makes sense not only to himself and his supervisor, but most importantly to his students. Planning allows a teacher to visualize the sequence of activities that will take place over a period of time, be it a half-hour lesson, two-week unit or throughout the semester.

Planning includes organizing for very short periods of time as in lesson plans, intermediate as in unit plans, and long-range periods as in semester or course plans. As the plans move from long range to individual lesson, they become less general and more specific. But as in all organizations, there is a supportive relationship between each planning effort.

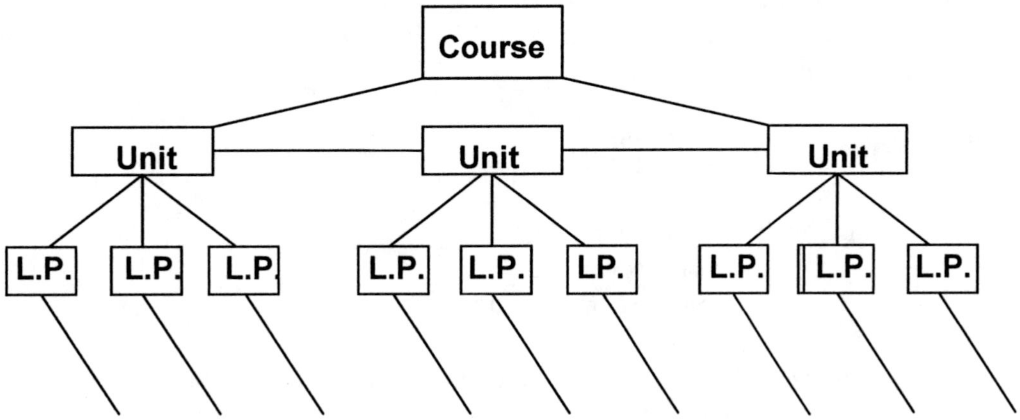

The course represents the larger goal or objectives that are to be accomplished. Within the course are several units that all related in some way to the course goal. The operational end of the planning is done via the lesson plans; this puts the objectives into action.

Some reasons for planning are:

1. **To see the *direction* in which you are taking your students.**
2. **To be able to *prepare* yourself for the activities which you're to teach.**
3. **To give you a *sense of continuity* from one day, week, to the next.**
4. **To assist you in *evaluating* what you have taught and what students have learned.**
5. ***Self-evaluation* allows you see your strengths and weaknesses.**
6. **Allows you to have a *reference* for future work.**

Steps in the Planning Process

Whether you are short or long- range planning, the basic steps are as follows:

1. ***Determine what your goal, purpose and objectives are. Establish a direction that you want to move in.***

2. ***Establish what level of understanding your pupils are at with the subject matter.***

3. ***Identify some pathways of teaching and lead your students to the subject.***

4. ***Determine various means of evaluating and measuring the pupils' process.***

Units Plans

Definition: ***A unit consists of a series of ideas and concepts unified by a particular theme or topic. A unit represents a general outline of the processes and not the specific procedures as in a lesson plan.***

Elements of the Unit Plan

I. ***Background Data:*** Unit Name: ____________________
# of Lessons: ____________ Time (weeks): ________
Subject: (Course Title): ____________________

II. ***Unit Objective:*** The objectives are broadly stated and reflect generalizations and concept development: i.e. the student will understand that families are basic social units of people who live together and usually care for one another.

III. ***Materials:*** A list, printout or nonprint media that would be used to teach the unit. Specific books, chapters, films or tapes would be cited.

IV. ***Procedures:*** A brief identification or a sequence of activities used
material.

1. ***Discussion:*** **What is a family?**
2. ***Film:*** Who Are We? – 15 minutes
3. ***Dramatic Play:*** Students can choose different family roles

V. ***Evaluation:*** A description of the methods used in evaluating the specific objectives of the unit and/or lesson objectives.

1. ***Essay Test: (each unit)*** **------- 30% of grade**
2. ***Unit Project:*** **------------------- 30% of grade**
3. ***Homework:*** **-------------------- 20% of grade**
4. ***Quizzes:*** **------------------------ 10% of grade**
5. ***Participation:*** **----------------- 10% of grade**

VI. ***Special Activities:*** Activities that take the student out of the classroom should be identified (field trip)

Lesson Plan

The most important aspect in the planning scheme is the ***lesson plan***. In it represents the ***step-by-step process of teaching specific "ideas."*** The lesson plan offers the teacher security in knowing what, where and how he is to teach the lesson. A good lesson plan leaves few unknowns with which the teacher must deal in conveying the actual presentation. The lesson plan is inclusive and gives the teacher a true sense of direction for teaching.

Lesson Plan Categories & Explanations

I. ***Background Data:*** This category identifies for the teacher what the "givens" are for the lesson. It sets up the rest of the lesson in terms of specific data such as time, place and subject.

Name: ________________ Date: __________ Time: __________ Grade: ______
Place: ________________ # of Students: __________ Subject: ______________
Unit: ______________________ Lesson Topic: ____________________

II. ***Core/Behavioral Objectives:*** A series of statements that reflect what you want the student to learn. For a given lesson there could be one or several objectives that you would teach toward or emphasize.

____

____

III. ***Materials:*** Anything that is used for the lesson that is ***not permanently*** in the classroom. Also include the quantity of each material used (i.e., books, handouts, experiments or laboratories).

____

____

t: Each lesson has an assignment, and the assignment given for ted and identified here. Assignments are given for two basic *pare* the students for the upcoming lessons and 2) to ***reinforce*** ork.

____

____

ctor will list the sequential steps by which he plans to ough the lesson. Those steps include a *very* detailed outline of activities for each method employed. Within the category of procedures there are several subheadings.

- ***Set:*** Before each lesson, the instructor introduces or gets the students ready to participate. (See chapter 8).

- ***Organization:*** Any time the instructor changes the normal seating pattern or structure of the class, it is noted in the plan. If the instructor moves from lecturing to small-group discussion, the change is noted, as well as possible conformation of the groups.

- ***Illustrations:*** When the instructor uses examples other than verbal, such as pictures, charts, models, graphs or tapes, an indication is made in the plan as to when and where they are to be used.

- ***Time:*** A running log is kept on the approximate amount of time it takes to conduct each part of a lesson. This accounting of time allows the instructor to see where the emphasis is placed in the lesson.

Exercise: *See Storm Chasers pgs. 52-53*

Organizations & Illustrations	**Procedures**	**Time**
	Set:	
	Lesson/Strategy:	
	Closure/Evaluation:	

- ***Closure/evaluation:*** The final subheading under procedures is a summary and an informal evaluation. The instructor states the key points of the lesson and draws conclusions. An informal evaluation can be conducted through questions and answers of the students' basic understanding of the objectives. Mastery is not expected during the first lesson.

VI. ***Related activities:*** This category reflects a mini lesson plan within the larger plan. It represents the possible, maybe and could be, if there happens to be more time than expected. A teacher always plans for more time than necessary, and those extract activities relate to the basic thrust of the lesson.

____

____

VII. ***Assignment (New):*** The assignment for the next lesson is given. Assignments can be writing, viewing, collecting, questioning, reading and listening. All assignments do not have to be written.

____

____

VIII. ***Ongoing activities:*** This category is a statement of various activities or events that will be taking place in the future. It is similar to a long-range assignment telling the students about and preparing them for upcoming "activities."

____

____

IX. ***Lesson Comments:*** After the lesson has been completed, the instructor evaluates his and the student's performance. The instructor makes notations as to the strengths and weaknesses and what changes should be made for the next time this lesson is taught again.

____

____

Sample Student Lesson Plan (Storm Chasers)

I. Background Data: (Time: 7–10 minutes)

Name: Ken Smith ***Date:*** 4/25/06 ***Time:*** 12:15 P.M.
Grade Level: College ***Place:*** SSB111 ***# of Students:*** 28
Subject: Storm Chasers ***Unit:*** Weather Phenomena
Lesson Topic: Examining Earth's Atmosphere

II. Behavioral Objectives

A. The student will understand who and what storm chasers are.
B. The student will learn how chasers find storms.
C. The student will learn why people decide to chase storms and of what purpose or value this holds.
D. The students will learn the terminology used by storm chasers.

III. Materials

Whiteboard, dry-erase markers

IV. Previous Assignment:

Discuss in one page or less how an average person could predict weather patterns by using simple instruments such as a barometer, thermometer, weathervane and an instrument to measure humidity.

V. Procedures:

Set: Your previous assignment may have made you realize that our weather is not incredibly predictable. Professional meteorologists use high technology to follow storm fronts and predict our weather. A few others who are called amateur meteorologists are storm chasers who predict and chase the weather using little other than what you had to write your homework. Today, we will learn about these amateurs and try to understand what motivates them to endanger their lives to follow severe weather.

Organization: Arrange the chairs a three-quarter circle so they all face the teacher.

Teaching strategy: (Informal Lecture)

A. Introduce a typical storm chaser:

1. Jack Corso, a mailman, and Time Dorr, an advertising executive are common average people.
2. Explain that they are amateurs who use their vacation time to follow storms two weeks a year.

B. Where they chase storms:

1. Every May, the two men meet in Oklahoma City and set out on a two-week journey with their weather radios.
2. **The Southern Great Plains States** – Highest frequency of tornadoes in the world.
3. **Mid-Great Plains States** – Best thunder and lightning storms in the country.

C. How they chase storms:

1. They listen to the radio for updates on storms or patterns.
2. Explain that the pair "monitors" the sky by looking at cloud formations to predict weather movement.
3. They drive at high speeds to be in front of a storm front so they can be there before anything happens.
4. The chasers try to find a ***dry line*** (area where moist and dry air come together and the two fronts meet).
5. The chasers try to find this line to the ***triple point*** (area where the dry line and warm front intersect), a hot spot for twisters.

6. Some chasers decide to ***core punch***, a dangerous idea that entails driving to the triple point while the storm is mounting.
7. The chasers get excellent photos and videos if they're lucky, which they sell to finance their expensive hobby.

D. Who chases storms:

1. Researchers who study the atmospheric conditions using storms.
2. Thrill seekers who core punch and challenge nature.
3. People who are impressed with the awesome power of storms and admire the force.
4. People who record the images of storms for profit

Closure: In just a few minutes, you have learned how chasers track a storm and some of the terminology they use. If this is of interest to you, you may want to consider studying meteorology.

E. Related activities:

1. " Meteorology" DVD
2. " Experiencing a Tornado" reading

F. New Assignment:

For tomorrow, describe in a one-page paper, your opinions or theories on how the sun, the moon or other celestial bodies affect or control our weather.

G. Ongoing Activities:

Every student has a one-page paper to do, (four times a week), which will be applied to a term report at the end of the semester.

H. Lesson comments:

Write a summary of this DVD.

Summary

Planning is essential for good teaching. The two most widely used plans by teachers are the unit and the lesson plan. The unit plan brings together several lessons under a unifying theme or topic. The individual lesson plan guides the teacher in the actual presentation of the activities, spelling out the routes that will be taken by the students.

Chapter Notes & Additional Information:

____

____

____

Chapter 7: Technical Skills of Teaching: Questions

A series of individual skills that are an integral part of the presentation process regardless of method or style …

Chapter Topics:

Introduction	**Factual Questions**
Questioning Skills	**Descriptive Questions**
Fluency in Asking Questions	**Probing Questions**

Introduction

There are several "***technical skills***" of teaching that are common to all styles, forms and teaching strategies. The definition of technical skills used for the purpose of this lesson is as follows:

Definition: ***A series of individual skills that are an integral part of the presentation process regardless of method or style.***

These skills assist the teacher to become a more effective presenter or teacher. However, they are not considered as ends in themselves, but only as supports to the teaching process. All master teachers utilize the skills no matter what method, style or conditions (classroom structure and organization) are present.

Each of the skills can be learned independently of method and style and then incorporated into variations of teaching.

The technical skill of teaching included in this lesson is: ***Questioning skills***

Exercise:

Write down the questions a teacher asks. Even include questions that the teacher raises and answers himself. These are called rhetorical questions.

Class: ______________________ Dates: ______________________

Questions:

1. ____

____

2. ____

____

3. ____

____

4. ____

____

Questioning Skills

The purpose of studying and practicing questioning techniques is to help the teacher develop a repertoire of questioning skills that can be used to stimulate interesting discussions and productive thoughts. Once the teacher decides what kind of thoughts he wants his students to think, he can channel the thought process in the desired direction by skillful questioning.

Questions range from the concrete to the abstract and from the simple to the complex. There are basically four categories of questions:

- ***Factual and descriptive questions***
- ***Probing questions***
- ***Higher-order questions***
- ***Divergent questions***

This section will only concentrate on factual, descriptive and probing types of questions.

Fluency in Asking Questions: Emphasis is on the number of questions asked. You will be required to ask as many questions as you possibly can. The questions will usually be simple ones. Factual and descriptive questions are not the kind teachers most need to practice, but they are the most appropriate for an exercise in fluency. When you have achieved fluency, you will find it easier to acquire the three most sophisticated and important skills in questioning.

Asking Probing Questions: The teacher will ask probing questions in response to superficial answers or statements from the students. Skillful use of probing techniques helps the teacher both to bring more out of the students and to keep a classroom discussion interesting.

The thinking process stimulated by effective oral questioning should be reinforced by effective written questions. Once you have acquired skills in asking questions in the classroom, you should be able to write better examination questions. The following are general rules for asking questions. They should be considered when you are practicing any of the questioning skills; they will remind you of the characteristics of effective questioning.

1. Distribute questions among the students so that many are encouraged to speak, and the discussion is not monopolized by a few.
2. Balance the kinds of questions by using factual, probing, higher-order and divergent questions as appropriate.
3. Encourage students to give lengthy responses. Ask questions that require such answers and use probing techniques.
4. Allow students enough time to think over the question.
5. Ask clear and coherent questions. Rephrasing should not be necessary.
6. Encourage student-to-student as well as teacher-to-student interactions.
7. Ask questions that cannot be answered merely with a "Yes" or "No".

Fluency in Asking Questions

Probing questions, higher-order questioning and divergent questions are sophisticated techniques. Fluency is not; however, fluency is basic to the development of more complex questioning skills. Experience has shown that the teacher, who achieves fluency in asking questions of any kind, acquires the other questioning skills more easily than the teacher who does not acquire fluency. The achievement of fluency, then, is a prerequisite for developing the more important and complex skills of asking probing, higher-order and divergent questions.

In this exercise, the focus is on asking questions fluently. The objective of the exercise is for you to ask as many questions as you can during the lesson. It is recommended that you emphasize questions that can be answered from memory or by sensory description. The questions of this sort are uncomplicated. Is not difficult to ask them; however, it may be difficult to be fluent in asking them.

Basically, two kinds of questions are answerable from memory or by sensory description. They are usually called factual questions and descriptive questions.

Factual Questions

The words ***who, what, when and where*** often figure in this kind of question. Factual questions usually ask the students to recall specific information they have previously learned. There are at least three kinds of facts. Some facts, such as constitutional rights, blood types and driving regulations are important in themselves. Other facts form part of a common knowledge that members of a culture are expected to possess. A third category of facts is essential to building concepts and generalizations Concept formation and generalization are among the higher intellectual processes of human.

Examples of Factual Questions:

1. What is eight times ten?
2. How many quarts are in a gallon?
3. What is the capital of California?
4. What is the largest state in the union?
5. Name four vegetables.

Descriptive Questions

At first glance one might think that descriptive question should be classified as higher-order questions. On closer examination it can be seen that, although more complicated than factual questions, descriptive questions still require that the student answer simply from memory or by sensory description. However, the student must recall or describe not isolated facts, but facts organized into some logical relationship. Descriptive questions usually require a longer answer from the student than factual questions do.

Examples of Descriptive Questions:

1. How is bread made?
2. What is the difference between a microcomputer and a minicom-puter?
3. Describe how to change a flat tire.
4. Explain the process of cell division.
5. Describe the process of osmosis.
6. How do policemen serve the community?
7. ______________________________
8. ______________________________
9. ______________________________

In this exercise, you will be asked to teach a short lesson in which you should ask as many questions as you can. The kind of question you ask is unimportant. Factual and descriptive questions require little more of the students than remembering or describing. Since these kinds of questions are simpler than abstract questions, they are usually easier to ask. They will probably occur to you more readily; however, you need not limit yourself to a particular kind of question in performing this exercise.

Exercise:

Write as many questions as you can on the topic of your choice. You do not need to know the answer to the question.

Topic: ____

____

____

____

____

____

____

____

____

____

____

____

____

Probing Questions

Teacher:	"Would you say that inflation in the United States is greater or less than it was 10 years ago?"
Student:	"Greater."
Teacher:	"You are correct. Why do you think so?"
Student:	"Because there are easier credit terms."
Teacher:	"Yes, but that is only part of it. Can anyone else give me more reasons?"
Class:	(Silence)
Teacher:	"Well, basically it is because . . ."

A teacher wants his class to discuss the topic. He asks a question and receives a courtesy answer that adds next to nothing to the discussion. The discussion drags. It evolves into an unprepared lecture. In many cases, this is the teacher's fault. Teachers may ask questions that are embarrassingly simple; however, it may be that the students are shy, afraid of answering incorrectly or just naturally taciturn.

Effective teachers keep discussions going by asking questions that require more than superficial answers. They do this in two ways. The first is to forestall answers by asking questions to which such answers cannot be given. This is what higher-order questions do. The second approach is based on techniques that may be used after a student has given a superficial response. Once this has occurred, the teacher, instead of advancing to another question, ***probes*** the student's response by means of one of the techniques outlined below.

More than any other skill in this cluster, ***probing*** will require you to give an unrehearsed response. Because the ***probe*** depends on the students' response, you will rarely be able to prepare ***probing*** questions in advance of the lesson. By practicing ***probing*** questions with a variety of responses, you can develop a repertoire of question formats to apply when appropriate in the classroom.

The following ***probing*** techniques can be used in any situation where student participation is necessary to realize the goals of the lesson. Any given technique may be appropriate in one situation but not in another.

1. The teacher seeks clarification and may ask the student for more information or clarification by saying:

    a. "What, precisely do you mean?"
    b. "Please restate that phrase."
    c. "Could you elaborate on that idea?"
    d. ______________________________
    e. ______________________________

2. The teacher seeks to increase the student's critical awareness. The teacher wants the student to justify the response. Examples of appropriate probing questions are:

   a. "What are your assumptions?"
   b. "What are your reasons for believing that it is so?"
   c. "Are there other points to look for?"
   d. "How many points are we trying to raise here?
   e. "How would an adversary of this idea respond?"
   f. ______________________________
   g. ______________________________

3. The teacher refocus is the response. If a student has given a satisfactory answer, it may seem unnecessary to the probe it. However, the teacher can use this opportunity to refocus on a related issue. Examples of probing questions that might also refocus a response are:

   a. "If this is correct, what are the implications for…?"
   b. "How does Linda's answer conform to…?"
   c. "How does Pete's reply apply to …?"
   d. "Can you relate this to…?"
   e. "Let's analyze that answer."
   f. ______________________________
   g. ______________________________

4. The teacher prompts the student. The teacher gives the student a hint to help answer the question:

   Teacher: "Ken, what is the square root of 94?"
   Ken: "I don't know."
   Teacher: "Well, what is the square root of 100?"
   Ken: "Ten."
   Teacher: "And a square root of 81?"
   Ken: "Nine."
   Teacher: "Then, what do we know about the square root of 94?"
   Ken: "It is between nine and ten."

5. The teacher redirects the question. This is not a probing technique per se, but it does help bring other students into the discussion quickly, while still using probing techniques. The teacher changes the interaction from himself and one student to himself and another student.

   Teacher: "What is the theme of John Steinbeck's story, *Grapes of Wrath*?"
   Terry: "It is about migrants."
   Teacher: "Arnold, can you add to Terry's answer?"

These techniques have two main characteristics in common. They are initiated by the teacher immediately after the student has responded, and they require the student to think beyond an initial response.

Exercise:

Select a topic of general knowledge and write three questions based on the topic. You'll be asked to use those three questions, plus your probing techniques to keep a discussion moving for a period of 10 minutes with two other students. You may only ask questions, not give information as a discussion leader. List the questions and possible follow-up questions.

Question 1:

____

____

Follow-up:

____

____

Question 2:

____

____

Follow-up:

____

____

Question 3:

____

____

Follow- up:

____

____

Summary

Questioning skills are one of several technical skills that are incorporated into all teaching methods. Questions allow the teacher to probe and guide the students through the subject matter. Both fluency in asking questions and the types of questions asked are critical skills in teaching.

References:

Allen, D.W., K.A. Ryan, R.N. Bush and J.M. Cooper. *Questioning Skills*. Canada: General Learning Corporation, 1969.

Chapter Notes & Additional Information:

Personal Thoughts & Drawings

Chapter 8:

Technical Skills of Teaching: Set & Closure

Those who love teaching help others love learning.

Chapter Topics:

- **Introduction to Set**
- **Types of Sets**
- **When to Use Set**
- **Illustration of Set**
- **Examples of Set**
- **Closure**
- **Using Closure**

Introduction to Set

Many teachers spend outrageously little time preparing their students for classroom activities. Often this preparation consists only of telling their students to read some story by the next class session or to watch some demonstration carefully. With such a limited introduction, could any teacher expect students to be attentive and eager to learn the material? The purpose of this exercise is to stimulate you to think of better ways of preparing your students for learning.

Definition: ***A set is defined as a predisposition to respond or to put in simple terms. A set gets your students ready to participate in the learning activities.***

Several psychological experiments have demonstrated the importance of set induction in learning. Research indicates that activities preceding a learning task influence the performance of the task. The research also indicates that the effectiveness of a set depends somewhat on the situation to which it is applied. Therefore, a teacher must find those kinds of sets most appropriate to the purpose and must modify the sets to fit the specific classroom situation.

Exercise:

How did the teacher in your last class use "set"?

____

____

____

____

Types of Sets

There are three basic set of ways of establishing set for an activity. The teacher may select one or all of them depending on the purpose, learning, sequence and time.

1. ***Sequence of Activities:*** The emphasis on the set is to help the student become aware of the lessons sequence. It allows the student to anticipate, think ahead and prepare for the next phase of the lesson. The set may focus the students' attention on the following:

   a. ***Various learning activities of the lesson***
   b. ***Key or critical concepts of the lecture or discussion (objectives)***
   c. ***Time frame of the lesson***

Exercise:

Write a set for a sequence of activities.

____

____

____

____

____

2. ***Review of Assignment***: Each student should have had an assignment prior to the lesson, and at some point the teacher should refer to the assignment. This gives the student and teacher a common reference point to start a lesson with material that is familiar. By beginning or referring to past material, a teacher allows the student to do the following:

   a. ***Review past material (reinforcement)***
   b. ***Forces attention on experiences that are familiar***
   c. ***Use as a connection between the past, present and future***

Exercise:

Write a set for review of assignments.

____

____

____

____

____

3. ***Motivational:*** A teacher who uses this type of set, he is attempting to stimulate the curiosity of the students and get the students to commit themselves. This set encourages the students to become me emotionally involved with the learning. This type of set can be conducted in the following ways:

    a. ***Asking questions or making discrepant remarks***
    b. ***They use of visuals to stimulate response***
    c. ***Taking polls***
    d. ***The use of stories and anecdotes***
    e. ***Asking rhetorical questions***

Exercise:

Write a motivational set.

____
____
____
____
____

In most cases the initial instructional move of the teacher should be to establish a set. The set focuses his students' attention on some familiar person, object, event, condition or idea. The established set functions as a point of reference around which the students and the teacher communicate. The teacher uses this point of reference as a link between familiar and new or difficult material. Furthermore, an effective set encourages student interest and involvement in the main body of the lesson.

When to Use Set

The establishment of a set usually occurs at the beginning of a class period, but it may occur during the session. Set induction is appropriate whenever the activity, goal and/or content of the lesson are changed so that a new or modified frame of reference is needed. Set induction is also used to build continuity from lesson to lessen and from unit to unit. Thus, a new set may be linked to an established set or to a series of sets.

Everyone has experienced the influence of a set induction on his responses to a situation. If we have been told that some person is a brilliant scientist, we would respond differently than we would if we have been told he was a star athlete. What we "learn" during our conversation with this person will depend in part on what we have been told about him. Similarly, whatever information a teacher gives the students about the degree of difficulty and format a test will be will affect the way they study for it.

Sets are appropriate for almost any learning activity. For example, a set is appropriate:

1. ***At the start of a unit***
2. ***Before discussion***
3. ***Before a question and answer.***
4. ***When assigning homework***
5. ***Before hearing a panel discussion***
6. ***Before student reports***
7. ***When assigning student reports***
8. ***Before a film or movie***
9. ***Before a discussion following a film or movie***
10. ***Before a homework assignment based on a discussion that followed the film or movie***

Illustration of Set

Suppose that a teacher wants his students to read chapter 6 in their textbooks as homework. Suppose Chapter Six is about the Constitutional Convention of 1787. What remarks or activities will produce the most learning for the next day? The teacher could say, ***"Now class, for tomorrow, I want all of you to read chapter 6 in the text."*** Such a weak set would normally produce a weak response. The next day the teacher might discover that half the class had not read the assignment, and that the other half, although claiming to have read it, was unable to discuss it in any depth.

The teacher might have said, ***"For tomorrow, I want you to read chapter 6 in the text and come to class prepared for a discussion."*** This set is an improvement. It gives the students more information about the instructional goal. They are to prepare for a discussion. But, the students need a good deal more information before they will be able, or disposed, to prepare themselves for an interesting, stimulating discussion. Exactly what will be discussed? What points should they consider as they read? What should be the focus while they read? How should they use previously learned material? Should they study facts or principles? Should they compare or contrast? Both? Neither?

The teacher could take a completely different approach to the Constitutional Convention of 1787. A different set, one more likely to motivate the students might be something like the following:

Teacher: Suppose you are setting up a colony on a distant planet. Since this colony will be self-governing, the colonists have to draw up some kind of rules governing themselves. For tonight, I want each of you to pretend that you're a columnist on the planet, and that tomorrow you'll begin discussions to draw up some sort of constitution. Think about who will do the ruling, how the ruler will be chosen, and what kinds of rights each individual will be guaranteed. Also, consider what the colony will do when its population exceeds to over one million people. Each one of you should answer these questions and be prepared to discuss them tomorrow in class.

After spending a subsequent class period discussing these and related questions, the teacher could assign appropriate reading and conduct discussions about the problems that confronted the Founding Fathers in 1787. The teacher would have established a significant set, one that both stimulated the students and prepared them for the learning activity.

Examples of Set

Some of the most efficient sets are those that catch the students' attention and interest them in the material. The following examples present learning activities or less on material with ideas for appropriate sets:

1. Lesson: A chapter on the Civil War
   Set: Ask the students to think about how they would have tried to prevent the war had they been the president.
2. Lesson: Understanding fictional characters
   Set: Ask students to choose a character from a book they have read and to pretend that they are that person being interviewed on a television show.
3. Lesson: Student book reports.
   Set: Give examples of good book reports.
4. Lesson: Ordering and categories in behavior.
   Set: Give the class 35 CD cases. Ask them to sort the cases into four categories.
5. Lesson: Cultural differences.
   Set: Ask the students to imagine that they are Japanese and that you, the teacher, are an American walking down the street in Tokyo. Ask them if and how they would tell you were an American.
6. Lesson: Any historical situation in which a nation faced a problem.
   Set: Define the problems but don't identify the nation. Ask the students to find a solution.
7. Lesson: Government
   Set: Make up a set of questions about the constitution. Have the students give this test to members of the community.
8. Lesson: Density and specific gravity.

Set: Put an ice cube into each of two beakers filled with a clear liquid. In one beaker the cube floats, in the other it sinks.

Exercise:

1. ***Write a set for teaching the following concept*:** ____________________

____
____
____
____
____

2. ***Write how your last instructor closed topics and class.***

____
____
____
____
____

Closure

Closure is more than a quick summary of the material covered in a lesson. Besides pulling together the lessons main points and acting as a link between past knowledge and new knowledge, closure provides the student with a needed feeling of achievement.

Definition: *Closure can be defined as the unification of the covered subject matter.*

Closure is also used at specific points within the lesson so that students may know where they have been and where they are going. It is applicable at the end of a session in which a lesson was completed as planned.

Closure is complimentary to set induction. A teacher uses a set to establish a link between his students past experiences and knowledge and the material to be presented. Once the "***door***" has been opened, it must be closed or else there is a chance that students will not fully grasp the meaning of the concept. Closure allows the student to see the end and to see the relationships of the material covered.

Using Closure

A teacher can do a number of things to help students achieve closure. First, by organizing the content around a central theme, generalization, construct, model or analogy, the teacher helps the students themselves to organize the material. Second, the teacher can capitalize on the cueing power of such statements as "Five main parts follow," or "There are three subtopics under each major heading." Third, the teacher can draw attention to completion of the lesson or lesson part. The teacher should leave an adequate amount of time at the end of the lesson for summary, which should include the major points covered in the lesson. It is often effective to review major points several times during the lesson. The repetition helps many students assimilate the ideas. At any point during the lesson, the teacher can "consolidate" the students understanding of the main ideas up to that point.

> ***Teacher:*** *Before continuing, let's see if we can draw any conclusions from the discussion so far.*

If the lesson is built around some basic principle, the teacher can relate what has occurred during the lesson back to this principle.

> ***Teacher:*** *I think we can see from our discussion that organization is the key to writing a book report.*

The teacher may want to use a lesson outline to review major points of a lesson.

> ***Teacher:*** *Looking over the outline of the lesson, let's review the major points.*

The teacher should, whenever possible, connect lesson content with previously learned material. This helps the students fit the new material into their existing, cognitive structures (their present knowledge and past experiences). Frequently, it is also possible to connect the lesson with future learning as well. The teacher can review the sequence that was followed in advance from familiar material to new material.

> ***Teacher:*** *Let's go back to the beginning and trace our steps in arriving at this conclusion.*

Also, the teacher can apply what has been learned to similar cases.

> ***Teacher:*** *We have been discussing one characteristic of mammals; that they nurse their young. The example we have been using is humans. Can anyone think of additional examples?*

And whenever possible, the teacher can extend the covered material to new situations.

> ***Teacher:*** *Compare images from:*
> *A cheek's kiss*
> *Palm caressing my face*
> *Large canvas lips awaiting my face*
> *As I favor my cherries*
> *The memory returns ...* to another love sonnet.

Finally, one very effective way to help students achieve closure is to let the students demonstrate what they have learned. Demonstration offers feedback to both the students and the teacher. If the students cannot demonstrate what they're supposed to have learned, the teacher knows that closure has not been achieved. Two ways students can indicate their acquisition of the material are, to practice the material and to summarize the material. Of course, while one student may be able to summarize the material, thus evidencing he has reached closure, other students may not. Hence, the teachers should not assume that one student's summary is an indication of closure for the whole class.

Achievement of closure means that, at the end of the lesson or lesson part, the students know where they have been and what they have learned. Furthermore, they are able to integrate the new material into their cognitive structure.

Exercise:

Write a closure for teaching the concept of: ______________________________

Summary

Set and closure are two complementary technical skills of teaching. Set prepares the student for the various activities that will take place throughout the learning process. Closure, on the other hand, summarizes and integrates the knowledge and activities that have been learned. Both set and closure are done often throughout the lesson.

References:

Allen, D. W., K. A. Ryan, R. N. Bush, and J. M. Cooper. *Creating Student Involvement.* Canada: General Learning Corporation, 1969.

Chapter Notes & Additional Information:

Chapter 9:

Teaching Strategy: The Discussion

Teachers are a special grade of people in a class all by themselves.

Chapter Topics:

Definition	**Student's Role**
Purpose	**Teacher's Role**
Classification	**Strengths**
Organization	**Limitations**
Preliminary Preparation	**Sample Student Lesson Plan**
Discussion	**Valuative Discovery Discussion**
The Discussant	

Definition: ***A discussion is a meeting of people who communicate face-to-face, in order to fulfill a common purpose. The purpose maybe to share information, solve problems, seek evidence or find solutions.***

There are several specific formats for discussions: debate, panel, small-group, brainstorming, problem-solving, Socratic and buzz sessions. This chapter only concentrates on the characteristics of discussions in general.

The definition of a discussion implies several important characteristics:

1. ***Cooperation is paramount to discussion. There may be a disagreement or argument during a discussion, but all members must cooperate in the search for a product that will be as satisfactory as possible to all.***

2. ***Interaction occurs continuously. The members are constantly reacting, adapting and modifying their behavior in response to each other.***

3. ***A group exists. Each member has some personal feeling of need as well as shared values and norms that he or she hopes will be satisfied via the discussion.***

4. ***Speech is the primary medium of communication. Words and vocal characteristics are the major means by which members interact, although interaction will take place through gestures, touch and writing.***

Exercise:

From your last discussion, outline the topics and processes.

Topics:

____

____

____

____

Process:

____

____

____

____

Purpose

Discussions, whether they are used in an educational setting or for general use, have well-defined purposes.

- ***To Inform:*** Several forms of discussions, panels, symposiums, debates and seminars, have purposes to present information for participants' enlightenment. Instead of using the traditional lecture, discussions can effectively be used to inform students.
- ***To Stimulate Interest:*** Discussions are often used to stimulate interest in important questions and problems. If relevant information is presented in an interesting matter, students are encouraged to participate in contributions of information and questions.
- ***To Solve Problems:*** Problem solving is often a discussion technique used not only in education, but also in business and government agencies. A problem is identified and the group's task is to find an acceptable solution(s).
- ***To Stimulate Creativity:*** Brainstorming, a form of problem solving, is a discussion technique used to develop new ideas. The freewheeling technique of "idea" acceptance from all the members enhances the possibilities of discovery.

Classification – (refer to chapter 3)

Physical: Responsive
Cognitive: Secondary
Affective: Secondary

Organization

Preliminary Preparation

Select the topic and identify the objectives for discussion. Each discussion has a theme and objectives that are to be discussed and achieved during the given period of time.

Assign readings and materials that are to be reviewed by the group prior to the discussion. Limit the materials to those readings that will give the students a basic understanding of the topic. Additional materials can be assigned to different students that emphasize various aspects of the topic, but each student should share the general information.

Identify subgroups and the student composition of the groups. Oftentimes because of the size of the class or the type of discussion being conducted, it is necessary to divide the class into smaller groups. Some of the characteristics used in designing group composition are: knowledge and experience, attitude, articulation and leadership. The size of the group is usually limited to three to five members. Groups smaller and larger generally have difficulty carrying out discussion problems.

Organize the physical arrangements for conducting a discussion. These include the tables and chairs, audiovisual equipment, graphics, reading materials and whiteboard. Generally, the type of discussion, panel, symposium or seminar will determine how the tables and chairs will be organized; however, there are some general guidelines that can be adhered to:

1. ***A slightly overcrowded room is better than a half empty one.***

2. ***Auditoriums and formal settings are not appropriate for small-group type discussions.***

3. ***When interaction of all members is expected, chairs should be arranged to allow for face-to-face contact.***

Discussion

Although there are several ways in proceeding with a "discussion", the following can be used and modified to fit the specific needs of the instructor.

- **Step 1:** ***Definition of Terms and Concepts***

To lessen the chances of the group's becoming involved in useless arguments; terms are defined and clarified for discussion purposes. It is not necessary that all members agree on terms, but only that they are aware that the definitions are the ones to be utilized.

- **Step 2:** ***General Statement of Author's Message (theme or discussion).***

  The purpose of this step is to obtain some grasp of the overall meaning of the assigned reading. It demarcates the area to be discussed; it zeros in on the topic for discussion. The students should be able to state the general purpose of the assignment in their own words.

- **Step 3:** ***Identification of Major Themes or Subtopics***

  Most material can be broken down into a number of important subtopics. As a new step two, the students should be able to identify the related theme in their own words.

- **Step 4:** ***Allocation of Time***

  To ensure that each topic of the discussion is covered fairly, a schedule of time allocation is devised. Often this is done by the teacher prior to the discussion, but students are still informed of the general sequence and time constraints. Of course, flexibility is necessary in any scheduling process, but unless time is organized and students are able to pace themselves, the discussion may become a bias forum.

- **Step 5:** ***Discussion of Major Themes and Subtopics.***

  The previous four steps were preparation for the body of the discussion. Coordinating the actual discussion is demanding and requires a great deal of skill on the part of the discussion leader. Some hints for keeping a discussion moving are:

1. **State** an opinion or ask a thought-provoking question to begin the body of the discussion.
2. **Inject** questions on vital points that bear on the problem.
3. **Outline** the discussion on the board and record important points
4. Make your questions and points require comments.
5. **Find** some justification for each view expressed and make the contributors feel they are helping.
6. **Avoid** premature introduction of new topics and keep members from wandering away from the subject.
7. **Encourage** all to contribute and do not allow anyone to dominate the discussion.
8. **Summarize** frequently the contributions that directly aid the discussion and conclude each topic.
9. **Be ready to** come up with a comment or question to redirect discussion if it is leads to a dead end.
10. **Use** a whiteboard, PowerPoint or handouts to keep the group together on each point.

- **Step 6:** ***Integration of Material with Other Knowledge***

  To assist in the connection between concepts, a conscious effort is made to relate knowledge of the discussion to knowledge acquired in previous lessons or other learning experiences. Students begin to see the relationship of one lesson to another and the integration of concepts.

- **Step 7:** ***Application of the Material***

  Whenever possible the instructor should assist the student in the application or implications of the subject matter. Subjects such as government, psychology and health, often have direct application and can be easily be pointed out to the students. **Others may have less personal application, but theoretical implications can be shown to students.**

- **Step 8:** ***Drawing Conclusions and Summarizing***

  The summary is the review of the salient points of the discussion. These points can follow the outline with elaboration and insertion of students' point of view.

  The conclusions can be made on several aspects of the discussion, including the author's writing ability, the solution or alternatives, generalizations, hypothesis and theories for the future. In all discussions the students are led to the formation of a conclusion even though it may be open ended or a compromise. They are not left hanging in midair.

The Discussant

The discussion is limited only by the ability and preparation of its members. The discussants should be adequately prepared for their role.

1. ***Communicate openly:*** The effective discussant reacts so that others can be constantly aware of his or her state of mind. Response and reaction are essential to good interpersonal relations. When you agree or disagree, show with a nod, frown or smile. If you have a question, ask it!

2. ***Speak effectively:*** When speaking effectively, several things should be kept in mind.

   A. Speak as if you want to be heard. Emphasize your remarks and project your voice.
   B. Speak to the group, not just the leaders, but to all members.
   C. Organize your thoughts in a pattern. Relate contribution to what has already been said; state the idea, developed and supported, and connect the contribution to the topic or phrase of the problem being discussed.
   D. State one point at a time; otherwise the impact may be lessened.
   E. Speak concisely and state ideas as simply and briefly as possible.

F. Use appropriate language and speak in concrete terms. Do not use vague or ambiguous terms.

3. ***Don't monopolize:*** Offer information when you contribute something new and relevant, and realize that you are one of the many that may wish to speak.

4. ***Listen to understand:*** Without effective listening skills, much of what is said during a discussion is a rehash and a waste of time. Listen critically to what the discussant is saying; be able to restate his or her point of view. Good listening is a process of understanding what another speaker meant from their perspective, then evaluate the significance and dependability of the comments.

Student's Role

Beyond the role of a discussant, the student has the obligation to be prepared with the subject matter and to keep an open mind or mature perspective when discussing highly emotional topics.

Teacher's Role

Besides being the discussion leader and guiding the students to steps of a discussion, the teacher must refrain from dominating the discussion and turning it into an informal lecture.

Strengths

1. ***The method utilizes the knowledge of the group.***
2. ***It helps to develop higher levels of thinking in questioning skills.***
3. ***It assists in bringing about modifications of viewpoints and changes in attitudes, interests and values.***

Limitations

1. ***Without adequate preparation, digression to rap sessions is imminent.***
2. ***Leading students to conclusions is difficult.***
3. ***It is very easy to wander off course and move into unrelated areas.***

References:

Borman, Ernest. *Discussion and Group Methods: Theory and Practice*. 2nd ed. New York: Harper and Row Publishers. N.Y., London, Evanston, 1975.

Brillhart, John K., Gloria J. Galanes, and Katherine Adams. 10th ed. *Effective Group Discussion: Theory and Practice*. Dubuque, IA: Wm. C. Brown Company Publishers. 2001.

Hill, William. Fawcett. *Learning Thru Discussion.* Rev. ed. Beverly Hills, CA: Sage Publications, Beverly Hills, London1969.

Exercise:

List 10 magazine articles that may be used in discussion topics.

1. ______________________________
2. ______________________________
3. ______________________________
4. ______________________________
5. ______________________________
6. ______________________________
7. ______________________________
8. ______________________________
9. ______________________________
10. ______________________________

Sample Student Lesson Plan

Valuative Discovery Discussion

I. ***Background Data***:

Name: Sally G. Deak ***Date:*** 4-23-06 ***Grade:*** College
Hour: 7-8:30 P.M. ***Subject:*** Sociology 202 ***Place:*** NAS 210
Lesson Topic: Abortion—Right or Wrong? ***Unit:*** Social Issues

II. ***Behavioral Objectives:*** The student will:

1. Be able to identify the six medical techniques commonly used in performing an abortion, and the risks, complications, advantages and disadvantages of each.
2. Have a better understanding of the pro-abortion and pro-life sides of the issue.
3. Have a better understanding of the history of abortion laws and practices.
4. Have a better understanding of how personal and individual the stands are that people take on abortion.
5. Realize and be more aware of the importance of exploring and discussing the issues of abortion and other confrontational social issues.

III. *Previous Assignment:*
Read the handout "Medical Techniques for Abortion," and give some thought to your own feelings concerning abortion.

IV. *Related Activities:*
Discussion, if time permits on the decision of having children or not having children and the feelings surrounding the issue.
1. How do women with children feel about women who do not want any?
2. Why do some women choose not to become mothers?

V. *Procedures:*
Set:
1. Review topics discussed in class over the past two weeks.
2. State topic for today's discussion, "abortion-right or wrong?"
3. Sequence of events:
    a. Background information on history of abortion laws and practices
    b. Readings from both points of view: pro-life and pro-abortion
    c. Open discussion on any and all issues surrounding abortion
    d. Summary and conclusion

Organization of class: Have students arrange chairs in a semicircle.

Teaching strategy
A. Review (five minutes)
1. The topics discussed over the past two weeks: gun control, busing.
2. Abortion, along with the others, is all confrontational, social issues.
3. Very personal issues; no right or wrong answers, even though today's topics is "Abortion – Right or Wrong?"
4. What is meant by that is: there is a right or wrong for every individual in their own mind; not a general basis for all society.
5. All confrontational issues affect us in one way or another, therefore, they're important to explore and discuss.

B. Today's topic (five minutes)
1. ***Abortion:*** each person's opinion and feelings about it depend on various things:
    a. If you have children of your own
    b. If you've ever had an abortion or know someone who did
    c. If you are the husband, or boyfriend of a woman who had an abortion or, contemplated having one
    d. Your religious beliefs
    e. Your age and marital status
    f. If your physical condition, meaning whether or not you've had a hysterectomy or a vasectomy.
2. Each person's ***feelings*** on abortion and their reasons for feeling that way are valid and right for that person.

3. Discussion, not debate, not here to decide whether abortion is right or wrong for everyone, only for yourself.

C. **Background Information** on history of abortion laws and practice (five minutes)
1. Tolerated in Europe for centuries
2. Nineteenth-century laws passed making it a crime
3. Pope Pius IX: "murder"
4. 1980's—outlawed, except for saving a woman's life
5. Women will seek abortion whether it is legal or not
6. Trauma of illegal abortions
7. Illegal profits
8. Discrimination against poor women
9. Mid 1960's, woman organized to try to change the laws
10. Reformed laws came about
11. 1970—New York State
12. 1973—U.S. Supreme Court – Legal

D. **Two Points of View (15 minutes)**
1. **Pro-life:** Read excerpts from "Handbook on Abortion."
2. **Pro-abortion:** Read excerpts from two personal experiences—legal and illegal.

E. **Discussion (45 minutes)**
1. ***Introduction***
    a. Does hearing things such as what I have just read to you make anyone less sure and/or firm on their "stand" on abortion, or does it make you feel more sure and firm? Why?
    b. How many of you know exactly how you feel about abortion?
    c. How many of you are uncertain how you feel?
    d. What are your feelings about the excerpts that I read?
2. ***Have you ever really thought about how you feel?***
3. ***Is it important to you to have an opinion on abortion?***
4. ***Do you feel both sides have good arguments?***
    a. **Pro-Life**
        1. Fetus is a "person" from the moment of conception, therefore, abortion is murder.
        2. Our legal system is founded on the equal protection by law of all living humans.
        3. Physically harmful to the woman.
        4. The right of the child to live is greater than and supersedes any right that a woman may have to the privacy of her own body.
        5. Every Child is a Wanted Child: Planned Parenthood slogan. Should add… and if not wanted, kill!
        6. Right of the father.
    b. **Pro-Abortion**
        1. Basic right of the woman to decide if to have children and when to have children.

    2. Diagnosis of birth defects
    3. Rape
    4. Right of the father, even if he leaves the woman
    5. Alternative is illegal abortion—butchering by nonprofessionals
    6. Young girl who gets pregnant
    7. Incest
5. Do you know what ***YOU*** would do if you got pregnant now? (Meaning, your life as it exists right now, whether it would be with your two other children, or with no one else around, if you are single.)
6. What about the rights of the father?
7. Should there be a universal law for all women concerning abortion?
8. What are the rights of women?
9. What do you feel the emotional impact of abortion is on a woman? Her family? Husband? Boyfriend? Relatives?

F. **Summary and Conclusions (10 minutes)**

1. Review major points and feelings brought out in the discussion.
2. Does anyone feel differently now about abortion than they did when the discussion began? Why?
3. Emphasize that the discussion showed us how personal an issue abortion is, how there are many opinions on it and they are all valid.
4. What did you get from the discussion?

VI. Assignment:

For the next class, think about your feelings concerning ratification of the ERA: Do you think it will pass? Do you want it to pass? Why? Why not? Do you think it will benefit women if it does pass?

VII. Lesson Comments:

Exercise:

List the content questions from the previous lesson.

1. ______________________________
2. ______________________________
3. ______________________________
4. ______________________________
5. ______________________________
6. ______________________________
7. ______________________________
8. ______________________________

Chapter Notes & Additional Information:

Personal Thoughts & Drawings

Chapter 10:

Teaching Strategy: The Lecture

The lecture is a systematic way of transmitting information and ideas orally by a speaker to a group of listeners.

Chapter Topics:

Definition
Purposes
Classification
Limitations
Special Limitations
Organization
Preparation
Introduction
The Body
Repetition
Summary and Conclusion
Student's Role
Teacher's Role
Strengths
Limitations
Sample Student Lesson Plan

Definition*:* ***The lecture is a systematic way of transmitting information and ideas orally by a speaker to a group of listeners.***

The material presented in a lecture is arranged in a logical and orderly manner with the planned use of illustrations and examples to make comprehension and note taking easy.

- ***Formal Lecture:*** A formal lecture is purely verbal, the communication is basically one way from speaker to audience, and is designed to offer information and solve problems for the learner. The formal lecture is generally used when addressing large groups of people where interaction is impossible.

- ***Informal Lecture:*** During informal lecture, the communication process is opened to permit questions and comments from the audience and is not strictly a teacher-to-student interaction. The informal lecture requires the student to work mentally with the lecturer and is effectively used with smaller groups of students.

Exercise:

Describe the best and the worst lecture of your college career.

Best:

Worst:

____

____

____

____

Purposes

There are several reasons for using the lecture other than to convey information. This is not to diminish the importance of imparting knowledge, but to bring forth other possible goals of the lecture.

1. ***To Reinforce Written Work:*** A lecture covering lessons reinforces student learning through repetition. Use of this sort of lecture should be limited to emphasis of the main points of the material.
2. ***To Change Pace:*** Any teaching strategy, used exclusively, is boring. A teacher who relies heavily on discussions might profit by lecturing occasionally.
3. ***To Synthesize Many Sources:*** Lecturing is economical, in that the teacher is able to synthesize several sources of information and present them to the class.
4. ***To Inform Students of Expected Results:*** A lecture can be a means of informing students of expected outcomes of a learning activity. When used in this matter, it functions as an introduction to the activity by directing the students' attention to the critical aspects of the material.
5. ***To Convey Enthusiasm:*** A lecture can convey to the students the teacher's enthusiasm for a topic. An exciting lecture demonstrates that instructor's interest and will undoubtedly stir the students also.

Classification – (refer to Chapter 3)

Physical: Passive
Cognitive: Primary
Affective: Primary

Limitations

Time: One hour for adults
Audience: Minimum 25—40 Formal

Special Limitations

There are several instances or situations when a lecture would be inappropriate.

1. The objective is other than the acquisition of information.

2. The objective involves the application of skills.
3. The objective involves the changing of attitudes or behaviors.
4. The knowledge acquired is to be retained for a long time.
5. The material is extremely complex or abstract.
6. Student participation in the learning activity is required.

Organization

There are four phases to the lecture method: ***Preparation, Introduction, Body and Conclusion.***

Preparation: Concentrates on the three factors in the design of the lecture that include:

- **Classroom Organization:** Students should be seated so they can ***clearly see*** the speaker and any illustrative devices used in the presentation. In classrooms with movable furniture, it would be better to have the desks and chairs arranged in a ***semicircle***, rather than in rows.

  The room should contain a whiteboard large enough for students to see, which can be used for noting key points, outlining and diagramming. In lieu of or in conjunction with a whiteboard, PowerPoint demonstrations are an excellent means of ***visually showing information*** for student use.

  A microphone is necessary if the room and audience are large, or the acoustics are poor, to give appropriate voice projection throughout the room. Finally, a podium or lectern for the speaker is necessary for the placement of notes, centralizing students' attention and requiring the instructor to have a standing delivery.

- **Material and Illustrations:** The material in the lecture should not be the same as the textbook; new and supported information should be given. If a textbook is used as a primary resource for the lecture, it would be best to use the time to allow the students to read it instead of listening to the instructor orally repeat it.

  Confine the material to what the audience can receive and understand within the given period of time. ***Do not attempt to overwhelm*** the audience with too many topics and details. Keep the lecture down to a few main points and limit the amount of trivia and extreme detail that is used. Details are important to ***support the main ideas*** and are eagerly sought by students, but a constant barrage of facts and figures tends to become boring.

  Both verbal and visual illustrations can be valuable tools for the lecturer to clarify concepts. It motivates listeners by showing them how the topic under study has occurred in real-life situations; it holds their concentration because they visualize the image; and it promotes reaction by stimulating past associations or experiences with the concept.

The aids do not have to be elaborate; a ***simple*** chart or diagram on the whiteboard would complement a lesson. PowerPoint presentations, models, graphics or audio recordings all have a place in a well-organized lecture. ***Verbal illustrations*** such as frames of reference, analogies and anecdotes help to clarify, just as diagrams, charts and pictures do. Whatever type of illustration is used, it is important to plan ahead and select only those examples that your audience can relate to.

- **Audience Analysis*:*** Before the selection of material for a lecture, an analysis of the potential audience is examined. How much do they know about the topic? What are their general life experiences with the subject? What was taught in past lessons or other courses?

  It is important to determine the extent of the audience's knowledge, for it is useless to relate concepts they already possess or present complicated ideas that they cannot understand because they lack the information needed to learn the more advanced concepts.

  By ***understanding the makeup of the audience,*** the instructor is able to ***organize*** the material in terms of their motivation and also in their comprehension of the subject. All the illustrations and organization of material are of little use unless the instructor is able to ascertain the primary understanding of the students' abilities and background with the assigned topic.

Introduction

The first few minutes are critical to the success of the lecture, and during this brief period the instructor has to provide a foundation for his or her thoughts. The opening statements of the lecture should do at least two things:

- ***Track the students' attention and interest:*** Several techniques may be employed and plotted: post hypothetical questions, discrepant remarks, anecdotes, dramatic statements and personal experiences. It is not necessary for the instructors to be entertaining, but they must be able to ***motivate*** student interest with their words and symbols.

- ***Explanation of the purpose:*** The main points for the body of the lecture are stated or outlined. The students are made aware of the main topics and their sequence. The important thing is to pinpoint your purpose in terms of what you want your listeners to do as a result of them hearing the lecture. The points and purposes should be stated clearly at least once before moving on to the body of a lecture.

The Body

The lecture is organized into manageable units of thought. Each unit is supported with data and illustrations. These partitions of ideas should not be more than what the audience can digest at any given period of time. It is better to have fewer main ideas and spend more time clarifying, than to overwhelm the audience with several concepts. Unless your students are unusually alert and able, they cannot digest more than a half dozen major concepts in one hour. A lecturer can cover material a great deal faster than an audience can take it in. Design the lecture so that you follow each important fact or idea with a lot of discussion or explanation of the idea.

The main ideas of the lecture are sequences in a ***logical pattern*** that can readily be seen by the audience. The lecturer has a ***rational plan*** for presenting his ideas, which includes a ***carefully thought out*** approach to the subject that doesn't take the student on a trip of rambling thoughts. The listeners are unable to get a sense of the lecture that wanders with no perceptible pattern, following no organizational plan that they can see. It is therefore important that the ideas presented are ***sequenced*** and ***organized*** in a discernible pattern.

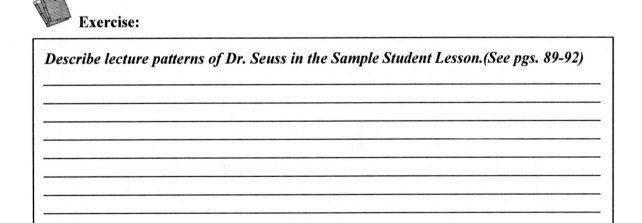

Exercise:

Describe lecture patterns of Dr. Seuss in the Sample Student Lesson. ***(See pgs. 89-92)***

Repetition

Because the strategy is primarily verbal, and students are required to take notes, it is necessary to use repetition. Planned repetition increases the students' opportunity to remember the main ideas. There are several forms of literal repetition that can be used during a lecture.

- ***Simple Repetition:*** Ideas or statements are repeated immediately following the initial presentation.

- ***Spaced Repetition:*** Repetition at various intervals during a lesson. The identification of key words or concepts and repeating them periodically increases the chances that student will remember them.
- ***Cumulative Repetition:*** Repetition of all the prior concepts in a sequence must be established before new ideas are presented.
- ***Massed Repetition:*** All the important points or concepts are repeated together as a sequence. This usually occurs at the conclusion of the lessons or at any time the teacher believes a summary is necessary.

Informal Lecture Explanation

The informal lecture opens the communication process to allow student involvement via asking or responding to questions. When students participate in the lecture, it prevents the most prevalent criticism of the method—students who are passive recipients of information.

The participation in the lecturing process comes through two avenues:

1. ***Responding to the lecturers questions, and***
2. ***Asking questions for the clarification and expansion of ideas for areas of interest.***

When and how questions may be asked should be indicated at the onset of the lecture. This is clarified by a simple statement such as:

"Questions may be asked at any time"
"Please hold your questions to end of the lecture."

The lecturer must ***"select"*** between the advantages of immediate clarification, constant feedback and comprehension by all students, versus the destruction of the class by a small minority, digression from prepared remarks, loss of the flow of the lecture, and the possibility of not finishing the prepared remarks. Whatever choice the instructors make, they should ***be flexible*** in both how they allow questions to be raised, and the deviation from the prepared text.

Any time questions are raised there is the possibility that the instructor will vary or change emphasis from the main topics. This is certainly permissible and the instructors allow for this flexibility in their preparation of the lecture. However, it is not as stable to be constantly deviating and changing directions in that continuity from one point to another, and from lesson to lesson, is needed for the student.

Summary and Conclusion

Definition: ***The summary is a form of massed repetition whereby the main points of the lecture are reviewed and restated.***

The instructor may wish to draw conclusions or allow the students to form them in a short critique period following the body of the lecture. During the critique (five to ten minutes), points may be expanded or clarified, conclusions formulated, theories processed and questions answered. This is an important part of the lecture because it provides feedback to the instructor on how well the students understand the basic concepts.

Student's Role

For the lecture to be a success, the student must be able to listen critically and to record those thoughts into notes. Listed below are some hints on successful note taking:

1. ***Use an outline form to list the main points of the lecture.***
2. ***Write or paraphrase only the important concepts.***
3. ***Listen for clues such as: "There are two key points here . . .", "The most important factors are . . .," "In summary ...," or "In review of ...."***
4. ***Write neatly enough so that reorganizing notes would not be necessary.***
5. ***Leave room in your notes to add your own thoughts and questions. It is advisable when first introducing the lecture to students, to either outline the lecture on the board or duplicate an outline of the lecture for the class.***

Teacher's Role

There are two parts to preparing a lecture:

1. ***Doing the research***
2. ***Delivery***—Putting the research into a form that students will learn most effectively.

The lecture should develop the following characteristics:

1. Speak in a ***conversational manner*** using a word or phrase as a lecture guide. Do not read your notes.
2. The vocabulary should be appropriate to the abilities of the audience with new words and concepts ***explained*** and ***defined***. Talk to the students, not over their heads.
3. Your ***voice should be vibrant and lively***. Use a pitch and a volume to emphasize important points; refrain from talking in a monotone voice.
4. The personality of the lecturer should be ***warm, friendly and confident***. Appropriate and spontaneous humor should stem from remarks or events.
5. The pace should range between 115 and 160 words per minute, depending upon the complexity of the material.
6. ***Avoid annoying mannerisms*** such as: overuse of the words "like" or "um", or fidgeting with hands or note cards.

7. ***Observe*** your audience and take cues from them on how they are receiving the message.
8. ***Look at your audience***, not only at your notes.

Strengths

1. Lecture is economical use of time and material.
2. Provides all students with the universal body of information.
3. Allows outstanding authorities to teach large groups.

Limitations

1. Lectures, if given improperly, are dull and boring.
2. The method is overused and used inappropriately to teach attitudes, feelings and skills.
3. The method relies solely on the teacher as a final authority.

Sample Student Lesson Plan

I. Background Data:

Name: Rae Barr ***Date:*** 4-6-2005 ***Grade:*** College Level
Hour: 9-11 ***Subject:*** Children's Literature
Place: BCC Room 218 ***Lesson topic:*** Dr. Seuss and his works
Unit: Authors of Picture Books and Easy Readers

II. Behavioral Objectives:

Introduce Dr. Seuss. Students should be able to identify his artwork, writing style and important motivations in his work.

III. Previous Assignment

Ask students to familiarize themselves with one or two works by Dr. Seuss.

IV. Related Activities

Question and answer session. Reading of: *The Cat in the Hat*

V. Materials

The Cat in the Hat, If I Ran the Zoo, And To Think I Saw it on Mulberry Street, Fox in Soxs and *Dr. Seuss's ABC*

VI. Procedures

Set—You will remember that last week we discussed the characteristics of picture books and easy readers. Remember that there are three basic requirements for an easy reader, which are: ***standard book size,***

standard print size and a limited vocabulary for first and second graders. The picture book, on the other hand, has no restrictions on size of book or print. The most important factor is its ***ability to tell a story by its pictures.***

We will begin today with a series of authors in these two genres. Today's author is Dr. Seuss.

Organization—No change in classroom setting is necessary. Have Dr. Seuss books on hand to show to class when speaking of them.

Teaching Strategy—(Lecture)

A. Introduction of Dr. Seuss (4–5 minutes)

1. Name: Theodore Seuss Geisel
2. Born: March 4, 1904–Deceased
3. Raised:
    a. Springfield, MA
    b. Close-knit family, especially to his father

4. Father taught him the importance of:
    a. Perfection
    b. Persistence

5. Father's Life
    a. Worked in brewery, (President)
    b. Lost job
    c. Prohibition hit home
    d. Immediately began to work for Springfield park system and ran the zoo.
6. Education
    a. High School in Springfield—Wrote for school paper.
    b. Dartmouth—Master's, wrote for a humor magazine and an entertaining magazine.
    c. Oxford—discouraged
7. Professional Work
    a. Advertiser—The standard oil of N.J., Flint-insect repellent during depression, seasonal work, restless
    b. Binding contract, hires lawyer, finds loophole, can write children's books
8. *And to think I Saw it on Mulberry Street* ***(Show the Book)***
    a. 29 publishers
    b. Best seller, unique and different
    c. Penned the name Dr. Seuss
        1. Dr. Joke
        2. Seuss–Mothers maiden name

3. Save Theodore Seuss Geisel for great American novel

B. Although Dr. Seuss was a very successful advertiser, and he was a famous illustrator/writer, he never took an art course. (4–5 minutes)

Artwork

1. High school art class was a disaster. His teacher humiliated him. He left and never returned.
2. Never lost love of the craft. He continued privately.
3. Began artwork on large pads and doodles became characters. He began to interact with his characters.
4. Naming his characters the easiest part of the process. He drew a grinch and it was known as "Grinch."
5. Most of his characters are male animals. He had trouble drawing females in any form. Women's groups had given him a hard time. He felt he should do what he did best.
6. Style:
    a. Cartoon-like, flat, color within lines, like a child would draw.
    b. Used bold and energetic colors.
    c. Vivacious movements.
    d. Unique and timeless facial expressions.
    e. Humorous, repetitious and rhythmic

C. Dr. Seuss was very serious and particular about his writing. (4–5 minutes)

1. He may work on one book for over a year.
2. He felt one page in a children's book was equal to one chapter in an adult book.
3. Can't lose a child reader! You must take the child further with each page of the book.
4. Doesn't oversimplify. Doesn't talk down to children.
5. His books cover a wide range of topics from conservation to pure fun and imagination.
6. Stories come from many sources:
    a. Life Experience
        1. *If I Ran the Zoo* ***(Show the Book)***
        2. *McElliot's Pool* ***(Show the Book)***

    b. Accident–*Horton Hears a Who* ***(Show the Book)***
    c. Dare–*The Cat in the Hat* ***(Show the Book)***
7. Opposed to using his books for political causes or to caricature racial or ethnic characters.
8. Very interested in words. He studied Latin. He felt books should be phonetic and are meant to be read aloud.

9. He felt TV was a great fault in children not reading as much as they used to.
10. Extremely conscientious and very successful as a result.
11. Has written over 40 books, which have been translated into several languages including: Japanese, African and Braille.
12. He has received 3 Academy Awards and did not plan to retire.

Closure—Today I have introduced you to Dr. Seuss. You should remember that his father had a great influence on building his character and in giving him several topics for his books. We learned how and why he chose his pen name, Dr. Seuss. We examined his art style, colorful, cartoon-like and energetic. We learned that most of his characters are male animals and that he made no apologies for them. We discussed his writing, repetitious and humorous writing style and his integrity in writing seriously for children.

D. Ongoing Assignment

Please read *I'll Fix Anthony* by Judith Viorst and be prepared to discuss for writing style as well as Arnold Lobel's artwork.

Media: Enthusiasm in the Lecture

Exercise:

A. List at least ten different ways that Professor Fraterrigo generates enthusiasm in the lecture.

1. ______________________________
2. ______________________________
3. ______________________________
4. ______________________________
5. ______________________________
6. ______________________________
7. ______________________________
8. ______________________________
9. ______________________________
10. ______________________________

B. ***Summarize the lecture in not less than 100 words.***

____
____
____
____
____
____

C. ***Draw a map of the Battle of Lexington and Concord.***

D. ***Explain how poetry can be used to teach history.***

Chapter Notes and Additional Information:

Chapter 11:

Teaching Strategy: Demonstration Performance

Any subject can be taught effectively in some intellectually honest form to any child at any age of development.

Chapter Topics:

Definition	**Strengths**
Classification	**Limitations**
Limitations	**Sample Student Lesson Plan**
Organization	**Instruction to Begin Lesson**
Sample Format (Plan)	**Magic Squares**
Student's Role	**Magic Square (5X5)**
Teacher's Role	**Lesson Plan**

Definition: ***Demonstration is the process of showing how to do a physical or cognitive skill.***

It incorporates both visual as well as the auditory senses in the illustration of the skill. After the teacher demonstrates, the student performs the skill; thus the strategy demonstration – performance. The primary purpose of the method is to give the student a complete (iconic) image and explanation for the skill that they are asked to master.

- ***Formal Demonstration:*** An instructor plans and demonstrates a skill before a group in an organized manner. The formal demonstration usually precedes any type of informal demonstration.

- ***Informal Demonstration:*** An instructor demonstrates a skill to one or two individuals, as in coaching. It differs from the formal method in that one is preplanned and the other is on the spot or is given as the situation is needed.

Exercise:

List the skills that you have learned via the demonstration. (Ex: Addition, drawing or music scales)

____

____

____

____

Classification- (refer to chapter 3)

Physical: Responsive
Cognitive: Secondary
Affective: Secondary

Limitations

Students: 1– 30
Dependent on the Skill
Time: None

Organization

There are four major phases to the demonstration method: ***Demonstration, Explanation, Performance and Evaluation.*** Depending on the complexity of the skill and the student's abilities, the phases may be separated and distinct or combined.

Pre-Demonstration: Prior preparation to the actual demonstration is necessary to the success of the lesson. Three organizational decisions should be clarified before the onset of the demonstration.

1. ***Classroom Organization:*** The students should first be organized so that they can clearly see the demonstration and are not obstructed by fellow students. If the skill is minute, or difficult to see, then more than one demonstration is to be given to smaller groups.

   After the demonstration, the students should be arranged in such a manner that they have enough room to perform the skill. If the students are to demonstrate on or with another student, the pairing should be identified first.

2. ***Materials and Equipment:*** The materials and equipment that are required for the demonstration and the students' performance should be identified and available. Be sure that you have double checked for the amount that is needed, as well as any particular type or quality. If appropriate, the materials and equipment should be distributed prior to the demonstration. If not, procedures for its distribution should be clarified to the students.

3. ***Illustrations:*** Besides the demonstration of the skill by the instructor, there should be other forms of illustrations. Such devices as charts, models, various media and drawings are commonly used to complement the initial demonstration of the instructor. At times, handouts are given to students to use and to take notes on while the demonstration is being conducted.

***Phase I* - Demonstration:** The skill is presented to the student as a holistic image of the activity. The image presented in the demonstration should represent a clear picture of the whole as well as its parts.

The demonstration should:

1. ***Establish a sequence of steps.***
2. ***Provide a clear starting and ending point.***
3. ***Provide a standard for evaluation.***

Phase II* - Explanation**: This step is the formal explanation of the demonstration which should include a series of clear statements reflecting the process in each sub-step. Extensive explanations will tend to lose students; therefore, the phrases used in explanations should be ***clear and ***concise***.

In both Phase I and II, it is necessary to ***repeat the demonstration***, as well as the explanation, several times for the students. Each time the demonstration is repeated, the checkpoints should be emphasized. Often within Step I, a ***verbal explanation*** can be given, but it should not preclude the formal explanation after the demonstration.

***Phase III*- Performance:** The students are expected to execute the skill at this time. After a series of demonstrations/explanations, the class is then organized to perform the skill. The performance step can be done in either of two ways, depending upon the complexity of the skill in the abilities of the students.

1. ***If this demonstration is simple with only a few steps, and the students are familiar or had experience with the concepts, then the performance phase can be left to the students as a whole.***
2. ***If the skill is complex, the students should be led through the performances step by step until they have some familiarity with the process.***

Phase IV* - Evaluation:** During the student's execution or performance of the skill, the instructor begins the evaluation process. This process includes the ***assessment of performance and the use of the informal demonstration to assist in correcting faults. As the students practice the skill, assistance is given to help clarify weaknesses such as incorrect form or sequence, or to improve the level of the performance. The instructor will use the informal demonstration to ***explain*** and ***illustrate*** the skill in its entirety or in select parts.

Sample Format (Plan)—Spiking Volleyball

Pre-Demonstration: Explain what to watch for in the illustration of the skill. (i.e., Starting position, Take off and follow through)

Demonstration: ***Spiking Skill in Volleyball***

The demonstration of spiking should be shown as a whole rather than broken down into parts. The speed of the skill demonstration should be both at normal speed and half speed to allow the conceptualizing.

Explanation:

Step 1: Take off with both feet balanced, nearly a full crouched position, slightly behind the balls path. As you jump, thrust both arms violently upwards to a full extended position.

Step 2: At the height of the jump, bring your hitting hand and arm to a cocked position. Contact the ball at the highest point by extending your hand and arm.

Performance: Students will be led through the various steps by the instructor until the parts of the whole are clear in the students mind.

Step 1: Instructor: "Ready position. Jump!" (Repeat 2–3 times)

Step 2: Instructor: "This time jump, then cock your arm and jump again." (Repeat 2–3 times)

Evaluation: The instructor evaluates the class as a whole in their performance of the skill, along with individual evaluations. Errors in execution are pointed out to the class at large, while giving informal demonstration to assist individuals in their performance.

Evaluation to class: "Most of you are jumping too early for the ball; time your jump to reach the ball at its maximum height."

Evaluation to individual: "Mary, watch the cock of my arm on the jump. See how my elbow is flexed?"

Student's Role

This student must be a keen observer to benefit from the method. He must be able to visualize the part in its relationship to the whole, and place it in proper sequence. With appropriate cuing by the instructor, the student can become an accomplished observer.

Teacher's Role

The teacher's main responsibility is to provide the student with a quality instruction or image of the skill that will represent a model to the student. The instructor should carefully plan the demonstration to illustrate the skill as simply as possible, eliminating unnecessary complications during the first of a series of demonstrations. If the teacher is unable to demonstrate the skill, media or other forms of illustrations should be provided to the student for visual conceptualization.

Strengths

1. It provides the student with a holistic image.
2. The demonstration points to a success level.
3. It strengthens the position of the teacher (performer) as an expert or authority.

Limitations

1. Requires a great deal of planning and preparation on the part of the teacher.
2. The demonstration can lead to imitation without true understanding.
3. The model of excellence may be an unreachable and frustrating goal for some students.

References:

Staton, Thomas. *How to Instruct Successfully.* New York: McGraw Hill Book Company. 1960.

Hoover, Kenneth. *The Professional Teachers Handbook.* Boston: Allyn and Boeing. 1963.

Exercise: The Windsor knot

Outline the steps of demonstrating how to tie the Windsor knot.

1. ______________________
2. ______________________
3. ______________________
4. ______________________
5. ______________________
6. ______________________
7. ______________________
8. ______________________

Sample Student Lesson Plan—Magic Square

I. ***Background Data:***

Name: Francine Papierman *Date:* 10-25-06 *Time:* 30 minutes

\# of Students: NA *Grade Level:* College

Subject: Magic Square *Unit:* 1

Lesson Topic: The Learning Method to Complete the Magic Square

II. ***Behavioral Objectives:***

1. Students will learn the history of the Magic Square
2. They will see how the Magic Square works.
3. Students will see teacher demonstrate a Magic Square and then the students will proceed to complete a Magic Square on their own.

III. ***Materials:*** Whiteboard, Dry Erase markers, Handouts with written rules and any additional handouts that may aid the students in completing a Magic Square.

IV. ***Illustration Procedures:***

1. Describe the history of the Magic Square. ***(1 minute)***
2. Draw a completed Magic Square on the whiteboard. ***(2 minutes)***
3. Demonstrate how the square works. Have students add numbers in all directions, including the diagonal. ***(3 minutes)***
4. Ask students if they have ever seen this done and if any of them have experience in doing the square. ***(1 minute)***

Instructions to Begin Lesson

I. Hand out a list of rules and 2 blank Magic Squares allowing enough time for students to review rules. ***(2 minutes)***

II. Conduct a mini review and a question and answer session. ***(2 minutes)***

Exercise:

Phase II—Explanation instructions: Write out instructions for rule number one on page 100.

____

____

____

____

____

____

III. Erase the box on the board and draw it a second time filling in the numbers with the help of the students. Repeat the rules whenever necessary. ***(4 minutes)***

IV. Erase the box on the board and have the students fill in their own Magic Box using the rules. Give them assistance if necessary. ***(3 minutes)***

V. For those who wish to continue with this, give them the handout of the large box with 25 squares. ***(2 minutes)***

VI. Peer Evaluation form should be handed out and the student should be given a test grade. ***(2 Minutes)***

Magic Square

A Magic Square is one in which the columns, rows and the diagonals all add up to the same number.

The formation of magic squares has been an amusement for centuries. They were sometimes said to possess magical properties; one particular square was inscribed on a silver plate and was carried as a protection against the plague.

Magic squares can be constructed by trial and error, but the task is very time consuming. Thanks to a rule discovered by De la Loubere in 1693, it is possible to complete odd numbered squares with these. There are formulas for even numbered squares, but they will not concern us at this stage.

	15	**15**	**15**	
15	8	1	6	**15**
15	3	5	7	**15**
15	4	9	2	**15**
	15	**15**	**15**	

De la Loubere's rule is stated as follows:

1. Always place the numeral 1 in the middle of the top row.

	1	
		2

2. Proceed to place the successive numbers moving upwards, diagonally to the right. However, if the top row is reached, one moves to the bottom row as if it had been above the top row. Thus numeral 2, goes to the bottom right hand corner.

	1	
3		
		2

3. If the right hand column is reached, one moves to the left hand column as if it had been next to the right hand column. Thus, numeral 3 goes to the middle, left hand cell.

4. If, when moving diagonally, you find another numeral filling a cell, then move to the sell immediately below that cell. Thus, numeral 4 goes below numeral 3.

	1	
3		
4		2

5. When the top, right corner cell is reached, place the next numeral directly below. This is a special case and only occurs in the square once. Thus, numeral 7 goes below numeral 6.

	1	6
3	5	7
4		2

6. Now the right column is reached so the numeral 8 goes in the left column. This reaches the top line, so the numeral 9 is placed in the bottom row.

8	1	6
3	5	7
4	9	2

Conclusion: When any cell is full, go directly below where the last numeral was placed.

Magic Square – 5 X 5 Square

Let us apply the rules to a 5 x 5 cell square. All rows and columns add up to 65.

17	24	1	8	15
23	5	7	14	16
4	6	13	20	22
10	12	19	21	3
11	18	25	2	9

Exercise:

Now, try a 7 x 7 cell square.

Lesson Plan

***Teaching Strategy*: Demonstration Performance**

I. ***Background Data:***

Name: Dr. Paoni *Date:* 2/15/07 *Grade:* College
Time: 60 Minutes *Subject:* Dance *Place:* BCC 211
# of Students: Max. 25 *Unit:* Ballroom Dance
Lesson Topic: The Fox Trot

II. ***Behavioral Objectives***

a. The student will be able to explain how to dance the basic Fox Trot and the Basic Box Step.
b. The student will be able to demonstrate the following components of the dances:
   1. Ballroom positioning for starting the dances.
   2. Male: Individual steps and positions
   3. Female: Individual steps and positions
   4. Dance box step to music

III. ***Previous Assignment:***

a. In our last class, we learned where the dances originated.

b. We discussed many dances, including the Fox Trot and Box Step.

IV. ***Materials:***

a. CD of Music and a CD Player
b. DVD of the dances
c. Ties for students to designate male from female, in an all female class.
d. Lesson Plan
e. Whiteboard and Dry Erase Markers

V. ***Related Activities:*** Listen to a variety of music and determine what dance is appropritate for each title.

VI. ***Procedures:***

Set: Last week, we learned the Cha-Cha, the Crossover Step and the Chase. (Demonstrate the moves as you discuss them). Have two students also demonstrate the moves. Today, we will cover the Fox Trot and the Box Step.

Organization and Illustration: Class is arranged in a semi circle in an empty or cleared out classroom. (Show DVD's before beginning each step.

Demonstration: (repeat twice)
Play DVD of Box Step and dance the positions. Focus on the starting foot for male and female including body positions.

Explanation:
Break the step into two parts;

Dance Position: **Male & Female**

Step 1: Male – (Explain and Demonstrate)
Weight on right foot with left foot forward.
Right foot follows with a touch step.

Step 2: Weight on left foot, right foot moves to the side, left follows (side closes) weight on left foot.

Step 3: Right foot back and left follows. Touch step and then to side (original posion), right follows.

Fox Trot – Male Steps: Fourth count, slow, slow, quick, quick.

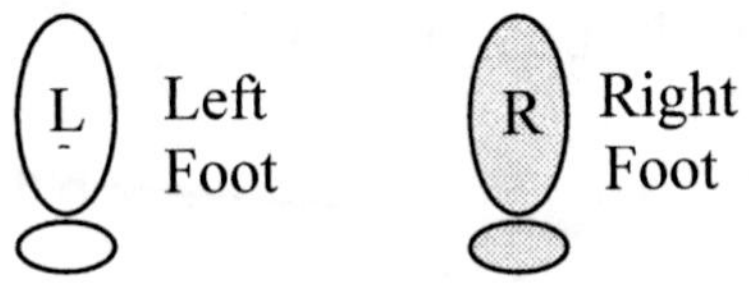

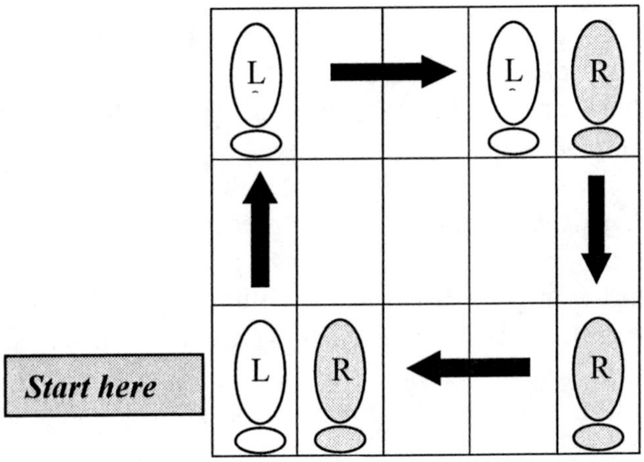

Fox Trot – Female Steps

The foot positions may seem backwards, but remember that you are standing opposite your male partner.

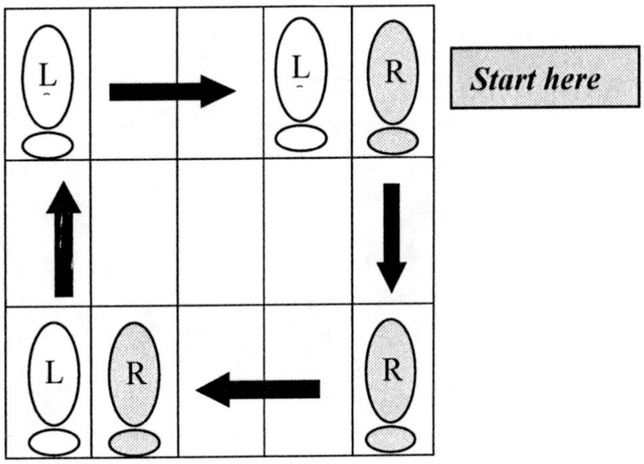

Organization and Illustration: Pass out the ties to all female students dancing the male roles. Arrange students in lines. Cue the CD and DVD.

F F F F F
M M M M M

Performance: Re-demonstrate complete Box Step focusing on the shifting of the weight. Demonstrate with a partner to music.

Steps 1–3: Repeat as in Explanation Phase, but with the roles for females separately.

While the students are in pairs, do the following: ***(5 Minutes)***

1. Check their dance positions.
2. Walk them through the first 4 counts. Step on the second 4 counts. Repeat this 4 times.

Demonstrate with a partner to music. Repeat preceding step with music.

Evaluation: Review all the steps both with and without the music. Have two or three couples demonstrate also. ***Change partners at least 2 times. (2 minutes)***

Assignment: Review the Cha-Cha, Fox Trot and Box Step. Be able to write and discuss steps in all dances.

Ongoing Activities: Optional field trip to Roseland, New York City, 3-15-07

Chapter Notes and Additional Information:

Chapter 12:

Teaching Strategy: Simulation Game

Educated persons must be more than doctors, teachers or scientists. They must be effective citizens and human beings.

Chapter Topics:

Definition	**Debrief**
Purpose	**Student's Role**
Classification	**Teacher's Role**
Organization	**Strengths**
Guidelines for Selection of Games	**Limitations**
Sample Formal (Plan)	**Sample Student Lesson Plan**
Introduction	**Closure and Evaluation**
Scenario	**Simulation Game**
Halt Game	**Lost at Sea**

Definition: ***A simulation game is a form of role-playing that combines an imitation of a real-life process in a game context. Simulation is an operational imitation or replication of real life. (Courtroom, business, government or social condition)***

Games are contests with goals, rules and roles.

- ***Goals:*** Each game has specific purposes and values that determine the expected outcome.
- ***Rules:*** Provide guidelines and sequence for the play.
- ***Roles:*** Players take on the role of decision maker and become responsible for their choices.

Exercise:

List educational games that you have played in the classroom.

Elementary	Secondary	College
____________________	____________________	________________
____________________	____________________	________________
____________________	____________________	________________
____________________	____________________	________________

Purpose

There are several purposes that may be achieved through simulation games other than the primary goals of engaging students in decision-making roles.

Terms and Concepts: The games expose the student to new vocabulary and correct usage.

Facts: Each game has a base of information that is necessary to learn in order for the game to be played properly.

Intellectual and Social Skills: Skills of both intellectual and social values are learned by providing incentives and the opportunity to practice them. Incentive is the result of learning skills that enable a person to do well in the game and the opportunity to practice comes from playing the game.

Attitude Change: Within the real-life situation, a student has the opportunity not only to learn new information, but to also experience inner feelings as he or she participates in various roles.

Exercise:

Explain what educational purposes were learned by playing these games.

Game: (Stock market)	Purpose: (Facts, skills on trading stock)
______________________	______________________
______________________	______________________
______________________	______________________
______________________	______________________

Classification—(refer to Chapter 3)

Physical: Responsive
Cognitive: Secondary
Affected: Secondary

Organization

Selecting the game: The game that is selected must fit into the unit of instruction and be able to reflect one or more unit objectives. The game should emphasize aspects of the real situation that are ***important*** and ***worth teaching***. The problem is not so much what games to select, but which ones are ***most applicable***. Simulation games are widely used and available in commercial form for every subject and grade level.

Guidelines for Selection of Games

1. The game should allow all of the class to participate. If the class is too large, divide them into groups and assign alternate activities.

2. Games should not require more time than available for classroom activities. Most simulation games require at least one hour to play.

3. The game should be able to be played in the normal classroom or existing facilities with little disturbance (noise and excitement) to adjacent rooms.

4. The game selected must meet the abilities and limitations of the students who are able to be the participants. The game should not demand more than what a student is able to give. (reading levels, abstractions and concepts).

5. The rules and guidelines should be clear and easily understood by the students. They should not be so complex as to distract from the actual play.

6. Does the game create a real-life situation that allows meaningful roles for the students? There should be more to the simulation game than the roll of the dice or spin of the wheel. The game must give the students an opportunity to experience that simulated life process.

Step 1: Introduction of Game: The sequence of the first three to four steps may be altered depending on the game. Explain to the class what the general characteristics of the game are. Explain as ***simply*** as possible what the situation is, who of the players are and what the goals of the game are. The initial introduction should be ***brief*** and without a great deal of detail and exact information.

Step 2: Assign Roles: The class is divided into appropriate groups as the individual game dictates. The assignment of groups and roles is usually done by the teacher. The makeup of a group and the roles played by the students are critical to a successful game experience. Slower and faster students may be assigned together to provide fairer competition and to allow the slower to learn more quickly. The selection of groups is an excellent opportunity for the teacher to take advantage of peer learning: gifted/slow, aggressive/meek and silent/talkative.

Step 3: Present the Scenario: The objectives, purposes and context of the game are now explained to the class in more detail. The scenario and situation of the game are reviewed, and the specific unit objectives are ***outlined*** and ***emphasized.*** Remember that the game is only a means to an end—***to acquire knowledge, skills or values.*** If the objective/purpose is glossed over, the game will have lost its purpose. Explain to the class that during the game they should be aware of their actions in relation to the purpose and objective. During this phase or the next, materials are distributed to the class, if needed.

Step 4: Explain the Rules: The rules and pattern of play are explained and whenever possible, illustrated. If the rules are complete, duplicate them for individual use and have the students review them the day before. If that is not possible, write them on a whiteboard or use a PowerPoint demonstration. Once again, keep the explanation simple and brief; if time allows, have a trial run of the play before the actual game.

Step 5: Play the Game: When students are engaged in playing the game, there are several tasks for the instructor.

1. **Take notes** as to how individuals react and play the game. These observations will be critical in the debriefing session. Look and listen for conversations, decisions, consequences, attitudes, moods and feelings expressed by the students.
2. **Answer any questions** about the rules and pattern of the game, making sure that the students are following them. Handle disputes only when students cannot settle them themselves.
3. **Make adjustments** in the game as needed. Disregard rules that are complex, shorten time or eliminate sequence. Usually, most modifications will be made prior to the game, but situations arise where it is necessary to change the rules during play.
4. **The Students Game:** Do not play the game, make decisions for the students or infer value judgments. The game is for the students, and it has its own internal value system, which allows you to be an observer, not an evaluator. As an important observer, you can focus on the art of teaching rather than an evaluator of the student.

Step 6: Halt Game: Give the students a warning (five minutes) prior to stopping the game. After the materials are collected, ask the students to jot some quick notes on various aspects of the game. Allow students time to think about the game before beginning the debriefing session. This time is important for them to collect their thoughts and to also gear down for a discussion.

Step 7: Debrief: The debriefing session is the final phase of a simulation game. It ties together the objectives, the play and the outcomes. The there should be ample time left in the period so that a thorough discussion of the game's activities can be discussed. Many of the questions in the observations made during the game will provide the basis for discussion.

The following are general guidelines for the conducting the discussion:

1. **Begin Discussion:** To start the discussion, encourage the students to talk about their experiences during the game: What decisions were made? What were the consequences? What were the causes?
2. **Reflection:** Have the students reflect on their feelings and attitudes: Did their beliefs change? Did they experience a new feeling? What were the feelings of your group?

3. **Relate:** Using the first two types of questions as a focal point, have the students relate specific events or actions of the game that reflect cause-and-effect relationship. Use your notes as an observer of the game to remind them of their actions.

4. **Compare** and relate the game to real-life situations: Ask students to visualize themselves in a real situation and ask whether they would make the same decision or act in the same manner. It is important during this phase that the students can relate the game to activities in their real lives.

5. **Summarize, Generalize and Conclude:** Bring together the objectives of the game, the play and the outcomes for the students. The reasons for playing the game as well as the resultant actions could be clarified and the reinforced. Conclusions can be drawn on how the learning process "***simulation game***" can be applied and utilized in their future lives.

Sample Format (Plan)

The following is the simulation game BA FA, A Cross-Cultural Experience. The ratings are those extracted from the instructor's manual.

Introduction

The purpose of the orientation is to ***briefly explain*** the objectives of the simulation and outline the procedures that will be followed. It is very easy to overwhelm people with instructions in the orientation. This should be avoided as the participants can become so frustrated that their ability to effectively participate in the simulation can be reduced. On the other hand, enough information should be given so that the students are assured that you, as director, know what you are doing and that the objectives of the simulation are worthy of their interest and time. The broad outlines of the experience should be apparent.

You should also feel free to ***tailor*** the simulation experience to fit the needs of a particular course of study or interest of the participating group. For instance, if the experience is being used to sensitize persons preparing to visit or live in a foreign culture, psychological barriers and blocks that one can develop while attempting to learn a foreign language. Then, in his orientation, the director might want to ask the participants to make special note of the feelings surrounding their attempts to speak and understand the language of the Beta Culture, so that they can discuss those feelings at the end of the simulation.

Scenario

The following is a suggested outline for the orientation. Explain to the group that the specific purposes of the simulation will become evident as a simulation progresses, but basically the experience is intended to:

- Create a situation that allows us to profitably explore the idea of culture.
- Create feelings that are similar to those they will likely encounter when traveling to a different culture.
- Give participants experience in observing and interacting with a different culture.

Before the game begins, write each of the italicized headings on the whiteboard. Explain that you will provide more detailed instructions as the game develops, but that the general outline of what happens is as follows:

1. ***Divide into two cultures:*** You will be divided into the Alpha Culture and the Beta Culture as soon as we are finished with the orientation.

2. ***Learn and practice your new culture:*** In the real world, cultures develop shared meanings and ways of interacting over many centuries for many different reasons. Likewise, a person living in a culture learns the different rules and reasons for various behaviors over an entire lifetime. In this experience, we are going to give you those rules and ask you to learn them in a short period of time. They may seem complicated at first, but as you practice them, they will appear very clear and reasonable.

3. **Select an Observer:** Each group is to select a person to travel to the other culture to observe the ways they behave with an eye toward helping future travelers. The observer should try and figure out what rules govern the behavior of the other group by carefully observing their actions. It is not permissible for the observer to ask a member of the other culture about the rules; they are to be figured out on the basis of observation and later trial and error.

4. ***Exchange of Observers:*** Once the Alpha Culture and the Beta Culture are well established, the observers will travel to the other culture. They will be wearing a badge with the name of their home culture on it. Each observer has approximately two minutes to learn as much information as they can about the foreign culture. It should be remembered that they must learn from intelligent observation. Asking questions about the rules is not allowed.

5. ***Report of Observers:*** The observers will return to their home culture and describe what they saw and any ideas they have about the values, more and

rules of the other culture. Everyone in the group should be encouraged to develop ideas about the meaning of the observer's report so that future visitors will have the benefit of the entire group's thinking.

6. ***Exchange of Visitors:*** Once each group has had the chance to discuss the report of their observer, then each culture continues as they were before the observers report. Once each culture is reestablished, visitors will then be exchanged. Visitors will be required to wear a badge with the name of their home culture on it. They will be given cards, chips or whatever is used in the culture to be visited. The purpose of the visit is to successfully interact with the other culture. We will indicate how many visitors should be exchanged and the length of time each group of visitors should stay in a different culture.

Halt Game—*End of game*

Once everyone has a chance to visit the other culture, the game will be ended and we will discuss the implications of the experience.

Debrief—*Discussion and Analysis*

The strength of the simulation for many people is that it allows the director to surface the feelings, anxieties, misperceptions and counterproductive attitudes of people who, by choice or circumstance, are required to interact with another culture or subculture. For others, the advantage of the experience lies in being able to help them realize that people with whom they are presently dealing (women, Blacks, Orientals, Chicanos or Anglos) may belong to a different culture and be operating from another set of rules. There are many different uses which the simulation may serve by giving careful thought to what questions and topics will be debated in the post-game discussion. However, in almost all cases, the following questions should be asked before going on to the task of relating the experience to more specific objectives.

These questions, if asked in the sequence outlined below, allow each group to see how they were perceived, and more importantly, misperceived, by the other group.

1. Ask the Beta members to explain the Alpha Culture.
2. Ask the Alpha members to explain the Beta Culture.
3. Ask the Alpha members how the Beta visitors appeared to them.
4. Ask the Beta members how the Alpha visitors appeared to them.
5. Ask Alpha members to describe their feelings and thoughts when they visited the Beta Culture.
6. Ask Beta members to describe their feelings and thoughts when they visited the Alpha Culture.
7. Ask Beta members to explain the Beta Culture.
8. Ask Alpha members to explain the Alpha Culture.

9. Ask members of each culture in which culture they would prefer to live and why.

Student's Role

The primary role of the student in simulation games is to be an active participant, making decisions that determine the course of action. The word "***active***" is stressed because the strategy is dependent on the willingness of the students to engage in roles that force them to make decisions. The student should be prepared to experience new feelings and values and share in the consequences of winning and losing.

Teacher's Role

Play the game prior to classroom use for the purpose of finding the trouble spots, length of play and complexities. The modifications of the game should be made prior to its classroom use. It should be noted that it is perfectly permissible to modify the game to fit the needs of your students. The game should not dictate your needs and objectives.

The teacher should also refrain from making judgments about students' decisions within the game in that the game has its own standards and values.

The teacher should stress the purpose of playing the game versus the entertainment of the game.

Strengths

1. Games are self-motivating and appealing.
2. Role-playing and simulation games have been used throughout the students' lives to help them learn.
3. Simulation games encourage critical thinking.
4. Simulation games encourage better communication between student and student, and teacher and student.
5. Students learn to cope with unpredictable circumstances and look into future roles.

Limitations

1. Students may become too competitive.
2. Simulation games are often artificial and overly simplified. They do not offer an accurate picture.
3. The game may become the important activity and not that the game is really for the transfer of experience.
4. Simulation games need a large block of time to conclude properly.

References:

Boocock, Sarane S., and E. O. Schild. *Simulation Games in Learning*. Beverly Hills, CA: Sage Publications, 1968.

Livingston, Samuel A. and Clarice S. Stoll. *Simulation Games*. New York: Free Press, 1973.

Sample Student Lesson Plan—Simulation Game

I. *Background Data:*

Name: Genoveva Margues, Diane Lang *Date:* 3/32/07 *Time:* 10 a.m.
Grade: College Level *Place:* Brookdale Community College.
# of Students: N/A *Subject:* Sociology
Unit: Individual Culture & Society *Lesson Topic:* The Meaning of Culture

II. *Behavioral Objectives:*

1. To understand the terminology used in this chapter (see attached page), its application in our culture and any culture that students have encountered.
2. Explore the ideas of culture by creating a situation in which the student encounters a new culture. (Use of the simulation game.) Let them become aware of their emotions, frustrations and what techniques were used to interact with the new culture. (Use of symbols. Did they conform or not? What social interaction was used?)

III. *Materials:*

1. BA FA Game
2. CD and CD player
3. Milk and cookies
4. Masking tape
5. Extra room for division of the groups

IV. *Previous Assignment*: Ask students to remember past experience they may have had when traveling. *Travel not necessarily to another country.*

V. *Procedures*:

Set—Last week students were asked to remember a past experience when they traveled. As what the students major difficulties were: language barriers, values, how the culture was ordered (male dominated), time organization or dress. We will try to present everyone with a new culture. Begin simulation game.

Teaching Strategy: (Simulation Game)

A. **Orientation:** Explain the objectives
   1. Explore the idea of culture and what it means to the students.
   2. Become aware of your feelings and frustrations when encountering different cultures.

3. What various techniques were used to interact with different cultures?

B. **Listen** to CDs describing the new culture.
   1. Learn the rules of the culture.
      a. Demonstrate the rules.
      b. Choose a patriarch.
      c. Divide group again into males and females.

   2. Have class **practice** their culture.

   3. **Choose observer** and explain their duties.
      a. Observe actions of other cultures.
      b. Try to figure out the other culture's rules. Cannot ask any questions.
      c. Report findings to own group.
      d. Write down observation of group.

   4. **Choose visitors** (# of students: 2)
      a. Send in visitors to interact with culture.
      b. Receive necessary material for interaction with the other culture.
      c. Return and report what they have experienced.
      d. Cannot ask any questions.

C. **Begin actual simulation game**
   1. Start cultures
   2. Send observer and report back
   3. Send visitors and report back. Repeat until all visitors return (5 minutes each).

D. **Group Discussion and Analysis** (No discussion until the entire group is back together.)
   1. Ask the Beta observer to explain the Alpha Culture.
   2. Ask the Alpha observer to explain the Beta Culture.
   3. Ask the Alpha observer how the Beta visitors appeared to them.
   4. Ask the Beta observer how the Alpha visitors appeared to them.
   5. Ask Alpha observer to describe their feelings and thoughts when they visited the Beta Culture.
   6. Ask Beta observer to describe their feelings and thoughts when they visited the Alpha Culture.
   7. Ask Beta observer to explain the Beta Culture.
   8. Ask Alpha observer to explain the Alpha Culture.

9. Ask members of each culture in which culture they would prefer to live and why.
10. Did the experience remind you of any trip you might have taken overseas? Why?
11. Can one experience explain how and what a foreigner would feel in the United States?

Closure and Evaluation: We have several important things from this experience;

1. What we perceive of something is not always true.
2. Culture goes beyond surface appearance to include purpose, tradition and reason.
3. We must be aware of how others perceive us.
4. We must not judge others hastily. We can make it easier for others to understand us.

VI. ***Assignment:*** Read Unit 4 on Family Structure - How would you describe the structure of your family? Describe both past and present.

VII. ***Ongoing Activities:*** Get as much information as you can on your family back-ground so that it can be used for the construction of your family tree.

VIII. ***Lesson Comment:***

Simulation Game:

Vocabulary:

- ***Culture***—The system of values and meanings shared by a group or society, including the embodiment of those meanings in material objects.

- ***Subculture*** —The culture of a segment of society such as a social group.

- ***Culture Trait***—The simplest and most significant unit of a culture. (eating breakfast or bathing)

- ***Symbolic Interactionism***—A social and psychological theory that stresses the importance of communication through language and gesture, in the formation and maintenance of personality and social relationships.

- ***Ethnocentrism*** —The attitude that one's own culture or group is by nature superior and the evaluation of another culture in terms of one's own culture.

- ***Conformity***—Behavior that is in accord with the norms of a social group or society.
- ***Value***—An abstract and generalized conception of what is good, beneficial, desirable and worthwhile.
- ***Resocialization***—A process involving a radical change in both role behaviors and values, to a new way of life that is inconsistent and incompatible with the former one.
- ***Patriarchal Family***—A form of a family organization in which the father is dominant.

Exercise:

Explain how the games Monopoly or Stock Market may be used in the classroom to teach educational concepts.

Lost at Sea

Group: ____

Instructions: This is an exercise in group decision making. Your group is to employ the group, consensus method in reaching its decision. This means that the ranking for each of the 15 survival items must be agreed on by each group member before it becomes a part of the group decision. Consensus is difficult to reach; therefore, not every ranking will meet with everyone's complete approval. As a group, try to make each ranking one with which all group members can at least partially agree. Here are some guidelines to use in reaching a consensus.

1. Avoid arguing for your own individual judgment. Approach the task on the basis of logic.
2. Avoid changing your mind if it is only to reach an agreement and avoid conflict. Support only solutions that you are able to agree to at least somewhat.

3. Avoid "***conflict reducing***" techniques such as the majority vote, averaging or trading in order to reach a decision.

4. View differences of opinion as a help rather than a hindrance in decision making.

Assignment:

You are adrift on a private yacht in the South Pacific. As a consequence of a fire of unknown origin, much of the yacht and its contents have been destroyed. The yacht is now slowly sinking. Your location is unclear because of the destruction of critical, navigational equipment and because you and the crew were distracted trying to bring the fire under control. Your best estimate is that you are approximately 1,000 mi. SSW of the nearest land.

Below is a list of the 15 items that are intact and undamaged after the fire. In addition to these articles, you have a serviceable, rubber, life raft with oars large enough to carry yourself, the crew and all the items listed below. The total contents of all survivors' pockets are: a package of cigarettes, several books of matches and five $1.00 bills.

Your task is to rank the 15 items below in terms of their importance to your survival. Place the numeral 1 by the most important item, the numeral 2 by the second most important item and so on through to numeral 15, the least important.

_____ Sextant
_____ Shaving mirror
_____ 5 1-gal. cans of water
_____ Mosquitoes netting
_____ One case of U.S. Army C-rations
_____ Map of the Pacific Ocean
_____ Seat cushion (flotation device approved by the U.S. Coast Guard)
_____ 2 1-gal. cans of oil/gas mixture
_____ Small transistor radio
_____ Shark repellents
_____ Twenty square feet of opaque plastic
_____ 1 qt. of 160 proof, Puerto Rican rum
_____ 15 ft. of nylon tape
_____ Two boxes of chocolate bars
_____ Fishing kits

Exercise:

Using the simulation game "Lost at Sea," explain the purpose of the game and how it can be used to teach educational concepts in the classroom.

____
____
____
____
____
____

Chapter Notes & Additional Information:

Personal Thoughts & Drawings

Chapter 13:

Teaching Strategy: Field Trip

The sooner we all get out of the stuffy classroom, the better it will be for everyone.

Chapter Topics:

Definition and Purpose	**Teacher's Role**
Classification	**Strengths**
Limitations	**Limitations**
Organization	**Lesson Plan**
Sample Format Plan	**The Metropolitan Museum of Art**
Student's Role	

Definition and Purpose

Definition: ***The field trip is a planned, purposeful and educational study undertaken other than in the normal classroom environment.***

The purpose of the field trip is to **observe** and to ***clarify concepts*** in their functional setting. The field trip offers a bridge between the classroom experience and the real world of ideas. Field trips can be categorized into four different types:

- ***In-school trips*** that take place within the school environment (i.e. to the library, cafeteria or school grounds).
- ***Inter-school trips*** that take place between schools of the same district or different systems.
- ***Community trips*** that are planned so they can take place within the normal day.
- ***Extended trips*** that require more than a day to complete.

Classification

Physical: Interactive
Physical: Acquiring and Organizing
Affective: Attending and Receiving

Limitations

Time: 1 to 1 ½ hours

Exercise:

Write a summary of your most/worst memorable field trip and what educational purposes it served.

Best field trip:

Educational Purpose/Objective:

Worst field trip:

Why:

Organization

Pre-Trip: The extent of the arrangements for any trip depends on its length and purpose. It is therefore expected that the time to prepare an extended trip is considerably more than for an inter-school or community trip.

The success of a field trip is dependent on the ***planning*** and ***preparation***. For all field trips, students should have at least one to two weeks of prior study and preparation.

The teacher should ensure that the students have:

- ***Adequate background for the concept to be viewed and studied***
- ***Skills necessary to take notes, observe and collect items***
- ***Know the precise purpose and their tasks and responsibilities***

1. ***Clarify your legal responsibility*** and liability concerning field trips.
    a. **School Policy:** Most schools have a written policy statement as to the hows, whys and limitations of organizing field trips.
    b. **Obtain Parental Permission Slips:** Include in the cover letter a complete explanation of the field trip and its purpose.

2. ***Clarify site arrangements*** through visitation (if possible)
    a. Onsite supervision requirements
    b. Limitations of sight facilities
    c. **First aid procedures:** Bring a first aid kit, on all field trips
    d. **Time arrangements:** Arrival time, tour, lunch and departure times.

3. ***Plan for adequate supervision by:***
    a. Organizing students by the buddy system
    b. Including one adult for every five students. The ratio can be increased depending on students and activity.
    c. Explaining responsibilities to parents aides and chaperones ahead of time

4. ***Establish standards of behavior and dress code.***

5. ***Plan for travel, lodging and tour arrangements range ahead of time.***

6. ***Gather equipment and materials.***

7. ***Establish the purpose and objectives of the trip.***

On-Site: The students should be clearly organized into appropriate groups with a clear set of tasks and objectives. It is not necessary that all students do the same activity, but, there should be some common activities to the field trip. Much of the pleasure of a field trip is in sharing of your ***"discoveries,"*** which in part means that each trip should have some flexibility for student choices. Make sure that your schedule is realistic with plenty of rest and quiet time. Do not over-saturate or try to get everything in on one visit.

1. Confirm arrangements with your onsite personnel. Clarify any changes on your or their part.
2. Explain the purpose and objective of the field trip again to the class. (See field trips sample format [Plan].)
3. Establish meeting times and places when the class does not move as a group.
4. Plan for appropriate "rest stops" according to the age group and duration of the field trip.
5. Check to see that students have not left anything behind and that "thank you's" are given to the hosts.

Post-Trip: After the trip, the ***evaluation*** and ***assessment*** of the success of the experience is completed. You, as an instructor, have to determine if it was beneficial to your students for the time and effort expended. First, was it a ***positive, educational*** experience that added to or expanded on the unit of study? Was it just a day out of the classroom? If the field trip was positive, then, plan another field trip.

Second, did the students learn and experience things that are not possible in the classroom? Were the students ***active learners*** or ***passive observers*** of the experience? The field trip should be an opportunity for students to be active learners.

1. Send formal thank-you notes to the hosts of the field trip as well as involved parents.
2. Evaluate the trip in terms of the established purpose. Was the field trip worth the effort and time expended?
3. Conduct classroom follow-up activities. (See field trip sample format [plan].)

Exercise:

Make a list of ten possible activities students may do on the sample trip (Seahorse Trip).

1. ______________________	**6.** ______________________
2. ______________________	**7.** ______________________
3. ______________________	**8.** ______________________
4. ______________________	**9.** ______________________
5. ______________________	**10.** ______________________

Create several different ways of evaluating students for the field trip. (knowledge, skills or attitudes).

1. ______________________	**6.** ______________________
2. ______________________	**7.** ______________________
3. ______________________	**8.** ______________________
4. ______________________	**9.** ______________________
5. ______________________	**10.** ______________________

Sample Format (Plan)

"Pre-Trip"

I. Establish a purpose and objectives for the field trip.

The purpose and objectives of the field trip need to be clearly identified for the trip to be educationally successful. Generally, the field trip is planned as a culminating activity for a unit. The field trip allows a firsthand experience of observing ***"ideas"*** in their functional setting, after they have been discussed in the classroom.

The objectives of the field trip should be clarified in terms of what is to be learned and how it is to be accomplished.

Field trip: To the seashore for the study of marine life

Objectives: Identify and collect mollusks
Identify and collect crustaceans
Identify and collect water vegetation

Process: Students are divided into groups of five to collect and record items listed above.

"On-Site"

II. Explain purpose and objective prior to action.

The whole purpose and objectives should be clarified once more prior to the active learning experience. The learning experience, whether it is viewing, collecting or doing, must be clearly established in the students' minds. This is not to say that there isn't any flexibility within the experience, but that there is a purpose and a means to accomplish it.

Process: If possible, use worksheets as a guide for students as they observe, touch and collect.

"Post-Trip"

III. Conduct classroom follow-up activities

The follow-up activities are critical to the benefits that students will derive from the field trip. It is necessary for the students to conceptualize the relationship between the field trip and the classroom lessons; otherwise, it becomes an isolated aspect of the unit. Try to plan follow-up activities that relate to the major learning activities of the field trip.

Objectives: Categorize the mollusks, crustaceans and vegetation collected.
Relate samples to other types of sea life.
Discuss interrelationships of sea life.
Build an in-house aquarium.

Student's Role

The student's role in the field trip is as an ***active participant*** in the process of observing, recording, collecting and questioning. The specific learning activity that is needed during any field trip must be within the student's capacity, if not developed by the teacher. Adequate preparation for the field trip, in terms of reading and assignments, are also the responsibility of the students in order for them to take full advantage of the experience. Finally, it is the student's responsibility to have ***self-discipline*** and present a

positive image to the public. Rules, behavior standards and dress codes should be established prior to the trip so that the students are aware of their expected behavior.

Teacher's Role

A great deal of teacher planning is necessary for a field trip to be successful. The organization of a field trip requires at least three days; one for just planning, the trip itself and, follow-up activities. The specific responsibilities related to the planning stage were identified under "***organization***."

The teacher's primary responsibility, besides the task of organizing, is to ensure that the field trip is an ***"educational experience"*** and not just a trip or day away from the classroom. The experience does not have to be drudgery, but can be very exciting and enjoyable if the teacher does adequate preparation.

Strengths

1. Field trips provide for firsthand experience and an opportunity for students to relate classroom learning to reality.
2. The community becomes an effective resource of the classroom.
3. Students have an opportunity to see their community as well as to learn how to take advantage of its resources.

Limitations

1. Field trips take a great deal of preparation and time, and are exhausting to both teachers and students.
2. The field trip is a multi-learning experience and too much stimulation reduces the effectiveness of the experience.
3. Discipline problems become pronounced on a field trip.

Exercise:

Explain possible reasons and solutions for discipline problems on a field trip.

Problem:

____

____

____

Solution:

____

____

____

EDU216 Lesson Plan

"Field Trip"—Metropolitan Museum of Art

I. *Background Data:*

Name: Mary Smith, Joe Olds, Kate Newtown *Date:* 2-17-07 *Time:* 10a.m.
Grade: College Level *Place:* Metropolitan Museum of Art.
# of Students: 24 *Subject:* Art
Unit: The Impressionists *Lesson Topic:* "Experience the Met"

II. *Behavioral Objectives:*

The students will:

3. Complete museum "scavenger hunt" checklist
4. Observe paintings from the Impressionist Movement (American and French)
5. Relate lecture material on Impressionist painters to observations
6. Participate in a guided, walking tour of the French Impressionist Galleries

III. *Materials:*

1. Transportation for 30—40 students (bus)
2. Information packet for each student, including
   A. Museum floor plan
   B. Day's schedule
   C. Scavenger hunt checklist (See Page 128)

IV. *Previous Assignment*: Discuss and lecture on the artists and provide an introduction to the Metropolitan Museum of Art including the field trip.

V. *Related Activities:* Assign an artist to each student to explore and provide a brief summary to the class. Take a tour of Henry R. Luce Center for the Study of American Art.

VI. *Procedures*:

Set: (On the Bus):

1. Welcome the students and their guests to the trip.
2. Give the students a brief overview of the day's activities.
3. Introduce the group leaders and assign their groups.
4. Assign groups to specific artists for research.
5. Review information that is to be gathered.
6. Review post assignment activities.
7. Discuss free-time activities:
   a. Frederic Remington: the Masterworks
   b. Paintings in the Renaissance Sienna: 1420-1500
   c. Ingres at the Metropolitan
   d. Victorian Dress: 1837-1877

8. Discuss exit time and meeting places.

After the Museum: Visit to Little Italy for sustenance

Organization & Illustrations: Students and their guests divide into two groups.

Group 1:	***Group 2:***
Paintings of:	Paintings of:
Manet, Monet	Cassatt
Cézanne	Whistler
Pissarro	Homer
Van Gogh	Artists/Paintings as previously noted
Degas	Artists/Paintings as previously noted
Toulouse-Lautrec	

Teaching Strategy (Field Trip)

I. *Schedule:*

Arrive at Museum 9:00 A.M.
Free Time (Lunch Break) 11:30 A.M.–1:00 P.M.
Finish Museum 1:00 P.M.–2:30 P.M.

II. *Group Assignments and Schedules:*

A. **Group 1:** Meet in the Great Hall (1st Floor)
   1. Walking tour of French Impressionist Galleries
   2. Observation of Paintings
   3. Review Painters
      a. Discussion by group leaders and students
      b. Question-and-answer period
      c. Comments
   4. General Summary of Impressionism

B. **Group 2:** Meet at the Great Hall Balcony (2nd Floor)
   1. "The Great Metropolitan Museum of Art Scavenger Hunt"
   2. Tour of the American Wing
   3. Review Painters
      a. Discussion by group leaders and students
      b. Question-and-answer period
      c. Comments
   4. Tour of Charles of Engelhard Court (1st Floor)

III. *2:30-3:30 P.M.*

Groups 1 & 2 will reverse activities:

A. Group 1:
   1. "The Great Metropolitan Museum of Art Scavenger Hunt"
   2. Tour of the American Wing

B. Group 2:
   1. Walking tour of French Impressionist Galleries

2. Observation of Paintings

IV. ***3:30-4:30 P.M* – Free Time**

V. ***4:30 P.M*** - Meet outside the Museum to board bus and go to Little Italy.

VI. ***6:00 P.M.*** – Board the bus to go to Brookdale Community College.

VII. ***7:00–7:30 P.M.*** – Arrive at Brookdale Community College

Closure & Evaluation:

General discussion of the day's activities.
What did the students do with their free time?
Discussion of Impressionist paintings ("In the Flesh")
Short debriefing with Dr. Paoni

VIII. ***Assignment :***

A. Bring "Scavenger Hunt" checklist to the next class.
B. Prepare questions and be prepared to discuss the field trip.
C. Debriefing of field trip.

IX. ***Ongoing Activities:***

A. Finish the unit on Art in the Twentieth Century.
B. Class Lecture
C. Introduction the Museum of Natural History
D. Field Trip: The Museum of Natural History

X. ***Lesson Comments:***

Exercise:

List 10 field trips that you would take your class on in Monmouth County. What is the educational purpose for each trip?

1. ______________________________
2. ______________________________
3. ______________________________
4. ______________________________
5. ______________________________
6. ______________________________
7. ______________________________
8. ______________________________
9. ______________________________
10. ______________________________

The Great Metropolitan Museum of Art
"Scavenger Hunt"

Name: ________________________________ Date: ____________

1. It is much smaller than the original. It is only a model. Your stomach must be grumbling. What is the name of the famous Greek temple?

____

2. Who has just lost their head to Perseus? (HINT: Great Hall Balcony – 2nd floor)

____

3. Which artist would agree that these shoes "were made for walking"? (HINT: Andre Meyer Galleries)

____

4. Monet painted which European government building? (HINT: Andre Meyer Galleries)

____

5. There is only one self-portrait in the French impressionist exhibit. Who is it?

____

6. Of the impressionists in this exhibit, which is not French?

____

7. When you think of this name, you usually think of expensive jewelry, but, you would not want to hear the sound of breaking glass from this man. (HINT: American Wing Garden Court)

____

8. This young lady's cousin stands atop Madison Square Garden. "Who and what is she? (HINT: American Wing Garden Court—1st floor)

____

9. There is something "church-like" about the first floor of the Garden Court. Why, or should we say, what?

____

10. This painting features our first president's most famous, aquatic adventure. What is the title? (HINT: American Wing Entrance—2nd floor)

____

*** Bonus: As you walk through the museum, you will notice little boxes on the floors. What purpose do these gadgets serve?

____

Chapter Notes & Additional Information:

Personal Thoughts & Drawings

Chapter 14:

Teaching Strategy: Observation

The desire for knowledge increases with its acquisition. Those who really thirst for knowledge usually get it.

Chapter Topics:

- Teaching Strategy: Observation
- Definition
- Purposes
- Classification
- Organization
- Continuous Experiences
- Short-Term Observation
- Observation Experience
- What to Observe
- How to Observe
- How to Record
- Follow-Up
- Scheduling
- Student's Role
- Teacher's Role
- Strengths
- Limitations
- Sample Observation Questions/Activities
- Metropolitan Museum of Art
- Sample Student Tasks
- Field Trip Exercise (Observations)
- Field Trip Written Assignment

Teaching Strategy: Observation

Definition: ***Observation is the act of noting and recording a situation for a study. The observer may be viewing a particular action, group process or a series of events. This observation can be a singular viewing or a process that may involve several continuous visitations.***

Exercise:

In the observation process of viewing a work of art, describe how the senses may be used.

Sight:

Sound (imagine the sound of crashing waves):

Smell:

Touch:

Taste:

Purposes

Through the process of observation, a student is able to achieve several educational ends.

1. ***Give Meaning to Ideas:*** When a student has little or no direct experience with an area of study, ideas will have a limited meaning. Direct contact with ideas through observation allows for a more accurate understanding of the ideas.

2. ***Determine Needs:*** Through viewing a *situation*[2], a student is able to see a complete picture and determine the necessary requirements for mastery. As in the teaching strategy or demonstration performance, a student is given the opportunity to view the whole and record the parts that comprise the concept.

3. ***Evaluate Quality:*** Through critical study, a student is able to establish standards of performance. Even though the observation may offer a range of standards, the students soon develop an objective set of criteria for reference purposes.

4. ***Develop Positive Attitudes:*** Observing an excellent or quality demonstration can inspire the viewer's interest and enthusiasm. Even through a negative observation, the instructor can instill a positive will to improve the performance.

Classification

Physical: Responsive
Cognitive: Primary (Acquiring and Organizing)
Affective: Primary (Attending and Receiving)

Organization

Types of observation experiences: Observation experiences generally fall into two categories: **Continuous Experiences** and **Short-Term Observation.**

Continuous Experiences

Continuous experiences are observations that are more than one or two viewings and reflect learning over a long period of time. When observing a situation on a continuous basis, a student is better able to see the process (situation) in a truer light than in a singular observation. The observation, over a period of time, can be organized in several ways: *weekly, biweekly, daily* (concentrated observation), *full day, half day,* hour or other periods of scheduling. In all cases the viewing is on a regular basis and scheduled to offer the observer learning in a sequential manner.

---

[2] Situation is defined as an action, process, event, skill, idea or concept.

Example: Field experience for various collegiate courses such as psychology and education, where students observe an elementary school, class or grade.

Short-Term Observation

Singular or short-term observations are more common in the educational process and are often incorporated into field trips. This type of observation is easier to arrange and does not require the administrative organization that longer periods of observation will. Examples of short-term observations are: ***visiting other classes, community organizations, special exhibits, conferences and demonstrations.*** The short-term observation differs from the continuous observation by presupposing that the learner can acquire the necessary insight through one or two observations.

Preparation:

Helping the student to become an intelligent observer will ensure a quality experience.

1. Provide background data on the person or situation to include: history, age, abilities, characteristics, interests and needs.

2. Explain how the observation relates to the area being studied.

3. Explain the expected activities and sequence that students will be observing.

4. Explain the environment (Physical –psycho-socio) and conditions in which the observation will take place. In some observations situations, students will be isolated from the situation by a one-way mirror and glass partitions for railings.

5. Identify any rules for procedures that may be required during the observation. In some situations students are asked not to move about, talk or disrupt the normal routine as in the laboratory schools. Other observations may provide a mixture of activity in which the observer may participate.

Observation Experience

The observation, whether a short or continuous experience, should have an established purpose. Certainly many other concepts will be identified along with the stated objectives, but it is important that the teacher emphasize the central purpose of the observation and what is to be identified and recorded.

What to Observe

Depending on the nature of the observation (first or only), the teacher should cue the students as to the range of possibilities of experiences that this situation may yield. Do not overload the experience by asking the student to see everything, but limit the observations to a few, critical aspects for recording purposes.

How to Observe

When explaining what to observe, the instructor should also ***demonstrate*** how to listen and see. Skill in observing is being able to ***analyze differences*** between the important and unimportant, determining ***cause*** and ***effect*** and finding relationships. The teacher, in illustrating these procedures, should use concrete examples of the skills.

How to Record

Note taking and recording the observation experiences can be done in several different ways. The use of ***recorders, videotapes*** and ***writing instruments*** all can be employed to record the observation. Depending on the situation, prior approval is usually required when taping (audio or visual) is to be employed.

When using note taking as the primary means of recording, the teacher may wish to provide a checklist and question or observation sheets to assist the student in organizing the material. However, if the checklist and observation sheet are too extensive, they may take too much time from the actual viewing.

Follow-Up

Observations are of value only as they are put to use in helping students better understand the related concepts. Steps to ensure the benefits of the experience are:

1. **Discuss** each experience.
2. **Plan** discussions to follow closely after the observation.
3. Allow each student to **contribute** and **record** his data.
4. **Analyze** data and observations in relation to purpose.
5. **Prepare** students for the next observation.

Scheduling

In scheduling the observations, consideration is given to the following:

1. The number of students that can be accommodated.

2. The amount of time needed to adequately make the observation a worthwhile experience.

3. The need for all students to have the same observation experience. Would all students benefit, or would other observations offer greater rewards?

4. The time of day that best serves the ***"agency"*** accommodating the observers.

Student's Role

The observation experience requires two important traits from the student.

1. ***To express either in writing or verbally the student's "views" of the observation.***
2. ***The ability to concentrate and be passive for periods of time during the observation.***

Teacher's Role

The skill of teaching how to observe is the critical role of the teacher in teaching strategy observation. Besides teaching technical aspects of observation, the teacher is responsible for making the observation an ***objective versus a subjective process***.

Strengths

1. Student is able to view concepts in a realistic atmosphere.
2. Develop powers of ***"observation":*** listening, seeing and reasoning.
3. Observations are an excellent ***"enrichment"*** strategy.

Limitations

1. It is difficult for the observer to be totally objective.
2. Many observation situations do not provide excellent examples.
3. Short-term observations can distort the picture.

Exercise:

Make a list of observations (activities) that you would have your students do during or after listening to a symphonic orchestra.

1. ______________________	***6.*** ______________________
2. ______________________	***7.*** ______________________
3. ______________________	***8.*** ______________________
4. ______________________	***9.*** ______________________
5. ______________________	***10.***______________________

Sample Observation Questions/Activities

Metropolitan Museum of Art

- Sketch in the style.
- Color in the style.
- Describe the setting.
- Identify the main focus.
- Compare scene to a personal experience.
- Take pictures, buy posters and duplicate the setting (a vase of flowers or poses)
- Describe the use of color and range.
- Explain color usage (foreground or background).
- Realism of the scene versus impresssion.
- Texture of the painting.
- Size of the painting.
- Frame a painting.
- Discuss the title and the meaning.
- Give an alternate title for a subtitle.
- Count the number of people, trees or flowers in the painting.
- Describe the faces and the meaning of their expressions.
- The balance of positioning.
- Identify types of trees or flowers.
- Discuss clothing and style.
- Brushstrokes.
- What sound does it picture make?
- Write a story about the scene.
- Write a dialogue between characters.
- Discuss the emotions or moods.
- Sequence several paintings together with a storyline.
- Identify music appropriate to the painting.
- Make up a poem about the scene.
- Mix colors to create a new color.
- Brainstorm to describe feelings.
- Create your own island, woods or scene.
- Taste the fruit or food of the painting.
- Read stories about the place depicted.
- Record descriptions or others comments.
- Select your favorite from the artist, grouping or section.
- Use a variety of media to create the same scene (crayons, chalks, oils, watercolors or mixed media).
- Make your own mobile with specific focus on the theme.
- Locate "place" on a map.
- Select paintings for home.
- Spend money to furnish home or gallery.
- Research the cost of paintings.
- Discuss the lifestyle of an artist.
- Discuss an art colony.
- Discuss periods of art.
- Create your own sculpture using clay.
- Create similar models or sculptures using papier-mâché.
- Discuss how bronzes figures are made.
- Describe the shapes and representations.
- Why are there empty spaces in paintings?
- Discuss contrast (colors and figures).
- Define collage.
- What materials make up a collage?
- Reasons for symbols in collages.
- Describe or explain why photography is an art form.

Sample Observation Questions/Activities Continued

Metropolitan Museum of Art

- Reflect on black-and-white versus color - Greater or lesser impact?
- Compare a photograph and a similar painting.
- Take a photo of a painting scene.
- How do different lenses affect the image?
- How does the artist portray women, children and men?
- Explain children and animal art forms.
- Explain paintings and art form from the perspectives of men or women.
- Using plaster, create a similar sculpture.
- Have a student model various poses.
- Describe the feeling (touch) of various surfaces (bronze, plaster or wood).
- Compare the sculpture to the real object.
- Explain three-dimensional aspects of sculpture.
- List other art forms: "quilting, furniture, glass, jewelry or needlework).

Samples Student Tasks

Lila Acheson Wallace Gallery

Iris & Gerald Cantor Hall – 2nd Floor

Cheva Cobo, a painting called *January 23 and April 15, 1986*: Types of Fish? Why the title?

Clifford Still, a room of paintings (abstract, blotches*): **Draw*** in the style.

Chuck Close, *Lucas*: Compare to Seurat.

Roy Lichtenson, *Stepping Out:* Describe.

Mark Tansey, *The Innocent Eye Test:* Find a picture with three cows.

James Rosenquist, *House of Fire:* Explain representations.

Phillip Pearlstein, *Female Model in Eaves Street*: Retitle the picture.

Fairfield Porter, *Elaine di Kooning*: Make up a story.

Ellsworth Kelly, *Blue Panel:* Why is it askew?

Milton Resnick, *Wedding*: Can you find the wedding?

Al Held, *Taxi Cab 111*; Explain.

Frank Kline, *Black, White and Gray:* What is this painting a vision of?

Jackson Pollock, *Autumn Rhythm #30:* Draw in the style.

Milton Avery, *White Rooster*: Describe the colors.

Field Trip Exercise (Observation): Sample Experiences

Required Tasks

1. ***Locate your artist and describe one of these works*** (colors, style, scene or mood)
   a. With your coloring instruments, draw or copy any one of his paintings.
   b. Reflect on your lecture and what you might add if you did it a second time.

2. ***For your house or apartment, select one painting for each room. Describe each painting and why you made your selections.***

3. ***Visit the store and buy a postcard of one of your artist's works.***

4. ***Visit either the Astor Court or the American Wing Garden Court (Charles Engelhard Court), Temple of Dendur.***
   a. Sit and observe your surroundings.
   b. Record your thoughts and describe the view from your seat.

5. ***Design six activities that you would have your class do (observe) at the museum.***

Field Trip Written Assignment

By Helen Jersets

Task 1: My artist, Ansel Adams, was not displayed during our visit to the Metropolitan Museum of Art; there-fore, think I adopted the artist Paul Cezanne been for this exercise. I made a pencil sketch of his oil painting on canvas *Still Life—Apples and Pears*. The subject of this painting was a wooden table, upon which were placed two plates of fruit: four near each plate. Dark-toned walls and deep, shadows comprised the background of the painting. The painting measured approximately 24 in. by 30 in. and was executed in shades of brown, blue, gray, green, gold and red.

One important characteristic of the painting was that the perspective was off when Cézanne portrayed the table. I believe this was done intentionally to create a broader focal point for the composition: especially when you see how the space between the plates of fruit draws your attention to the center of the painting. Overall, the painting was very soothing to the eye and I included it among my choices to furnish my home. (See sketch.)

Task 2: The following selections of art have been chosen to furnish my home.

a. **Living Room:** I have chosen a large 4' X 5' landscape, an oil painting titled *Merced River,*

Yosemite Valley by Albert Bierstadt (1830-1902). It pictures people on the banks of a river with huge, rocky mountains in the background. The earth tone colors of this painting will work very well with the color scheme of this room as I hang it over the sofa.

b. **Dining Room:** I have chosen a massive marble and semi-precious stone table called *The Farnese Table.* It was designed and constructed by Guglielmo della Porta (1565-1573) in Rome, Italy. The predominant color of the marble is putty and the accent are in shades are white, beige, gold, green, mauve and wine red. It measures approximately 4' X 8' and would seat ten people comfortably I believe this will look spectacular with a plain, base china and silver flatware. Because of the extremely hard material it is made of, I could use it without a tablecloth especially since it would be a shame to cover up such a magnificent piece of craftsmanship.

c. **Master Bedroom Suite:** I have selected an oil painting by Willard Metcalf (1850-1925), titled T*he North Country.* It features a tranquil, mountain landscape in soft, muted shades of blue, mauve and gold. These are the colors I used to decorate the rest of the room. Because it is a rather large painting, 3' X 4', I would hang this over my long dresser, along the largest, uninterrupted wall of the room.

d. **Master Bath**: Another oil painting has been selected for this room adjoining the master bedroom. It is called *Study for Eaglehead, Manchester*, by Winslow Homer (1836-1910). It is a beautiful seascape, measuring 8" X 20" in shades of blue-green, blue, brown and mauve. This was selected because of its compact size so it would not overpower the room.

e. **Kitchen:** For this room I have made two selections, one was mentioned earlier, *Still Life Apples and Pears* by Cézanne. The second is titled "*Tyrolean Interior*", by John Singer Sergeant (1856-1925). This painting also uses shades of brown, beige, blue and gold, with a touch of red as it depicts four people sitting around a kitchen table having a conversation. I like the messages conveys by illustrating entertaining in the kitchen. This somehow always seems to happen in my home.

f. **Bedroom #2:** I've decided to place another oil painting by John Singer Sergeant entitled *Two Girls with Parasols at Fladbury.* It features two women with parasols to match. The colors predominating are shades of green, blue and aqua. This painting will enhance the similar color scheme of the room.

g. **Bedroom #3**: I have chosen an oil painting by John Frederick Kensett (1816-1872) with a beautiful blending of colors in this sunset on a river. It is titled *Twilight on the Sound* and features tones of pink, green and brown. The serene mood of the painting and the coordination with the color scheme of this room again prompted me to make this selection.

h. **Bath # 2:** My selection for this bathroom is a 10" X 14" seascape by William Trost Richards (1833-1905). This oil painting depicts waves crashing on the rocks and is aptly titled, *Surf of the Rocks*. This is an absolutely gorgeous rendition of the sea with shades of green, blue, brown and gray that he used throughout the painting.

i. **Foyer:** For this area, I have selected a few of the photographs of Ansel Adams. The stark, white walls and the black, tile floors are enhanced by his black-and-white photography style. The selections are: *Church, Taos Pueblo, New Mexico; Untitled* (Mesa Verde National Park, Colorado*): Acoma Pueblo, New Mexico* and *Church, Acoma Pueblo*. All of these photographs carry a similar theme as they depict adobe or stucco buildings.

j. **Hallways:** Here again, I have selected Ansel Adams photographs because of the continuation of the black-and-white color scheme. For display, I have chosen photos which are alike as they depict clouds, mountains and water, (rivers or lakes). The selections are: *Canyon de Chely, The Tetons, Snake River; Evening McDonald Lake, Glacier National Park; Yellowstone Lake, Mt. Sheridan*; *Untitled* (Glazier National Park) and *Grand Teton.*

Task 3: See the attached postcard.

Task 4: I decided to write my observations to the Charles Engelhard Court in the form of a free verse poem.

An experience and environment
unlike the exhibits, so exact.
An open atrium; bright sunlight and airy,
adorned by mixed mediums sculpture;
amid the greenery.

Adults and children come and,
walk along the cross hatched brick paths.
Unhurried and at leisure: open eyes
take in all that surrounds them.
Amid the greenery.

Notice the heavy, black urns planted
with flowering cherry trees in bloom.
The pollen has dusted the surface of
shiny pathos leaves below them,
Smell the greenery.

Breathe in the cooler air here.
Not as stuffy as the enclosed,
main halls of the museum.
The air is cleaner and fresher here
thanks to the greenery.

Task 5: Activities:

a. Inspired by the varied glassware exhibits, I would have my students, (ages 6-10), make their own artistic glass back in the classroom. Using thinned, oil-base paint, to make it transparent, have the students' paint ordinary, drinking glasses or empty jars with one or more colors. Encourage originality and the use of more than one color. When completed, display the glass art in front of a classroom window for a colorful, sunlight effect. Another variation would be to have the students make a design or figure on the surface of the glass using glue and then carefully roll the glass in granulated sugar to simulate an etched glass effect.

b. After visiting and relaxing in the courtyard, have students (ages 10-12) make a courtyard model when they have returned to the classroom. Individually or in small groups, they could glue bits of dried moss, dried flowers, branches, buildings, blocks, paper mosaics (for walkways), cardboard, toothpicks and other suitable materials to simulate gardens, walls and benches in the courtyard. Encourage original designs and creativity.

c. There was a lattice-work display on the wall near the Charles Engelhard Court. When young students (ages 5-8) return to the classroom, have them weave a lattice work pattern. Use a sheet of construction paper with parallel slits cut in the center area at least 1 inch away from the edges. They could weave strips of paper through the openings. Another method uses separate strips of construction paper in which they could overlap and glue into lattice work designs.

d. After viewing the furniture exhibit, have the students (child to adult age) set up a room floor plan (or entire house, floor plan) of their choice when they return to class. By taking a sheet of paper, they can draw the room dimensions using a suggested scale of 1 in. = 1 ft. Be sure to have them note window and door openings. Cut construction paper into shapes representing furniture using the same scale. For example: 2 in. squares = chairs or end tables; 1 in. circles = lamps. Encourage creativity and color coordination in the students' plans. (Note: there are pre-made kits available for adult use.)

e. When the quilts were viewed in the museum, an emphasis could be placed upon the mathematics and geometry used to construct them. Using handout sheets, have the students (child to adult age) answer problems related to the designs on display. For example: how many 3-in., right triangles are needed for a quilt that measures 5' X 6'? The answer: 960. Another variation for adult students would be for them to actually duplicate a cloth square of a quilt design that they liked. Place emphasis on originality and creativity.

f. After viewing the arms and armor, as a teacher, I could point out the significance of designs used in shields, which frequently bore a knight's family crest. For example: the lion was a popular English motif and the fleur de lis was a popular French design. Instruct the students (ages 5-10) to take notes or make small sketches of the various designs used. When they return to class, the students can make a cardboard shield in any shape they like. Cover the form with aluminum foil and glue construction paper cutouts to form their own crest. Encourage originality and creativity.

Chapter Notes & Additional Information:

Personal Thoughts & Drawings

Chapter 15:

The Laboratory

Schools should teach us all the different alternatives that are open to society, and they should also show that there is a basic foundation to life.

Chapter Topics:

Purpose	**Steps in Developing Classroom Centers**
Definition	**Student's Role**
Classification	**Teacher's Role**
Organization	**Lesson Plan**

Purpose

Traditionally, the laboratory is thought of as a formal means by which investigations and research take place. However, in recent years the definition of the laboratory has been expanded to include not only experimentation, but also mastery of skills. Subjects such as languages, reading, math, vocational and technical subjects have utilized the laboratory concept to explore, problem solve, investigate and also to master through the drill of repetition and practice.

Definition: ***A laboratory is defined as a place to labor. Labor meaning to work, to exert effort or to achieve.***

Running laboratory: When laboratory experiences are formally scheduled parts of the course curriculum, then it is said to be a running lab. This type of laboratory is highly organized, and laboratory assistants are needed to aid in the conduct of the lesson.

Interest Centers, Activity Centers and Learning Centers: In recent years, the laboratory has been brought into the classroom and has been part of the classroom environment. Physical areas within the class are set aside for students to work on their own or in small groups on various assigned tasks or interests.

The ***"interest centers"*** differ from the running laboratory in two ways:

1. All students are not expected to do the same work at the same time nor required to participate in each station.

2. The running lab has direct supervision whereas the students in interest centers are basically on their own.

Exercise:

Describe the most recent laboratory you have attended and the activities involved.

Laboratory: ____________________________ Course: ______________________________

Description:

____

____

____

____

____

____

Classification

Physical: Interactive
Cognitive: Secondary
Affective: Primary

Organization

Running Lab: The running lab meets once or twice a week on a regularly scheduled basis. The lab sessions are coordinated with large-group presentations. Prior to each lab session, the students should be introduced to the concepts, skills and problems that they will be expected to learn in the laboratory. The following are guidelines in organizing a scheduled laboratory.

Course/Unit Development: In most scheduled laboratory situations, the large group and laboratory materials are coordinated and sequenced in a logical pattern. Concepts are introduced in the large group and labs are arranged to expand, illustrate and demonstrate the idea. Very seldom should a student be expected to perform in a laboratory session without prior instruction to the general idea.

The units, (***lab sessions***) are expected to ask the students to apply, discover or put to use the information acquired in the large-group presentations.

After each laboratory session, there should be a time to discuss what took place and develop the relationship back to the larger idea (large-group session). This can be done by either allotting time at the end of a laboratory session or at the beginning of a large-group assembly.

Physical Arrangement: When the laboratory has a permanent location versus arranging a lab in the normal classroom for a single session, or unit, much of the planning has been done.

If, however, the classroom is to be utilized as a lab, consider the following:

1. The ***number of students*** actually participating in the lab; not all need to participate at once.
2. The ***activity*** in terms of physical space, noise level, equipment, lighting and number of students involved.
3. ***Movement*** from one station to the next when using a rotating lab.

The lab equipment and materials (***lab setup***) should be organized and distributed ahead of time to prevent confusion and waste of time at the beginning of sessions. Numbering and assigning equipment/materials to students is also more effective than random distribution; it allows students to learn responsibility.

After each lab the students are expected to ***clean up*** their laboratory station and return the equipment and unused materials. The cleanup, as well as the distribution of equipment, is a joint, class effort and not the responsibility of the teacher or the lab assistant.

Lab Session: Each laboratory session should have ***clear, detailed directions*** (instruction sheets or lab manuals) that enable the students to carry out the activities with minimal assistance from the instructor or laboratory assistant. The instructions should, whenever possible, have illustrations and small steps to help guide the students.

Some instructors like to ***demonstrate*** and ***explain*** each experiment before allowing students to proceed on their own. This first step is dependent upon the experience of the students and the complexity of the task.

The students are expected to ***record*** their findings in some orderly fashion, such as a notebook, lab manual or worksheet. The lab reports are to be turned in after each session for feedback and evaluation purposes.

Supervision: Whenever possible, pair or group students on a regular basis, changing groups only as problems arise or abilities change. For each session, make one person responsible for cleanup, organization or other tasks that give structure to the group.

Before an activity is conducted, ***review safety procedures*** with the class. Always post a set of rules or guidelines that are to be maintained during the laboratory hours, and constantly make sure students conduct themselves accordingly.

Interest and Learning Activity Centers: In planning the classroom laboratory, many of the guidelines that applied to the running lab are also applicable to the classroom laboratory; however, the classroom laboratory, although a spin-off of the running laboratory, does have some different characteristics.

1. ***Continuing the rearrangement of the centers***
2. ***Time expectations***
3. ***Separation of student role***

Skill Centers vs. Interest Centers: Skill centers are designed to give practice in particular skills such as fractions, translations or tennis techniques.

Interest centers capitalize on topics of current interest or attempt to stimulate new interests. They can provide enrichment and change of pace activities, such as designing a cartoon or listening to an opera.

Compulsory vs. Noncompulsory Centers: Compulsory centers are required of everyone or of designated students who need to practice on the task provided in the center. Skill centers are generally compulsory.

Noncompulsory centers are there for anyone who wants to utilize them. Although the work in these enrichment areas is usually more complex than in skill centers, students are attracted to them for their unique content.

Short-Term vs. Long-Term Centers: Short-term centers exhaust their usefulness when the skill for which they provide practice has been mastered, or when interest in the activity decreases.

Long-term centers are continually expanding as the area is probed in even greater depth and new materials and activities are added.

Steps in Developing Classrooms Centers

1. ***Identify an idea***
   a. From your own classroom experience for inspiration
   b. From someone else, your colleagues
   c. From sample centers you have seen
   d. From professional books

2. ***Adapt it to the needs of students***
   a. Examine your diagnostic data (Is the idea needed? Is it of interest?)
   b. How much background experiences necessary?
   c. Decide whether its purpose is interest or skill.
   d. Define your objectives and tasks.
   e. Determine appropriate levels.
   f. Decide whether it should be compulsory or noncompulsory.

3. ***Arrange the room and the equipment.***

4. ***Place in rooms and explain to class***
    a. Identify rules for use
    b. Explain responsibilities
    c. Illustrated or have samples at each station

Principles of Design: The following are essential in the development of the Interest Center Concept.

1. The teacher thoroughly understands the organization and purpose of the laboratory method.
2. Assessment of pupil's needs is the heart of the methodology.
3. Each center is conceived and created to meet some perceived interest or need of the students.
4. Each center is more or less self-contained.
5. The centers have been explained to the students and they have an understanding and ability for working independently or along with others to complete activities.
6. The teacher becomes a supervisor, assisting but not directing the class.
7. Everyone starts slowly and moves gradually, building a foundation to work from. Students are assigned to centers at first and eventually given freedom of choice.

Exercise:

Design a reading/language center. Include drawings as well as activities and notices.

Student's Role

The laboratory method requires the student to undertake activities with minimal supervision. The student must have a sense of responsibility and maturity to carry out assigned tasks without interfering with colleagues.

Teacher's Role

The significant task of the teacher in the laboratory method is ***organizing*** and ***designing*** a clear set of instructions which the students can follow in a semi- independent manner.

References

Blake, Howard E. *Creating a Learning-Centered Classroom.* New York: Hart Publishing Company, 1977.

McCloskey, Mildred G. *Teaching Strategies and Classroom Realities.* Englewood Cliffs, NJ: Prentice-Hall, 1971.

EDU 216 Lesson Plan (Sample Lab Experience)

Laboratory

I. ***Background***

Name: Beth, Carmen, Diana, Veronica *Date*: 12/11/06 *Grade:* College
Hour: 7-9:40 P.M. *Subject:* Health & Fitness
Place: BCC Room SSB 109 *Unit:* Technique
Lesson Topic: Stress Management

II. ***Behavioral Objectives***

a. Students will take a test to find out how stress resistant they really are.
b. Students will participate in various ways of relieving stress, temporarily, through the following laboratory experiences.
c. Students will discuss why or why not these experiences could help relieve their stress.

III. ***Previous Assignment***—Ask the students to think of a stressful moment and how they were able to deal with it, if they dealt with it.

Materials:

Lab Station #1: How stress-resistant are you?

1. Pencils (6)
2. Tests (6)
3. Handout—"Uptight? Call Time-out"

Lab Station #2: Stretch to beat stress

1. Table
2. Chairs (6)
3. Handout—"Stretch to Beat Stress"

Lab Station #3: Muscle Relaxation

1. Poster of the body
2. Handout—"How to tense muscle groups"

Lab Station #4: Autogenic training

1. CD player
2. Autogenic CD
3. Handout—"Imagery Training"

IV. ***Related Activities:*** If time permits, show a DVD about yoga as another form of relieving stress.

V. ***Procedure:***

Set: This evening we are going to experience ways of temporarily relieving stress. Most of our lives are like a roller-coaster ride. We all have our own way of dealing with this bumpy ride.

Some of us thrive on stress and enjoy the challenges that would overwhelm others. The following labs are for us "less-hearty" types who feel the need to reduce stress. These are some simple ways to temporarily relieve stress.

Organization/Illustration: (See Individual Lab Stations)

Lab Station # 1:

Organization/Illustration: Students will sit at a table
Hand out the article "Uptight? Call a Timeout"

Time: 10 minutes

Set: Students will find out how stress-resistant they are by taking a test found in *The Walking Magazine.* Students will receive a handout regarding ten easy ways to relieve stress.

Teaching Strategy: (Lab)

A. Take a test.
   1. Hand out test and pencils.
   2. Read the instructions.
   3. Make sure everyone understands the instructions.
B. Add the total points for each student.
C. Discuss the results.
D. Look at the handout, "Uptight? Call Time-out"
E. Discuss the handout, if time allows.

Lab Station # 2: Stretch to Beat Stress

Organization/Illustration: Set up chairs in a semicircle
Handout article, "Stretch to Beat Stress"

Time: 10 minutes

Set: Students will learn how stretching breaks up knots and releases lactic acid, which will help you feel more relaxed and help energize you.

Teaching Strategy: (Lab)

A. Explain how muscles will tighten up in a natural response to stress.
B. Explain how stretching breaks up the knots and releases lactic acid which will help you feel more relaxed.
C. Explain how stretching can help energize you.
D. Breathe, relax and enjoy (See handout, "Stretch to Beat Stress.")
E. Do you feel that this lab could be of any help to you the next time your muscles tighten up due to a stressful situation?

Lab Station # 3: Muscle Relaxation

Organization/Illustration: Chairs in a circle as comfortable as possible
Poster of the body
Handout: "How to Tense Muscle Groups"
Handout "Quiz"
Handout (take home): "How to Instruct Yourself" and " Log Sheet"

Time: 8 minutes

Set: We are going to learn to relax by studying opposing feelings of tensing and relaxing our muscles.

Teaching Strategy: (Lab)

A. Do not expect immediate results.
B. Do not be too concerned with your progress.
C. We're learning basic skills to use at home.
D. It will take **PRACTICE!**

The muscle groups have been broken down into four groups.

A. We will focus on one muscle area at a time.
B. Always work in this order.

a. Major Group 1:

A. Dominant hand and forearm
    1. Make a fist and hold it tight.
    2. Focus on points of tension. —fingers, and back of hand, wrist and forearm
B. Dominant biceps (part that bulges when you make a muscle)
    1. Arm flat—palm up
    2. Push with elbow down
    3. Focus on tension in biceps
    4. Alternative—bend arm at elbow, hand facing toward you and elbow free. Try touching your shoulder with hand while at the same time opposing movement. Will seem frozen in the air.
C. Non-dominant arm and forearm (same as above)
D. Non-dominant biceps (same as above)

b. **Major Group 2:** Forehead (tension is most often in the facial muscles, talk cry smile or frown). Frown or knit brows.
   i. Cheeks and nose—Squint your eyes and wrinkle your nose. Do not be afraid of making funny faces.
   ii. Jaw—Clench teeth together hard and pullback corners of mouth.
   iii. Lips and Tongue
      1. Teeth separated.
      2. Press lips together.
      3. Press tongue against roof of mouth
   iv. Neck and throat
      1. Pull chin down to touch chest
      2. Apply counter pressure
      3. Alternative—press head back

c. **Major Group 3:**
   i. Shoulders and upper back
      1. Pull shoulders up as if strings are attaching themselves to the ceiling
      2. Then arch back, trying to touch shoulder blades together
   ii. Chest
      1. Take a deep breath and hold for 5-6 seconds
      2. Exhale evenly and smoothly (not too fast or slow).
   iii. Stomach
      1. Make stomach hard
      2. Either pull in or push out

d. **Major Group 4:**
   i. Thighs and Buttocks
      1. Consciously try to tighten while pressing heels to the ground
      2. Alternative—Counterforce: Press knees toward each other while applying pressure to keep apart (pretend a rubber ball is preventing touch)
      3. Alternative—Try lifting your legs out in front of you.
   ii. Calves—Point toes upward
   iii. Feet
      1. 3-second periods
      2. Point slightly down
      3. Turning inward and curling toes

Lab Station # 4—Autogenic Training

Organization/illustration: Place CD in CD player
Hand out the article on "Imagery Training"

Time: 10 minutes

Set: Students will know the definition of ***"Autogenic"*** and how this relaxation technique helps control the heart rate, breathing and blood circulation. Students will experience a 10-minute lab an autogenic training.

A. Autogenic Training
    1. Definition.
    2. Ways to be used.
    3. Girl swinging who calmed irregular heart.
B. Deep Breathing Exercises
    1. Imagine ocean waves rolling in and out.
    2. Silently say, "Breathing smooth and rhythmic."
C. Heart rate regulation exercises
    1. Imagine slow ocean waves.
    2. Silently say, "My heartbeat is calm and regular."
D. Blood Flow
    1. Right arm and hand.
    2. Left arm and hand.
    3. Legs and feet.
E. Summing Up Phrase " I am Calm"
F. Return to activity—Count forward from 1 to 3
G. Group Response
    1. Ask how the students feel.
    2. Introduce Imagery Training.

Closure: Tonight we have learned how stress-resistant we are and various ways of helping us temporarily deal with the stress of everyday living. We'll learn that stretching can help the stress by doing six stretching movements and breathing. We have learned the definition of "a***utogenic***" and how this relaxation technique helps us control our heart rate, blood circulation and breathing. We discussed whether or not these lab experiences would help us with the stress that we may face from time to time.

VI. ***Assignment:*** Next week will be discussing problems that your body may experience as a result of constant stress. Your assignment is to read chapters 4 to 6 in your textbook.

VII. ***Ongoing Activities:*** During next week you will probably experience a stressful moment. You may experience many, stressful moments. When you feel stressed, try one of the lab experiences to help relieve the stress. Be prepared to discuss how you tried to relieve the stress and if the technique worked.

VIII. ***Lesson Comments:***

Exercise:

Create a lab situation for the previous lesson plan.

Chapter Notes & Additional Information:

Personal Thoughts & Drawings

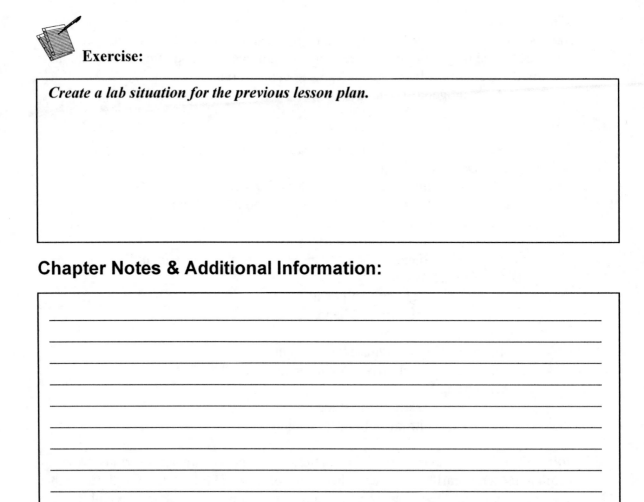

Appendices

TABLE OF CONTENTS

Appendices

Voting Rights	Sample Student Observation
Suspensions, NJ	Board of Education Interview
Oath of Allegiance	Certification Requirements
Mandatory Petition for Annual School Board Election	Test Requirements for NTE License in NJ
Nominating Petition of Annual School Election	Passing Scores Required for Licensure
Student Records	Elementary Certificate Test Description
Duties of the Board of Education (Middletown)	Substitute Applicant Information
Standard Resolutions for Executive Sessions	Application for Substitute Teaching
Time, Place, Notification of Board of Education Meeting	Secondary School Attendance and Discipline
Board of Education Observation Form	Teacher's Discipline Procedures
	Elementary School Discipline Code
	Middle School Discipline Code
	Governor Signs School Uniform Bill
	Child Abuse and Neglect
	Compassionate Class Trips

Voting Rights

2C:51-3. Voting and Jury Service

A person who is convicted of a crime shall be disqualified from voting in any primary, municipal, or special or general election as determined by the provisions of R.S. 19:4-1, and from serving as a juror as determined by the provisions of N.J.S. 2A69-1.

19:4-1. Constitutional qualifications; persons not having right of suffrage; right to register,

Except as provided in sections 19:4-2 and 19:4-3 of this Title, every person possessing the qualifications required by Article II, paragraph 3, of the Constitution of the State of New Jersey and having none of the disqualifications hereinafter stated and being duly registered as required by this Title, shall have the right to suffrage and shall be entitled to vote in the polling place assigned to the election district in which he actually resides, and not elsewhere.

No person shall have the right of suffrage:

1. Who is an idiot or is insane; or
2. (deleted by amendment)
3. (deleted by amendment)
4. (deleted by amendment)
5. (deleted by amendment)
6. who has been convicted of a violation of any provisions of this Title, for which criminal penalties were imposed, if such was deprived of

such right as part of the punishment therefore according to law, unless pardoned or restored by law to the right of suffrage: or

7. who shall be convicted of the violation of any of the provisions of this Title, for which criminal penalties are imposed, if such person shall be deprived of such right as part of the punishment therefore according to law, unless pardoned or restored by law to the right of suffrage; or

8. who is serving a sentence or is on parole or probation as the result of a conviction of any indictable offense under the laws of this or another state or of the United States.

A person who will have on the day of the next general election the qualifications to entitle him to vote shall have the right to be registered for and vote at such a general election and register for and vote at any election, intervening between such date of registration and such general election, if he shall be a citizen of the United States and shall meet the age and requirements prescribed by the Constitution of this State and the laws of the United States, when such intervening election is held, as though such qualifications were met before registration.

Suspensions, NJ (Suspension and Expulsion)

Conduct which constitutes good cause for suspension or expulsion of a student guilty of such conduct includes, but is not limited to, any of the following:

a. Continued and willful disobedience.
b. Open defiance of the authority of any teacher or person having authority over him.
c. Conduct of such character as to constitute a continuing danger to the physical well-being of other people.
d. Taking, or attempting to take, personal property or money from another student or from his presence by means of force or fear.
e. Willfully causing or attempting to cause substantial damage to property.
f. Participation in an unauthorized occupancy by a group of students or others of any part of any school or other building owned by any school district and failure to leave such school or other facility promptly after being directed to do so by the principal or other person then in charge of such building or facility.
g. Incitement which is intended to and does result in unauthorized occupation by any group of students or others of any part of a school or other facility owned by any school district.
h. Incitement which is intended to and does result in truancy by other students.
i. Knowing possession or knowing consumption without legal authority of alcoholic beverages or controlled dangerous substances on school premises, or being under the influence of intoxicating liquor or control dangerous substances while on school premises. (N.J.S.A 18A:37.2)

Oath of Allegiance

State of New Jersey:

: SS.

County of

I, ______________________________________,do solemnly swear (or affirm) that I will support the Constitution of the United States and the Constitution of the State of New Jersey, and that I will bear true faith and allegiance to the same and to Governments established in the United States and in this State, under the authority of the people.*So help me God.

Sworn and subscribed to

before me on this ________________ day of

_________________A.D. 20_____

*Not mandatory.

RS 41:1-1

Every person who is or shall be required by law to give assistance of fidelity an attachment to the Government of this State shall take the above oath of allegiance.

Mandatory Petition for Annual School Board of Elections (Middletown, NJ)

Qualifications

Candidates filing a nominating petition for board membership must meet the following qualifications:

- He/she is a registered voter in the district.
- He/she is a citizen of the United States of America.
- He/she must be at least eighteen (18) years of age to qualify for office.
- He/she must be able to read and write.
- He/she has been a resident of the municipality from which he/she is to be elected for at least one year preceding the date of the election.
- He/she shall not be directly/indirectly interested in a concern with or claim against the Board.
- He/she is not disqualified as a voter pursuing R.S 19:4-1.

Guidelines for Challenges to Candidates

Should the board Secretary, the board itself, another candidate or any legal voter of the district allege a lack of qualification on the part of a candidate or a deficiency in the petition (other than as described in N.J.S.A. 18A:14-12), or the violation of statute or regulation relating to the candidacy, he/she may file a petition with the Commissioner pursuant to the provisions of the N.J.S.A. 18A:6-9 and N.J.A.C. 6:24-1.1 et seq. within the required time period.

Please Note:

A candidate eligible for election to a school board may file for only one term even though two or more terms may be open on such board.

This information supplied by the Attorney General's Office[1] supersedes the Commissioners Decision in Recount of Ballots Cast at the Annual School Election in the Borough of North Caldwell, 1949-50 S.L.D. 52.

---

[1] Letter memorandum, file number 596, January 20, 1976.

NOMINATING PETITION FOR ANNUAL SCHOOL ELECTION

To, ________________________, Secretary of the ______________________________Board of Education:

A. **Nominating Statement**

We, the undersigned are qualified voters of the ________________________School District of
(Name of School District)

____________________________________in ____________________County, NJ. We hereby endorse,
(Name of Municipality) **(Name of County)**

________________________________, whose address is ______________________________as candidates
(Name of Candidate) **(Street, Number, Post Office)**

for member of the Board of Education representing ___________________________________ for the
(Name of Municipality to be Represented)

______________________term of ________________years, and we hereby request that the name of said
(Full or Unexpired) **(Number of Years)**

candidate be printed on the official ballot to be used at the ensuing election for the Board of Education to be held

__________________________ 20________________.
(Election Date)

B. **Signatories** (TEN SIGNATORIES ARE REQUIRED TO NOMINATE A CANDIDATE)

We, the undersigned, hereby certify that the said___________________________________ is legally qualified
(Name of Candidate)

under the laws of this State to be elected a member of the ________________________Board of Education.
(Name of School District)

	Name	Address		Name	Address
1.	______________	______________	7.	______________	______________
2.	______________	______________	8.	______________	______________
3.	______________	______________	9.	______________	______________
4.	______________	______________	10.	______________	______________
5.	______________	______________	11.	______________	______________
6.	______________	______________	12.	______________	______________

C. **Verification**

_____________________________________being duly sworn or affirmed according to the law on his/her oath
(Print Name of Petitioner Swearing/Affirming)

deposes and says: That the above petition is signed by each of the signers thereof in his/her own proper handwritings that the said signers are, to deponent's best knowledge and belief, legally qualified to vote at the election at which the candidate shall be voted for, and that the said petition is prepared and filed in absolute good faith for the sole purpose of endorsing the candidate therein named in order to secure his/her election as a member of the Board of Education.

SWORN OR AFFIRMED AND SUBSCRIBED____
BEFORE ME ON THIS _____________________DAY (Signature of the same petitioner listed on the line
OF ______________________________________. above in this section. This petitioner MUST be one of the signatories named in Section B.)

D. **Candidates Acceptance**

_____________________________, the candidate for membership on the board of education, named in the foregoing petition, does hereby certify that he/she is qualified to be elected a member of the ________________________as a member of the said body. He/she affirms and declares that he/she is not
(Name of School District)

disqualified as a voter pursuing to R.S.19:4-1. ____
(Signature of the candidate)

Student Records

The educational interests of the student and of society require the collection, retention and use of information about individual students and groups of students. The welfare and progress of students is inextricably related to the maintenance of a thorough and efficient system of public schools; the latter cannot be achieved nor assessed in the absence of appropriate information about the former.

It is no less the interest of society to protect the right of each of its members against an unwarranted invasion of privacy. Society's need to know, then, must be balanced by the individual's right to privacy and self-determination. The primary justification, therefore, of student record keeping shall be the educational welfare and advancement of the student.

The Board of Education has primary responsibility in this district for the compilation, maintenance, access to and security of student records. Only records mandated by the state or federal government for the following may be compiled by the staff:

1. Observations and ratings of individual students by professional staff members acting within their sphere of competency.
2. Samples of student work.
3. Information obtained from professionally acceptable standard instruments of measurement such as: interest inventories, aptitude tests, vocational preference inventories, achievement tests, and standardized intelligent tests.
4. Authenticated information provided by a parent or adult student concerning achievements and other school activities that the student wants to make a part of the record.
5. Verified reports of serious or recurring behavior patterns.
6. Extracurricular activities and achievements.
7. Rank in class—and academic honors earned.
8. Sibling order.
9. Language spoken.
10. Student Description Summary (Secondary Schools).
11. Photographs of individual students.

In addition to the foregoing, the administration is authorized to compile such districtwide information on ethnic groupings as required for state and federal reporting such ethnic groupings to designate Black, Caucasian, Oriental, Spanish, American Indian, or Other. No other records may be accumulated unless the collection of such facts has been authorized by the Board. Permitted records shall be preserved for a period of three years after graduation or after the student has left the district.

The superintendent shall prepare an administrative guide for the implementation of this policy in which he shall define a record, indicate the matter of maintenance, describe the form of the record, identify those who shall be granted access to the records and under what conditions, and provide a procedure for challenging the contents of a student's records.

Reference: 18A:6-9,18A:36-19, 18A:40-19,47:1A-1,47:1A-2, NJAC 6:3.21 et seq, 6:20-1.1 6:27-1.10, 6:28-2.4(g), 6:28-3.21(c2), 6:28-3.22(b), 6:29-4.2(a5), 6:29-4.4, 6:29-6.4(c), 6:39-1.1

Date Adopted: 9/8/75

Date Revised:

Duties of the Board of Education (Middletown, NJ)

Section 1. ***Board***—Those duties which a Board member must perform to comply with the statutes and the directives of the Board of Education are:

A. Educational Program

1. Provide courses of study suitable to the age and attainments of all students between the ages of five and twenty years. (18A:33-1)

2. Provide suitable facilities and convenience of access thereto for the implementation of the educational program. (18A:33-1)

3. Determine annually the dates between which the schools of the district shall be open in accordance with law. (18A:36-2)

4. Provide textbooks and other necessary school supplies free of cost to all students. (18A:34-1)

5. Identify and ascertain which children five through twenty years of age cannot be properly accommodated through school facilities because of their handicaps. (18A:46-6)

6. Report to the County Superintendent all children in special educational instructional services and any known handicapped children who are not attending school. (18A:46-7)

7. Provide suitable facilities and programs for all children classified as handicapped (except those that are neither educable nor trainable), whether or not such facilities exists in this school district. (18A:46-13)

8. Pay tuition whenever a handicapped child is confined to a hospital, home or institution and is enrolled in an educational program approved in this article. (18A:46-14)

9. Make rules for safekeeping and proper care of textbooks and keep account of monies expended for textbooks and other supplies, in accordance with booking directions prescribed by the State Board. (18A:34-2)

10. Adopt a course of study in community civics, geography, history, and civics of New Jersey, and privileges and responsibilities of citizenship. (18A:35-3)

11. Teach the nature and affects of alcohol and narcotics. (18A:3-3 and 18A:4-28.7)

12. Give regular courses of instruction in accident and fire prevention.(18A:6-2)

13. Give regular courses of instruction in the Constitution of the United States. (18A:6-3)

14. Conduct courses in health, safety and physical education. (18A:35-5)

15. If maintaining a program of adult education, determine the courses, charge and collect tuition, and apply all such income to the adult school program. (18A:50-1,2,4 and 6)

16. Provide appropriate exercises for the development of a higher spirit of patriotism on the last day preceding (18A:36-13):

Lincoln's Birthday
Washington's Birthday
Memorial Day
Columbus Day
Veteran's Day
Thanksgiving Day

17. Approve annually the interscholastic sports program.(N.J.A.C. 6:29-6-4)

18. Provide appropriate exercises for the observation of:

Flag Day (June 14)
Arbor Day (April 28)
Commodore Barry Day (September 13)
Crispus Attucks Day (March 5)

19. Present to each student on his graduation from elementary school, a copy of the Declaration of Independence, the Constitution of the United States and the amendments thereto, and the Constitution of the State of New Jersey, and the amendments in thereof. (18A:36-18)

Standard Resolution for Executive Session

Resolution by ____________________, seconded by ________________________

WHEREAS, Chapter 231, P.L. 1975, also known as the "Sunshine Law," authorizes a public body to meet in executive or private session under certain limited circumstances.

AND

WHEREAS, said law requires the Board to adopt a resolution at a public meeting before it can meet in such an executive or private session.

NOW, THEREFORE, BE IT RESOLVED BY THE SCHOOL DISTRICT BOARD OF EDUCATION THAT:

1. It does hereby determine that it is necessary to meet in Executive Session on __________________ to discuss the matters stipulated, in conformant with the subsections of said act which are indicated. (Read an appropriate date.)

(**Select from the following topics.**)

7.b (1) Confidential matters
7.b (3) Student matters
7.b (4) Collective bargaining
7.b (6) Public safety
7.b (7) Contract matters or litigation
7.b (8) Property matters

2. The matters discussed will be made public when confidentiality is no longer required and formal action pursuant to said discussion shall take place only at a meeting to which the public has been invited.

ROLL CALL VOTES: Ayes Nays Absent Abstain

Time, Place, Notification of Meetings

Regular meetings of the board of education shall be held on dates and at times and places determined by the board at its annual organization meeting. Special meetings shall be called by the board secretary/business administrator at the request of the president or on a petition signed by the majority of the board members, and shall commence no later than 8:00 P.M.

Adequate Notice–Adequate notice shall be given for all regular meetings and for special meetings whenever possible. Adequate notice generally means written advance notice of at least 48 hours, giving the time, date, location, and, to the extent known, the agenda of the meeting. The notice must state whether formal action may or may not be taken at the meeting. The notice must be:

A. Promptly posted in at least one public place reserved for such announcements:
B. Communicated to at least two newspapers designated by the board because they have the greatest likelihood of informing the board's public; and
C. Filed with the clerk of the municipality.

The Board of Education may hold a meeting without providing adequate public notice if:

A. Three-quarters of the board members present vote to do so; and
B. The meeting is required to deal with matters of such urgency and importance that delay would be likely to result in substantial harm to the public interest; and
C. The meeting will be limited to discussion of and action on these matters; and
D. Notice of such meeting is provided as soon as possible following the calling of such meeting; and
E. One of the following:
    1. Either the board could not reasonably have foreseen the need for such meeting at a time when adequate notice could have been provided; or
    2. The need could have been foreseen in time but the board failed to give adequate notice.

Announcement of Adequate Notice—At the beginning of every meeting, the presiding officer must announce that adequate notice of the meeting was provided and must specify the time, place and manner in which the notice was provided. However, if adequate notice was not provided, the presiding officer must say so, and in addition, must state reasons why this could not be done.

Board of Education Observation Form

Introduction to Education

Name: ______________________________ Day or Section # __________

Directions: Be as specific as possible in notes and attach a newspaper account of the board meeting and agenda of the meeting. TYPED or NEATLY WRITTEN.

School: ________________________ Place: _____________________

Date: __________________ Type of Meeting: ______________________

# of Spectators: ___________ # of Board Members Present: ______________

Agenda: Whenever appropriate, make notes on the agenda items (i.e., # of Yes or No viewpoints, superintendent positions, board president position. Select four or five items and explain the issues.

Item I:

Item II:

Item III:

Item IV:

Item V:

Public Remarks:

Your thoughts and impressions of the meeting:

Sample Student Report of Board of Education Meeting

School District: Marlboro Township
Place: Board of Education Building
Date: Originally September 21, 1995
Rescheduled: September 27, 1995

Type of Meeting: Regular
# of Spectators: 7
# of Board Members: 9

I. Audit Report (#7 p. 7)

An auditor approached the board with the results from their audit this year. It was stated that the school district did very well. There were no recommendations or comments in the audit report. The board made a point to make sure that they made their improvements from their last audit. The audit report showed that they were very impressed with the way that the township acted on their grants. There were also very pleased with the job done by Operations. They were glad to see that the school accounts improved greatly. Over all, the district got a great report correcting all recommendations from the last audit.

II. Amended Employment and Salary (#19 p. 21)

This discussion came about when one of the board members made a comment about whether or not it was in the school districts favor to hire Mrs. A full time. The board member made the point that much of this teacher's time would be spent traveling to the four schools in which she would be working. Another board member made a comment about how difficult it is to find a good ESL (English as a Second Language) teacher. The point was also made about the increase of ESL students in the district to 67 students from the usual 25 to 40 students, most of them being kindergarten-aged students. It was finally settled that having Mrs. A as a full-time traveling teacher was in the townships benefit. I agree with the decision.

III. Job Descriptions (#1 p. 23)

It was agreed at this point that these three positions; Maintenance Foreman, Asbestos Management Person, and an Inventory Control Person would be hired to eliminate a full-time position. One board member brought up the point of whether or not it should be included in the job description that these duties did not take place during the school day. It was decided that it would not have to be included. This would be discussed during the interview. Another board member asked whether this job was being offered outside of the district, and if it wasn't, was that legal? The president replied that the job would not be offered outside the district unless they began to have difficulty getting responses in the district, and that it was not illegal to do so.

IV. Sunshine Resolution (p. 24)

The board decided which of the nine matters in the agenda would have to be discussed in an executive session. It was decided that items 1, 2, 3, 4, 7 and 8 be discussed at closed sessions. All board members agreed.

V. Other Items

Many items discussed at the meeting, but did not go into lengthy discussion. These included:

- **A.** Long-range bonds being sold
- **B.** Taxes this year being 1 to 2 cents lower than usual.
- **C.** Scope donated two computers and software to the school district for special education.
- **D.** The employment of substitute bus drivers.
- **E.** The perfect attendance of 13 staff members was also recognized and commended.

There were no public remarks made at this meeting. In the agenda it stated that public session would be limited to agenda items only, but the board opened it to any business. There was still no response. This did not surprise me because public turnout was extremely low.

I felt that the board themselves were very unorganized. It was as if they were unsure as to how to run the meeting. I originally attended the first meeting scheduled for September 21, but it was cancelled due to lack of attendance of board members, including the president. At the rescheduled meeting on September 27, the president apologized and stated that it should never have happened, AND would never happen again.

Overall I found the meeting hard to understand and very rushed. As the end of the meeting approached, I began to understand more about the way in which the meeting was being held. I began to understand roll call, approval of resolutions and matters, and voting. I felt that as I attend more meetings, I will learn to follow along and have a better understanding as to the discussions at hand. It will be at this time that the meeting will become useful and understandable to me.

Board of Education Interview

Interview a Board of Education member and ask the following questions:

1. What motivated you to run for office?

2. What has been your biggest accomplishment?

3. What has been the most frustrating aspect?

4. How do you think the general public perceives board members?

5. How do teachers view you?

6. How much time (on average) do you spend on board matters each week?

7. What changes are needed in financing schools?

8. What are the two biggest problems facing schools besides finances?

Test Requirements for NTE Licensure in New Jersey

Introduction

Applicants for New Jersey licensure in subject teaching fields must pass the appropriate PRAXIS II Subject Assessment test(s) for NTE Programs Specialty Area test. Applicants for licensure in elementary education must pass the NTE General Knowledge test of the Core Battery. The tests are required for all applicants including those applicants who are licensed in other states. Certain teaching fields are exempt as noted.

Applicants for the Speech-Language Specialist license must pass the Speech-Language Pathology NTE Specialty Area test.

Applicants for the Principal and/or School Administrator licenses must pass the Educational Leadership: Administration and Supervision NTE Specialty Area test.

Effective September 1, 1996, the content testing requirements are changed in several licensing areas. It is your responsibility to register for the correct test(s). Carefully check test requirements and test code numbers listed to ensure registration for the correct test.

Passing Score

Applicants must achieve the current required passing score(s) for licensed/certificate issuance. Passing scores are subject to change. The test score must be obtained within the last five years, and it must meet the current passing score to satisfy the test requirement.

Undergraduates must take Praxis/NTE test(s) in their senior year.

Test Scores Service Fee

There is a test score service fee of $10 per endorsement that requires a test. The test score service fee must be submitted with your **Application for Licensure** using a money order or a certified check payable to "Commissioner of Education." ***Do not submit this fee to Educational Testing Service with your test registration form.***

Introductions for Test Registration

Register for Praxis II: Subject Assessment/NTE tests directly through The Praxis Series. Test registration procedures, registration form and other information are included in **The Praxis Series *Registration Bulletin*.**

Bulletins are available from the educational testing service as follows:

The Praxis Series
Educational Testing Service
P.O. Box 6051
Princeton, NJ 08541-6051
(800) 772-9476

Scores on Praxis II: Subject Assessment/NTE tests taken in the State of New Jersey will automatically be sent to the New Jersey Department of Education.

If you are tested in another state, you must request to have your score sent to New Jersey by coding **R7666** on your registration form. You must also include your Social Security number when completing your registration form and answer sheet. **Only** official score reports from Educational Testing Service are accepted for licensure. Coding the Department of Education (R7666) and your Social Security number precludes the delay in license/certificate issuance.

Instructional Endorsement	**Required Praxis H: Subject Assessment NTE Tests**
Agriculture	Exempt
Art	Art: Content Knowledge: (10133)
Bilingual/Bicultural Education	Exempt
Business Education	Business Education (10100)
(All Endorsement)	
Elementary (K-5)	Elementary Education: Content Knowledge (10014)
Elementary Teacher with Subject Matter:	
Language Arts Literacy (5-8)	Middle School English Language Arts (10049)
Mathematics (5-8)	Middle School Mathematics (20069)
Science (5-8)	Middle School Science (10439)
Social Studies (5-8)	Middle School Social Studies (20089)
English as a Second Language	Exempt
Family and Consumer Services	Family & Consumer Sciences (10120)
Foreign Languages:	Exempt
French (6-8)	French: Content Knowledge (20173)
German (6-8)	German: Content Knowledge (20181)
Spanish	Spanish: Content Knowledge (10191)
Other Languages	Exempt
Health Education	Exempt
Health and Physical Education	Health & Phys. Ed.: Content Knowledge (20856)
Marketing Education	Marketing Education (10560)
Mathematics	Mathematics: Content Knowledge (10061)
Music	Music: Content Knowledge (10113)
Physical Education	Physical Education: Content Knowledge (10091)
Pre-School – Grade 3	Exempt
Psychology	Exempt
Reading	Introduction to the Teaching of Reading (10200)
Science:	
Biological Science	Biology: Content Knowledge, Pt. 2 (20232)
	General Science: Content Knowledge, Pt. 1 (10431)
	General Science: Content Knowledge, Pt. 2 (10432)
Chemistry	Chemistry: Content Knowledge (20241)
	General Science: Content Knowledge (10431)
Earth Science	Earth/Space Sciences: Content Knowledge (20571)
	General Science: Content Knowledge (10431)
Physical Science	Chemistry: Content Knowledge (20241)
	Physics: Content Knowledge (10261)
	General Science: Content Knowledge (10431)
Physics	Physics: Content Knowledge (10261)
	General Science: Content Knowledge (10431)
	Exempt
Social Studies	Social Studies: Content Knowledge (10081)
Special Education	Speech Communication (10220)
Speech Arts & Dramatics	Theatre (10640)
	English Language, Literature, Composition: Content
Teacher of English	Knowledge (10041)
	Technology Education (10550)
Technology Education	Theatre (10640)
Theatre	Exempt
Vocational Education	Speech-Language Pathology (20330)
Speech-Language Specialist	School Leaders Licensure Assessment (11010)
Principal/School Administrator	School Superintendents Assessment (11020)

Passing Scores Required for Licensure

Code	Text	Passing Score
10014	Elementary Education: Content Knowledge	141
10041	English Language, Literature, and Composition Content Knowledge	162
10049	Middle School English Language Arts	156
10050	Technology Education	570
10061	Mathematics: Content Knowledge	137
10081	Social Studies: Content Knowledge	157
10091	Physical Education: Content Knowledge	148
10100	Business Education	580
10113	Music Education: Content Knowledge	153
10120	Family and Consumer Sciences	550
10133	Art: Content Knowledge	150
10191	Spanish: Content Knowledge	159
10200	Introduction to the Teaching of Reading	560
10220	Speech Communication	560
10261	Physics: Content Knowledge	135
10431	General Science: Content Knowledge Part 1	152
10432	General Science: Content Knowledge Part 2	142
10439	Middle School Science	145
10560	Marketing Education	630
10640	Theatre Education	570
11010	School Leaders Licensure Assessment	148
11020	School Superintendent Assessment	151
20069	Middle School Mathematics	152
20089	Middle School Social Studies	158
20173	French: Content Knowledge	156
20181	German: Content Knowledge	157
20232	Biology: Content Knowledge Part 2	147
20241	Chemistry: Content Knowledge	134
20330	Speech-Language Pathology	550
20571	Earth and Space Sciences: Content Knowledge	145
20856	Health & Physical Education	151

Passing scores are subject to change.

Elementary Certificate Test Description

Following are brief descriptions of the NTE Programs tests required for New Jersey certification. The number of items for each test may vary slightly within different editions of the test. Also note that, on occasion, a decision may be made after the administration of a test not to score one or more of the questions in the test.

Elementary Certificate Tests

The Core Battery Test of General Knowledge assesses examinees' knowledge and understanding of various disciplines and their interrelationships. The test consists of four separately timed 30-minutes sections: Literature and Fine Arts, Mathematics, Science, and Social Studies.

The 35 questions in the Literature and Fine Arts section of the test are based on passages from literature, photographic reproductions of artwork, films stills, and photographs of theater or dance performances. The questions using these kinds of materials are designed to assess examinees' skills in analysis interpretation.

The 25 questions in the Mathematics section of the test are intended to assess examinees' cumulative knowledge of mathematics from having studied throughout elementary school, for at least one year in high school, and possibly for one year in college. Questions are selected from such topics as comparing and ordering numbers; estimation; interpreting graphs, charts, and diagrams; use of ratio, proportion, and percent; reading scales; measurement; interpreting formulas and other expressions written in symbols; logical reasoning; and recognition of more than one way to solve a problem.

The 30 questions in the Science section of the test are designed to measure knowledge and understanding of certain themes that are major areas of scientific interest and current concern. Questions selected emphasize important principles, theories, concepts, and facts of science; application of these theories and facts; and the methods of science. The science questions are based on important themes from the biological, physical, and earth sciences.

The 30 questions in the Social Studies section of the test assess and understanding of major U.S. historical and cultural events and movements, political institutions and political values; an understanding of prominent characters of society culture; an understanding of relationships between culture and individuals; an understanding of economic concepts and processes; knowledge and understanding of geographical features and characteristics of human settlement and culture; and an understanding of social science methodologies, methodological tools, and data resources.

Monmouth County Superintendent 3435 Highway 9, PO Box 1264 Freehold, NJ 07728 (732) 431-7826	Middlesex County Education Office 1501 Livingston Avenue New Brunswick, NJ 08822 (732) 249-2900 ext. 112	Ocean County Education Office 212 Washington Street Toms River, NJ 08753 (732) 929-2078

Substitute Application Information

Dear Substitute Applicant:

We are happy that you are interested in substituting in the (district name). New Jersey law and administrative procedures require that you provide certain documentation to be eligible to substitute in New Jersey.

The following information should be completed before contacting the personnel office to schedule an interview;

1. Certification
   a. If you hold a New Jersey certification, bring the original of your New Jersey regular teaching certificate to be recorded.
   b. If you do not hold a New Jersey certification, but have a County Substitute Certificate, bring your original for recording.
   c. If you hold no type of certification, bring the following to the interview:
      1. Official transcript of all college credits.
      2. A certified check or money order in the amount of $30, payable to the "Commissioner of Education."
      3. Oath of Allegiance" form (Notarized)
      4. Complete application for substitute certificate.

2. Proof of TB tests (Mantoux) within the last three years.
   a. If you have proof of test, bring proof of such test to interview.
   b. If you do not have proof of test:
      1. Report to the nurse at ________, two calendar days prior to your interview (between the hours of 9:00 A.M. and 11:00 A.M., or 12:30 P.M. and 2:30 P.M.) She will administer the test.
      2. See school nurse prior to your interview and she will read the test.
      3. At the conclusion of the interview, see ________________ in the Personnel Office to complete information for your personal file.

If you have questions regarding the aforementioned information, please contact the Personnel Office at ______________________________.

Application for Substitute Teaching

Name: ______________________________

Address: ______________________________

Telephone: ______________________________

Social Security Number: ______________________________

Education Preparation:

Name of School & Location   Dates Attended   Graduation Date   Degree

____

____

If you hold a New Jersey Teaching Certificate, give exact title and date it was recorded in Freehold:

____

Do you have a New Jersey Substitute Certificate? ______________________________

Date Substitute Certificate expires: ______________________________

Teaching Experience:

Place: Grade or Subject

Dates

____

____

What is your subject or grade preference? ______________________________

If your availability is limited to a particular school or schools, please list:

____

____

References:

____

____

Date: ______________ (Signed): ______________________________

Date Interviewed: ______________________________

To: All Substitute Teachers
Re: School Tuberculosis Testing

Under the rules and regulations of New Jersey State Department of Education, you are required to have an intradermal test for evidence of tuberculosis infection. Board of Education policy requires that this be a Mantoux test, as is it has been determined that this test is more reliable.

1. All employees who are tuberculin negative shall be retested with an intradermal test every three years.

2. Any employee shall be exempt from intradermal testing on presentation of documentation of a prior positive reaction (i.e., 10 mm or more of induration) following a Mantoux test with five (5) tuberculin units of stabilized PPD tuberculin, or by a presentation of a medical contraindication form signed by a physician which specifically states the reason(s) for the exemption.

3. All employees who are positive reactors (10 or more mm of induration) or who have been exempted from the Mantoux test shall be required to have a chest X-ray or produce documentation of a prior chest X-ray, unless one year of chemotherapy has been completed.

4. If the chest X-ray of a positive tuberculosis reactor is negative for evidence of tuberculosis, he/she requires no further testing for tuberculosis infection, but should be referred to his/her family physician for chemoprophylaxis or prevention therapy.

5. A positive tuberculin reactor who is certified in writing by a licensed physician to have completed one year of prevention treatment (Chemoprophylaxis) with Isoniazid (INH), shall not be required to undergo any further testing for tuberculosis infection.

Please contact the high school health office to make arrangements for your tuberculin test or to provide the required documentation.

Secondary Student Attendance and Discipline

Board of Education, Middletown Township, NJ

The Board recognizes and accepts its responsibility to provide a thorough and efficient education for every student within the district. The full cooperation of parents and students in maintaining high levels of school attendance and discipline is required in order that the Board meets its responsibility.

Absence from school restricts and inhibits the ability of the student to complete successfully the prescribed curriculum requirements; it also may violate New Jersey State Law, which requires students to attend school regularly. Good discipline is necessary so that the instructional process is not disrupted.

Teachers have the responsibility for maintaining a suitable environment for learning.

Administrators have the responsibility for maintaining and facilitating the educational programs. The principal is authorized by State statute to suspend students for cause. Rules and regulations regarding attendance and discipline shall be published, disseminated to parents and reviewed with students at the opening of each school year and posted in each school library.

In order that infractions of the rules established for students attendance and conduct may be treated equitably and consistently, the Board has directed the Superintendent to prepare procedures for the district's schools. The professional staff shall administer discipline within the guidelines defined in District Administration Procedures No. 5131R and other specific policies relating to student attendance and behavior adopted by the Board.

The intent of these procedures is to provide parents and students with a definition of the limits of acceptable attendance and behavior and to assist school administrators or their designees in the fair and just administration of school district rules given the circumstances of the individual case. Additionally, administrators shall have the authority to take other reasonable disciplinary action which they warranted by situations not covered in procedures.

Date Adopted: 7/7/78
Date Re-Adopted: 11/2/87
Date Revised: 12/5/88
Date Re-Adopted: 9/1/92

Teachers' Discipline Procedures

Board of Education, Middletown Township, NJ

Classroom disruptions are to be handled using the following steps:

Step One: Talk with the student in private and proceed with the following process:

1. Describe the behavior you observed.
2. Explain the effect of the student's behavior on the class and/or on you.
3. Explore alternatives to the behavior of observed and agreed on a plan of action.
4. Implement plan of action for student improvement.
5. Record in a matter of the teacher's choosing, the procedures followed at this step.
6. Inform student's guidance counselor for preventive action.

Step Two: Repeat the same procedures and explain to student that parents will be contacted by phone.

1. Communicate to parents what has happened up to that time and ask the parents help in implementing the plan to improve the student's behavior.
2. Set a specific date for a follow-up conference or letter.
3. The teacher should help the parents and student understand the behavior that you want improved.

Step Three: Refer to administrative action with explanation and/or documentation of student improvement plan implemented.

Elementary School Discipline Policy

Board of Education, Middletown Township, NJ

The Board of Education believes that a safe and orderly school environment helps ensure the effective delivery of instruction and curriculum. The cooperative interaction among students, parents, teachers, and administrators is necessary in order to ensure that the continuity of the instructional purpose is not disrupted.

Within their level of maturity, the Board expects students to conduct themselves with proper regard for (a) the rights and welfare of others, (b) the educational purposes underlying all school activities and (c) the care of the facilities, equipment and materials.

The best discipline is self-imposed and students must learn to assume and accept responsibility for their own behavior as well as the consequences of misbehavior. Staff members who interact with students shall use preventive disciplinary action and place emphasis on each student's ability to grow in self-discipline. Each child's personality, disposition, and unique characteristics should be given full consideration before taking disciplinary action.

In order that infractions of the rules established for student conduct may be treated equitably and consistently, the Board has directed the Superintendent to prepare procedures for the district's schools. The intent of these procedures is to provide parents and students with a definition of the limits of acceptable behavior and to equip administrators or their designees in a manner which they deem just, given the circumstances of the individual case. The professional staff shall administer discipline with the guidelines of these procedures and other specific policies relating to student behavior adopted by the board.

Date Adopted: 9/1/92

Middle School Discipline

This table represents the most common infractions of school regulations and guidelines for determining penalties. Penalties may vary because of the frequency and/or the intensity of the infraction. All discipline matters will be handled on an individual basis and administrative discretion will be used in the final evaluation. Parent will be notified for each infraction. The parent may choose to appeal the suspension to the assistant superintendent for secondary education.

Type of Student Behavior	First Offense	Second Offense	Third Offense
Destroy or defacing property	Possible suspension 1-7 days: notify police: monetary restitution and/or physical restoration		
Malicious damage of school personnel's property	Suspension, 9 days: monetary restitution		
False alarms	Suspension 9 days: notify police and Fire Prevention Bureau: notify Child Study Team		
Endangering the safety of others	Saturday detention	Suspension 1–5 days; parent conference	
Threatening another student	Detention	Saturday detention	Suspension 3–5 days
Attacking another student	Suspension 3–9 days: notify parent	Suspension 3–5 days; parent conference;	Suspension 3–9 days; meet with police officer assigned to district
Threatening school personnel	Suspension 9 days: notify parent	Suspension 3–9 days; parent conference; meet with police office assigned to district	
Attacking school personnel	Suspension 9 days: parent conference: expulsion hearing with Board of Education	Suspension 1–3 days; parent conference	
Extortion/shakedown	Saturday detention	Notify police; notify Child Study Teams	Suspension 3–5 days; refer to SRC

Elementary School Discipline

In accordance with Policy No. 5129, the following rules and regulations are issued concerning student discipline in the elementary schools:

1. These rules and regulations shall be published and disseminated to parents and reviewed with students at the opening of each year.
2. All students are expected to follow the rules and regulations for acceptable behavior in the school. Disciplinary action will be taken for students who violate the rules and regulations for acceptable behavior set forth by the principal/teacher.
3. The principal has the responsibility of monitoring student behavior and maintaining discipline in the school. He/she is also charged with the responsibility of informing parents and students of the rules and regulations for acceptable behavior in the school. The principal is authorized by state statute to suspend students for cause.
4. Classroom discipline is affected by the nature of the program provided, and the development and consistent application of appropriate behavior and work standards. Therefore, teachers have the responsibility for informing parents and students of the rules and regulations for acceptable behavior in their classes. They are expected to monitor student behavior and handle disciplinary infractions.
5. Infractions considered as cause for immediate disciplinary action by the teacher/principal may include but are not limited to:
   a. Continued disregard of minor infractions
   b. Fighting
   c. Disrespect or defiance of authority
   d. Endangering the health or safety of others
   e. Profanity or obscene gestures
   f. Stealing
   g. Vandalism
   h. Truancy
   i. Smoking on school property
   j. Possession of alcohol, drugs or weapons
6. Depending on the seriousness in the child/children involved, disciplinary infractions may be handled by but not limited to the following actions:
   a. Conference between the teacher and student
   b. A written note or letter to the parents
   c. A telephone call to the parents
   d. Conference with the parents
   e. Detention
   f. Excluding the student from extracurricular or school activities
   g. A conference between the teacher and the principal
   h. Referral to the principal
   i. Suspension from school
   j. Referral to special services

Dates adopted: 9/1/92

Governor Signs School Uniform Bill

School boards now have the authority to adopt a dress code policy. The governor signed the School Uniform Law which permits a school board to establish dress codes, which could require school uniforms. The law also authorizes boards to prohibit clothing indicating membership in certain gangs.

Why did this law come about?

The legislature believed that a dress code could positively influence student behavior. Legislators pointed out crimes that have occurred relating to the clothing of children.

Is the law a mandate?

The law permits each board of education to develop a dress code and to determine whether this policy would require a school uniform.

How will policy be developed?

The board may develop a policy at the request of the principal, staff, and/or parents. The board must hold a public hearing prior to the adoption of the policy and cannot implement the policy with less than three months notice to the parents or guardians of the students. The specific uniform selection will be determined by the principal, staff, and/or parents of the individual school.

What about those students who cannot afford a uniform?

Any policy adopted that requires a uniform must include a provision to assist economically disadvantaged students.

What about those parents who choose not to participate?

The board of education may provide a method whereby parents may choose to comply with an adopted school uniform policy. If the board provides such a method, a student can not be penalized.

NJEA members should work through their local school boards to ensure that this provision is included.

What is NJEA's policy?

When this legislation was introduced, NJEA's Youth Services Committee received it and made a recommendation to the Executive Committee. The Committee recommended that school uniform policies be instituted only as a part of a comprehensive violence reduction plan at school sites that have demonstrated a specific need for the elimination of independent dress styles.

They also recommended that a school uniform policy: allow and encourage students, parents and staff to participate in the school uniform process; contain one or more mechanisms that will provide uniforms to children who cannot otherwise afford them; stipulate that a student cannot be penalized academically or otherwise if his/her parents choose not to comply with the code for reasons stated in a formal petition to the school board.

Child Abuse and Neglect

The Board of Education is deeply concerned with the physical, emotional and psychological health and well-being of the children within this district, not only as a prerequisite to learning through the formal education process, but also in principle. Children may be abused, molested and/or neglected by their parents, guardians and/or other persons, including school employees. In an effort to prevent and intervene in instances of child abuse or neglect, this district will cooperate fully with the **Division of Youth and Family Services (DYFS)**, and Department of Human Services in the early identification and immediately of suspected child abuse cases or allegations thereof, whether or not substantial corroborative evidence is available. The Board will respond to findings at each stage of the investigation as it affects any child or school personnel.

The Board of Education directs the chief school administrator to implement this policy and procedures/rules and regulations in compliance with law and code requirements pertaining to allegations of child abuse.

The chief school administrators/designee shall act as a liaison between **DYFS** and the district. The liaison show facilitate communication and cooperation between the district and **DYFS** and act as a primary contact between the schools and **DYFS** with regard to general information sharing and the development of mutual training and other cooperative efforts. Referrals are not to be screened or referred through the liaison.

Educators and other school employees are able to observe the physical, emotional and behavioral changes of children on a day-to-day basis and are in a unique position to make early identification of children at risk. All district employees shall cooperate fully with **DYFS** in the investigation of child abuse cases.

Information about child abuse, neglect and the prevention of early identification shall be incorporated into the family life curriculum. The chief school administrator or designee shall require all the employees and regular volunteers to receive in-service training annually to assist those in the recognition of possible child abuse neglect cases, the instructional methods and techniques relative to issues of child abuse in the local curriculum, and to inform them of their responsibilities to the abused child pursuant to **NJSA 9:6-8.10 et seq**. This training shall include information regarding the identification and reporting of allegations of child abuse to **DYFS**, as well as the investigative process conducted by **DYFS.** Additionally, the employees shall be made aware of their rights and responsibilities according to law and code.

A person making the report in good faith is immune:

"Anyone acting pursuant to this act in the making of a report under this act shall have immunity from any liability, civil or criminal, that might otherwise be incurred or imposed. Any such person shall have the same immunity with respect to testimony given in any judicial proceeding resulting from such report." (NJSA 9:6-8.13)

Failure to make a report is a violation, and the person is subject to a $1,000 fine and up to six months in jail.

Any person knowingly violating the provisions of this act including the failure to report an act of child abuse having reasonable cause to believe that an act of child abuse has been committed is a disorderly person. (NJSA 9:6-8.14)

No school personnel will be discharged from employment or in any manner discriminated against as a result of making a good faith report or causing to be reported an allegation of child abuse (NJSA 9:6-8.13)

Due process rights will be provided to school personnel who have been reassigned or suspended in accordance with NJSA 18A:6-10 et seq., 18A:25-1, 18A:25-6, and NJSA 9:6-3.1. Temporary reassignment or suspension of school personnel alleged to have committed an act of child abuse shall occur if there is reasonable cause to believe that the life or health of the alleged victim or other children is in imminent danger due to continued contact between the school personnel and a child. (NJSA 18A:6-10 et seq and NJSA 9:6-3.1)

Compassionate Class Trips

Throughout the school year, teachers, school administrators and PTAs across New Jersey arrange school trips for children that are intended to fascinate, stimulate curiosity and educate. Many of these trips do, but some, like trips to circuses, zoos and aquariums perpetuate the belief that it is acceptable to imprison animals for purposes we deem appropriate. Listed below are alternate trips that do not involve institutionalized animal abuse and exploitation. This list is provided as a courtesy and is by no means exhausted. There are hundreds of educational class trip opportunities for children that would be impossible to list here.

- **Allaire Village: Allaire State Park**
  Wall Township, NJ: A living history park.
  (732) 938-2253

- **American Museum of the Moving Image,**
  Astoria, NY: Explore what it is like to work in a TV control room or a radio editing room. (718) 784-4520

- **Aviation Hall of Fame and Museum,**
  Teterboro NJ: Aircraft, artifacts and photographs commemorating NJ's 205 -year aeronautical history.
  (201) 288-6345

- **Batsto Historical Village**
  Wharton State Forest, Washington Township NJ: A major center of iron and glass manufacturing from 1766-1867. Interpretive programs, including exhibits and guided tours of Batsto Mansion. (609) 561-0024

- **Buehler Challenger & Science Center**
  Paramus, NJ; Experience being an astronaut and/or a mission controller, hands-on science series, and more.
  (201) 262-0984

- **Children's Museum of Manhattan**
  New York, NY; Exhibits and activity center.
  (212) 721-1223

- **Curriculum Travel of America**
  Allentown, PA; Exciting science travel programs designed and led by education professionals for school groups (grades 5-12). (800) 541-6606

- **Dey Mansion**
  Wayne, NJ; Washington Headquarters Museum; Revolutionary War reenactments. (973) 696-1776

- **Discovery House Museum**
  E. Brunswick, NJ; Hands-on interactive children's museum for kids under 12. (732) 254-3770

- **Drumthwacket**
  Princeton, NJ; Tour this Greek Revival mansion, the official residence of NJ governors. (609) 683-0057

- **Edison National Historical Site**
  West Orange, NJ; Tour Thomas Edison's Laboratory, hoe and library. (973)736-0050

- **Franklin Mineral Museum**
  Franklin, NJ; Learn about geology and mining. Children can collect and identify minerals and rocks. (973) 827-6671

- **Garden State Discovery Museum**
  Cherry Hill, NJ; Hands-on activities about the earth, dinosaurs, music and more. Ages 1-10 (856) 424-1233

- **Gateway National Recreation Area**
  Sandy Hook, NJ; Programs of flora and fauna on this peninsula.
  (732) 872-0015 or (732) 872-5970

- **Geology Museum (Rutgers University)**
  New Brunswick, NJ; This museum features exhibits on geology and anthropology with an emphasis on the natural history of NJ.
  (732) 932-7243

- **Imagine That! Discovery Museum for Children**
  Middletown, NJ; hands-on science, art, computers, social studies and more. (732) 706-0900

- **Immigration Museum**
  Ellis Island, NY; Tour Immigration Hall, where thousands of Europeans first set foot on American soil. Ferry service from Liberty State Park. (212) 363-3200

- **Intrepid Sea Air Space Museum**
  New York, NY; the museum has a vast permanent ship, aircraft and tank collection. (212) 245-2533

- **Jersey Explorer Children's Museum**
  East Orange, NJ; exhibits and ongoing programs. (973) 673-6900

- **Liberty State Park Ferry**
  Jersey City, NJ; Take the ferry to Statue of Liberty and Ellis Island. (201) 915-3400

- **Museum of American Glass**
  Millville, NJ; This working museum offers educators the opportunity to enhance their curriculums on NJ history, as glassmaking was instrumental in the region's growth. (856) 825-6800 or (800) 998-4552

- **NJ Children's Museum**
  Paramus, NJ; Hands-on exhibits for children under 8. (201) 262-5151

- **NJ State House**
  Trenton, NJ; Learn about representative government and how bills become law. (609) 633-2709

- **NJ State Police Museum**
  West Trenton, NJ; (609) 882-2000 ext. 6400

- **NJ Vietnam Era Educational Center**
  Holmdel, NJ; A full complement of educational programs and reference materials and provided at the Center. Guided tours of the Memorial and Educational Center are available. (732) 335-0033

- **NY City Fire Museum**
  New York, NY; Real fire engines and equipment housed in old-fashioned firehouse. (212)691-1303

- **NY Public Library**
  New York, NY; (212) 726-9757

- **Please Touch Museum,**
  Philadelphia, PA; Hands-on museum for young children where activities are educational and fun (215) 963-0667

- **Pocono Environmental Education Center**
  Dingmans Ferry, PA; Design a program from over 30 classes, including orienteering, wildlife studies and hiking. (570) 828-2319

- **Raritan Valley Community College**
  North Branch, NJ; Planetarium programs. (908) 231-8805

- **Sterling Hill Mine & Museum**
  Ogdensburg, NJ; NJ's only underground mine tour, exhibit hall, fluorescence mineral displays and more. (973) 209-7212

- **The Old School House**
  Mount Holly, NJ; NJ's oldest schoolhouse, built in 1756. Children try on colonial costumes, hold a Quaker meeting using scripts or go on an archeological dig. (609) 267-6996 or (908) 782-7079

- **United Nations**
  New York, NY; (212) 963-1234

- **Wetlands Institute**
  Stone Harbor, NJ; Field trips explore laboratories and natural habitats. (609) 368-1211

OTHER INTERESTING TRIPS

- Ballet, Concerts, Opera or Theatre Programs
- Children's Peace Fair, Brookdale Community College
- Lincroft, NJ

- Craft Fairs
- Ethnic Festivals
- Hiking Trips
- Oceans, Lakes & Rivers
- Planetariums
- Radio Stations & Newspapers
- River Canoeing, Cruises, Rafting, Touring, Tubing
- Sporting Events (Baseball, Basketball, Football, etc.)

Resources:
Libraries, Local Telephone Directories, Internet, New Jersey Calendar of Events–provided as a public service by the NJ Department of Commerce and Economic Development, Division of Travel and Tourism, CN 826, Trenton, NJ 08626 (609) 2470

NEW JERSEY ANIMAL RIGHTS ALLIANCE (732) 446-6808

Reflections

A new idea is a rare thing.
It is easier to adapt an old idea,
rather than create a new one.
When a new idea appears,
those with intelligence recognize it,
develop it, and bring it to fruition.

It takes no intelligence
to react negatively
toward a new idea.
It is just a reflex action
of those
with no imagination
to create an idea.

INGENUITY CREATES,
REACTIONISM NEGATES.

M.K.P.